The Secret Battle For Britain

The RAF's Handling and Interrogation of Luftwaffe Prisoners of War 1939-1940

The Secret Battle For Britain

The RAF's Handling and Interrogation of Luftwaffe Prisoners of War 1939-1940

M.S. Morgan

AIR WORLD

First published in Great Britain in 2025 by
Pen & Sword Military
An imprint of
Pen & Sword Books Ltd
Yorkshire - Philadelphia

ISBN 978 1 03613 573 7

A CIP catalogue record for this book is available from the British Library.

Typeset in INDIA by IMPEC eSolutions
Printed and bound in England by CPI Group (UK) Ltd, Croydon, CRO 4YY

The Publisher's authorised representative in the EU for product safety is Authorised Rep Compliance Ltd., Ground Floor, 71 Lower Baggot Street, Dublin D02 P593, Ireland.
www.arccompliance.com

For a complete list of Pen & Sword titles please contact

PEN & SWORD BOOKS LIMITED
47 Church Street, Barnsley, South Yorkshire, S70 2AS, England
E-mail: enquiries@pen-and-sword.co.uk
Website: www.pen-and-sword.co.uk

or

PEN AND SWORD BOOKS
1950 Lawrence Rd, Havertown, PA 19083, USA
E-mail: uspen-and-sword@casematepublishers.com
Website: www.penandswordbooks.com

FSC www.fsc.org
MIX
Paper | Supporting responsible forestry
FSC® C013604

Contents

Luftwaffe Ranks and Their RAF Equivalent

Oberst	Group Captain
Oberstleutnant (Oberstlt.)	Wing Commander
Major (Maj)	Squadron Leader
Hauptmann (Haupt.)	Flight Lieutenant
Oberleutnant (Oblt.)	Flying Officer
Leutnant (Lt.)	Pilot Officer
Stabsfeldwebel (Stab Fw.)	Warrant Officer
Oberfeldwebel (ObFw.)	Flight Sergeant
Feldwebel (Fw.)	Sergeant
Unteroffizier (Uffz.)	Corporal
Obergefreiter (OGefr.)	Leading Aircraftman
Gefreiter (Gefr.)	Aircraftman First Class
Flieger (Flgr.)	Aircraftman Second Class

Introduction

As a former police detective and senior investigating officer (SIO), I have spent a great deal of time re-examining a number of mysterious and secretive episodes concerning the Royal Air Force during the Second World War.

In my previous books, I have examined the little-known Czech pilot Augustin Preucil, who flew an RAF Hurricane back to the Nazis, before becoming a Gestapo stool pigeon; as well as re-examining the Second World War deaths of Guy Gibson and Prince George, the Duke of Kent.

I have examined Dulag Luft at Oberursel near Frankfurt – the Luftwaffe's main reception centre for captured allied airmen, an establishment which later employed similar tactics to those of the Royal Air Force Air Intelligence interrogation team, known initially as AI1(k). The investigation into Dulag Luft and the behaviour of some of its RAF prisoners, stimulated my interest in the reciprocal RAF interrogation of Luftwaffe airmen during the early years of the Second World War.

As well as being a former senior investigator, I spend many years in the field of intelligence and I was a trained advanced interviewer. It is because of my personal history and the book on Dulag Luft, that I decided to examine the interrogation and handling of Luftwaffe prisoners of war.

In 1941, Oberleutnant Franz von Werra – more commonly known as the *One That Got Away* – escaped from Canada having been shot down during the Battle of Britain. Von Werra's exploits and his efforts to escape, were the subject of a number of books and a 1957 movie of the same name starring Hardy Kruger. However, very few people know when he returned to Germany, he briefed the Luftwaffe High Command on the tactics used by RAF Air Intelligence when interrogating captured German airmen. Similar interrogation skills were then put to great use in a similar system developed by the Luftwaffe.

In the movie *The One That Got Away,* the first thirty minutes concentrates on von Werra's capture and interrogation in September 1940. It is in many ways, a compressed version of his treatment. It is very enlightening, but omits a number of alleged RAF intelligence tactics which can only be found in German texts written around the same time (in the 1940s and 50s).

After completing my book *Hitler's RAF Collaborators* and having read and watched various accounts of RAF Air Intelligence and Franz von Werra, it seemed natural for me to take a closer look at the section responsible for the interrogation of Luftwaffe airmen at the start of the war. There have been a number of books and articles in magazines and newspapers touching on the treatment of Luftwaffe prisoners of war in the early part of the war, but most were written before the RAF Air Intelligence files were released into the public domain in and around 2004.

Once these files and other similar interrogation documents were released by the UK National Archives, it was only natural for researchers and historians to aim for the proverbial *bullseye* – German war crimes, the Holocaust and the so-called V-weapons. Most of the surviving files detail verbal statements and private discussions between senior officers and some lower ranks, many obtained via covert microphones, as well as via interrogation, stool pigeons and simple kindness and good manners.

These tactics were developed in the first months of the war and the time leading up to and during the Battles of France and Britain. This period produced large numbers of German airmen and the new tactics and skills were honed on these unsuspecting guinea pigs.

After spending many months examining the files on countless visits to The National Archives where they are now contained, one is left with the clear impression many files are still being withheld or have been destroyed. Those that are available for public scrutiny are the initial Air Intelligence field reports, completed after the preliminary interrogation of airmen and a number of compilation reports from other primary and secondary interrogations. Sadly, it would appear the main interrogation reports have disappeared, although elements have been incorporated into the compilation reports.

Most of the available intelligence logs from Air Intelligence section AI1(k), are signed by the unit's commander – Denys Felkin. Although he was the number one interrogator at Trent Park during the Battle of Britain, it appears beyond the capability of any human being to have interrogated so many POWs alone. It is therefore more likely he 'signed-off' the reports gathered from the initial intelligence officers, many of them *out in the field* across the country, but he undoubtedly undertook many of the secondary in-depth interrogations himself.

Many of the preliminary AI1(k) intelligence reports were completed soon after the prisoners capture, but many of these men were hospitalised and clearly not in a fit state to attend Trent Park. Among the initial intelligence reports signed off by Denys Felkin, are a number of more detailed reports, concentrating on subjects such as aircraft, bombs, individual Luftwaffe units, training and morale. These reports were written using intelligence gleaned from one or more prisoners of war.

With a vast number of secondary and other in-depth interrogation reports missing from the archives, there is little doubt the British authorities have either chosen to withhold or destroy the files detailing the lengthy supplementary interrogation of their prisoners; possibly to protect the identities of the prisoners or the tactics of AI1(k). Personally, I believe the files have been destroyed to protect the individual prisoners, because, as we shall see in this book, Denys Felkin wrote a secret report detailing the units tactics at the end of the war.

Although many interrogation files are missing, the transcripts of prisoner discussions recorded via the covert M-Room microphones, are still available and very revealing. These were probably saved from the Air Ministry shredder because 99% of them are anonymised. Although the first M-Room reports gave the names of those involved, from early 1940 onwards, the individuals concerned were given a code number. Despite this, with some cross-referencing, it is possible in a number of cases to identify those concerned.

The Luftwaffe prisoners, most believing in 1939 and 1940 that victory was inevitable, provided Air Intelligence both wittingly and unwittingly, with a treasure trove of information which covered not only technical and tactical intelligence, but also possible war crimes, civil and military morale, the Nazi regime and much more.

RAF Air Intelligence used tactics and procedures that any modern-day interrogator will recognise. The separation of a prisoner from his colleagues, examination of his personal belongings, documents and aircraft, all created an unwelcoming hostile atmosphere. Expecting a hard time, prisoners were expecting the worst, only for their interrogators to confound this impression with charm, kindness, the offer of alcohol, cigarettes and other homely comforts. This confusion could be very disarming for a young, frightened and possibly wounded airman.

However, if the prisoner was obstructive, arrogant or a hardened Nazi, the suggestion of physical threats, intimidation and harsher conditions, was always available to an interrogator, together with character assassination or just an awkward period of prolonged silence.

From 1939 onwards, Air Intelligence built up quite a library of information gleaned from various sources, many of which we would now call open-source material. This included newspaper articles, magazines, radio broadcasts, old photographs and information from previous prisoners of war and refugees. Carefully collated and analysed, in time Air Intelligence would build-up a detailed picture of numerous pilots and airmen, their aircraft, units, friends and even the general social situation around a unit or airfield community.

A prisoner who refused to give anything but his name, rank and number was often shocked to be told their unit, aircraft details and recited a 'who's who' in their squadron. Many prisoners thought there was no use in holding back, as it was clear their interrogator knew everything about them and their unit. Their interrogation it seemed was just a formality, before they were moved on to a permanent prisoner of war camp. This would often lead to the prisoner relaxing and divulging even more information to his interrogator.

After a period of solitude and interrogation, a prisoner would be put in a room with a colleague, one they possibly knew. Highly sensitive covert microphones, hidden in the walls, furniture or fireplaces, allowed German speaking *listeners* to tune-in as the men discussed not only the interrogation they had just endured, but often what they had not told their interrogators!

In some cases, a stool pigeon would be introduced. Often a German or Austrian refugee, sometimes Jewish, they would often glean extra information after divulging their own cover story or *legend* to the recently arrived prisoner.

Air Intelligence was initially based in 1939 at the Tower of London, before relocating to Trent Park, Cockfosters, north of London. The man who would take command of the Air Intelligence effort until the end of the war was Squadron Leader and later Group Captain Samuel Denys Felkin (usually known as Denys Felkin). Felkin would become known to the German prisoners as Squadron Leader King and he would play a central part in the processes and interrogations at Trent Park. (He would often introduce himself as Major Konig – Squadron Leader King).

The files in the UK National Archives, indicate that many of the prisoners were interviewed while still undergoing medical treatment and recovering from wounds and injuries. Many had been held at the Royal Herbert Military Hospital in Woolwich, South-East London. The wards had soldiers standing guard with fixed bayonets as the men received the best medical care available, but were the men interrogated in compliance with the Geneva Convention?

As someone who worked as a senior investigating officer, trained in advanced interview techniques, technical intelligence gathering and covert human intelligence source controlling, I found this subject of Air Intelligence and interrogation to be fascinating.

This book will examine the development of the Air Intelligence interrogation branch from just before the war in 1939, to the end of the Battle of Britain on 31 October 1940. It will consider the unit's senior officers, tactics and formation, before examining the intelligence gleaned from the prisoners, its value to the war effort and how it was used.

We must remember, Britain was gripped by a fear of imminent invasion and expected no mercy, the nation was fighting for its life, but despite this, the personnel involved from the RAF interrogators to the soldiers provided by the Guards Regiments, professionally handled the German airman, extracting information from them piece by piece. It is said, many airmen did not realise they had given anything of value to the interrogators, having apparently left after a pleasant chat, a glass of whisky and having smoked a few cigarettes by the fireside.

As mentioned earlier, although many of the documents available in the UK National Archives are anonymous, especially those obtained via hidden microphones, they do give details of times, places, aircraft types and units.

The SRA documents detailing the covert recordings of many prisoner conversations, have been assessed and where possible I have identified the prisoners concerned, or at least those I believe were concerned. This process was assisted by the low number of Luftwaffe prisoners in the first six to seven months of the war, but it became much more difficult to identify individuals during the summer months of 1940 and the Battle of Britain. As well as using the individuals rank, position and the date of the report, it is possible via some of the more detailed transcribed exchanges to identify the men concerned.

It is now approximately eighty-five years since these records and their intelligence was created, most, if not all of the men involved have now passed, and I have therefore decided to name the individuals I believe to have been involved. Most of the prisoners gave their information unwittingly and were not traitors. The character and behaviour of these men covered a broad spectrum. Some were arrogant individuals, confident of a German victory, while others just wanted the war to end and to return home to their families.

Acknowledgements

I would like to thank the staff at The National Archives in the United Kingdom for their assistance, and also the RAF Air Historical Branch.

I would like to thank Stuart Leasor for his kind permission to use elements of his father's book, *The One That Got Away*. I am very grateful and highly recommend a read of it!

I would also like to thank the following: In no particular order, for allowing me to use their images in this book, Chris Goss, Nigel Parker, Andy Saunders, Martin Mace, and Historic Military Press.

Finally, and by no means least, I would like to thank Kate Francis, Project Administrator at Trent Park, for her kind assistance and providing images for this book from the Trent Park Trust's archives. In the next year or so, a museum will open at Trent Park covering its wartime intelligence work and I hope this book will whet your appetite and prompt a visit.

Chapter 1

Oberleutnant Franz Von Werra

One name that will always be synonymous with Air Intelligence and its interrogation section - AI1(k), is Oberleutnant Franz von Werra, otherwise known as '*The One That Got Away*'. Before we delve into the AI1(k) system, it is worth considering this man and his interrogation.

The British book of the same name and the movie starring Hardy Kruger as von Werra, have long been a favourite of wartime movie audiences, but can we trust their content and more specifically, the first part which covers his capture, treatment and interrogation by AI1(k) at Trent Park?

A separate book was published in Germany titled *Einer Kam Durch* which translates as *One Came Through*. Both the British and German books used an original manuscript dictated by Franz von Werra upon his return to Germany, after his escape in 1941. The Nazi authorities never published *his* book because it is alleged, they deemed his comments about the enemy and their treatment of German POWs to be too fair. Nazi propaganda demanded a reason to hate the enemy, not respect him. Von Werra had experienced the RAF system in 1940 and he was very impressed, so much so, he could hardly wait to tell his masters of its abilities.

The two books are similar, but the German version gives extra detail about the subterfuge used by RAF Intelligence in a bid to get von Werra to talk. Clearly, in the 1950s, the British public may not have thought the tactics to be sporting and fair! As we shall see, some would have been shocking to the post-war British audience.

Whether the tactics were sporting or fair is immaterial, Franz von Werra was impressed by his treatment and the skills of the RAF Intelligence service, so much so, that he gave a detailed account to the Luftwaffe High Command.

After the escape of British prisoners from the POW camp and Luftwaffe prisoner reception centre at Oberursel near Frankfurt, compounded by Gestapo allegations the system was too lenient; Franz von Werra was sent to inspect the camp and the interrogation of RAF prisoners of war. It is because of his findings and recommendations the Luftwaffe changed their interrogation tactics to mirror those used at Trent Park by AI1(k).

Von Werra tells of his own detailed interrogation by an RAF officer known as Squadron Leader King (Denys Felkin) at Trent Park. So, who was von Werra and was he really the lovable rogue portrayed by Hardy Kruger in the 1957 movie?

Before we examine the conception, development, role and tactics of AI1(k), it is worth examining the story of Franz von Werra in some detail, using both the books and the publicly available records on Franz von Werra in 1940.

By amalgamating the two books and comparing their details, we get a good impression of what was waiting for von Werra when he made his forced landing at Winchet Hill, Marden, Kent on 5 September 1940.

After exiting his Messerschmitt Me 109E, Franz von Werra was immediately captured by a group of soldiers from a nearby anti-aircraft site. A guard was placed on his intact Me 109E and it was covered in branches to hide it from marauding German aircraft.

Von Werra was initially housed in a police cell at the Kent Constabulary headquarters in Sutton Road, Maidstone, before being transferred to the town's barracks. (Sadly, the cell block at the Police Headquarters has now been demolished.) Von Werra remained alone in his cell overnight – no one came to question him.

On 6 September, both books and the movie claim he was transferred to London and Kensington Palace Gardens, the home of the so-called London Cage, but this is questionable and shall be discussed in the next chapter. Wherever he was in London, and whatever unit dealt with him, it seems he was locked in a bare room, No.13, with a hard bed and no soft furnishings. By the window was a piece of penciled graffiti, apparently left by a previous prisoner, it stated in German: 'You'll laugh Tommies, but you will still lose the war!' It was signed Leutnant Manhart; this was Walter Manhart, a Messerschmitt Me 110 pilot of 6/ZG26, shot down over Essex two days before von Werra.

The comment made von Werra smile to himself, but the door opened and he was told to follow the soldiers. They led him to a room where he was met by an Army Captain, an older man. He did not appear threatening or mysterious and offered the young pilot a cigarette. The British officer was kind and pleasant, so much so, that von Werra immediately suspected a trick. Von Werra told the officer he would only give his name, rank and number, he would not divulge any military information, but this British officer just wanted to talk about politics in Germany.

This was his preliminary interrogation, but von Werra did not know this. The officer, possibly assisting the RAF because of the high number of new arrivals in September 1940, was examining the character and ideals of the young German pilot. He was assessing von Werra and considering whether he should be sent directly to a POW camp or sent for further interrogation at Trent Park?

What von Werra did not know, however, was that the RAF already knew a considerable amount about this young firebrand from other prisoners and information gleaned from the German media. In addition, his aircraft had already been assessed and the information passed on to Trent Park by AI1(g) the technical section of Air Intelligence.

In the movie, the initial interrogating officer refers von Werra on to Trent Park because of his attitude, but the RAF already knew a lot about this man and they wanted to speak to him in greater depth.

On 7 September, Oberleutnant Franz von Werra was escorted to Trent Park, Cockfosters. He knew upon arrival this was no ordinary prison camp – a high wall, barbed wire fences and numerous patrolling sentries with fixed bayonets. The conclusion of his journey was the main mansion house, a grand façade although inside it was a little austere.

Von Werra was taken into a room in the cellar where he was medically examined before being deposited in another bare room on an upper floor. This time there were four iron beds with folded rough blankets, a table and chairs with coconut rugs on the wooden floor. He was the only occupant of this new prison cell and it was clear the other beds were unoccupied.

As darkness fell that evening, von Werra lay on his bed looking at the single uncovered light bulb dangling from the ceiling. As darkness grew, he wanted to turn the light on, but like the earlier room in London, the switch was on the other side of the locked door.

Suddenly the door was unlocked and a torch shone in his face. 'Stay there!' said a booming voice in German. A guard entered the room, examined the window before placing a black-out shutter over it. Another guard in the corridor switched on the light and he noticed a tray on the table. It contained a cup of cocoa and three slices of bread with jam and margarine spread thinly on them. The solider in the room was a Sergeant and he said, 'Your dinner – leave the blackout alone', before leaving the room and locking the door.

The next morning the Sergeant returned with another meagre meal, but he would not engage in conversation and always replied 'Spater', the German word for later. Von Werra would later discover other prisoners called him Feldwebel Spater, translated into English as Sergeant Later.

Franz von Werra had no further human contact until the evening of 8 September, three days after he crashed his Messerschmitt in rural Kent. The house was quiet and he had nothing to read and no cigarettes to smoke. His only 'entertainment' had been a distant air raid on London the previous night, which he could see in the distance above the tree line. Franz von Werra was feeling very low, but little did he realise this was all part of the softening-up process.

At dusk, von Werra heard marching boots in the corridor outside. They stopped outside his door which was unlocked. He was marched by the soldiers down long corridors to another part of the mansion and halted outside a door. The lead guard knocked on the door and a voice inside told them to 'Come in'. Von Werra was about to meet Squadron Leader King – actually Denys Felkin – the commander of this unit and its lead interrogator.

Von Werra and one of the soldiers entered the room, a wood paneled office with a large desk, comfortable chairs and various fixtures and fittings. The overhead lamp was dim, but the table lamp cast a bright light upon the desk where an RAF officer was writing. The officer's hair was thin and swept, he wore a uniform with pilots' wings and medal ribbons. In front of him on the desk was box with a silver model of a Spitfire on it.

The officer sat writing, his face out of sight, before the soldier spoke, 'Corporal Bates with the Werra prisoner, sir.' The officer told the soldier to wait outside the door. As he left the room, von Werra finally saw the officer look up. He had a narrow, lined face, bushy arching eyebrows and a twirled black mustache. His eyes were dark and sunken, but this was a perfect description of Denys Felkin (see the images section).

In fluent, but accented German, the officer said: 'I am Squadron Leader King. Sit down Oberleutnant von Werra.'

Von Werra clicked his heels, bowed and sat in a leather chair in front of the heavy wooden desk. The RAF officer sat writing in silence for at least two minutes. As the silent atmosphere built up the tension, the German pilot began feeling uneasy.

Suddenly a side door opened and another RAF officer entered with a number of files. Without saying a word, the junior officer placed the files on the desk and left the room, switching off the main ceiling light so that only the table lamp illuminated the room. This was probably all part of the choreography.

Once he had finished writing, the squadron leader offered von Werra a cigarette from a box. This was accepted. Sat outside the beam of the desk lamp, the officer began his interrogation in German: 'Thirteen shot down and half a dozen destroyed on the ground, this is a very commendable success, Oberleutnant. As a minor ace of the First World War, it is a very special honour to meet one of the great heroes of the Second World War.'

The squadron leader's tone was one of derision and sarcasm, von Werra was immediately thrown off his stride, clearly this would be different to his first interrogation with the army captain. It was a common tactic causing the prisoner to feel affronted and challenged. Von Werra reportedly replied that he was honoured to meet a First World War ace, but could not recall seeing King's name when studying that war. He added that if he wanted military information from him, the squadron leader would not get anything, not even his unit.

The arrogant, bombastic young Luftwaffe Oberleutnant continued mockingly, 'Undoubtedly you are the enemy who shot me down?'

The squadron leader sat in silence without comment. The silence lasted so long von Werra thought the interview was over. However, as any trained interrogator will tell you, these periods of silence can be more productive than any words or gesture.

The air raid sirens started to sound again and von Werra sat back in his padded chair smiling with satisfaction. Not only was he putting this old RAF officer in his place, his colleagues were bombing London.

The squadron leader stood up, turned off the desk lamp leaving the room in darkness and with the aid of a cane, he walked to the window, closed it and the black out curtains. He returned to the desk and turned the lamp back on. The officer seemed to limp and von Werra thought he had a prosthetic leg, causing him to apologise immediately to his host. The squadron leader remained silent and handed von Werra a crystal ashtray from the desktop.

The RAF officer rested his backside against the desk in front of von Werra and starred at him, before asking if he had just said something about his unit. Von Werra started to lose his patience and struck a fist onto the padded arm of his chair, denying this and repeating that he would give no military information. This use of an incorrect line or a deliberate mistake was another simple tactic which would often catch an airman off guard, but not Franz von Werra.

Unperturbed, the squadron leader launched into a pre-planned diatribe: 'And I would actually like to know, which of your squadron colleagues – Fuhrer-staffel of II Gruppe of 3 Jagdgeschwader, right? … will look after your lion cub Simba now that you are gone? Your friend Sanni will have to do that – right?'

With one swift sentence the squadron leader had announced that he knew quite a bit about Franz von Werra. The German pilot was dumbstruck. How did he know all this and what else did he know? Just one sentence threw the cocky Oberleutnant completely off balance, but he remained calm as the squadron leader continued sarcastically: 'The Great War produced the air hero Manfred von Richthofen, it seems this war continues the noble tradition and gives us Franz von Werra.'

Von Werra sat in silence and the RAF man continued: 'I must congratulate you on your skill enlisting the press, particularly remarkable given the fierce competition among Luftwaffe fighter pilots. From unknown leutnant to air hero on the cover of a magazine in just a few weeks. How is it done? … Well, its childishly simple, isn't it? Other pilots have a dog, a pig, or a hunting falcon, but you get a little lion and get on the front pages … One of our brave young fighter pilots with Simba, his beloved little lion, Franz von Werra the red devil, terror of the British air force!'

Not only was the RAF man telling this German officer he knew all about him, he was challenging his honour and pride. It was a tactic meant to induce a response from his prisoner.

Anti-aircraft guns pounded and bombs started to fall on London in the distance, but the RAF man continued despite the frequent explosions and the rattling of the window frames. Von Werra finally snapped and responded, belittling the RAF man's argument about lion cubs when his Luftwaffe colleagues were dropping bombs on London. He again told the RAF man he would say nothing.

The squadron leader moved the interrogation up a notch and pulled a copy of the German radio newspaper *Hot mit mir* from a file. It was dated 24 August 1940, just two weeks before the interrogation. On the cover was a Luftwaffe leutnant leaning against the wing of a Messerschmitt Me 109E with a lion cub … It was clearly Franz von Werra – even his distinctive signet ring was visible. The squadron leader read out the newspaper caption: 'This is the squadron lion "Simba", who has taken the place of the British lion, as he rarely ventures into the neighbourhood of German fighter pilots.'

Though struck by the increasing amount of evidence, von Werra laughed mockingly at the RAF officer. Nevertheless, the Englishman continued, challenging stories about shooting down two French Potez bombers and six British bombers which were painted on the tail of his Me 109E.

Von Werra felt the rage building inside him and forcefully stated: 'Squadron Leader, I am a German officer and demand to be treated accordingly. I will not be insulted!'

The squadron leader continued questioning the veracity of the media stories and his combat claims, but the German would not buckle. Instead of giving up, the RAF man continued with another batch of accusations: 'We have only mentioned the victory symbols for two French and six British bombers painted on the tail of your aircraft … and that brings us to the five British fighters shot down in dogfights. Wouldn't you like another cigarette?'

Von Werra refused and shook his head as the squadron leader carried on: 'So, the British fighters you shot down, you told all sorts of heroic stories in the radio broadcast that you spoke to, yesterday a week ago at 6pm on the German radio station.'

The squadron leader pulled a written transcript from a file and placed it in von Werra's hand. He then moved towards what appeared to be a record player-like device, saying, 'This is the text of your broadcast. If you want, you can also listen to the recording.'

Von Werra read the transcript. It detailed his exploits only a few days before, when he reportedly shot down four Hurricanes and destroyed five others on the ground. The British officer had him cornered, but he would not give in and retorted having noticed the rank was incorrect and a simple spelling mistake with his name: 'A remarkable story Herr Major, but what does this Leutnant von Werrer have to do with me?'

The interrogator was like the proverbial cat playing with a mouse: 'Remarkable! The announcer calls it the greatest aerial feat of the entire war and you just call it remarkable! Surely you don't want to claim this broadcast, just because your rank was given as a Leutnant and the name isn't produced correctly? Maybe you would recognise your own voice if I played the broadcast for you?'

The RAF officer started the recording and von Werra listened to his own voice reciting the words in the transcript he held in his hand. Von Werra responded arrogantly: 'I have no idea about the matter.'

The interrogator was reaching a pinnacle and smelt blood: 'What you mean to say is that you are ashamed to admit that the greatest flying feat of the entire war was fabricated from start to finish – a typical example of Werra's boasting.'

Von Werra remained quiet and the squadron leader grew impatient with the German pilots incredulity. An exhibition of controlled impatience and even anger was another tactic the officers of AI1(k) would utilise in other interrogations: 'Werra, you don't have your grandmother in front of you who would perhaps believe your story about attacking landing Hurricanes. Do you think the tail end pilot is not particularly vigilant in the dangerous moments of landing? Can you really believe he could mistake a Messerschmitt for another Hurricane? And that the other five pilots probably didn't have rear view mirrors? And since they were all flying in a cozy circus and had permission to land, they had no contact with Flying Control? Let's assume that by some miracle the pilots didn't spot you – don't you think they would spot you from the ground?'

Still von Werra denied any connection to this man, but the interrogator continued: 'Are you aware that you have become a figure of ridicule in the Royal Air Force? The red devil on the attack!'

The RAF squadron leader continued his lecture, telling von Werra it was lucky he was alone at the time of this extraordinary feat of flying with no Luftwaffe witnesses – he was nothing but a shameless fraud. He then challenged the German on his nerve to report such an account to his own commander. Von Werra finally stayed quiet and the interrogator leaned over him before shouting at him: 'Where was this British airfield? It must be somewhere in Kent or Essex, now talk!'

Von Werra remained silent and the officer asked forcefully once more. Finally, the German pilot spoke saying he knew nothing about it and had nothing to say. The squadron leader paused then told him both the RAF and von Werra knew nothing like this had ever happened.

Running out of tactics, the RAF interrogator went to one of his last resorts – a threat. He told von Werra he would soon be transferred to a POW camp where he would meet many squadron friends, but what would they say if they found out his heroic deed was a fraud? Von Werra knew the interrogator had exhausted his bag of tricks and responded accordingly: 'Squadron leader, do you want to know what I would say, if I were in the position of this Leutnant von Werrer who made this broadcast. I would tell you that you can tell the others what you want. If the RAF lost nine Hurricanes' they would hardly admit it! On the contrary, who would they believe, you or a fellow German officer.'

Von Werra would not budge; he would not give any military information to his interrogator. The RAF man switched the main lights back on and offered the German another cigarette, he knew he was beaten this time. The guard returned von Werra to his room and he remained alone all night.

There is no doubt that Squadron Leader King was Denys Felkin, the lead interrogator and commander of AI1(k) at Cockfosters. The description is certainly that of Felkin, and, as we shall see, his tactics were those he would advocate and use for the remainder of the war.

Felkin signed-off the short preliminary report about von Werra's interrogation. It can be found in The National Archives at Kew under AI1(k) Report No.465/1940. After giving various details of his identity disk and Ausweis (identity card), the crash site location and aircraft, its markings and his unit (II/JG3 – identified from those markings and other information) it states the following:

> 'The pilot landed in the aircraft and has refused to give any details whatsoever. From interrogation of other prisoners of war from the same Gruppe, it has been established that he is the Adjutant of the above unit. This is confirmed by the fact that his identity disk is three below that of 6/JG3. Other prisoners of war state that according to the German wireless, this pilot carried out an attack on an aerodrome near Rochester, about ten days ago when he shot down four Hurricanes which were about to land, set fire to a hangar with incendiary ammunition and riddled five more Hurricanes which were on the ground.'

The report noted that the pilot was unwounded, his morale was very high, that he was confident, and that he was the holder of the Iron Cross First Class. It was signed by Denys Felkin and dated 8 September 1940.

Clearly this report was only a summary and it is very likely there were other more detailed reports which have not been released to the public or have been destroyed. AI1(k) clearly had an excellent administrative system which collected and analysed information before preparing detailed files on enemy airmen.

Over the next two weeks, von Werra would be subjected to further interrogations and various tactics in a bid to make him talk, most were not included in the British book or movie. These included a further one-to-one talk with a different RAF officer who gave him cigarettes and whisky. One night, a group of RAF officers reportedly burst into his room and took him to their Mess, plying him with more alcohol. One officer clearly talking about Squadron Leader King (Felkin) winked at von Werra and told him he had gone and was a terrible guy, they were different. But von Werra remained silent.

On another occasion a man arrived in a civilian suit wearing a bowler hat. He told von Werra that he knew he didn't talk, but all he had to do was blink when he read out a series of Feldpost numbers and he heard his own number. The man read the list and von Werra did not respond. The man therefore made him an offer – he could take him out of the mansion house to the West End of London, he could have dinner, go to a club and even arrange time for him to be alone with a girl. It was an extraordinary offer, but von Werra still refused.

This offer seems incredible, but we know that later in the war, high-ranking prisoners were treated in this way. So, why not make such an offer to a prisoner of von Werra's calibre in September 1940?

One interrogator offered to put von Werra in with a fellow prisoner if he recognised anyone on his list of prisoners. As he read out the list, von Werra remained silent. They would not get his unit from him that way – he would not talk. Eventually, von Werra told the officer he would go in with anyone.

He was taken to a room and the door was opened. Inside was a face he immediately recognised – it was Oberleutnant Karl Westerhoff of 6/JG3. He had been shot down on 31 August 1940, making a forced landing on the ranges at Lydd in Kent. Westerhoff had set fire to his Me 109 and papers. He had refused to give any details other than his name, rank and number, though he did let slip that he belonged to JG3. However, the interrogators did not believe him as his identity disk and his Feldpost numbers did not tally with that Geschwader, when compared to AI1(k) intelligence records.

Von Werra tried not to show any recognition of Westerhoff. He clicked his heels and introduced himself as Oberleutnant von Werra, but his friend immediately recognised him and said, 'Sonny! Man, what a surprise.' 'Sonny' was von Werra's nickname in the Officers' Mess, but it did not matter that this statement confirmed von Werra belonged to JG3, the RAF already knew that. What it did confirm was that Westerhoff was a member of the same Geschwader. The ploy had worked, but that was not the end of it. The RAF officer smiled and left the room; the door being locked again.

The two German pilots chatted happily and Westerhoff asked if von Werra had been interrogated by Squadron Leader King, but suddenly von Werra was suspicious. He suspected the room was bugged and a quick search found what he believed to be a microphone in an air vent. Whispering, he told Westerhoff they would play a game and make up details of pilots and aircraft for the British *listeners*. This continued for some time, but it appears the *listeners* knew this was made-up and fake intelligence, as there are no apparent matching M-Room records for this event in records at the National Archives.

The next morning, Westerhoff went to the window and opened it. Unlike the other windows, this one could be opened. Von Werra quickly identified this could be another trick and bounded out of bed, asking his friend to help him look for another hidden microphone by the window. Von Werra called out, 'Hello RAF Intelligence, Oberleutnant von Werra is calling RAF Intelligence, I'm trying to find a microphone hidden by my window.'

A short time later, the men were separated and moved to different rooms. This time there were five other Luftwaffe officers in with von Werra; they were taken out one at a time for further interrogation.

Later, von Werra was placed in a room with a man who introduced himself as Leutnant Kleinert of JG26. The man claimed to be an Austrian who had worked as an engineer with Professor Willi Messerschmitt, but had been sent to the front to gain combat experience. Unfortunately for him, he was shot down on his first flight and now the British had him.

Leutnant Kleinert started to talk freely and told von Werra he was very interested in all the technical details of the Messerschmitt fighters, and they had a lot of trouble designing a launching device for the Jabos (bomb carrying Me 109s), i.e. the mechanism for releasing the bombs. Kleinert asked von Werra if he had any experience with the device himself, but the latter was no fool and told his new companion to shut up. He quickly told Kleinert that 'Walls had ears.'

Von Werra said Kleinert looked surprised and asked him if he thought there were hidden microphones, before dismissing the idea as complete nonsense. This sent von Werra's suspicious mind into overdrive and he told Kleinert he could be a spy and, in the same manner, von Werra could be the spy. Leutnant Kleinert laughed uncomfortably as he sat sowing and repairing his socks, but a short time later, the Austrian was taken away for further interrogation. Von Werra never saw him again.

Leutnant Kleinert is not listed as a member of, or a loss from, JG26. Could he have been a stool pigeon, placed in the room as one last bid by AI1(k) to get von Werra to talk about military matters? Other prisoners in 1940 had been experts seconded to the front for experience. Could this have been used as a stool-pigeon's *legend*?

Eventually, Franz von Werra was moved to Grizedale Hall POW camp near Coniston in the Lake District. The German camp leader was Major Willibald Fanelsa of Stab III/KG1, a man who would soon follow von Werra to Swanwick Camp in the Midlands. Von Werra would escape from both camps before being transferred to Canada, where he would successfully escape and return to Germany in 1941.

As we shall see in a later chapter, the team at Trent Park did get some revealing information from von Werra, detail that was less of a military value, but a lot more concerning. Information that completely destroys the image of the cheeky almost likeable Hardy Kruger character in the books and movie.

I wrote this opening chapter to give an immediate description of the work of Air Intelligence and AI1(k). The story of Franz von Werra may have been embellished by the man himself (just like his victory claims), but I believe it is a very good account of what an enemy airman could expect after being captured and interrogated at Trent Park.

In the next chapter we shall look at the origins and formation of AI1(k), before moving on to look at its tactics and techniques to gather intelligence from enemy airmen. Later, we shall look at some more detailed cases and the excellent results Air Intelligence obtained in 1939 and 1940.

Chapter 2

Formation and Planning

In January 1939, the intelligence branches of the War Office, Admiralty and the Air Ministry met to discuss their plans if there was another European war. After lengthy discussions, they agreed that a new technique called an 'M-Room' would be one of the tactics for extracting intelligence from any future prisoners of war. The 'M' stood for microphone and the plan was to utilise covert high-grade, sensitive devices to listen in on prisoners of war as they discussed their recent interrogations and other confidential matters.

According to documents held in The National Archives at Kew (file reference KV4/302), representatives of the various intelligence sections attended the Admiralty in London on 9 June 1939, to discuss further, how they would deal with any prisoners in the event of war. One report (No.18 in the file), states that it was suggested the 'Admiralty and the Air Ministry (the latter feeling very much in the dark), should each undertake their own interrogation of their own respective prisoners of war.' The report's unidentified author added that to get best results, they should make the best use of technical brains, methods and interpreters to pool experience, to co-ordinate intelligence received and to economise in these experts. The best plan was to acquire a combined central bureau for the detailed interrogation of new prisoners of war.

The report's author added that these experts, when not interrogating prisoners, could be used to examine captured documents, with the unit's new commander sending officers to interrogate prisoners at military depots across the country. The report also stated the different armed services did not particularly like the idea of utilising the Tower of London as a prisoner of war interrogation centre, as it was believed to be too vulnerable to attack and *The Tower* had a sinister atmosphere which might be twisted by enemy propaganda and even lead to reprisals.

Although the author of this report said those in attendance did not like the thought of using the Tower of London, the meeting had continued and discussed forming a Combined Services Detailed Examination Centre at the location. They suggested sixteen cells for prisoners of war and forty sets of married quarters for staff. The Salt Tower on the south-east corner of the inner curtain wall, was identified as having four rooms one above the other, each capable of housing three to four prisoners. At the time, the Salt Tower was not in use and appeared suitable for the installation of the proposed covert microphones. Two large barrack rooms in 'F' Block South were also identified with room for one hundred prisoners of war.

MI1 (Military Intelligence 1) would create a new sub-section – MI1(g) – which would handle, manage and interrogate all prisoners of war at the Tower of London. This would later become MI1(h). The report went on to give details of how naval prisoners would be handled, as well as those that were the responsibility of the Air Ministry/RAF.

Enemy air force prisoners of war would be given a preliminary interrogation carried out by an Air Force Intelligence Officer, stationed at the local Group HQ. Officers at the time were based at Abingdon, Wilton in Hampshire, Mildenhall, Linton-on-Ouse, Grantham, Norwich, Uxbridge, Hucknall, Gosport, Bristol, Farnborough, Halton and Eastchurch (Isle of Sheppey).

A further meeting was held at the War Office in London on 21 July 1939. It was attended by Captain G. Lucas and Lieutenant A.R. Rawlinson of the War Office, Commander F.J.C. Halahan from the Admiralty and Squadron Leader R.J. Montgomery-Moore from the Air Ministry.

Squadron Leader Robert J. Montgomery-Moore was a long serving officer, having joined the RAF some twenty years before. He was the Station Commander at Duxford in 1928 and retired before being recalled as another war approached. He was recommissioned and joined the Deputy Director of Intelligence Staff - DDI (1), being promoted to wing commander and going on to command AI1(a) in 1940.

At the meeting on 21 July, it was agreed the Tower of London plan would be actioned with accommodation consisting of fifty-six separate rooms, with four rooms in the Salt Tower and the barrack rooms. The Salt Tower had five-floors. The lower floor had been used in Tudor times as a dungeon for Jesuit priests. The four upper rooms – one on top of the other, could each hold three to four prisoners of war and were fitted with concealed microphones. (Later, the Broad Arrow Tower just along the inner curtain wall from the Salt Tower, was similarly used for secret listening via microphones.)

The War Office would arrange for the supply and fitting of the so-called *special apparatus* (covert microphones) and the necessary wiring, to the secret rooms where *listeners* would record the conversations. Where the listening room was located is unclear, but it could have been on the lower floor of the Salt Tower, as this has a separate access door. The report added details of staffing required, which in the case of the Royal Air Force initially consisted of two Air Intelligence Officers and a clerk.

The use of two medieval towers, together with their Tudor prisoner graffiti, dim lighting and arrow slits, together with the imposing edifice of the nearby Norman White Tower, must have shaken the firmest of prisoner nerves. The Tower, and in particular the Salt Tower, have a reputation as being somewhere you do not want to venture after dark; and in a later chapter we shall see this could have been used as a tactic with some of the prisoners of war.

Exactly who supplied and fitted the microphones and equipment in the Tower of London is unclear. A later covert order was made for high-quality microphones from the American RCA company. When they arrived, they were installed at Trent Park, Cockfosters, by a team of specially selected Post Office engineers who signed the Official Secrets Act.

A new form, AFW.3000, was created to cover all newly arriving Army and Air Force prisoners of war. This was to be completed and would accompany the prisoner on his transfer from section to section or prison to prison. It was agreed that an Air Force preliminary interrogating officer would examine each prisoner, before deciding whether they should be sent directly to a prisoner of war camp or on to the Tower of London for more detailed interrogation.

The various intelligence branches agreed that a series of tactics were required on top of the covert microphones, and prisoners of war should be handled in a specific manner. A new commander to oversee this new section was required, who was not only fluent in German, but one who had an excellent knowledge of the country and its armed forces. That man was Thomas Joseph Kendrick, a man with an in-depth knowledge of German prisoners of war during the First World War. In addition, he had lived and worked in 1930's Germany and was acutely aware of the Nazi mind and its philosophy.

Thomas Kendrick had served in the Army during the Boer War and the First World War, before entering the field of intelligence. In the 1920s he worked for British Intelligence in Germany and Eastern Europe. In 1938, he was involved in assisting Jews to escape the Nazis, while he worked in the Passport Office at the British Embassy in Vienna. Eventually, Kendrick was arrested by the Gestapo and interrogated repeatedly, but he did not admit anything. Three days later, he was released and smuggled out of the country and into Hungary, where he flew back to England via Holland and Czechoslovakia. Once in London, Kendrick was debriefed and eventually assigned to work for SIS in the United Kingdom, as he was now on the Gestapo's most wanted list.

Having been chosen as the man to head and implement the new regime for dealing with prisoners of war, Kendrick oversaw the arrangements for housing and interrogating prisoners in the Tower of London. These arrangements included not only the housing of staff and the prisoners, but the so-called M-Rooms and the necessary listening posts. With the plans already in place, Kendrick, who was given the Army rank of a major, prepared to open his new *business* in the Tower of London as soon as war was declared.

Wearing his army uniform, Thomas Kendrick was the commanding officer of the new unit, which comprised of intelligence officers from the Army, Royal Navy and the Royal Air Force. The two intelligence officers from the RAF were Squadron Leader Edmund Pollak and Flying Officer, soon to be rapidly promoted to Squadron Leader – Samuel Denys Felkin – usually known as Denys Felkin. Edmund Pollak had served in the Royal Flying Corps and the RAF during the First World War, being awarded the Military Cross. He later owned a hotel in Vienna during the 1930s and was an associate and friend of Thomas Kendrick.

In 1938, Pollak's hotel and his assets were seized and he was arrested by the Gestapo. Kendrick, who was not quite under Nazi suspicion at the time, managed, through diplomatic negotiation, to get Pollak released and he headed back to Britain. It has long been suspected that Pollak was like his friend, an intelligence officer in Vienna and upon return to London, he continued that profession, but as a commissioned RAF Officer.

Denys Felkin had also lived for a time in Vienna and knew Thomas Kendrick. He served in the Artists' Rifles during the early years of the First World War, before joining the Royal Flying Corps and later the RAF in 1918. At the end of the war, Felkin was posted to the Reparations Committee in Berlin, where he became fluent in German and attained a keen understanding of the nation, it's people and their idiosyncrasies. This knowledge was to prove invaluable, as in time he would command the RAF intelligence section handling and interrogating Luftwaffe prisoners of war. This would be known as AI1(k) or ADI as it was later redesignated.

In the 1930s Felkin worked in Paris as manager of the Ideal Radiator company and regularly travelled back and forth into Nazi Germany. This roving vocation allowed him to gather information and was a perfect cover for his intelligence work. With the approach of war, he returned to Britain and was recommissioned into the RAF.

On 1 September 1939, Germany invaded Poland and it was clear a new European war was imminent. Accordingly, the plan for the new unit was activated at the Tower of London. The day after war was declared by the British on 3 September, the War Office sent an urgent telegram advising all military units of the provisions for handling prisoners of war.

Four days later, on 8 September, the War Office sent another document directing that if Luftwaffe prisoners were held at Infantry Depots, they should contact, by telephone or telegram, the nearest RAF Group HQ or aerodrome contained on an attached list. The army depot should provide facilities for the primary interrogation of the prisoner by the attending RAF Interrogation Officer. The list included:

No. 2 Group HQ RAF Wyton, Huntingdonshire,
No. 3 Group HQ RAF Mildenhall, Suffolk.
No. 4 Group HQ RAF Linton-on-Ouse, Yorkshire.
No. 5 Group HQ RAF Grantham, Lincolnshire.
No. 16 Group HQ Chatham, Kent.
RAF Biggin Hill, Kent.
RAF Hornchurch, Essex and RAF Uxbridge, Middlesex.

It would seem that there were some initial teething problems with these new arrangements. Report No.18 in The National Archive's file, dated 17 October 1939, details the fact some prisoners were not being segregated when transferred by rail to the Tower of London, even when ample rail accommodation was available. It reminded commanding officers that segregation was essential for the successful examination of all prisoners of war. No prisoner should be allowed to confer with other prisoners and should be kept segregated from the point of detention, until handed over to the Combined Services Detailed Examination Centre at the Tower of London.

Later, on 2 November 1939, there appears to have been another issue. This time, newly arrived prisoners had been interrogated by civilian police officers before the RAF's Field Interrogator had arrived. The letter, from an unidentified author to Wing Commander J.O. Archer at the inter-services liaison section AI1(d), states: 'The only instructions we have regarding German Airmen who come down in this country are that they are handed over as soon as possible by the Police to the Military Authorities, who in turn hand them over to the nearest Military Depot. I understand there is no question of any lengthy interrogation until they reach the Tower.'

Despite this letter, as we shall see throughout the rest of 1939 and 1940, a number of prisoners of war were not segregated, were interviewed and/or had their personal and service items taken from them and appropriated by unknown persons. This caused a great deal of frustration for RAF Field Intelligence staff.

It soon became clear that the Tower of London was too small for the purpose of interrogating POWs and on 14 December 1939, a memorandum stated that the Combined Services Detailed Examination Centre was being transferred to Cockfosters Camp, also known as Trent Park, at Barnet in Hertfordshire. The telegraphic address would be PRISWAR BARNET and no reference was to be made in the written address, that this was even a prisoner of war camp – let alone an interrogation centre.

The main mansion house at Trent Park was similarly equipped to the Tower of London with M-Rooms, listening stations, administrative offices, living quarters and detention rooms for the prisoners, but on a much larger scale. Various other properties were built to house staff and prisoners alike, with a number of double barbed wire fences, concertina wire, guard posts and barriers being erected. The house was approached after passing through a guarded main gate house with a high wall. The road continued through a thickly wooded area, until it passed through another guard post and a gate in a barbed-wire fence. Several hundred yards further, there was another gate and a second high barbed-wire fence. Soldiers patrolled with rifles and fixed bayonets between the two fence lines.

In terms of the RAF Intelligence section, the administration unit and the file rooms would grow in size and contain a vast amount of information on prisoners, aircraft, Luftwaffe structure, politics, personnel and much more. The mansion house also had its own medical facility for the prisoners and sparsely furnished rooms containing iron framed beds with rough blankets, a wooden table and chairs, plus personal lockers. The windows were barred on the outside and locked. Black-out boards were placed over the apertures during the hours of darkness. A single uncovered light bulb hung from the ceiling providing the only light, this being controlled by an external switch outside in the corridor and out of reach of the prisoner in their locked room. The rooms did not look like a police or prison cell per se, but it was clear the occupant was a prisoner. The rest of the house that was accessible to prisoners was sparsely furnished, but those rooms available to the interrogators and staff were more comfortable.

Squadron Leader Edmund Pollak had left the RAF Intelligence Section and Denys Felkin was promoted to Squadron Leader, taking command of the unit at Trent Park. Before leaving the Tower of London in late October 1939, the

RAF element had been re-badged as Air Intelligence 1(k) more commonly known as AI1(k). Although Felkin managed the team, in 1940, he reported to Group Captain Francis Inglis who headed the unit at the Air Ministry in London.

Denys Felkin had his own office known locally as Room 'A'. It was comfortably furnished with padded leather chairs, filing cabinets, a good quality mahogany desk and a reading lamp. The walls had wood paneling and thick black-out curtains hung at the windows. The floor was fully carpeted.

Felkin was not only the commanding officer of AI1(k) at Trent Park, he was also the lead interrogator. He had access to alcohol and would often offer the prisoner a drink or a friendly cigarette as he tried to engage them in conversation. The stage was now set for Denys Felkin and his team to examine the expected influx of Luftwaffe prisoners of war in 1940.

Around the same time, Thomas Kendrick and his team were organising and implementing the new unit, which became known by the end of 1939 as the Combined Services Detailed Interrogation Centre, or CSDIC, at the Tower of London; another man entering the intelligence scene from the prisoners' arena was the controversial Lieutenant Colonel Alexander P. Scotland. Scotland was aged 57 in 1939. A Yorkshireman with Scottish ancestry, he had travelled to South Africa intent on joining the British Army during the Boer War, but ended up running a business on the border with German-controlled Namibia. With his German neighbours being regular customers, he became fluent in their language and, like the other intelligence men, attained an excellent understanding of their attitudes and behaviour.

Unbelievably, Alexander Scotland joined the German Army in Namibia and served for four years between 1903 and 1907. In his own book, *London Cage*, which was released after the Second World War, Scotland says he passed intelligence back to the British in South Africa.

In 1914, with Britian and Germany at war, Scotland was detained for espionage by the Germans and held until released by a British advance in 1915. He returned to the UK, obtained a commission in the British Army and served in France, interrogating German prisoners of war. Scotland always stated he used the same German tactics he had observed in Namibia while he was a prisoner. In addition to interrogating German prisoners of war, Alexander Scotland worked behind enemy lines in 1918, posing as a German-Namibian, but he had to flee when it looked like he had been recognised. For his work, Scotland received an OBE and, after the war, he worked in South Africa and South America, allegedly reporting back to the British authorities on the local Germanic community.

With the start of the Second World War, Scotland was recalled to military service, made a Major in the British Army and sent to the Continent to continue his work interrogating German prisoners of war. Scotland also trained young Army officers on how to deal with prisoners.

Like Kendrick, Felkin and Pollak, Scotland found the system of handling and interrogating prisoners of war to be inadequate. He would soon devise his own methods, which were apparently very different to those of Felkin's AI1(k).

After the withdrawal from Dunkirk, Alexander Scotland joined the Intelligence Corps and was given command of a different unit, responsible for handling prisoners of war – the newly-created Prisoner of War Interrogation Section, often referred to as PWIS. This unit eventually managed a number of so-called 'Cages', many of them based at various race-courses such as Lingfield, Kempton Park and Doncaster, as well as other locations around Britain. The first and most infamous of these 'Cages' was at Kensington Palace Gardens in London. Opened in mid-October 1940, it would become known simply as the London Cage. It received its first 'guests' on 23 October.

The Tower of London was the prime CSDIC site in 1939, but with an increase in the number of prisoners of war in 1940, other facilities were required. As we have already seen, the RAF section under Denys Felkin moved at the end of 1939 to Trent Park, Cockfosters, creating their own M-rooms in the large mansion house; and as we shall see later in this book, they handled the Luftwaffe prisoners throughout 1940 and the Battle of Britain.

At the Tower of London, Trent Park and the various Cages, the Army would provide the guards, escorts and administrative staff, although the other two services also had their own *listeners* and administrative personnel. Interestingly, it was the Household Foot Guards regiments that provided most of the guards by virtue of the fact that most members of these regiments were tall and strong – an imposing sight for any enemy prisoner.

Like Trent Park, Alexander Scotland's London Cage would become well-known for its handling of senior German officers, SS and Gestapo men later in the war. They would both play a part in the discovery of information regarding the so-called final solution, vengeance weapons and other war crimes. However, the London Cage would also become synonymous with the alleged ill-treatment of some German prisoners and with Scotland being in command, he would become the main suspect.

After the war, Alexander Scotland wrote and published his book *London Cage* in which he gave details of how the unit made obstructive and non-talkative

Nazis submit to their questioning. Allegations made against Scotland and his London Cage staff included verbal and physical abuse, threats and other forms of interrogation banned under the Geneva Convention. Access to the site was restricted and even the International Committee of the Red Cross would find their efforts to inspect the Cage thwarted.

The British Intelligence Services fought hard to stop publication of Scotland's book in 1954 and 1955, even sending Special Branch officers from Scotland Yard to seize the manuscript and any official papers still held by the now-retired Scotland. The book was eventually released, although heavily redacted, and many historians and researchers have continually questioned what really happened inside the London Cage at Kensington Palace Gardens.

On first inspection, it would appear the RAF and its prisoner interrogation unit AI1(k), under the command of Denys Felkin at Trent Park, handled all Luftwaffe prisoners of war during 1940 and into 1941. It was an expert and proficient unit, gaining as we shall see, valuable intelligence of Luftwaffe personnel, its formations, aircraft and technical advances from a variety of tactics. They also obtained information regarding German morale, industry and much more.

So, the question is why were a number of Luftwaffe prisoners sent to the London Cage for interrogation after it opened in late October 1940 and early 1941? We know this is correct, as their abbreviated files are held in The National Archives and are covered in a later chapter in this book.

Franz von Werra, in his own words, apparently stated he had been taken to both Kensington Palace Gardens (the London Cage) and Trent Park after being shot down. This was repeated in the book *The One That Got Away* by Leasor and Burt and published in 1956, as well as in the corresponding German text *Einer Kam Durch* which was published in 1957, the same year the film was also released. The problem is, von Werra could not have attended the London Cage, as it did not receive its first prisoner until after he arrived at No.1 POW Camp at Grizedale Hall in the Lake District. This raises the question of whether there was another POW reception centre in Kensington Palace Gardens or central London that von Werra attended in September 1940? He was said to have been interrogated there by an Army officer, so was the Army assisting the RAF due to the high number of Luftwaffe prisoners at the peak of the Battle of Britain? It is more than plausible.

In October 1954, the *Bookseller Magazine* reported that Scotland's book was due for release and the War Office considered some of its contents to be a possible breach of the Official Secrets Act. In February 1955, various national and regional newspapers, including the *Yorkshire Post and the Leeds Intelligencer,* were discussing the *London Cage* and the Ministry's attempts to prevent its publication.

Whatever the case, it is clear that Luftwaffe prisoners usually went to Trent Park, but in a number of cases, as we shall see, they were sent to Alexander Scotland's London Cage after it opened in late October 1940. The question is why and what sort of reception did they receive considering the later allegations of ill-treatment? We shall look at the London Cage's Luftwaffe prisoners and the allegations of mistreatment in later chapters.

In early 1940, AI1(k) sent a section of staff to assist the British Expeditionary Force (BEF) in France. They managed to send back a number of reports which went to Trent Park, but with the rapidly advancing enemy forces overrunning the British and French armies, many prisoners were returned to the Luftwaffe when the Wehrmacht overran the units holding the prisoners. In addition, there was little opportunity to thoroughly examine crashed Luftwaffe aircraft on the Continent. RAF Intelligence already had section AI1(g) which was responsible for the examination and technical assessment of crashed and captured enemy aircraft, and they would play a vital role during the summer of 1940.

In May and June 1940, AI1(w) was formed to provide a larger group of duty intelligence officers at airfields across Britain. This group of men was expanded by using suitably qualified RAF Volunteer Reserve officers who were proficient in the German language. The original seven locations at which they were based and mentioned earlier in this chapter, were now expanded to a total of twenty-four locations (see Appendix VI).

At Trent Park, Denys Felkin was supported by his deputy, Flight Lieutenant Guy Brooks Jepson, and four other officers. The latter were Flight Lieutenant H.O. Gregory, Flight Lieutenant C.H. Smith, Flying Officer W.A.O'M. Brayton and Pilot Officer H.N. Roffey. Brayton, Gregory and Smith had originally joined the team at the Tower of London as support in October 1939, but they were soon joined by Roffey. Sadly, Jepson, who served with AI1(k) and ADI throughout the hostilities, was killed in an autobahn crash in Germany in early December 1945. He is buried in the Hanover War Cemetery.

In addition to the ongoing expansion of the unit handling of POWs, a new specialist training course was created to train interrogators at Trent Park, while in August 1940, another group of intelligence officers were sent out to Malta to act as a local interrogation team. This was the set-up managed and further developed by Squadron Leader Denys Felkin at Trent Park. In time, he would be promoted to wing commander and then group captain.

In the next chapter, we shall examine the training and qualifications needed to be an AI1(k) interrogator, as stipulated by Denys Felkin himself in his post-war report. In the summer of 1940, the Directorate of Intelligence under Air Commodore A.R. Boyle was a very complex organisation and included AI1(k). Its main elements and officers were as follows:

DIRECTORATE OF INTELLIGENCE
Air Commodore A.R. Boyle

ASSISTANT DIRECTOR OF INTELLIGENCE
Group Captain P.R. Chambers

DEPUTY DIRECTOR OF INTELLIGENCE DDI (1)
Group Captain D.L. Blackford

AI1		J.B. Hogan
AI1(a)	W/C R.L. Montgomery-Moore	
AI1(b)	Air Ministry Bulletins	F/L H.H. Bolitho
AI1(c)	Ultra Liaison	W/C F.W. Winterbotham
AI1(d)	Inter-Service Liaison	G/C J.O. Archer
AI1(e)	Y-Service and Signals Intelligence	W/C E. T. Carpenter
AI1(f)	Foreign Liaison	Capt. (Retd.) Hon F/L W.E.N. Growden
AI1(g)	Technical Intelligence	W/C J.A. Easton
AI1(k)	POW Interrogations	G/C F. Inglis, S/L S.D. Felkin
AI1(s)	Internal Security	S/L (Retd) P.L. Plant
AI1(t)	Translating	Miss W.D. Wimble
AI1(w)	Intel. War Room	S/L Sir R.J.F. Chance
AI1(z)	Censorship	W/C W.H. Farrow

Chapter 3

Samuel Denys Felkin and AI1(k) Tactics

Samuel Denys Felkin was the man responsible for the development and successful tactics of AI1(k). Apart from the contents of documents and reports now held in the UK National Archives, very little would be known of how this man managed and oversaw the successful unit. One important document, not held by The National Archives, but by the RAF's Air Historical Branch, is Denys Felkin's post-war report on Air Intelligence and the handling of enemy air force prisoners. The document was an intelligence narrative written by Felkin and titled *Air Ministry Intelligence in War*. Initially a secret report, this lengthy document details the work of Air Intelligence and how it developed throughout the war.

The report starts with Felkin discussing the need for a unit to specialise in the interrogation of captured enemy airmen, how the unit was conceived and its expansion via the Tower of London to Trent Park and beyond. In Chapter 7 paragraph 25 of the report (paragraph 30 in the unredacted report), Felkin explains that from experience gained during the war, certain basic methods should be employed if reliable information is to be obtained. These basic methods include the use of hidden microphones, stool pigeons, the careful maintenance of a library and records section for the briefing of interrogating officers and for ascertaining the exact extent of *our knowledge* of the enemy. Results from interrogations should be collated, carefully analysed and provided in readable intelligence reports.

Denys Felkin was quick to identify that *field interrogation* of newly-arrived prisoners was important. A prisoner was at his most vulnerable while still suffering from the shock of being shot down and captured. As we have seen, a number of Field Intelligence officers were distributed across the United Kingdom and by July 1940 this number had risen rapidly (see Appendix VI for details).

Each Field Interrogation Officer was provided with a car and a driver. Their role was to undertake an immediate preliminary interrogation of any new prisoner and if possible, examine the aircraft or what remained of it. If the pilot or crew had been killed or were missing, the wreckage and any bodies would be examined to extract all papers, documents and any other material or facts deemed to be of intelligence value.

All papers, documents and information were to be sent to AI1(k) headquarters at the Tower of London and later to Trent Park with all possible speed. This was essential if intelligence such as codes and radio call signs were identified, the information being time critical if it was to be of any use to the RAF.

During the first months of the war, the preliminary interrogating officers would send the prisoners on to the Tower of London and Trent Park, but as the number of prisoners grew in 1940, they were given authority to filter the new arrivals. Those deemed unlikely to have anything of intelligence value were sent straight to prison camps, while those suspected of having vital information were sent to Trent Park.

As we have seen, in 1939 it was initially envisaged the Army would apprehend and guard all prisoners of war, but by the time of the Battle of Britain, this responsibility almost always fell upon the local civilian police. The police were content to undertake this responsibility having experience in handling, searching and housing prisoners in their cells. Once detained, the military authorities would be contacted and if possible, a RAF Field Interrogation officer would attend.

Eventually, the prisoner would be conveyed by the Army to AI1(k) at Trent Park for further interrogation or on to a POW camp. All Luftwaffe prisoners, even if they were part of the same crew, were to be separated and prevented from talking to other detainees, civilians or anyone else, before being formally interrogated by the RAF intelligence officers. Instructions were also given that the police or military should place a guard on any wrecked aircraft and if possible, camouflage it to prevent other enemy aircraft attempting to destroy it.

As already mentioned, the preliminary Interrogation Officer should, if possible, visit the wreckage to make a search of it while an officer from Technical Intelligence – AI2(g) – would attend to make an inspection, looking for any modifications or improvements not seen on earlier models.

Once the preliminary interrogation officer was armed with all these facts and documents, he would conduct an interview with the prisoner aimed at establishing a number of primary facts such as his name, rank, service number, unit, the aircraft type and his home airfield. These details were quickly sent to Trent Park on the relevant forms to be quickly followed by the individual if selected for further more detailed interrogation.

In his post-war narrative, Felkin was keen to state that a good interrogator is a practical psychologist, with a capacity for rapid appraisal of character and an understanding of how to deal with the different types of prisoners he encountered. As a former police senior investigating officer, detective and advanced interviewer, I would completely concur with this statement. Quickly identifying the strengths and weaknesses of an individual is essential when trying to gather human intelligence.

Felkin added that the officer should be a reasonably good linguist, although emphasis on an understanding of the language, is more important than an ability to speak the German language perfectly. In fact, experience showed that prisoners were suspicious of someone who spoke perfect or even regional accented German. Assumed imperfection and mistakes in pronunciation or the inability to remember certain words or phrases, would often cause a reluctant prisoner to talk and correct the interrogating officer. With the barrier removed, conversation often followed.

Felkin noted that the interrogating officer should not be too young as maturity gains respect. However, if too old, the prisoner may perceive the man to be of an older generation and not likely to appreciate his predicament, service and age etc. It was also found that it was an advantage if the interrogating officer was of a higher rank than the prisoner. German officers and non-commissioned men were used to strict discipline and more inclined to respect the higher rank, even if he was an opponent.

The interrogating officer must accumulate and maintain, an excellent personal general knowledge of enemy aircraft, well-known pilots, units, airfields, terminology, equipment, as well as an understanding of Germany and its politics. This information and knowledge would often catch a prisoner off guard and once disarmed by the RAF officers apparent widespread knowledge, he would talk.

In the first instance, a prisoner may assume there was no point in not talking, as the interrogator already knew everything. Secondly, any attempt by a prisoner to mislead and give false information could be counteracted. Denys Felkin was keen to point out, that the interrogating officer's method of approach to a new prisoner was vital and they must quickly assess and decide upon a tactic. They needed to judge whether a strict or friendly approach would be more beneficial. In addition, they must judge whether the prisoner can be *won over* by friendly discussion, argument, kind treatment or offers of cigarettes, alcohol or chocolate.

The interrogator, Felkin noted, must be possessed of patience, perseverance, an excellent memory, determination and a cool head. A show of anger or impatience may be required, but a total loss of temper was always fatal to the budding interrogator-prisoner relationship. To carry out this role, the interrogator must be a good actor. He must also be quick-witted and versatile, able to promptly identify an error or unguarded comment by a prisoner which could be used to challenge the man.

Interrogating officers must also consider that a prisoner can have his moments of courage, revolt and weakness. Many men would be talkative and blustering, some are vain and keen to promote themselves and their units. On the contrary, some will be frightened and expect poor treatment. Sometimes such prisoners will give information to improve their own treatment and perceived safety. While most aircrew were intelligent men, some were too foolish to realise that just a few misplaced words could complete a jigsaw of information gathered from other prisoners.

There was some vulnerability around the scientific and technical side of operational flying. Some prisoners were keen to give the impression they knew about new devices or technical developments, divulging a small amount of information they had overheard. Very often such unguarded comments could be very important, although the boasting prisoner may never have realised the value of what he said.

Some prisoners making misleading comments in the hands of an expert interrogator, would quickly fall into a verbal trap and be found wanting. The prisoner would then confess his lies and give a more honest account. However, there is also the intelligent prisoner who is cheerful and chatty to a point, but does not divulge any useful intelligence to his interrogator. He is bright and has clearly listened to security briefings, always suspecting verbal traps, hidden microphones and even stool pigeons. This, as we have seen, was the von Werra type of prisoner. However, as we also noted in von Werra's case, other information can be used to dismantle his persona and he will soon start to talk, or in von Werra's case, remain stubbornly tight-lipped.

Denys Felkin points out in his report that two or more prisoners from a single aircraft's crew had to be separated as soon as possible. This prevented the men inventing and agreeing upon a story, though even if they had created some falsehood, this could be broken down over time by an experienced interrogator. If one airman gave away the smallest piece of information, this could be used as a lever against the other members of the crew.

In Felkin's redacted report, which is now available in its entirety, he stated that occasionally it might be necessary to deliberately lead a prisoner to untruth or impoliteness, in order that the interrogator might take on a sterner tone. The interrogator would adopt a harsher tone and mention the prospect of a strict

POW camp. He might also suggest the possibility of the prisoner being handed over to another interrogator who may not be so pleasant. The interrogator should however, *couch* his words in terms that are not too definite, partly because he must leave a loophole in case the prisoner calls his bluff. This coercion, as we shall see later, was a breach of the Geneva Convention and it is probably due to this the paragraph was initially redacted from the report.

Another redacted paragraph details the use of a double act by two interrogators. One man who has apparently failed to get a prisoner to talk, would suggest the inclusion of another interrogator. This new man, like those mentioned in the last paragraph above, is much sterner and makes much harsher comments ... the classic good cop, bad cop routine.

Felkin was keen to state that an interrogator, 'Can only use words and had little else than his personality, determination and experience to assist him.' He added that the interrogator must be careful to avoid any suggestion of threatening the prisoner with violence, immediate, or in the future. The interrogating officer's art must consist of suggestion and innuendo rather than threats. This paragraph appears in some sense to conflict with the earlier paragraphs suggesting the use of implied threats or actions.

Paragraph 60 of the original unredacted report gives an insight into the implied hostility towards Luftwaffe prisoners. Felkin states that the fact the Army provided transport and guards, gave opportunities for the interrogators to say they had no responsibility for any lack of consideration towards the prisoner by these soldiers or even their sparse accommodation. Army guards were, 'ordered to be somewhat inconsiderate in their treatment' of the prisoner, allowing the RAF interrogator to ingratiate himself, by being much more pleasant to the prisoner. Over the decades since 1945, there have been a number of unsubstantiated allegations that Army guards were not only inconsiderate, but physical with prisoners, pushing and shoving them while shouting abuse at them. Although this would be the lower end of the scale of abuse, as we shall see, this paragraph in Felkin's report was probably redacted due to a perceived contravention of the Geneva Convention.

As the German people were indoctrinated with Nazi propaganda throughout the 1930s and the early war years, it was hardly surprising many prisoners were arrogant, sneering and confident of a German victory. Felkin mentions that a process of political indoctrination often proved to be successful. Prisoners having been segregated and isolated from his colleagues could be undone by proof their political beliefs were merely based on inaccurate Nazi propaganda. Pointing out that it was foolish to believe such nonsense, a prisoner would often crumble. Other prisoners who were not committed Nazis, could be placed in a cell with an ardent National Socialist. Their conversation would be monitored via the covert microphones.

A successful tactic used later in the war, was the entertainment of a prisoner with an outing to London, even including a visit to a West End show or restaurant. As we have seen, Franz von Werra claimed such offers, and more, were made to him in September 1940 by his RAF interrogators. Felkin corroborates such actions in his report. He states the problem regularly arose with keeping a prisoner engaged, especially if they were kept at the interrogation centre for a long time. These prisoners were taken to London or elsewhere for a day's outing and shown the sights, or perhaps taken to the theatre or cinema. They were brought back to the centre for the night and a renewed intensive period of further interrogation which often produced excellent results.

As we have already seen, some paragraphs were redacted from the earlier versions of Felkin's report and there is no corroboration of Franz von Werra's claims that he was offered the services of a girl and a room. However, this is hardly surprising.

Felkin notes that Germans in particular were so dependent upon the society of their fellows, that once deprived of their moral support or company they were prone to persuasion. When it was proven the Nazi regime was deliberately misleading its people, some prisoners not only changed their views, but would offer to join the opposite side to work against their government for the good of the German people at home. The report added that experience found very few German prisoners did not talk after a period of interrogation, which could last anything from two to nine days.

Intelligence gleaned from the interrogations was collated, analysed, edited and presented in reports for dissemination. The editor and the interrogating officer would work closely to ensure the reports reflected the intelligence they had gathered.

As already mentioned, covert microphones secreted into various M-Rooms allowed the interrogation staff to listen in to conversations between the prisoners. The placing of two or more prisoners into one of these rooms after an initial interrogation often paid dividends, while the application of a stool pigeon into such an environment was often successful. Although a useful tool, the *listeners* who sat listening to the conversations of prisoners, often had to overcome distracting sounds, technical interference or even breaks in the sound quality. This meant a sentence or crucial piece of information could be missed.

The historian Helen Fry, in her book *The M Room* (published 2012), states that usually only two prisoners would be placed in an M-Room cell. This was to allow the *listener* to differentiate between the two men and who was saying what. However, in the AI1(k) records for 1940, there are a number of occasions when three prisoners were recorded in the M-Room during the Battle of Britain. This was almost certainly due to the numbers of newly arriving captives.

Denys Felkin noted that considerable 'but friendly' differences of opinion between CSDIC and AI1(k) (later known as ADI(k)) took place during the war. These differences centred around the value of recorded interrogations as intelligence. The recordings offered interrogators the opportunity to assess the initial comments of a prisoner against their later private conversations with other prisoners. Despite the need and use of microphones, Denys Felkin clearly states in the report, that nearly all major intelligence obtained by Air Intelligence, came directly from one-to-one interrogations. It was also discovered on rare occasions, that prisoners may exaggerate during a conversation – even one with his compatriots. An airman could boast about their own involvement in something or could be deliberately misleading, this was especially so, if they suspected their new room-mate to be a British stool pigeon.

The use of German or Austrian refugees as stool pigeons was a logical development of the M-Room tactic. During the early war years, many of the stool pigeons were Jewish refugees, while others were political opponents of the Nazi regime. After initially being interned, some were assessed and recruited into the Pioneer Corps before heading to Trent Park to work as *listeners* and/or stool-pigeons. Later, the RAF would use German deserters, or even POWs who wanted to assist the Allies.

A stool pigeon needed a good working knowledge of the Luftwaffe and was given a thorough briefing about the prisoner they were about to meet. They would be advised about what the interrogators wanted to know and how this could be achieved. Uniforms with relevant rank insignia and decorations were required to convince a genuine prisoner they were talking with a captive colleague.

The stool pigeon would be given a detailed *legend* to cover their pseudonym. This had to be detailed to prevent any prisoner suspecting he was a stool pigeon. The *legend* could be used a number of times before it had to be altered or changed, as prisoners undoubtedly talked among themselves in the prison camps.

Stool pigeons had to be great actors with a high degree of confidence. It was soon found that a successful tactic for introducing a stool pigeon, was to use one from a different armed service to the genuine prisoner. However, this could be unsuccessful, as can be seen by the alleged use of a seconded engineer to the Luftwaffe in von Werra's personal story of Trent Park.

The refugees from Germany and Austria made excellent M-Room *listeners* as they could understand certain dialects and accents better than any Briton, even one who was fluent in text-book German. Again, the *listeners* themselves had to be well briefed and have considerable knowledge about Germany, the Luftwaffe and its terminology.

If a particularly valuable prisoner was being interrogated, he would be kept in solitary confinement before being treated in a kind and friendly manner. This was to allow an in-depth assessment to be made of his attitude and the apparent reliability of his personal knowledge. Once the initial stage was complete, a decision would be made about which tactics to use to obtain more detailed information.

While the human intelligence and interrogations were vital, the inspection of crashed aircraft and captured documents was just as important to Air Intelligence. Papers captured with a pilot or airman gave the interrogators a starting point for an interrogation. Identity cards or an Ausweis often allowed the intelligence team to identify a prisoner's parent unit, his airfield or more. It was soon discovered that certain records were given serial numbers which could be attributed to a particular unit or location. For example, if a previous prisoner known to be from Jagd-Geschwader 2 (JG2) had an Ausweis with a certain serial number on it, it was highly likely a new arrival with a number just a few digits away in the numeric sequence was also from JG2.

Maps and briefing documents were often found in the possession of prisoners or in the wreckage of their aircraft. Together with identifying marks on the aircraft (see later chapter on this subject), these allowed an interrogator to surprise a prisoner with his knowledge about his unit, aircraft, call signs, codes and base etc.

In 1939 and 1940, it was clear security was lax among Luftwaffe airmen. They often flew with a wide range of documents and objects which were a treasure trove for the intelligence staff at AI1(k). Whether this lax attitude was due to an expected victory over Britain or something else is debatable, but there is no doubt this was a security risk and the records from Trent Park regularly give details of items that should never have left the ground.

Once recovered or seized, documents, maps and the like would be dispatched with all haste to Trent Park and assessed by the intelligence team there. By the time of the Battle of Britain, vast quantities of papers were being sent to Trent Park and a large registry was compiled from these documents and the information provided from prisoner interrogations. Prisoners were even often found in possession of Luftwaffe intelligence reports, personal diaries, letters, lecture notes, code books and railway, theatre and cinema tickets.

The diaries and personal letters gave away a huge amount of intelligence before the airman had even been interrogated. Even a railway timetable could be of use to the interrogators, either with the airman concerned or a future *visitor* to Trent Park.

The code books, especially those containing radio codes and call signs for various Luftwaffe units, were indispensable information for the RAF's wireless listening unit known as the Y-Service. Y-Service personnel fluent in the German language would listen to the Luftwaffe air-waves, but codes and call signs would often change at short notice. However, if a new set of codes could be located in the possession of a prisoner or in a wrecked aircraft, they could be rushed to the Y-Service *listeners*, who would quickly identify the units assembling for an attack. Similarly, the intelligence from the *listeners* could identify and corroborate victory claims, target codes and other intelligence obtained verbally from prisoner interrogations at Trent Park.

Captured airmen were often found in possession of their paybooks and savings account books. Bank and post office stamps for deposits often gave away the location of the airman's airfield and by extension his unit. If the book had a number of stamps, the airman's movements over a period of time could be deciphered and when he was interviewed by the interrogation officer, his transfers recited to him leaving the man astounded.

Personal letters and diaries often gave lists of officers and men in the prisoner's own unit, again all very useful, not only in identifying the airman's unit, but also allowing the analysts to build comprehensive files on the various different Staffeln and their personnel. Felkin's post-war report added that one airman was found to be in possession of a key for a hotel room in Morgat, near Brest in France. This allowed the intelligence staff to quickly identify his unit.

In addition to the high number of personal and official documents, a large library was developed containing all manner of newspapers, magazines, radio broadcast recordings, newsreel films and items relating to the Luftwaffe. This, together with the registry of captured documents and papers, allowed Air Intelligence to build files on certain well-known individuals, in the hope they might one day be a guest of AI1(k). The file used to interrogate von Werra is a perfect example of this – it provided Denys Felkin with a history of his career, his unit and anything else that the intelligence system had gathered. This was very disheartening to many a prisoner of war, especially if he thought he could get away with just his name, rank and service number.

The library and records section would eventually become so large that it was given its own section number – AIK3. Indeed, the work of this unit cannot be over emphasised. Every small piece of information gleaned from a prisoner, his papers, the aircraft and so on, was stored away, even if it appeared to be totally inconsequential, for it may one day be the final piece of the proverbial jigsaw.

AI1(k) had its own prisoner card index which contained a photograph and details of each man, but it also maintained a photographic card index of non-captured Luftwaffe personnel. This photographic collection usually came from previous prisoners who often carried images of their crew and friends in their wallet or diary. Other images were appropriated by British censors when prisoners tried to send the images home to Germany, but many came from foreign press and magazine articles. Felkin, in his post-war report, stated that few German airmen suspected the source of these images and many attributed them to the work of British Intelligence.

A list of serial numbers on identity disks, or dog-tags, was maintained, including information on the units that issued them. This was especially important, as it soon became apparent the Luftwaffe with characteristic Germanic thoroughness, allocated identity disks with a block of serial numbers to a single unit. If a prisoner gave just his name, rank and number, refusing to say anything else, his number alone could identify his unit and therefore his airfield, aircraft etc. The prisoner was naturally never told how the interrogator knew this information and he would remain in a state of confusion.

The Ausweis, an operational identity card allowing entry to military property, could also assist the intelligence section in identifying the owner's unit. Issued in varying colours and sizes, as well as different type sets and in differing papers or card, they also bore an authorising signature and often a serial number. The serial number, like that on identity disks, could reveal a location, and could be corroborated from the different colours and sizes, all of which could identify a unit or location of issue.

Another AI3(k) index held the airfield postal codes otherwise known as Feldpost nummers (Field Post numbers). However, the Luftwaffe soon learnt of its use by RAF Air Intelligence and changed the system in early 1941.

Detailed files were kept on each Luftwaffe Geschwader, their Gruppen, Staffeln and airfields, as well as the main personalities. In addition, an index of unit markings, crests and badges allowed intelligence officers to quickly identify the owner of a specific aircraft.

Finally, an index of the names and signatures of parachute packers and their home airfields, allowed the RAF intelligence staff to identify where a parachute originated, even without physically seeing or possessing the pilot or his aircraft!

In addition to Trent Park and all its resources, it was, as already mentioned, important an initial examination of an aircraft wreck and a subsequent report be made as soon as possible. The civil police, Army and Observer Corps were quick to report downed enemy aircraft and the intelligence officer and their driver would quickly attend the scene. If they could not attend, an airman or soldier would complete a report and forward it as soon as possible to Trent Park. To assist this process, a proforma was designed to be used. This was often called-in by telephone, but, in special cases, a written report would be submitted consisting of the following details:

A. Date and location of crash and map reference.
B. Type of aircraft.
C. Identification and distinguishing marks.
D. Type of engine/s.
E. Cause of crash, type and distribution of bullet strikes and condition of aircraft.
F. Armament,
    i) Guns of all types, positions, quantity.
    ii) ammunition, state number of magazines.
    iii) bombs and bomb installations.
    iv) mines and mine carriers.
G. Armour plating, quantity, positions, thickness and if penetrated.
H. Number of crew and fate.
I. Leading edge and if protected against balloon cables by cutters.
J. State if sample can be obtained of petrol or oil.
K. Internal equipment, condition, bombsights, navigational, wireless and other instruments and wireless settings.
L. General remarks.
M. Recommended disposal.

This widespread collection of information from personnel, documents, wreckage and even the German media, allowed AI1(k) and its records section – AIK3, to build a vast data base of intelligence. This information gave the interrogators who used the aforementioned tactics, a distinct tactical advantage in extracting further intelligence from hundreds of Luftwaffe airmen in 1939 and 1940.

Chapter 4

Deciphering the Luftwaffe's Structure and Markings

One of the main strands of work for Air Intelligence was deciphering the Luftwaffe structure and identifying its various operational units. The RAF had a relatively simple system made up of Commands (Fighter Command, Bomber Command and Coastal Command etc.); and the commands were made up of various Groups, for example No.11 Group, Fighter Command, which covered the South-East of England. The various Groups were split into Sectors, each one made up of a number of airfields which housed one or more fighter squadrons.

The Luftwaffe had a similar system with Air Fleets instead of Commands. Unlike their British opponents, each Air Fleet would contain bomber, fighter and dive bomber groups. In essence, each Air Fleet was like a small air force in its own right. For example, on the 17 August 1940, Air Fleet 2, which had its headquarters in Brussels, contained no fewer than seven bomber groups (Kampfgeschwader), a dive bomber group (Stuka Geschwader), five fighter groups (Jagdgeschwader) and two Destroyer groups (Zerstorer fighter Geschwader) equipped with the twin engine Messerschmitt Me 110. There were also a number of smaller units for reconnaissance, night-fighting, air-sea rescue and coastal patrol work.

Air Fleet 2 was a significant force and was replicated by Air Fleet 3, with its own headquarters in Paris and the smaller Air Fleet 5, which was based in Norway. Like the RAF, each Luftwaffe unit had its own number, badge or crest (some official and some unofficial).

In the 1930s, RAF fighter aircraft often bore squadron colours comprising of a band along the upper wing between the roundels and on either side of the fuselage roundels. These bands displayed the squadron's identifying colours. No. 74 Squadron for example, known as the tigers, had an alternating gold and black band along its upper wing. This was repeated either side of the fuselage roundels and the squadron crest (in this case a Tiger's head) was placed in front of the fin flash on the vertical stabiliser. Many modern RAF squadrons still use such identification colours to this day.

It was also common practice to have the squadron commanders pennant below the cockpit. This was a small badge similar to a flag-pennant with the squadron number visible on it. This practice died out in the first years of the war, but again it can still be seen on the RAF's modern jets.

In the years leading up to the war, the RAF ensured that their new Spitfire and Hurricane fighters were not only camouflaged, but did not display their squadron colours and badges. In time, they would be given a two-letter squadron code to be displayed on the fuselage of their aircraft, together with that particular aircraft's identifying letter. For example, Nos. 610 (County of Chester) and 32 Squadrons at Biggin Hill had the respective squadron codes 'DW' and 'GZ' in August 1940. An aircraft with the individual identifying letter 'C' in each unit, would therefore display the fuselage code DW-C or GZ-C. It was a simple system and easy to understand, a similar system being used in both Bomber and Coastal Commands.

The Luftwaffe, however, had a system which, while simple to understand once explained, was more complicated than the British version. To make matters even more difficult for Air Intelligence, the pre-war Luftwaffe unit designations were changed in a large number of cases. For example, KG355, a pre-war bomber unit, changed to KG55, and, although aircraft markings changed accordingly, crewmen very often still carried documentation or parachute packs with the old unit designation marked upon them.

Luftwaffe single seat fighters like the Me 109E, belonged to various fighter wings or groups called Jagdgeschwader (which translates to *hunting wing*). Each wing was given a title and a number, e.g. Jagdgeschwader 26, which is often shortened to just JG26. Each Jagdgeschwader was made up of a number of Staffel, usually totaling nine Staffeln, together with a Stab or Headquarters section. Each Staffel was given a number e.g. 1 Staffel, 2 Staffel, 3 Staffel and so on. The number of aircraft in each Staffel could vary depending on serviceability, but most of the time it was slightly smaller than a full RAF fighter formation of twelve machines.

An aircraft from 5 Staffel of Jagdgeschwader 26 would have the shortened title of 5/JG26, while one from the Stab or Headquarters section would be identified as Stab/JG26.

Staffel aircraft had an identifying number between 1 and 14 allocated to each machine. Different colours were used in the summer of 1940 to signify a particular

Staffel's aircraft and generally speaking, aircraft from the 1st, 4th and 7th Staffel had white identifying numbers, those from the 2nd, 5th and 8th had black numbers, while those from the 3rd, 6th and 9th bore yellow numbers. However, this rule was not always adhered to, and in the summer of 1940, it was not unusual to find an aircraft attached to a Staffel bearing another Staffel's coloured number. This was often because of serviceability issues and aircraft were *borrowed* from sister units. In addition, this may have been due to the movement of an aircraft or a pilot being attached to another Staffel at the time he was shot down.

In the latter stages of the Battle of Britain, some aircraft had completely different number codes. For example, one aircraft brought down from 3 Staffel of JG51 (3/JG51), bore a brown number on its fuselage and one from the 4 Staffel of JG53 (4/JG53) was noted by Air Intelligence as having an orange number. There were other peculiarities as well. Unteroffizier Braun of 6/JG26 had a brown fuselage number when he was shot down ... almost certainly a personal touch linked to his family name.

While most 5 Staffel aircraft used black numbers, JG27 used both black and red, while JG53 and JG54 used red outlined in black. AI1(k) managed to decipher and understand this colour coding system, but after the summer of 1940 Luftwaffe fighters started to use a variety of colours including green and blue letters and fuselage bands near the aircraft tail.

The nine Staffeln of each Geschwader were divided into three Gruppen, numbered I, II and III. I Gruppe contained the aircraft from Staffel 1, 2 and 3 with their white, black and yellow identifying fuselage numbers. II Gruppe contained aircraft from Staffel 4, 5 and 6 with their similar white, black and yellow numbers and on with the III Gruppe (except were already noted, when some used different colours).

Very often an aircraft from the 4th Staffel of a Geschwader, would be listed as an aircraft belonging to the II Gruppe instead of its own Staffel. For example, an aircraft of the 4th Staffel JG3 could be listed as belonging to either 4/JG3 or II/JG3. This complicated the system for Air Intelligence and took some time to unravel. In addition, the Headquarters or Stab section of JG3 would be listed as Stab/JG3. Each Gruppe would also have its own Stab flight and an aircraft from the I Gruppe Stab flight would be shown as Stab I/JG3 and the others Stab II/JG3 and Stab III/JG3.

The aircraft of each Jagdgeschwader's senior officers bore identifying symbols rather than numbers and these can be seen in the following table:

Top row left to right: Geschwader Kommodore and Geschwader Technical Officer.
Second row: Gruppe Kommodore and Gruppe Technical Officer.
Third row: Geschwader Adjutant and Geschwader Operations Officer.
Bottom row: Gruppe Adjutant and Geschwader Chief of Staff.

In addition to the coloured fuselage identifying numbers and symbols, the Jagdgeschwader Gruppen sometimes employed symbols on the fuselage to indicate the Gruppe. Very often, the I Gruppe used no symbol at all, but the II Gruppe used a horizontal bar on the tail side of the German cross on the fuselage. Together with the individual aircrafts number, aircraft 8 would be displayed as:

8 + –

The III Gruppe often used a vertical bar or a wavy line and aircraft 8 would have the following markings:

8 + | or 8 + ~

The Adjutant of the III Gruppe may have the following insignia on his Messerschmitt, but these *rules* were not always adhered to:

< + ~

The III Gruppe Technical Officer may have the following insignia:

<O + ~

In addition to this system of identifying symbols and coloured numbers, each Jagdgeschwader liked to apply their own unit crest or badge to their aircraft. JG26 was known as the *Schlagater* Geschwader and regularly used a black Gothic letter 'S' on a white shield under the cockpit. Various JG26 Staffel also used their own motifs and the 9th Staffel of JG26 used a *Hellhund* (hellhound), which looked like a black sitting griffon or demon in addition to their *Schlagater* Geschwader 'S' shield and the aircrafts individual number and or markings.

Through this combination of coloured numbers, symbols, crests and motifs, Air Intelligence staff could quickly identify the aircraft and a pilot's unit. Add this to the pilot's identity tags, Feldpost numbers and any Ausweis details he carried, and the pilot need not talk at all, to be quickly identified by AI1(k) and their Field Intelligence staff. If a non-communicative pilot was subsequently bombarded with facts about his unit by his interrogator, his lips were soon loosened.

From mid-August 1940, Me 109s from various different Jagdgeschwader started to appear with a variety of yellow engine cowlings, spinners, rudders and rudder tips. Wing tips were also added to this mix and initially, it was suspected by RAF pilots and Air Intelligence, this was something akin to Manfred von Richthofen's brightly coloured *Flying Circus* during the First World War, and these aircraft belonged to crack units and selected pilots. JG26 were one of the first Jagdgeschwader to carry such markings and Adolph Galland's team certainly fitted the bill of a crack unit, but there were far too many aircraft for this to be the case.

Oberleutnant Ulrich Steinhilper of JG52 noted in his own diary, that yellow paint arrived at their aerodrome on the 24 August 1940, with orders to paint the engine cowlings of their Messerschmitt's immediately. The order he said, came directly from Hermann Göring. Eventually, it was said the orders had been issued as there was an urgent need to identify German fighters due to the number of friendly fire incidents and the loss of pilots. At the time, many Luftwaffe pilots believed the markings were being applied as some form of invasion marking (a bit like the Allied invasion stripes in June 1944).

Oberleutnant Anton Stangl of 5/JG54 was brought down on 1 September 1940, near Ashford, Kent. He quickly told his RAF interrogators that the yellow nose of his and other Messerschmitt 109s was so they could recognise their own aircraft in combat.

A recorded conversation in an M-Room dated 11 September 1940, tends to confirm Steinhilper and Stangl's claims. In the transcript (ref. SRA498), a Leutnant pilot, believed to be Karl Stix of 4/ZG2, claims it is difficult to distinguish between a Messerschmitt 109 and a Spitfire, that is why the noses of 109s are painted yellow.

On 19 September, prisoner A483 – Oberfeldwebel Gotthard Goltzsche of 1/JG77 – stated in response to another pilot's claim that the Spitfire looked like a Messerschmitt 109: 'Now the '109 has a yellow ring round the nose, so that you can distinguish them.'

The first identified Messerschmitt to be lost and crash in the United Kingdom with its yellow markings, appears, from AI1(k) records, to have been that flown by Oberleutnant Helmut Tiedmann of 2/JG3 on 18 August 1940. It is possible others had crashed before this date, but this was the first in which there was sufficient wreckage left to allow an examination and an assessment.

A number of other Me 109s from JG2, JG3, JG26 had crashed on the eighteenth, but they were too badly damaged for any markings to be visible. Two JG27 machines came down and one was examined at Shanklin Down on the Isle of Wight, but no yellow markings were noted. However, as we shall see, reporting officers or airmen sometimes missed off such crucial information when submitting their reports to Air Intelligence.

The next aircraft to come down sufficiently intact for its markings to be noted, was that of Unteroffizier Wilhelm Kaiser of 9/JG3 on 24 August. This was noted as having a yellow tail and wing tips. On the same day, the aircraft of Oberfeldwebel Fritz Beeck 6/JG51 was noted as having yellow wing and tail tips. However, not every Me 109 that day was noted as having such markings and the aircraft of Feldwebel Herbert Bischoff of 1/JG52, had no yellow markings at all.

Over the final week of August, aircraft from 4/JG2, 2/JG3, 3/JG26, 1/JG54 and 4/JG54 were identified with a variety of yellow markings. On 30 August, RAF Intelligence staff noted that the Messerschmitts of Feldwebel Ernst Arnold and Oberleutnant Erwin Axthelm, both of 3/JG27, had their engine cowlings painted orange – clearly something had gone wrong in the paint supply chain!

Although most Jagdgeschwader appear to have adhered to the official directive, three Me 109s of 3/JG3 came down on 31 August 1940 and no yellow markings were noted. Similarly, an aircraft from JG26 also came down that day without the yellow markings, but the aircraft of Oberleutnant Hans-Jurgen Ehrig, Leutnant Jura Petrenko and Feldwebel Gunter Kramer of 1/JG77 were all noted as having yellow engine cowlings. On 1 September 1940, Leutnant Josef Burschgens of 7/JG26, belly landed his Me 109 at Iden, near Rye in Sussex, and it bore no yellow markings. The last aircraft in this period noted with a yellow nose, was that of Oberleutnant Anton Stangl of 5/JG54 when he crashed near Ashford in Kent.

Suddenly, without notice and for reasons that have never really been understood to this day, the yellow (and orange) markings changed to white. Whether it was believed this was a better and more visible colour, or there was some other reason, is debatable. (RAF training aircraft about twenty years ago changed from red and yellow paint schemes to a black and yellow scheme, as it was deemed to be more visible.)

What we do know is that between 2 and 7 September 1940, a number of Me 109s were brought down and noted with white markings. These included the von Werra's aircraft. The list includes the following:

2/9/1940	Fw. Verlings	1/JG52	White wing tips and tail
	Uffz. Elbers	8/JG54	White wing tips and tail
5/9/1940	Lt. Schnabel	1/JG3	White wing tips and rudder
	Uffz. Grabow	3/JG3	White wing tips and rudder
	Oblt. Von Werra	Stab II/JG3	White wing tips and rudder
	Haupt. Meyerweissflog	Stab/JG53	White wing tips and rudder
	Lt. Deutsch	7/JG53	White wing tips
	Uffz. Hotzelmann	1/JG54	White wing tips and rudder
6/9/1940	Uffz. G. Schulte	7/JG53	White wing tips and rudder
	Fw. W. Gottschalk	6/LG2	White wing tips v rudder
	Gefr. Holzafel	7/JG26	White wing tips and rudder
	Oblt. Metz	8/JG2	White cowling

On 7 September 1940, the Me 109 of Leutnant Hans Krug of 4/JG26 came down at Pluckley in Kent with a yellow cowling and rudder. It was followed half an hour later by that of Oberleutnant Adolf Gotz of 1/JG2, who came down at

West Hougham in Kent, this was noted as having a yellow rudder and spinner. Others soon followed and it was clear the white Me 109 markings had returned to yellow, though not every Me 109 bore these markings.

From the AI1(k) intelligence logs, these changing colours do not appear to have been identified by the analysts as being a particular concern. Such was the identification scheme the RAF interrogators and intelligence staff had to untangle in 1940, though it did not take long to unravel and AI1(k) quickly used it to their advantage in interrogating many bemused fighter pilots!

The Kampfgeschwader (bomber groups/wings) of the Luftwaffe in 1939 and 1940, used a different system to identify their aircraft and units. This system was also used on the Messerschmitt Me 110 heavy fighters and Junkers Ju 87 Stuka dive-bombers. Aircraft were given a fuselage code of a letter and number to the left of the German cross with two letters to the right. The letter and number to the left of the cross identified the Geschwader, while the first of the two letters to the right, identified the aircraft's individual letter and the second its Staffel. The individual aircraft letter was colour-coded like the numbers on Me 109Es. By way of example, the famous Leaves Green Dornier Do 17, brought down near Biggin Hill on 18 August 1940, bore the fuselage code:

F1 + DT

F1 identified the aircraft as belonging to Kamp Geschwader 76 (KG76). The fuselage code was written in black, but the aircraft letter **D** was in yellow. The letter **T** signified it was part of the 9th Staffel, III Gruppe of KG76 (9/KG76). The Staffel colour was yellow and so the individual aircraft identifying letter - **D** was painted in yellow.

Stab sections usually used a blue or green letter to identify their aircraft, while those of the 1st, 4th, 7th and 10th Staffel (bombers Geschwader could number up to 12 separate Staffeln), bore white letters. The 2nd, 5th, 8th and 11th Staffel had red letters; while the 3rd, 6th, 9th and 12th Staffel bore yellow letters.

An individual aircraft's Staffel colour was occasionally painted on the spinners of the aircraft engines and sometimes, but rarely on other parts of the airframe. Some Geschwader also added different coloured fuselage bands in addition to unit crests or badges identifying their particular Gruppe or Staffel. The fuselage bands were usually near the tail of the aircraft, but sometimes near the cockpit.

The aircraft from the Bomber or Kampfgeschwader were just as difficult to identify as their colleagues in the single engine fighter units. Very often the

Geschwader crest or badge might have a difference in size or colouring, but generally they remained the same. Sometimes this colouring would reflect the aircraft's Staffel and its coloured identification letter on the fuselage, e.g. a red letter might also be repeated with a red crest/emblem.

The following table gives some examples of KG26 Heinkels brought down on land in 1940 and how they displayed their unit markings – if at all:

Date	Location	Unit	Crest/Badge	Aircraft letter
28/10/40	Humbie, Edinburgh	Stab KG26	Green sitting Lion, facing left on a white shield under cockpit with motto *Vestigium leonis* above it.	Green 'J' 1H+JA
03/02/40	Sneaton, nr. Whitby	4/KG26	Red sitting Lion, facing left on a white shield under cockpit with motto *Vestigium leonis* above.	White 'F' 1H+FM
09/02/40	North Berwick Law	5/KG26	Red sitting Lion, facing left on a white shield under cockpit with motto *Vestigium leonis* above.	Red 'E' 1H+EN
03/04/40	Sea off Whitby	Stab II KG26	Not known if crest was visible.	White 'AC' 1H+AC see below
08/04/40	RAF Wick, Scotland	6/KG26	Red sitting Lion, facing left on a white shield under cockpit with motto *Vestigium leonis* above.	Yellow 'D' 1H+DP
12/07/40	Aberdeen	9/KG26	Not known if crest was visible.	Yellow 'F' 1H+FT
09/08/40	In sea off Whitburn, Sunderland	7/KG26	Not known if crest was visible.	White 'E' 1H+ER

N.B. The letters AC in white indicated this was the lead aircraft in this unit (Stab II / KG26).

RAF Field Intelligence interrogators and other specially trained staff were quick to identify and report the markings on a recently shot down aircraft. This information was quickly transmitted to AI1(k) at Trent Park, where the intelligence analysts sought to link it to information already held in the rapidly expanding archives of German aircraft, units, airfields and aircrew.

The RAF Field Interrogators were quick to add to their initial aircraft examination, adding any papers and documents found in the wreckage or in the personal property of the captured airman. Even before their first interrogation at Trent Park, airmen did not realise the Air Intelligence staff had in most cases, already built a detailed history of the prisoner and his background. By the time he sat in front of Denys Felkin, or one of his junior interrogators, they usually had a great deal of information on the prisoner. Sitting and remaining silent in many cases was pointless, the interrogator would do all the talking, giving the dumb-founded airman a resume of his aircraft and unit.

Eventually, many would break and while not divulging military secrets, they would be happy to admit their name, rank, unit, airfield, aircraft and even discuss some of their unit's personalities. They did not realise it, but this small aperture into their inner most thoughts, allowed the AI1(k) interrogators to plant seeds of doubt and suspicion, which in some cases led to further intelligence from extra sessions of interrogation or simple M-Room surveillance.

As we shall see in subsequent chapters, many Luftwaffe airmen went back to their rooms to meet with other prisoners, not realising that their every word was being listened to and recorded. Many returning prisoners were very satisfied with their efforts to confound the interrogating officer and they were keen to discuss what they had been asked, as well as what they had and had not told their interrogator. This information, some of it highly sensitive, was gratefully received by the M-Room *listeners* and disseminated to the relevant departments.

Chapter 5

The First Prisoners

September – December 1939

AI1(k) and the wider CSDIC team were primed and waiting for their first arrivals at the Tower of London when the war started on 3 September 1939. Although air raid sirens sounded across the South-East of England, the Luftwaffe failed to make an appearance and an air of anxiety settled across the nation.

The first intelligence report that was received concerning the Luftwaffe arrived in late September 1939 from France. Its author was Flight Lieutenant Duncan Grinnell-Milne MC DFC*, a First World War fighter ace and prisoner of war, Grinnell-Milne had been recommissioned and dispatched to France. What exactly his role was in September 1939 is unclear, but in June 1940, he was working as a liaison officer with the French Air Force; it would appear he was already in a liaison role in 1939.

Grinnell-Milne's four-page report, dated 27 September 1939, gave details of the interrogation of two Me 109 pilots, both of whom were captured on 24 September. Shot down by the French Air Force, both men were unharmed and went on to be interrogated by the French. Grinnell-Milne noted that these were the first Luftwaffe POWs to have been taken. The British officer also stated that he had interrogated the prisoners himself.

In his report, Grinnell-Milne states that the first man he interrogated was Gefreiter Adolf Hesselbach. He had been badly treated by the French police, with poor housing, food and clothing. He therefore responded to kinder treatment from the RAF officer. A cigarette soon loosened his tongue and the Gefreiter spoke freely. It transpired that the 21-year-old former engineering student was keen to renew his studies in Germany, but was fairly ignorant of world events. He claimed to have been brought down in his first engagement, but he believed anti-aircraft fire had brought him down and not the French fighters he encountered.

Continuing, the young German pilot gave a full description of his last flight, his unit and airfield at Biblis, near Worms.

Hesselbach stated that French Morane fighters had engaged them, with about six aircraft per side. He added that he was sorry to have lost 'his' Me 109, a type he believed to be the finest aircraft in the world. However, although his machine was faster, he did concede the French Morane was more maneuverable.

The two men discussed the French and German anti-aircraft, or flak, units, before Grinnell-Milne sympathised with his boredom of captivity. The German pilot was quick to reply, 'Oh, but it's going to be a very short war.' Despite this comment, Hesselbach told his interrogator that Germany would never attack France, as she had no issue with the French.

The conversation continued and the young pilot openly discussed the plentiful food in Germany, the fact Hitler was very popular and that no one understood why Britain and France were making war with Germany. He blamed Poland and said he had seen photographs of atrocities committed by the Poles. Grinnell-Milne was quick to summarise the young man as a product of a Nazi upbringing and propaganda.

The second captured Me 109 pilot was Leutnant Kurt Rosenkranz. Although not a Nazi Party member, he had a similar outlook to his younger colleague and was a fervent believer in the Nazi philosophy. Small in stature, Grinnell-Milne said the Leutnant reminded him of Joseph Goebbels.

Rosenkranz said he admired Hermann Göring, a man he described as a skilled airman and a great organizer. He seemed to like Rudolf Hess, but the name Heinrich Himmler brought just a shrug of the pilot's shoulders. On the contrary, he believed Winston Churchill and Anthony Eden were warmongers. He stated that they did not hate England and just wanted their colonies back and the right to live. Rosenkranz also blamed the Poles for atrocities and added that German prisoners had been tortured to death, burnt alive and had their eyes gouged out. Grinnell-Milne asked whether he had seen this himself, to which Leutnant Rosenkranz acknowledged he had not, but he heard about this from his brother who was in Poland.

Rosenkranz's comments on Adolf Hitler were very enlightening for the RAF officer when he said: 'There are hundreds to take his place if he should fall … The Fuhrer is always right, only the Fuhrer can decide, only the Fuhrer knows, the Fuhrer principle is that everything is life, it must be everything, nothing else matters.'

Rosenkranz admitted listening to foreign radio broadcasts, but could not comprehend why Britain and France should allow anything to be said against the German leader. Like Hesselbach, Rosenkranz was sure Germany would not attack France. He had received orders not to fly across the frontier, but it was difficult to obey when at altitude and seeing an enemy aircraft. He also believed the Me 109 was the best aircraft, faster than the Spitfire and the Morane, but he had yet to encounter the British machine. He knew the British had attacked Wilhelmshaven, but they had suffered terribly heavy losses. He was sure Germany would never attack London.

Grinnell-Milne's report ended with a comment that both men; 'Would seem to be products of a well-trained, well-drilled Nazi youth. Their morale is excellent, they are keen, convinced, loyal – and ignorant ... They know everything they have been told is true; only defeat in the field will disillusion them.'

As the Phoney War settled over the Continent, enemy aircraft started to probe British airspace – especially over the north of England and Scotland. Many aircraft were undertaking reconnaissance flights, looking for the Royal Navy at Rosyth and Scapa Flow in the Orkneys. On 26 September 1939, a Dornier Do 18 flying boat, on one such mission, was attacked and brought down by Fleet Air Arm Skuas over the area of Great Fisher Bank in the North Sea. Damaged by the naval fighters, the pilot, Leutnant zur See Wilhelm von Reitzenstein, a naval officer attached to the Luftwaffe's 2/KuFIGr506, landed and the crew of four surrendered to the destroyer HMS *Somalia*. The ship then sent the Dornier to the bottom of the sea with gunfire.

It was nearly three weeks before any further enemy aircraft were brought down. On 16 October 1939, Junkers Ju 88s from KG30 were sent from Germany to attack warships in the Firth of Forth. Two machines were attacked by Spitfires and brought down.

Hauptmann Helmut Pohle of 2/KG30 came down in the North Sea off Crail, Fife. Pohle was wounded and ended up in Edinburgh hospital, were he remained for some time. Sadly, his three crewmen were all killed. Pohle's injuries included a fractured jaw and severe facial injuries.

It appears that despite his injuries, Pohle was interrogated in his Edinburgh hospital bed. There is a report detailing his preliminary interrogation by an RAF Flying Officer, noted to be the Chief RAF Interrogation Officer, on 20 October 1939. This was probably Denys Felkin.

The report states that Pohle admitted his aircraft had been damaged by anti-aircraft fire, before being attacked by the Spitfires. He gave full details of his Ju 88's defensive armament and crew. He was quick to state he was the Staffelkapitan and a personal acquaintance of General Bodenschatz and Hermann Göring. He then surprised his interrogator when he asked him to telephone Berlin and request that a specialist doctor fly over in a Red Cross aeroplane to treat him!

Pohle admitted to being the leader of the raid, but he could not name all the pilots on it. He did, however, accept that Hauptmann Schnorr von Karolsfeld may have been on the raid without his knowledge. Pohle also admitted to having spent two months fighting in Spain during the Civil War with the Condor Legion.

Hauptmann Pohle gave a full description of the number of aircraft and their tactics on the raid to the Firth of Forth. This information was corroborated by a report from Captain Dee of HMS *Jarvis* and the commander of HMS *Falatine*, (possibly an error as there was no ship of this name), who witnessed the air attack.

Meanwhile, Oberleutnant Hans Storp and his crew of 1/KG30, came down in the North Sea off Port Seton in East Lothian. Their air mechanic was killed, but the other three men clambered into their dinghy – soon to be captured and dealt with by the interrogators. The interrogation of Storp will be covered in a later chapter, but Flying Officer Denys Felkin submitted two reports to his Commanding Officer, Squadron Leader Pollak, on and just after 20 October 1939.

The crew, as a collective, gave details of their mission, stating that they did not obtain navigational assistance from home-based radio beacons. They also did not receive any radio messages sent to British fighters. They gave details of their aircraft escape procedures and rubber boat drill.

The wireless operator, Oberfeldwebel Hans Hielschar, complained that the arc of fire for his machine gun was impeded by the Ju 88's tail structure. He modestly added that if his field of fire had been better, he was sure he would have accounted for one of the attacking Spitfires.

The crew of four were experienced airmen, the observer and wireless operator having been in the Luftwaffe since 1934. They had, it was revealed, taken part in the attack upon the British fleet on 26 September, and both Hielschar and Hohncke, the observer, had been awarded the Iron Cross for that single action.

Although there appears to have been a good deal of conversation, it is clear from the reports that Denys Felkin believed they were the crew of a Heinkel He III, when in fact they had been flying a Junkers Ju 88.

Two days after these reports, Felkin submitted another longer report which detailed the interrogation of Oberfunkmaat Hilmar Grimm. A wireless operator, Grimm's aircraft, a Dornier Do 18 flying boat – 8L+DK of 2/606 – had flown from Sylt to carry out a reconnaissance of the Firth of Forth and search for any ditched Luftwaffe aircraft on 17 October 1939. They were accompanied by another aircraft piloted by their flight commander, but they were intercepted and shot down by British fighters off the Isle of May. The flight commander's aircraft escaped, albeit it returned once the RAF fighters had departed.

Grimm was a very talkative man. He revealed that he was the wireless operator and assistant observer, that he had been in the Kriegsmarine for eight years, and that it was to his regret that he had been transferred to the Luftwaffe. The first observer was Oberleutnant zur See Siegfried Saloga, a man he said had been in the navy since 1935, but attached to the Luftwaffe since 1938. Feldwebel Grabbet was the pilot. He had joined the Kriegsmarine in 1930, but transferred to the Luftwaffe in 1934. The air mechanic, Unteroffizier Seydel, was killed by gunfire from the British fighters.

In his interrogation, Grimm gave a lot of detail about his unit and where they had been based in peacetime, he also stated there was no 1st or 3rd Staffeln in the Gruppe. They had been based at List, but only stayed there for three days before arriving at Kiel for four days, when their aircraft were given a thorough overhaul. They were then sent to Hornum and List and their aircraft were not kept in hangars at either location.

Grimm stated that 2/506 was currently based at Hornum, as was 2/406, whose aircraft carried the fuselage codes M2+-L. The Staffel based at Nordeney used the Heinkel He 115 and he provided details of their armaments and future cannon armament.

Grimm gave details of how they carried out their reconnaissance flights, their altitudes and speeds, as well as confirming the loss of an aircraft on 26 September 1939. He added that each aircraft had its own call sign and each used a different radio wavelength given to them on the day of their operation. Grimm also named the accompanying flight commander as Hauptmann Wodarg.

Grimm was in possession of a notebook when he was detained and this contained a great deal of information concerning radio beacon codenames. This was immediately passed on to AI1(e), which supported the Y-Service and Signals Intelligence.

This airman was clearly very happy to talk and Denys Felkin was keen to interrogate him again in much more depth, so a further very lengthy report followed. This report detailed not only the action which brought down Grimm and his colleagues, but also the backgrounds of his fellow airmen. He added details about the Do 18 and the fact they had not practiced blind-landings on their Staffel, but all pilots had been trained in this skill at flying school on Junkers Ju 52 aircraft.

Grimm gave a very detailed list of the eleven other aircraft in his Staffel and the full names and ranks of each crewman. This extremely valuable information included details of how the unit kept eight machines at one hours readiness and three at two hours readiness. Engines would be warmed up by ground personnel, the aircrews sleeping in their clothes at the barracks when at readiness. Aircraft with heavy loads would use Rantum to take off, as the waters were calmer there.

The amount of information provided by Hilmar Grimm was extensive and undoubtedly of great assistance to Air Intelligence. In addition, Unteroffizier Seydel's diary was recovered and found to contain details of all their flights since 31 August 1939.

After less than two months of war, it was clear some German airmen were happy to talk quite freely and discuss all manner of information, tactics and aircraft capabilities. In addition, it was noted that some were heavily indoctrinated with Nazi philosophy and their morale was high. Most, if not all of the captured airmen, expected a German victory.

The number of enemy aircraft brought down before Christmas 1939 was still low when compared with the events of 1940, but it allowed Denys Felkin and his colleagues to gain experience and knowledge. The foundations that would lead to such an expert and efficient unit in 1940 and beyond, were being laid at the Tower of London.

On 21 October 1939, two Heinkel He 115s were shot down during an attack on a convoy off the East Coast of England. A report dated 30 October, signed by the squadron leader of AI1(k), almost certainly Edmund Pollak, stated that the crew had been kept together after their capture and no information could be elicited from them. This would lead to a directive that all prisoners must be separated upon capture, kept away from one another and incommunicado.

On 28 October 1939, a Heinkel He III, 1H+JA of Stab KG26, was brought down by a combination of anti-aircraft fire and Spitfires at Humbie, south of Haddington to the east of Edinburgh. Previously, most aircraft had come down in the North Sea, but this Heinkel, which made a forced landing, was virtually intact and ready for inspection by Air Intelligence.

According to the preliminary intelligence report, two of the crewmen were killed and the pilot seriously wounded. The observer, Leutnant Rolf Niehoff, managed to escape without injury. The pilot was interrogated at Edinburgh Castle despite his severe injuries, but he refused to discuss anything of military value.

In a report for Squadron Leader Edmund Pollak, dated 4 November 1939, Denys Felkin described the interrogation of Leutnant Niehoff and the various documents recovered from the Heinkel.

Like previous airmen, Rolf Niehoff was very forthcoming and happy to talk with the RAF officer. He explained that they were part of the Stab of KG26, whose peacetime base was at Luneburg, but they were currently based at Lubeck-Blankensee and its Feldpost number was 22774. Their mission had been a reconnaissance flight over the Firth of Forth and the west coast of Scotland.

They were hit by anti-aircraft fire, then a number of fighters attacked them. The cloud layer was too thin to conceal the aircraft and they were hit again, their pilot being badly wounded. Despite his injuries the pilot made a good forced landing and Niehoff exited the Heinkel making no attempt to destroy any of his maps or documents. He was almost immediately surrounded by civilians and detained, giving one man his pocket knife.

Leutnant Rolf Niehoff was happy to discuss their previous operations and stated the whole Geschwader had been in action in Poland and did not sustain any casualties. He told his interrogator that the unit had a specialist reconnaissance staffel, as well as the Stab Staffel which comprised of eleven aircraft. Niehoff named his earlier Staffel Kapitan as Oberleutnant Fricke, a man who held the Pour le Merite, a First World War decoration, but he had now been transferred and Hauptmann Moeller was in command.

Various documents were found in the wreckage, including one from which the intelligence staff were able to identify that KG26 had two Gruppen, each consisting of three staffeln, as well as their Stab sections or an Aufklärungsstaffel (dedicated reconnaissance staffel). Other documents included the Form K3 – a navigational flight report, Form K15 – a preparation report or briefing for an attack form; and Form F5 – Calculations for flying on a beacon. In addition, it was noted that the observer used a Kleemeyer circular slide rule for his calculations. This information together with a separate report on wireless intelligence was sent to AI1(e).

Rolf Niehoff stated their deceased wireless operator had recently applied for pilot training, but this had been turned down, simply because the man was a wireless operator and highly valued.

On the 30 October 1939, AI3(b) completed an overall assessment of prisoner interrogations to date. The report stated: 'The political views of most prisoners were those of the orthodox Nazi. Although the airmen may not actually be members of the party, they exhibited the doctrine which makes them disinclined to criticise the regime adversely or indeed at all.' The prisoners were also noted as viewing conditions in Germany, through 'The rose-coloured spectacles of Nazi ideology.' In summary, every Luftwaffe prisoner was assessed as having no political views of his own.

Most Luftwaffe prisoners were assured in their belief, the war would not last very long. The Josef Goebbels inspired propaganda since 1933, was noted as being responsible for the disappearance of the defeatist temper, which followed the end of the First World War.

The POWs came from across the class divide and were noted as being well-educated, intelligent and filled with a sense of duty. All had received some form of political training and this reinforced their military discipline, 'Rendering each prisoner impervious to argument or enticement of individual profits.'

The report stated that prisoners either stated their unit name or this was obtained from their identity disc numbers. The fact the Luftwaffe put unit details on these discs was surprising, especially as they made other efforts to ensure secrecy.

To date, the interrogation and intelligence assessments had identified six units to which the prisoners had belonged, these were:

1 x Long range reconnaissance unit (Authors note – I(F)/122)
3 x Coastal units (Authors note – 2/KuFIGr506, 1/KufIGr406 & 2/KuFIGr606)
2 x Bomber units (Authors note – KG26 & KG30).

The report noted that Air Intelligence had only known one of the two bomber units previously, while the divulged bases for the reconnaissance and coastal aircraft merely confirmed previously held intelligence.

In summary the report stated:

> 'Although most prisoners have, on the whole, been fairly communicative, very little information regarding air force matters has been obtained that is not already known by this section. This is thought to be due, not only to a natural desire to refrain from divulging information, but also to ignorance of service activities outside their own particular sphere.'

One airman who seemed to buck this trend was Unteroffizier Fritz Ambrosius, a 24-year-old wireless operator attached to 2/KG30. His Junkers 88 (4D+EK) received a direct hit from an anti-aircraft shell as it approached Scapa Flow on 17 October. The aircraft caught fire and Ambrosius successfully bailed out with minor injuries, but sadly his three colleagues were killed.

Fritz Ambrosius was so communicative with his interrogators, he remained in their custody for many weeks, before finally being sent off to a prisoner of war camp.

Ambrosius explained that his pilot had been Oberleutnant Flaennig who had served in Spain with Hauptmann Pohle the commander of the Gruppe, (captured the day before on 16 October). Ambrosius had worked as a telegraphist in the Berlin General Post Office, but in 1937, he joined the Luftwaffe and signed-on for twelve years. He gave detailed information about his wireless training, but this had been curtailed due to his previous experience at the Post Office.

Ambrosius initially joined KG257 (later re-designated KG26 in 1939) and started flying. In May 1939, he transferred to KG25 which was formed from elements of KG26. This in turn became KG30, his current unit.

The young airman was happy to discuss the deployments of his unit and its personalities such as Hauptmann Pohle, whom he said was a personal friend of Hermann Göring. He added that if Pohle had not been captured, he would have moved to a role at the Air Ministry in Berlin.

Fritz Ambrosius explained that the crest for their Gruppe at KG30 was a plain cross with a folded umbrella diagonally across it. He then discussed their training and war flights in great depth, as well as the Junkers 88 as a machine, its performance and engines. His comments were certainly of great assistance to Air Intelligence and he was repeatedly interrogated over the next few weeks.

On the 7 November 1939, a further report was received at Air Intelligence from RAF HQ France. The author is not identified, but it may have been Flight Lieutenant Duncan Grinnell-Milne again.

The report concerned two airmen from a Heinkel III, shot down at Hazebrouck on 2 November. The two airmen – Oberleutnant Wilhelm Ohmsen and Unteroffizier Wilhelm Jung had already been examined by the French at length and were therefore *difficult* when interrogated by the RAF man.

Despite being described as *difficult,* Ohmsen eventually divulged a great deal of information about his previous attachment to 2(F)/122, based at Goslar. The unit operated Dornier 17's, but these had been replaced with Heinkel III's. There were two Staffeln in their Gruppe, which had been commanded by Major Kreipe up to the end of 1938, he was now on the personal staff of General Eduard Milch. Ohmsen also appeared to have been part of Milch's staff in 1938.

At the start of the war, Wilhelm Ohmsen claimed the first Staffel went to Poland attached to the Kampf-Geschwader's Stab Staffel, while the second Staffel joined KG26 and was active over the North Sea and Scotland (as already seen with previous POWs). The RAF Intelligence officers clearly noted that most of what Ohmsen stated was corroborated by previous intelligence reports. Both prisoners continued to talk freely, discussing aerodromes, types of aircraft and their opinions regarding Hurricane fighters and even the Spitfire, although they had never encountered one.

Wilhelm Ohmsen asked the RAF interrogators about two friends – Leutnant Paul and Leutnant Streng of KG26, both missing on operations to Scotland and believed to be prisoners. Sadly, Air Intelligence had no knowledge of the two men and they were assumed to be missing, presumed killed.

Wilhelm Ohmsen openly discussed a secret apparatus on the aircraft and this shall be examined in a later chapter of this book.

Although both men could not give any information about German army deployments, strength or plans, they stated there were considerable numbers on the Dutch and Belgian frontiers.

By the end of November 1939, Denys Felkin had taken command of the Air Intelligence element of CSDIC – AI1(k) at the Tower of London as an acting squadron leader. Many of the first prisoners, both Luftwaffe and Kreigsmarine had been dispatched north to the No. 1 (Officers) POW Camp at Grizedale Hall, near Ambleside in the Lake District.

On 12 November 1939, it appears Felkin sent a report to DDI3 concerning a visit by himself to Ambleside – almost certainly to the Grizedale Hall POW Camp. The reason for this visit appears to have been a private conversation between two airmen discussing glider bombs or rockets.

On 2 November, M-Room *listeners* heard Oberleutnant Gustav Awater and Leutnant Arndt Fischer – the pilot and observer of a 1(F)/122 Heinkel III brought down on the 22 October, discussing such weapons. In their transcribed conversation (ref. SRA 1), they stated:

> Awater: 'I think you can shoot at England from Germany. Tell me, how much can the 88 do?' (*Listener's* note: JU88??) (Author's note – more realistically 88mm gun.)
> Fischer: 'Yes, about 14 kilometers.'
> Awater: 'That's too small.'
> Fischer: 'Yes, with the gliding rocket, then it will be fine.'

This short tantilising exchange appeared to refer to a new secret weapon and Air Intelligence needed to know more. Felkin, or one of his deputies, therefore attended Ambleside to interrogate the earlier prisoners about this new weapon. Unfortunately, the report does not name who was interrogated, but it is safe to assume both Awater and Fischer were probably re-examined, together with Oberleutnant Hans Storp and Hauptmann Helmut Pohle who both flew Junkers 88 aircraft and may have known about this new weapon.

The report states that the visit in relation to gliding bombs was entirely fruitless and no information could be obtained. Despite the overheard conversation, it was possible the men had no information about this matter. Despite this statement, Felkin did add that one prisoner spoke about an experimental station for glider bombs in Austria, but this could not be accepted without corroboration.

Over the next three weeks, there were no newly arrived Luftwaffe prisoners delivered for interrogation. That changed on the 20 November, when a Heinkel III of 4(F)/121 (T5+LH), was brought down by Spitfires over the North Sea near the mouth of the Thames Estuary. The aircraft had been on a reconnaissance flight over the English Channel and south-east England, when it was intercepted by three Spitfires of No. 74 Squadron and shot down off the Dutch coast.

The pilot ditched the Heinkel and the three-man crew took to their dinghy, which was carried by the tide towards England rather than the Dutch coastline. The crew spent approximately 24 hours adrift, before they were picked up by HMS *Gypsy* off Southend and brought ashore.

The crew of three consisted of Leutnant Wilhelm Meyer aged thirty-one years, the aircraft commander and observer, recently commissioned from the rank of Feldwebel in October. He was a pre-war reservist who had been a wireless operator with the German national airline – Lufthansa. The pilot was Feldwebel Gerhard Rickertsen, aged thirty-one years and another pre-war reservist. The wireless operator was Unteroffizier Theodor Streyer another reservist.

It soon became apparent to Felkin's team that the structure of this crew was unusual. Instead of a four-man team, this crew consisted of just three men. The crew upon interrogation were happy to inform their interrogators that the standard wireless operator's seat had been omitted and covered over – increasing the aircrafts speed by 10-20 kilometers per hour. However, this meant there was no rearward upper firing machine-gun position.

Leutnant Meyer had been severely injured during the ditching, as he was treating the wounded Wilhelm Streyer. As the Heinkel hit the sea, Meyer was thrown the length of the crew compartment, sustaining a serious scalp wound and spinal injuries.

The pilot – Gerhard Rickertsen had been a qualified pilot since December 1930 and was qualified to fly seaplanes and to undertake 'exhibition flying' i.e. display flying. Rickertsen had been expecting to be commissioned to the rank of Leutnant when they were shot down.

The wireless operator/gunner Theodor Streyer had serious wounds to his knee. He was a wireless operator with Lufthansa pre-war, but this was his first flight with his two colleagues. He had yet to receive his identity discs or a unit paybook.

The three airmen wore electrically heated flying suits and gloves for high-altitude work, their flight altitude initially being 8,500 meters (nearly 28,000 feet). The reconnaissance flight to England was not meant to be an operational one, but merely a training flight. The crew had departed from Jever and they were to fly on to a different aerodrome. Rickertsen had spent the previous nine days in a hotel in Jever, paying his bill before boarding the Heinkel with a suitcase containing his personal possessions and clothing.

Despite being a practice reconnaissance flight over enemy territory, the only camera the crew possessed was a Leice, which Meyer had used to take a few images.

Rickertsen and Meyer admitted to undertaking numerous flights with passengers to Budapest, Vienna and Konigsberg, both men having been awarded the Iron Cross Second Class for flights over France. At least one of the airmen stated the head of their Gruppe was Oberstleutnant Rowehl and there was only one Staffel in the Gruppe at that time.

The crew spoke in detail about being shot down and that Streyer was wounded at the start of the Spitfires attack. They dived steeply from 27,000 to 6,000 feet in a bid to enter the cloud layer, but they were spotted again and attacked by the Spitfires. Once again, they hid in the clouds and managed to shake off the fighters, but their engines seized-up due to the cooling jacket of one engine being shot through, while the propellor gearing of the other was damaged in the attack.

The crew had entered the dinghy after ditching, but could not reach the Dutch coast due to the tides. They could see the Dutch lighthouses and saw a steamer which they did not hail, as they though it was heading for England.

The 'Phoney war' as it was called, took hold in December and January 1939-40 and there was very poor weather with heavy falls of snow. Only three aircraft were reported to AI1(k) as being brought down during December, a Heinkel

115 from 3/KuFIGr406 at West Beach, Sheringham, Norfolk (the crew of three being killed); and two Heinkel IIIs of 1/KG26 which were brought down off the coast Scotland, again there were no survivors.

This break in aerial activity allowed Air Intelligence to arrange its affairs and take stock of their interrogations and tactics to date.

AI1(k) relocated to Trent Park at Cockfosters at the end of 1939, and a more extensive and elaborate operation was put in place with extra accommodation, better M-Rooms and extensive records and administration offices. It was clear there was likely to be an increase in activity in the new year and with that, further new prisoner arrivals.

Denys Felkin was now in command and by the spring time of 1940, he would be a substantive squadron leader with a number of other interrogators and administration staff at his disposal. The foundations were now in place for the Nazi invasion of Western Europe and then the Battle of Britain.

Chapter 6

Unteroffizier Gerd Kahle

The new year started quietly for AI1(k) and their new home at Trent Park, Cockfosters, the poor wintery weather had seen to that.

In January 1940, the poor weather continued and although there were some air operations against Britain, only three enemy aircraft were recorded at the time as coming down on or around the shores of the United Kingdom.

The 4th Staffel of KG26 lost another Heinkel III (1H+KM) and its entire crew off Croquet Island, Northumberland, while a reconnaissance Heinkel III (T5+-H) of Aufkl.Gr.Ob.d.L came down with the loss of its entire crew off Dyce, Aberdeenshire. A few bodies were recovered from the sea, but there was very little in the way of intelligence to be found.

One airman was very lucky to survive on the 13 January when his Heinkel III (F6+LH) of 1(F)/122 was shot down by RAF fighters off the coast of Fife. Three of the crew died, but the pilot, Unteroffizier Gerd Kahle somehow managed to survive a number of hours in the cold North Sea before an RAF Rescue launch pulled him out and transferred him to Tayport.

Like Fritz Ambrosius in the last chapter, Gerd Kahle would become yet another Luftwaffe prisoner who was more than happy to converse with his interrogators at Trent Park, but the question is whether he gave too much information and could he have been assisting his captors?

After being transferred to Trent Park, Gerd Kahle, over a number of weeks, would provide enough material for the interrogators to complete nearly thirty pages of reports and intelligence assessments. In addition, he was placed in the M-Rooms with a number of other Luftwaffe prisoners. Whether he knew he was in a microphoned room is unknown, but he certainly continued his long conversations with his compatriots – much to the joy of the AI1(k) *listeners*.

It is unclear how long it took to transfer Gerd Kahle from Scotland to Trent Park, but the first intelligence report relating to him, (Intelligence report No. 2/1940), is dated 20 January 1940, a week after his arrival in British custody.

This first and very lengthy intelligence report, comprises of nine and a half pages and was completed by a junior interrogator – Flying Officer Guy B. Jepson, a man who would soon be promoted to flight lieutenant and act as Denys Felkin's deputy at Trent Park.

The report stated straight away, that there was little doubt Kahle's aircraft belonged to 1(F)/122 and probably bore the markings F6+LH (a correct statement on both counts). The place of take-off could not be ascertained, though it was known to have occurred at 0745 hours German time. This meant the aircraft had originated from 'well-inland' or it had taken an indirect route across the North Sea to Scotland. (It was later ascertained that the place of origin had in fact been Munster in Germany.)

The crew of four were described by Jepson as a *scratch* crew, but Kahle and the wireless operator – Unteroffizier Dietz had been together for some time. They had both been trained in *blind flying* and seconded to the Gruppe for war flight experience. The two other deceased crew members were part of 1(F)/122.

Gerd Kahle gave full details of his last flight and how the crew used tail bearings on the radio beacon at St Peter's every half hour for their navigation. Their landfall was made correctly in the middle of the Firth of Forth at 0950 hours GMT. Although the flight over the North Sea was through thick cloud, as they approached Scotland, the weather cleared and the visibility was good. Their task was to photograph the Scottish coastline and their Heinkel was equipped with two cameras – one built into the fuselage and the other a large hand-held device.

They were to fly along the coast avoiding Dundee, as they believed fighters were based there. They would then fly over the Highlands and return from the West of Scotland to the Firth of Forth and home again.

The second objective of their mission was to make a weather report. This would not be transmitted over the wireless to prevent interception, but would be sent when over the North Sea and near their home base.

By early 1940, AI1(k) reports started to refer to prisoners by an identifying code. Gerd Kahle was identified as prisoner A29, the A stood for airman and the number was his numerically sequenced identifying serial number. He was an airman and the twenty-nineth prisoner in AI1(k) custody.

The intelligence report noted that 'POW A29' (i.e. Kahle), said it was, in his own opinion, possible for German aircraft to send and receive radio messages over Scotland, without the British detecting them. He intimated that this was due to the use of short-wave transmissions and he thought this could be conducted within a range of 650 miles. He told the interrogator they had received two messages near Scotland, but they did not send any replies to avoid detection.

Gerd Kahle gave details of their combat. The wireless operator had shouted 'Fighters', but he was so excited, he did not give a position for the enemy aircraft. They were at an altitude of 20,000 feet and Kahle started an immediate dive. The first attack did not appear to inflict any damage to their Heinkel and he continued the descent turning back out to sea. At 12,000 feet he located a cloud bank, but this was too thin to provide cover and the fighters attacked once more.

Kahle claimed their air mechanic who was manning the rear lower gun was killed without firing a shot and the wireless operator fired just ten to fifteen rounds with the upper gun, before he too was killed.

The Heinkel received about six hits, some seemed to be heavier than others and Kahle believed one of the attackers was armed with cannon and not just machine guns. In reality, the fighters were just standard Spitfire Mk.1's, armed with eight .303 Browning machine guns.

During the second attack, the port engine was put out of action and Kahle entered a steeper dive with the Heinkel's air speed indicator displaying 600 kph (about 375 mph). He managed to pull out of the dive about fifteen feet above the sea, when the fighters made a third attack and bullets could be seen splashing into the water in front of him. The right-hand engine was then hit and oil spewed out over the exterior of the glass cockpit.

Struggling to handle the machine as it lost power, the Spitfire's made another attack, which he believed was aimed at hitting him in his seat. Miraculously, bullets seemed to outline his head without striking him and he landed on the water.

The undercarriage, or rather the hydraulics, appear to have been hit, as the wheels hung down limply and as he landed the Heinkel *dug in* and sea water smashed through and flooded the glazed cockpit. Within two minutes the Heinkel sank and Kahle managed to exit the aircraft with his observer who was wounded, but they could not release the dinghy from its compartment. Kahle gave an opinion that the dinghy should have been at the front of the machine and not the rear, where it got shot up and was useless. He managed to inflate his own lifejacket and went to assist the observer who had a left sided chest wound, but a bullet had pierced his life jacket and it would not function.

Somewhat bizarrely, Kahle claimed he believed two objects were more likely to be spotted than one by a rescue craft, so they split up. The observer was believed to have drowned and after three and a half hours in the sea, a RAF rescue launch picked a frozen Kahle out of the water.

Initially, Kahle was reluctant to say anything about his time in the Luftwaffe, but the interrogator managed to piece together a history from the pilot's personal papers and some indirect questions about these documents.

Kahle was described as belonging to a *better class of German*. He had a fairly international outlook, having spent two years exploring and flying in South America. He had been the pilot and part financier of the expedition. He had been flying for a number of years and had piloted his own private aircraft.

Kahle was identified as being a pilot of some experience and had attended many training courses. Pre-war he was the pilot of a flying classroom, stationed at the Testing Station at Travemunde. He would make long-distance flights to Hammerfest in northern Norway while testing the Dornier 18 flying boat. Before the war, he was engaged in designing a new machine for his own use on future expeditions, but this came to nothing.

When he knew war was inevitable, Kahle wanted to be operational, but the authorities deemed him to be too valuable an asset. He therefore applied for a commission to fly either the Junkers 88 or the Messerschmitt 110. He was told he could have a commission, but he would be non-operational and would work in an administrative capacity. To circumvent this directive, Kahle joined the Luftwaffe as a basic Flieger with the chance of a commission after eight months. He was promoted to Gefreiter and Unteroffizier in late 1939 and should have obtained a commission in March 1940, if he had not been shot down.

Kahle's paybook was issued on 26 August 1938 for the Wettererkundungsstaffeln OB.d.L at Berlin-Gatow airfield – a meteorological unit. He was also noted by interrogators as wearing his original identity disc. Despite this, Kahle had not undergone a course at the weather school at Tempelhof, although he said observers undertaking daily reconnaissance flights over the North Sea had done so.

Gerd Kahle had left the Weather Forecasting Staffel in November 1939 and joined KG40, which was commanded by an officer called Petersen at Bremen. The unit was either an entirely new unit or one re-equipping with the Focke-Wulf Fw.200 Condor. Kahle added that this process had yet to be completed in January 1940.

When captured, the pilot was in possession of a pass to the Focke-Wulf factory in Bremen, issued on 10/11/39. Why exactly he had the pass was not known, but he did say he acted in an advisory capacity as a Test Pilot.

Although Kahle had yet to be commissioned, he told his interrogator that all pilots on KG40 were Oberleutnants. He had been with KG40 engaged in training pilots in navigation and blind-flying.

Whatever Guy Jepson said to Kahle, it must have been very successful, because he soon divulged a great deal of detail on his own flying skills, the aircraft types he had flown and various other flight details. He was clearly, on first appearances, a very skilled and experienced pilot, but he did admit to crashing a Heinkel three weeks before he was shot down. His wireless operator at the time, being the same man on his final mission.

Kahle gave quite a lot of information on blind-flying, stating that the ultra-short wave blind flying equipment was not used for a blind take-off, as the bank and turn indicators were sufficient for the pilot.

On 11 January 1940, new machines were not ready for KG40 (i.e. Focke Wulf 200 Condor), so Kahle was seconded to 122 Gruppe to undertake some 'war flights'. Despite this admission, he would not state where he had taken off on his final flight, but the interrogator correctly assumed it was Munster, as two previous aircraft had originated from that airfield in October 1939.

Gerd Kahle could only remember part of his aircraft's fuselage code (+LH). The first letter was 'F' which denoted 'Fern' meaning long-distance and then a number. Jepson and his team managed to correctly work out from previously held intelligence, that it was safe to assume this was a 1st Staffel machine of 122 Gruppe and therefore the full code was F6+LH.

Kahle said he was fearful of a bombing war and thought the size of the two opposing bomber forces could mean the end of civilization. He also believed an assault on the Maginot Line would be supported by an intensive bombardment with as many as two hundred dive-bombers.

He believed there were several faults with German aircraft designs, but the Luftwaffe had depots full of machines. He happily discussed with his interrogator the arrival of new machines, like the Heinkel 112 and the Heinkel 117.

It was clear to Guy Jepson, Denys Felkin and AI1(k) that they had a very special prisoner in their hands and one who would happily talk.

Almost immediately, on 23 January, Kahle was placed in an M-Room with the earlier talkative airman – A24 – identified as Unteroffizier Fritz Ambrosius, a wireless operator of 2/KG30. He had been shot down and injured on 17 October 1939 off Scotland. The two men struck up a long conversation which was recorded as a transcript reference SRA16 and amounted to ten pages of information.

Gerd Kahle told Ambrosius that the war was just foolery, the Luftwaffe's machines were too heavy and too heavily armoured. Cannon, he claimed were quite good, but they were too heavy for aircraft.

Fritz Ambrosius was quick to reply, stating that if Hitler would send over 1,000 aeroplanes, he might achieve something; but he was quick to add that the British already had German photographs, maps and weather reports. They even knew what areas German aircraft were forbidden to fly in – it was in his opinion a disgrace and came from the stupidity of German organisation.

The two men were quite vociferous in their condemnation of German aircraft and preparations. Kahle added that the British defences were quite good and that he had six to seven Spitfires on his tail when he was brought down.

Ambrosius said the Germans should build other aircraft like the Junkers 88, which had a record of 2,000 kilometers at 500 kph. If all the Luftwaffe aircraft did 500 kph, no British fighter could catch them he claimed. Ambrosius had been reading an English newspaper which claimed German bombers had attacked fishing boats. He said the claims were ridiculous and that the English dreaded a large-scale attack.

Gerd Kahle told his colleague German aircraft had a lot of defects and were not ready, but new ones like the Heinkel 112 and the Heinkel 117 were first class machines like the Junkers 88.

Ambrosius carried on reading and translating his English newspaper. He told Kahle that talk of the so-called 'English hate' was nonsense. The English he had encountered were 'splendid fellows' and treated you as a human being. They were different from the 'Russian rabble'. He believed the British had as many flyers as Germany, thanks to the week-end flying scheme (RAF Volunteer Reserve) and the RAF were in certain respects superior to the Luftwaffe. However, he said British bombs were no good and they dropped many duds, while Spitfires did things he had never seen before. To the *listeners* this must have been music for their ears.

Kahle said the war was ghastly, his now deceased observer had only just been engaged to be married. Fritz Ambrosius replied that the English soldiers hated the war and his hospital doctor had told him both English and German people were good, but Hitler wanted war.

The two men discussed whether U-Boats were better than battleships and the Red Cross, which Ambrosius called a big swindle. Ambrosius was soon asking his companion if he knew Oberleutnant Schneise and a friend of Hermann Göring called Franke.

Schneise was on Junkers 88's and Ambrosius discussed dive-bombing in the aircraft and the arming and bomb release mechanism on the JU88. Kahle called the Heinkel III a brute of a machine and said he could not understand why the authorities were not building more Junkers 88s. The two men continued to discuss the performance of the Junkers 88 in fine detail, details that were gratefully recorded by the *listeners*.

The two men then discussed two earlier prisoners – Hauptmann Pohle and Oberleutnant Storp. Ambrosius claimed Storp only had the Iron Cross because he flew with Franke. They claimed they had sunk the aircraft carrier HMS *Ark Royal*, but clearly, they hadn't.

Kahle asked who else had served with Ambrosius and he gave the names of Oberleutnant Hass, Hauptmann's Diesing and Rosendal, as well as a man named Kuschke, a very young dive-bomber pilot.

Kahle questioned why Ambrosius did not have the Iron Cross if Storp had been awarded it. Ambrosius said Storp had it, because his brother was a captain on the General Staff – even though Storp was a rotten airman. This information was undoubtedly of enormous value to AI1(k) and it must have taken many hours to update their files.

The pilot continued to question Ambrosius, asking him if Flaenning (Ambrosius's pilot) had served in Spain. Ambrosius stated that he once had a pilot called Galler, who was known as 'Kapitan' as he was one of the best pilots.

Kahle continued to ask questions – information that was gratefully received by the *listeners*. He asked if Ambrosius knew Oberleutnants Salor, Schoeppke and Beckhans, but he did not know them. Neither did he know Stoffregen, another so-called crack pilot.

Whether Gerd Kahle was just happy to talk with a fellow German or not, he could not stop himself and the *listeners* writing hands must have been cramping up.

Fritz Ambrosius asked if Kahle knew the abbreviated signaling procedure used by wireless operators – in this you only sent the first letter, instead of the whole word. Kahle asked him what Lubeck's signals were? Ambrosius stated, '260' before he was interrupted by Kahle, who corrected him with '265 degrees.'

Ambrosius then explained that when they passed the curve of 271 degrees, the wireless operator would send the signal '271 degrees', but thereafter he would send only the last figure e.g. a '6' instead of '276'. This was probably all new information for AI1(k) and would be sent on to the RAF Y-Service for their information.

As they continued discussing the radio signals and beacons, Ambrosius stated that the FuGe 3 radio was better than the FuGe 10 system. Kahle countered that the FuGe 10 was better on long-wave, but Ambrosius said the other system was more exact and the FuGe 10 frequency was very unsteady.

The two men continued chatting and discussing further named personnel, but at the end of this transcript, Kahle said the interrogators still did not know where he took-off. He asked Ambrosius if the interrogators had asked him if he knew where Kahle had taken-off. Ambrosius told him they asked if he knew him.

Kahle said, 'You see, they try to worm-out everything. The snippets of information which may seem quite harmless to us, are of great importance to them. How many prisoners are there here?'

Ambrosius said there were about eighteen, six of them Luftwaffe men, to which Kahle replied, 'Well, if they only get a scrap from each of them, they will be able to piece together quite a story.'

Despite his comments, it appears Kahle did not suspect they were being listened to – or did he? Many airmen as we shall see, men like Franz von Werra suspected that there were hidden microphones, but this test pilot just kept going…

Another transcript was added on the 27 January (reference SRA17). Once again, Kahle was talking with Fritz Ambrosius. The two talked once more about Storp and Oberleutnant Flaenning as well as the Junkers 88.

The same day, there was another intelligence report completed relating to Gerd Kahle (reference No. 3/1940). Whether it was related to an interrogation before or after the last SRA transcript is unknown. This time, the report was signed by Denys Felkin and it appears he may have decided to talk to the prisoner himself, after Guy Jepson had interrogated him so successfully.

Denys Felkin reported that Kahle had without any doubt been a member of 1(F)/122 based at Munster. His Heinkel was quite new, as he had only just flown it from the factory. Five more typed pages of the report discussed in more detail the four fighter attacks made upon Kahle's Heinkel and his tactics to avoid them. They also discussed the possibility of German radio systems picking up British fighter wireless messages.

Kahle discussed in some detail, the airfield at Utersen and the dropping of bombs at Travemunde. Before he arrived at Travemunde, Kahle admitted to working as a test pilot at the research centre at Rechlin and knowing a Leutnant Franke (as discussed with Fritz Ambrosius in the M-Room). He said Franke, who was a well-known test pilot, had been awarded the Iron Cross First and Second class for sinking HMS *Ark Royal*. Franke never claimed or believed his bombs had sunk the aircraft carrier, but his observer had made the claim.

Kahle claimed to have flown the Arado 196 twin float monoplane and a version with a single central float. This he claimed was much more agile, but trickier to land than the twin float machine.

Denys Felkin asked Kahle about the Blohm and Voss 137 and the 140. He said he had tested the Blohm and Voss 140 which had twin engines and was an excellent aircraft, but it never went into production. Kahle claimed there had been problems with the steel tube struts connecting the floats to the aircraft when the sea was strength 3, but against his advice, the contract for a float plane had been given to Heinkel for production of the Heinkel 115.

Kahle said he had flown the three engine Blohm and Voss 138 and this was a good machine, but it also never went into production.

Although the above intelligence report by Felkin and the transcript from the M-Room were dated 27 January 1940, yet another M-Room transcript was completed for that day. Whether this was after the first transcript and the interrogation by Felkin is unknown, but clearly AI1(k) were keeping close tabs on their experienced and very valuable prisoner…

This time, SRA19 detailed a short conversation between Kahle and two other airmen believed to be Unteroffizier Walter Heckt (A6) of 2/KuFlGr506, brought down on 26 September 1939 and a Leutnant (A26), an observer. This man was initially thought to be Leutnant Ernst Korner of 2/KuFlGr506, but it seems unlikely now, as he spoke repeatedly about the JU88 and may have been captured away from the UK.

Gerd Kahle told the others that they had lost many reconnaissance machines in Poland. He then discussed money with the observer and having 200 marks in an account in Bremen. On the evidence of the transcript, it is easy to believe Kahle was trying to induce some kind of a response from the other two men, especially when he added: 'Depth charges must be devilish, but N125 (a naval POW and probable submariner) told me there is now something, a high-pressure arrangement so that the men can still get out.'

Unfortunately, the transcript does not state whether there was a lull in the conversation, but the next comment came from the leutnant observer who stated the Kondor (Focke Wulf 200) would be the right machine for here. The JU88 should have been in service a year before, but now was too late… they had already lost four JU88's he claimed.

Gerd Kahle added that there was a new dive-bomber, the four engine Heinkel 117. They carried two 1,000 kilograms bombs… He then stated that the Germans had no secret weapons and the Italians should enter the war.

Finally, it appears the observer replied, stating that the English were practically superior to the Germans at sea and in the air. He said there were not enough bombs to attack the Maginot Line and the Luftwaffe only had ten 1,000 kilo bombs at the start of the war.

Reading these M-Room transcripts and the amount of intelligence Kahle gave to both Felkin and Jepson, it is easy to speculate that he may have been 'turned' and was assisting his captors. Two days later, he was still apparently with the leutnant observer and Unteroffizier Heckt in an M-Room and still chatting away for the benefit of the *listeners*…

Transcript SRA20 details Gerd Kahle talking on 29 January, about the need for a big offensive, but the Fuhrer would not wish to waste lives on the Maginot Line. Instead, he speculated any attack would be made through Holland. The observer challenged this as there was no common frontier with France, but Kahle responded by saying that it would provide the Luftwaffe with airfields in Holland to attack England.

The unidentified leutnant observer bemoaned the fact Junkers 88 reconnaissance aircraft left a trail of white smoke and fighters only needed to follow this. Kahle the expert, added that at 7,000 meters the trail is practically no longer visible, but the observer explained that Spitfires followed the JU88's at 8,500 meters and had great maneuverability.

The conversation between the observer and Kahle turned to various personnel and their names and stations. Kahle spoke again about the Heinkel 112 and that it was difficult to land for a novice pilot, before talking about the Heinkel 117 and the fact it had two engines coupled together. Unteroffizier Heckt started to join in and asked if the 1st Staffel was at Goslar again. Kahle said he didn't know, but that an officer named Pappenhaus was the Staffel Kapitan.

The conversation flowed back and forth and Kahle mentioned the fact the interrogators found a Focke-Wulf factory pass in his possession. He said he had to say something, so he told them he was a test pilot and he had passes for various other works. Kahle added that the interrogator had already heard something about the Heinkel 117, but when the Messerschmitt 110 was mentioned, he had told his interviewer that the Messerschmitt 110 was all right for the Polish war, but there were new aircraft with four or five cannon and they would 'swipe everything'.

Gerd Kahle continued to talk and it is hard to decipher whether he was just full of bravado and bombast, trying to detract from his earlier comments to the interrogators or trying to prompt information from his fellow prisoners. The question is whether he realised there could be hidden microphones, knew they were there or he was totally ignorant of the fact?

A further M-Room transcript (SRA21) on the same day, detailed a short conversation between Gerd Kahle and the unidentified leutnant observer again. The observer had been taken for a walk by an officer and discussed politics prior to him being placed back in the M-Room with Kahle – a classic tactic of AI1(k).

The observer told Kahle, that the British officer had said the Fuhrer had not kept his word when he said he had no design on Czechoslovakia and then invaded the nation. Kahle agreed and asked what they could say to the contrary.

The observer, who was clearly somewhat dismayed with the politics, added that the Fuhrer was against communism and yet he had an alliance with Russia. The Fuhrer he said, promised a lot, but did not keep his promises. The British officer had said the whole German government must go before there can be peace. Despite these comments, the observer said he had told the British officer, Germany was one hundred per cent behind the Fuhrer and he did not believe they would lose the war.

It is clear the AI1(k) *listeners* were very happy with the information they were gathering from the observer and Gerd Kahle, as yet another M-Room transcript (SRA22) on the 31 January soon followed. The two men continued talking about dive-bombing of Poland and Warsaw, geo-politics and various other subjects.

On the 2 February 1940, Denys Felkin completed another Intelligence report concerning Gerd Kahle (reference No. 5/1940). It is clear from the paper trail, that Kahle was providing AI1(k) with a vast amount of information.

Kahle had continuously spoken about flying various German and now American aircraft in his capacity as a test pilot and this subject of conversation according to the report, went on for many hours.

Denys Felkin's report noted that Kahle had given information that although only the opinion of one individual, was to a large extent accurate. This included the statement that the Luftwaffe were only using aircraft and formations already known to the British, as there was a likelihood they might be captured. Kahle had also claimed many faults had been found on Luftwaffe aircraft in Poland and these were now being corrected. New types of aircraft were expected to be delivered in the near future.

Kahle had great faith in dive-bombing because of its accuracy, he suggested that as many as two hundred dive-bombers dropping 1,000 kilo bombs, were likely to be employed against the Maginot Line. (Clearly this did not correspond with the earlier claims recorded in the M-Room, that they only had ten such bombs at the start of the war).

Kahle claimed Germany was producing very large four-engine aircraft to be used as dive-bombers. The Heinkel 117 was one of this type and under test in July 1939, but Kahle had ceased work as a test pilot by that time. He claimed a new long-range, heavily armed machine which could fly at 34,000 feet was to be developed. This would be used against the west coast of England and the Atlantic Ocean. He had little doubt his Geschwader – KG40, would be equipped with this new machine in the spring time. The motors may be mounted in pairs – side by side and not tandem – coupled together with an overdrive clutch to one propellor he claimed.

Gerd Kahle continued discussing possible new developments, including a Heinkel 190, the Heinkel 177 and a specially adapted Focke-Wulf 200 Kondor.

What happened to Gerd Kahle between the 2 and 13 of February is unknown – perhaps he was giving even more details to Felkin and his team, but on the thirteenth he was back in an M-Room again. This time he was with a Feldwebel pilot (A30) who is believed to have been Hermann Wilms of 4/KG26, brought down on 3 February (see reference SRA27).

Gerd Kahle started the conversation by talking about German aircraft firing at fishing boats. Wilms thought the German crews may have thought the fishing boats had opened fire and he could not imagine anyone firing upon such boats.

Hermann Wilms explained how he was attacked and brought down, his crews injuries, and that he was part of KG26. He tried to destroy their aircraft, but could only burn his finger with the incendiary device. Wilms went on to claim that KG26 had no more aircraft and maybe no more crews left. They had lost practically a whole Staffel and had achieved very little. He added that Oberleutnant Hass was now a Hauptmann.

On 21 February, Kahle engaged an Obergefreiter air mechanic (A35), believed to be Heinz Hegemann, in another M-Room conversation (reference SRA31). Hegemann was also from KG26 and shot down on 9 February 1940. The air mechanic mentioned being asked by his interrogator about something called 'X-apparatus' or *X-Gerät*. (This is discussed in a later chapter of that name.)

On 23 February, Kahle was again in an M-Room, this time with both Hermann Wilms and Heinz Hegemann (SRA35 refers). This time they again discussed what they had said with their separate interrogators.

A further conversation that day (see SRA36) between Kahle, Heinz Hegemann and a pilot unteroffizier, believed to be Helmut Meyer (A34) followed similar lines. Four days later on the 27 February, Kahle was recorded in discussion with a pilot (A36) – believed to be Leutnant Erich Grote who was brought down on 22 February; the two men discussing similar matters once again (see SRA38).

The next day Kahle and Grote were again in an M-Room (see SRA39). This time Kahle started the conversation with something different – something which raises the question of whether he had been turned. He told Grote the (British) officers there were a frightful wind-up. Grote said he believed the British underestimated the German industrial strength, but Kahle said he believed they overestimated it.

Their discussion quickly changed to the merits of the Junkers 88 over the Heinkel III. Gerd Kahle claimed he hated the Heinkel III and had even spoken to Herr Heinkel about it.

Kahle said the British had about seventeen aerodromes (clearly incorrect) and that ten were really important. If two Staffeln of JU88's attacked each of the ten while flying high, it would be quite enough. This time Kahle suddenly said, 'I mustn't speak out loud, they may be listening outside!' He carried on explaining how they should bomb the aerodromes, factories and certain cities, causing ferment among the population. In time he claimed, the populace would throw out Churchill and Chamberlain. This view was enthusiastically endorsed by Grote.

Gerd Kahle had now spent about six to seven weeks in British custody and most of that was at Trent Park. Normally, prisoners would be interrogated and moved on to a camp in two to three weeks or even less. For Gerd Kahle to still be at Trent Park and still being placed in M-Rooms, makes one wonder whether he was not only saying too much, but knowingly assisting AI1(k).

On the 1 March (see SRA40), he was placed in an M-Room with Erich Grote and a feldwebel observer (A37), believed to have been Fritz Sprigarth from a Heinkel III (T5+OH), brought down in Berwickshire on 22 February 1940. Once again, their recorded conversations followed the usual pattern.

Other transcribed M-Room conversations were recorded before Gerd Kahle was finally moved on to a prisoner of war camp. Almost two months after being shot down and captured, it appears Gerd Kahle had exhausted his usefulness.

We now know that prisoners were often debriefed, both in British and German POW camps shortly after their arrival. The security sections in both Luftwaffe and RAF camps wanted to know if the new arrival was genuine and not a stool pigeon. They also wanted to know what the interrogators had been asking them.

In Germany this information was sent back to MI9 via coded messages and it is not hard to believe the Luftwaffe tried something similar with their own airmen.

What the German POW camp security must have made of Gerd Kahle is unknown. He had taken a considerable amount of time to make his way to a POW camp. He had engaged in conversation with at least nine other prisoners and a great quantity of intelligence was obtained by the M-Room *listeners*. The question is, did Gerd Kahle know he was being listened to? And if he did, why did he continue to talk? If he was ignorant of the M-Room microphones and *listeners*, how could such an intelligent man, an alleged test pilot, have not suspected something? We may never know the answers to these questions, but clearly Gerd Kahle was a very useful intelligence tool for AI1(k).

Chapter 7

The Raids February to April 1940

While Denys Felkin and his team were busy with Gerd Kahle, other aircraft were being brought down and this resulted in a steady flow of new prisoners from February to April 1940.

In February 1940, AI1(k) were informed of six Heinkel III's of KG26 being brought down over Britain or near its coastline. This resulted in twelve new prisoners, including Heinz Hegemann and Hermann Wilms mentioned in the last chapter. In addition, a seventh Heinkel III belonging to Aufkir Gr.Ob.d.L, came down in Berwickshire and the detained crew included Erich Grote and Fritz Sprigarth who also featured in the tale of Gerd Kahle at Trent Park.

In March and April 1940, further Heinkel IIIs were brought down, including two aircraft from KG30, one from 1/Aufkir Gr.Ob.d.L, four from KG26 and one from KGr126. They brought with them ten more prisoners for AI1(k), three of them were injured and twenty men were killed. This new group of prisoners included a very valuable man in the shape of a Gruppen-Kommandeur from KG26 – Oberstleutnant Hans Hefele.

Although AI1(k) did not know it at the time, this group of aircraft and prisoners would be every bit as valuable as Gerd Kahle, in fact even more so.

On 3 February 1940, KG26 dispatched a number of Heinkel III's on reconnaissance flights from Germany to look for shipping off the north-east coast of Britain.

At 0940 hours, Heinkel III (1H+FM) of 4/KG26 was shot down by three Hurricanes from No. 43 Squadron, the aircraft making a forced landing on Bannial Flat Farm, Sneaton, near Whitby, in the North Riding. It is said to have been the first enemy aircraft brought down on English soil.

The pilot was Feldwebel Hermann Wilms who spoke with Gerd Kahle, and his seriously injured wireless operator was Unteroffizier Karl Missy. The observer, Rudolf Leushake, was killed and lay inside the cockpit. His body was later pulled out of the wreckage and left by the aircraft's nose on the snowy ground, while the gunner – Unteroffizier Johann Meyer was seriously injured. Meyer and

Missy were later transported to the Whitby and District War Memorial Cottage Hospital for urgent treatment, Missy having a foot amputated and Johann Meyer sadly passing away.

In his book *Luftwaffe over the North* (Pen and Sword, 1993), author Bill Norman gives an account of the crash-landing and the comments of a number of civilian witnesses.

Special Constable Arthur Barratt and a number of farm labourers arrived to find Hermann Wilms crouching down inside the wrecked fuselage trying to 'burn his papers'. Meyer and Missy lay near him, clearly badly injured and in great pain. Arthur Barratt hung through the open top of the fuselage and tried to restrain the pilot, but Wilms broke free and managed to set fire to his papers. He then had the civilians assist his two injured colleagues, before he tried to fire a Very flare into the shattered nose of the Heinkel to destroy the aircraft. The civilian crowd quickly realised what he had done and managed to put the fire out with car extinguishers and shovelfuls of snow.

In his book, Bill Norman gives details of the crash in a letter from Special Constable Barratt to his brother the following day. Barratt explained that he could not stop the pilot (Wilms) from burning his papers and when he had completed the job, he exited the aircraft. Barratt detained him and told the civilians to look after him while he tried to get the injured men out of the wreckage. Unfortunately, Wilms then walked to the damaged nose and set fire to the aircraft. Barratt thought there would be a fifth member of the crew under the Heinkel, but there were only four men in the crew.

Ruth Smailes and a Miss Sanderson organised the removal of Missy and Meyer to the nearby farmhouse, before they were taken to the hospital. The body of Lueshacke was taken and placed in the coalhouse at the farm to await collection.

An initial intelligence log (No. 7/1940) by an unknown flight lieutenant dated 4 February, states that although the crew tried to set fire to the aircraft, it was only slightly damaged and papers, maps, cameras and a new type of optical bombsight had been recovered. From the crew's identity tags, the aircraft was believed to belong to the 4th Staffel of KG26.

Wilms had initially told his Field Interrogator they left a meadow aerodrome near Schleswig on a reconnaissance flight over the North Sea and British coast. They were working in conjunction with other aircraft. Wilms admitted that although they were on a reconnaissance flight, they had attacked a small cargo ship and a fishing boat off Scarborough. (A few days later Wilms was recorded talking to Gerd Kahle, when Kahle mentioned the allegations of bombers attacking fishing boats, Wilms immediately stated they must have thought the boats had fired at them. Clearly, Wilms knew what he had already told his interrogators.)

On the 5 February, Denys Felkin sent a message to an unidentified recipient. This had an attached list of documents salvaged from Wilms's Heinkel. It noted that the list did not include other documents left at the Air Ministry with AI1(e) the previous evening.

The list included:

- A copy of Weyer's *Taschenbuch Der Kriegaflotten 1939* – a sort of miniature *Jane's Fighting Ships*.
- A leaflet titled: General Information for soldiers.
- A number of old logbooks.
- A wad of *Flugvorbereitungsblatt zum Angriff auf* sheets. These were to be filled in just before and immediately after making a bombing attack.
- An old weather report.
- A correspondence pad and envelopes, including several letters.
- A loose-leaf pocket book with entries for call signs, frequencies, direction finding bearings, recognition signals for 24-27 and 28-30 January, the 31 January to 3 February – noted as ES1, ES111 and ES1.
- A small red notebook giving details of bombing practice against the warship '*Hessen*' in the Baltic Sea.
- A sheet of paper, torn in four giving particulars of direction finding '*Flugsicherung*' similar to the papers already sent to AI1(e).
- A Luftwaffe map covering grid 42-59 degrees, 30 minutes north and 6 degrees east to 9 degrees west.
- Meal cards showing various aerodromes from which the aircraft had flown, a pocket diary and other personal effects.

As we have seen, Feldwebel Hermann Wilms was subject to the M-Room procedure before he was finally passed on to a POW camp.

On the same day that Wilms was captured, two other KG26 Heinkel IIIs were brought down. According to intelligence report No. 8/1940, at 1100 hours 1H+HL of 3/KG26 crashed into the North Sea at Druridge Bay in Northumberland. The crew of four were killed and at 1600 hours that afternoon, the body of Leutnant Lutz von Bruning was washed ashore at Druridge Bay. His identity disc indicated that he belonged to 3/KG26, while papers on the body not only confirmed this, but gave a list of aircraft codes belonging to this Staffel, including those of two Junkers 52 transport aircraft attached to the unit for transport duties.

AI1(k) quickly deduced that the machine from which the body originated was 1H+HL, as this was written in pencil on one of the papers and that Feldwebel Petersen was the wireless operator. (This was confirmed when Petersen's body was washed ashore on the morning of the 4 February 1940.)

The intelligence report added that another document washed ashore, gave wireless instructions and it appears aircraft from 1(F)/122 were acting as *Fuhlungshalter* (monitoring of targets) aircraft for KG26. That document was dated 26 January 1940.

Fifteen minutes after this aircraft crashed, a Heinkel III of 2/KG26 was attacked by Hurricanes of No. 43 Squadron and brought down in the North Sea, fifteen miles off Tynemouth. The crew of five, which had two observers, had two men seriously wounded in the attack. The pilot – Oberfeldwebel Fritz Wiemer managed to ditch the Heinkel and the survivors exited it, but they could not release their dinghy before the aircraft sank beneath them.

The crew of the trawler *Harlech Castle* managed to fish four of the crew from the cold sea, but a fifth crewman was already floating face down and was clearly dead. This is believed to have been the gunner Unteroffizier Willi Wolf. Most of the crew were injured and Unteroffizier Karl-Ernst Thiede the second observer, was badly wounded.

In his book *Luftwaffe losses over Northumberland and Durham 1939-1945*, Bill Norman states that the skipper of the trawler – Thomas Trendall, told author Leo Walmesley in his 1941 book – *Fisherman at War*, that his crew had often discussed not rescuing downed enemy airman after a series of attacks on fishing boats and other unarmed merchant vessels. Despite this, they decided they could not leave the Germans as they were, 'Some mothers' sons.'

The airmen were taken below, given first aid, their clothes removed and given a hot drink. The crew were apparently concerned about how they would be treated, especially after they were told they were bound for the fishing town of Grimsby. Sadly, Karl-Ernst Thiede died en route to Grimsby. The trawlers skipper, Thomas Trendall, remembers there being a photograph of the man's wife in his uniform pocket.

At Grimsby the three survivors were handed over to the authorities along with the body of Karl-Ernst Thiede. Although the survivors thanked the crew of the *Harlech Castle*, there was reportedly a lot of animosity towards the Germans from the general fishing community. The crew were therefore taken quickly into custody and hospital before being visited by Field Interrogation staff and later sent on to Trent Park. Thiede was buried in Grimsby.

Two intelligence reports, No.'s 10 and 12/1940, detail the interrogation of (A32) one of the crew – believed to be Feldwebel Franz Schnee the surviving observer.

The Heinkel III was quickly identified as belonging to 2/KG26 and bore the code 1H+GK, the third letter being in red. Franz Schnee gave details of their take-off time and airfield, as well as their course from radio beacon 'St Peter'. He claimed bad visibility caused them to fly at just 300 feet with a tail wind and they soon arrived over Middlesborough.

Franz Schnee said the mission was purely reconnaissance, to locate convoys and report it by wireless. Intelligence had already been informed by the intercepting fighter pilots, that this Heinkel dropped a number of bombs into the sea when they attacked it, but Schnee pretended that he did not know his aircraft was carrying bombs. He claimed any bombs could have been jettisoned by any crew member. The intelligence report, signed by Felkin, noted that although this may be true, it was also possible Schnee feared the consequences of Luftwaffe aircraft attacking unarmed merchant shipping.

Schnee was impressed with the rapidity and speed with which the fighters attacked them. Their pilot had tried to take cover in the cloud layer, but with an engine out of action, they had little chance and he ditched the Heinkel. The aircraft sank within ninety seconds and they had no chance to get into their dinghy. They were pulled from the sea by the *Harlech Castle*, but one of their crew died soon afterwards.

Denys Felkin noted that while in the sea, the crew had ditched their identity discs, all their papers and even their wrist watches. One exception was found when a signals table similar to the one previously recovered that day was found in the pocket of a flying suit. This was dated 3 February 1940 and gave wireless frequencies and call signs for the entire Geschwader (KG26). In addition, it contained call signs and frequencies for 1(F)/122 which was acting as the *Fuhlungshalter* aircraft for KG26. This and similar aircraft were tasked with monitoring convoys, giving bearings and positions for the attacking Heinkel III's.

The second report, dated 10 February, went into much greater detail about the interrogation of Franz Schnee, who was probably interviewed a number of times after his arrival at Trent Park. The observer stated that aircraft from at least four KG26 Staffeln had taken part in the mission, three from the 1st, 2nd and 3rd Staffeln at Lubeck-Blankensee and the 4th Staffel from a meadow aerodrome near Schleswig.

The aircraft flew singly and his own Heinkel was the first aircraft of the 2nd Staffel. As the Heinkel flew at a height of about 1,000 feet, the Hurricane pilots had closed in and reportedly saw 'pom-pom' anti-aircraft fire from a ship the bomber had flown over. The observer however, did not report noticing any anti-aircraft fire from the vessel.

After interrogating Franz Schnee with a view to finding out if he had attacked any shipping, the report stated it was very improbable this aircraft had been involved in such attacks.

Schnee told his interrogator they would first fire a machine gun into the water in front of an unarmed merchant ship. This was to make the crew abandon ship before they carried out an attack. If the crew failed to abandon ship, a bomb would be dropped in front of the bow of the ship. If they still failed to leave the vessel, an attack would be made. Whether this was true is unknown, the question is would they waste a bomb just to make a crew abandon ship?

Denys Felkin noted that when they arrived at Grimsby on the *Harlech Castle*, there was a lot of hostile feeling towards the German airmen after repeated attacks on unarmed fishing boats. For this reason, the dead crewman was not given a military funeral and quickly buried.

Franz Schnee had explained that his Geschwader had undergone a period of training in the Baltic Sea to bomb shipping. Their target ship had been the *Hessen* and practice bombing took place from various altitudes. The observer would fuse the bombs and release them. In an emergency, the pilot or the radio operator could also jettison the bombs he added.

Schnee explained that he had undertaken a number of war flights with KG26. His pilot, Oberfeldwebel Fritz Wiemer, had taken part in an attack against the British Fleet in November 1939 and been awarded the Iron Cross Second Class after their observer reported hitting a ship. (This had been discussed with Gerd Kahle in the M-Room.)

Two of the crew were found in possession of orange-coloured triangles with tapes and hooks fitted to them. Franz Schnee explained that these were to be attached to their helmets if they landed in the sea, as orange was the best colour for rescuers to spot them.

Franz Schnee continued assisting the interrogators and discussed a notebook recovered from the aircraft brought down at Whitby on the same day. He explained that there was a series of six questions to be answered regarding any attack or mission. The answers would be sent by wireless back to base after an attack and on their way home over the sea.

Schnee said their aircraft was the first war loss for 2/KG26 and they had not been involved in Poland, although Staffeln 1, 3 and 4 had been engaged there. He said his Staffel Kapitan was Hauptmann Helm and Oberst Fuchs was in command of the Kampf-Geschwader. General Major Sieburg had previously been in command, but transferred in November 1939.

The interrogators discussed with Schnee that KG26 seemed to have been heavily engaged in the war with a considerable amount of work. Schnee agreed with this comment and said there had been a certain amount of dissatisfaction with this, as many other units had undertaken no war flights whatsoever. He did proudly add that this was because KG26 was experienced at flying over the sea.

Franz Schnee appears to have been very talkative and like Gerd Kahle, he seems to have overstayed with his time at Trent Park. Having arrived in early February, he was still there in mid-April, although this time, he appears to have been given a new code in the reports and was no longer referred to as A32, but A44.

A44 is listed as a Feldwebel observer in a number of M-Rooms transcripts, including SRA50 on 28 March, SRA56 on 3 April, SRA58 on 5 April and SRA59 on 10 April 1940. In these logs, A44 (Schnee) states he is from KG26 and they alone have been waging war on England. More details of these transcripts follow in later chapters, but it appears Schnee was very useful to AI1(k). The question is why change his code from A32 to A44? Was this an error or was there some other reason for this, possibly to distract attention from the length of time he was at Trent Park?

On 9 February 1940, another Heinkel III (1H+EN), this time from 5/KG26, was brought down by a combination of fighters and anti-aircraft fire while attacking a ship. The pilot made a forced landing at North Berwick Law in East Lothian and the aircraft was salvaged and repaired, before being sent to the Royal Aircraft Establishment for evaluation purposes.

Three of the crew were captured, including the pilot, Unteroffizier Helmut Meyer, the observer, Unteroffizier Josef Sangl and air mechanic, Obergefreiter Heinz Hegemann. The wireless operator Franz Wieners was killed during the fighter attack. Meyer and Hegemann have already been mentioned in the chapter on Gerd Kahle, as he spoke with them in the M-Rooms.

A large number of documents and maps were found in the aircraft and examined by AI1(k) and AI1(e). An intelligence report signed by Denys Felkin (No. 15/1940) states that the surviving crew members were interrogated in conjunction with the recovered documents and maps. Two maps were of particular interest and showed shipping routes and a convergence off the Firth of Forth – hence the attention paid to that area by the Luftwaffe.

A weather reporting map was first shown to prisoner A24 (the talkative Fritz Ambrosius who was still at Trent Park), before being discussed with this crew. This was because fragments of a similar map had been found in Ambrosius's possession when captured in late October 1939. It is interesting to note that Fritz Ambrosius was still at Trent Park many weeks after his capture, this being confirmed from the M-Room discussion he had with Gerd Kahle on the 25 January 1940 (SRA17).

Returning to the actual interrogation of the crew of this Heinkel, two of the crew had diaries from which a detailed war diary could be compiled for 5/KG26. Another recovered document was a 1:2,000,000 *Merkator Projecktion* map of Germany with a number of restricted areas drawn on it.

Although there was a slow flow of prisoners through Trent Park in February 1940, this allowed the interrogators to spend more time on individuals and the flow of intelligence was much greater in terms of value and detail. This would not be the case during the summer months of 1940.

On 22 February, a Heinkel III (T5+OH) was shot down by two Spitfires of No. 602 Squadron at Coldingham near St. Abb's Head, Berwickshire. The crew consisted of Leutnant Erich Grote (pilot), Feldwebel Fritz Sprigarth (observer), Unteroffiziers Wilhelm Berger (wireless operator) and Walter Bachmann (air mechanic). Grote and Sprigarth as we have already seen were the subject of M-Room conversations with Gerd Kahle at Trent Park.

The interception, crash and its aftermath was one that captivated the attention of the newly promoted Denys Felkin who was now a substantive squadron leader…

Felkin's signed intelligence log No. 23/1940, noted the crew had been extremely uncommunicative and thought they had destroyed all evidence of their unit and point of departure when they set fire to their Heinkel. Despite their best efforts, the AI1(k) system kicked into gear and quickly established a number of details for these men.

The aircraft markings had been noted and thanks to the identity disc of the wounded Walter Bachmann, several meal tickets, wireless instructions of the day and a diary, the aircraft was identified without doubt, as belonging to Aufkir. Gr. Ob. d. L.

From AI1(k) records it was known that the aircraft was based at Oldenberg at the start of the year and that they no longer used Jever as an advanced airfield on the coast. The identity disc of another crew member was recovered when he tried to flush it down the toilet at a local police station soon after his capture.

Denys Felkin and his team eventually managed to get the crew to accept these facts as correct and they stated they were the fourth loss for their unit. The crew started to talk openly – an excellent example of how the intelligence officers managed to break down their resistance with known facts.

The pilot, Erich Grote, stated that he had been a pre-war reservist and Lufthansa pilot. They gave full details of their flight, navigation and the fact they were not to send wireless messages of their attack or being attacked by RAF fighters.

The top gunner had spotted three Spitfires and the pilot thought that by diving they could outpace them. Two of the Spitfires attacked them from directly astern and the gunner could not open fire because the tail of the Heinkel obstructed his line of fire. The first attack caused most of the damage to the Heinkel, damaging the left engine and wing. Two minutes later, the left engine stopped. One of the Spitfires appears to have been armed with cannons as the report states, 'The crew did not realise that they had been fired at by cannon', although in February 1940, the unit is known to have only been equipped with standard Spitfire Mk.1's, armed with eight .303 Browning machine guns.

The top gunner claimed to have fired off seven to eight drums of ammunition in a fight that lasted five minutes. The lower gunner (Bachmann) was wounded in the fight. The observer (Feldwebel Sprigarth) was lying at his gun in the glazed nose. He was surrounded by bullets smashing through the nose and into the instrument panel, but he miraculously escaped injury.

The pilot (Leutnant Grote) said he had tried, after they were hit, to head towards the coastline, but Sprigarth criticised him for not diving immediately for the sea. As soon as the left engine stopped, the right one began to lose revolutions. The pilot ordered a ceasefire by his own crew and the fighters also ceased their attacks and followed the badly damaged Heinkel down. Grote made a forced landing at Coldingham and ordered his crew to dismount the machine guns to keep any civilians or the circling fighters from stopping them setting fire to the aircraft.

The bomber crew managed to ignite a special incendiary device next to the wireless set and after a ten second delay, the fuse set-off the mechanism and the nose of the aircraft was destroyed. As the fire burned, the crew threw most of their papers into the flames before the fuel tanks exploded and the camera film was also destroyed.

One of the Spitfires (flown by Squadron Leader Andrew Douglas Farquhar) tried to land nearby, but the aircraft tipped over onto its back. Sprigarth ran over and helped release the unfortunate and probably highly embarrassed Farquhar.

The crew stated they had left their paybooks at their base before the flight and this was the first time AI1(k) had come across this security tactic. It was also the second time in a month, prisoners had tried to ditch their identity discs.

One of the crew's personal diaries contained details of his previous flights, the aircraft used and the duration of his flights since the start of the year. One flight was in an aircraft coded D-AGIG, previous intelligence showing this to be a Junkers 52 attached to the unit and flown by a previous member of this Gruppe in March 1939!

There is little doubt that by early 1940, AI1(k) had an efficient intelligence system which was producing results and being continually added to as more prisoners arrived at Trent Park. Detailed files were being compiled on a number of units which would be very helpful in the coming months.

On 27 February 1940, KG26 made yet another foray against Scotland and the coast of Northumberland, once again their target was shipping in the Firth of Forth. This time two more aircraft from 2/KG26 were brought down in the North Sea off St. Abb's Head and Coquet Island in Northumberland.

Heinkel III (1H+-K) was shot down and the crew of five killed off Coquet Island. The crew included the Staffel Kapitan, Hauptmann Hans-Joachim Helm. The bodies of Helm and his observer, Unteroffizier Karl Lassnig, were later washed ashore and buried at Chevington, Northumberland. Lassnig came ashore at Whitby with a rubber dinghy a couple of days after the crash. When his body was searched, he was found in possession of cinema tickets from Delmenhorst.

The crew of the other Heinkel III (1H+AK), were captured and sent for interrogation at Trent Park.

On 7 March 1940, Denys Felkin signed off intelligence log No. 28/1940. The extensive and lengthy seven-page report states Air Intelligence had identified the take-off point for this aircraft as Lubeck-Blankensee. This was because other airfields were snow bound and the previous week, this crew had great difficulty in taking-off from Westerland.

The Stab Staffel was still based at Lubeck and members of KG26 now had their blood groups added to their identity discs. This, according to interrogations, was because during the Polish campaign, a number of injured men had needed blood transfusions and their blood groups were required.

One of the crewmen had an identity disc number indicating he was from 3/KG26, while the rest and the aircraft were from 2/KG26. The prisoners explained that because of losses to the 1st Gruppe, the first three Staffeln were now operating as a single unit – hence the confusion with this man's identity disc number.

The crew stated that they were now under strict orders not to fly over English territory, so that if attacked and shot down, the aircraft will sink and all secret papers would be lost.

The intelligence report noted that a small sausage shaped rubber bag was washed up on the shoreline. This contained a red dye which when added to water, would produce a wide expanse of orange for any would-be rescuers to spot the downed airmen.

Despite the best efforts of the crew, a number of documents were recovered from the sea and sent to AI1(k). These included various maps, one of which included navigational beacon locations and a number of bearings. Over the British Isles, a number of locations had a red square drawn in pencil. This the crew declared, was the position of known anti-aircraft gun sites.

A recovered personal notebook contained a number of pages detailing navigational calculations which could be linked to a number of previously known attacks by KG26. One mentioned 1 F.122 – clearly referring to 1(F)/122 who were acting at the *Fuhlungshater* aircraft for the KG26 attacks. The notebook also contained a number of diagrams which were tactics for attacking different sized convoys.

The report also noted that the observer of this aircraft, Unteroffizier Hermann Jonas, who was wounded, relied principally on dead reckoning, but did check this with radio beacons. Jonas added that the beacon at Norden was an alternative location for the Bremen station transmitter. It has been operating for some time, but A41 (believed to be this aircraft's wireless operator, Feldwebel Karl Henrici), said he had not found this station/beacon satisfactory for taking bearings. The report then noted that A24 (Fritz Ambrosius, himself a wireless operator), had stated there were UKW (beacon) stations on Sylt and Borkum – the Borkum transmitters had two beams at 267 and 20 degrees. This small piece of information would increase in importance in due course.

A41 (Feldwebel Karl Henrici) confirmed the intelligence previously given by Fritz Ambrosius, adding the Westerland beacon was near Rantum with its beam pointing westwards. He claimed these beams were to define the German frontier and to prevent them landing on foreign territory.

On 7 March 1940, while Felkin was signing off the last intelligence report, a Heinkel III (T5+AH) of 1/Aufkr Gr. Ob. d. L. was shot down by Spitfires of No. 603 Squadron, some sixty-four miles off the coast of Aberdeenshire. The pilot, Feldwebel Ernst Breiler, was wounded, but he managed to ditch the Heinkel, before inflating and clambering into the dinghy. The wireless operator was killed, but the other two crewmen, although badly injured, managed to exit the sinking aircraft. The wounded Brieler tried to pull them both from the sea into the dinghy, but they sadly drifted away and drowned.

Two hours later, the dinghy was spotted by a Bristol Blenheim and a motorboat picked up Breiler and took him to Leuchars the next morning.

Breiler was yet another experienced pre-war pilot. Over the next month he would be recorded a number of times in the M-Rooms giving a wide range of opinions under his prisoner code – A46 (see later chapters).

On 8 March 1940, a Junkers 88 of 1st Gruppe of KG30 was shot down by a Hurricane off the coast of Wick in northern Scotland. The crew were killed and a satchel was recovered from the sea by HMS *Griffin*. (The crew were later identified after a casualty enquiry from Germany via the International Red Cross in Geneva.)

Intelligence report No. 31/1940, states the satchel was similar to those recovered from aircraft of KG26 and contained a weather report from Westerland. For this reason, Air Intelligence staff initially assumed this was yet another Heinkel of KG26. Other documents relating to wireless and direction finding were sent to AI1(e), the most interesting of which was a description of an Ultra Short wave landing apparatus. This included instructions in connecting the apparatus up and tuning it in. Various photographic images of the device and its visual indicators were also included in the satchel. This information once again, would become very important in time.

The next aircraft brought down according to AI1(k) records, was a Junkers 88 (4D+AP) of 6/KG30 in Druridge Bay, Northumberland, on 29 March. The cause of the crash was unknown and no fighters made any corresponding claims, so it may have been an accident or a technical fault. Whatever the cause, the crew of four which included the Staffel Kapitan Oberleutnant Rudolf Quadt was killed. Their bodies were recovered and found along with the wreck to contain another treasure trove of documents and intelligence.

Five days later, on 3 April 1940, AI1(k) was presented with a very valuable KG26 crew. This time, it contained five crew members including the Gruppen-Kommandeur Oberstleutnant Hans Hefele, two Leutnants and two Unteroffiziers.

Their aircraft a Heinkel III of Stab II/KG26 (1H+AC) had taken off from Lubeck-Blankensee on an armed reconnaissance flight. They attacked a minesweeper with a number of 50 kilograms bombs off the coast near Middlesborough and Redcar, before the naval crew hit it with their own anti-aircraft fire. This caused the crew to ditch their remaining bombs and they turned for home, but they were soon intercepted by a Spitfire of No. 41 Squadron. The Spitfire pilot, Flight Lieutenant Norman Ryder, managed to put a good burst into the right wing and the Heinkel pilot, Leutnant Rudolf Benisch, decided to ditch the aircraft. Ryder circled as he watched the Heinkel settle on the sea.

A nearby armed fishing boat from Scarborough called *Silver Line* saw the unfolding drama. They had recently been attacked and as the Heinkel turned towards them, they expected another attack. The Heinkel passed low over the fishing boat and one of the crew opened fire with their Lewis gun. A number of rounds struck the aircraft and observer Leutnant Georg Kemper in the nose of the aircraft was hit in the head and seriously injured.

Benisch managed to get the Heinkel down in the heavy swell and it began to sink as the crew exited the aircraft and tried to inflate their dinghy. Unfortunately, the rubber boat had been punctured by Ryder's bullets and was completely useless. The *Silver Line* headed towards the downed bomber which sank, leaving only its tail visible and the crew in the cold sea. All five airmen were pulled from the sea by the crew of the fishing boat, who immediately took a pistol from one of the Germans.

In his book, *Luftwaffe over the North,* Bill Norman states that the captain of the fishing boat, Bill Watkinson, told the prisoners they were being taken to Scarborough and they would be well-treated. The commander of the airmen (Hefele?) apparently cheered and said, 'Make for England, we never wanted to fight you anyway!'

The German airmen were said to have been so happy, the pilot, Rudolf Benisch, gave Bill Watkinson his gold signet ring and one of the other men, gave his brother Tom Watkinson his wrist watch. The fishing boat arrived in Scarborough three days later on 6 April and the airmen were handed over to the authorities and transported to Trent Park.

Flight Lieutenant Ryder had unfortunately been hit by the Heinkel's return fire and had to abandon his Spitfire over the sea. He was also rescued and returned home safely.

AI1(k) logged an initial intelligence report No. 37/1940 for these prisoners, but a nine-page report (No. 42/1940) was submitted and signed by Denys Felkin on 10 April 1940. This report detailed the interrogation of the crew…

It was found that KG26 and KG30 belonged to the 10th Fliegerkorps and were based in the north-western coastal areas of Germany. The 2nd Gruppe of KG26 had moved from Schwerin to Lubeck from where this aircraft had taken-off. It was not possible to determine from this particular crew where the 1st Gruppe of KG26 was based, but they had left Lubeck.

It was noted that the unit coat of arms painted on the sides of Geschwader aircraft were normally different for each Gruppe, but with KG26 there an exception and the Lion on the crest was the same for both the I and II Gruppen.

KG26 had their own 'battle song' called, '*The motors are droning*'. The song had featured in a number of German radio broadcasts and the Kampfgeschwader claimed to have attacked over two hundred merchant and warships, forty-six of which they claimed to have sunk.

After interrogating the crew of this Heinkel, a full list of the senior officers of KG26 was compiled for future reference. The unit commander, Oberst Fuchs, was said to have recently received the Knights Cross. The crew provided details of actions in Poland and one man had a diary from which AI1(k) were able to list his operations since January 1940.

AI1(k) identified that a number of recently arriving prisoners were in possession of a new form of identity paper. This took the form of a linen cloth and bore the holders photograph and signature. The new prisoners from this aircraft, stated that this was for occasions when they landed away from their own aerodrome due to bad weather or orders.

A wireless signals table was obtained from this crew and there were noticeable changes to previous KG26 tables. These included the fact that III/KG26 and I/KG100 were both listed for the first time. Although AI1(k) were not aware at the time, these units would become very significant during the coming weeks and months of 1940.

Individual KG26 Gruppen were now set out separately with their own radio frequencies, codes and call signs. The radio frequencies for the *Fuhlungschalter* aircraft had not been changed. However, call signs and frequencies for aircraft of 1(F)/122 had now been omitted. Each Staffel now had its own call sign instead of just a basic Geschwader or Gruppe call sign. Finally, the procedure under the Direction-Finding Safety Service had also been modified.

The wireless operator for this aircraft, Unteroffizier Albert Wilhelm Weber, was asked about the new signals table. He stated that individual aircraft used a three-letter Staffel call sign and then added their own aircraft's identification letter. For example, 1H+FH of 1/KG26 would use call sign F6DF, the second 'F' being the individual letter of their aircraft.

Only when the Geschwader Kommodore or one of the Gruppen Kommandeurs gives an order to the whole formation, would the three-letter call sign be used. If the Kommodore or a Kommandeur was giving a standard radio signal, they would also add their own aircraft identification letter to the message.

It was also stated that the use of the letter according to the aircrafts position in the formation had now been dropped. In addition, the ground stations used the call sign of the Gruppen-Kommandeur, with the addition of their own identity letter according to the right-hand column of the Direction-Finding Safety Service section. Thus, SE8U was the code for communications between Lubeck and I/KG26.

One airman called Weber continued his very lengthy explanation of wireless operations, beacons and calibration of the systems on the aircraft; all of which was intelligence that would be of great assistance to the Y-Service when listening to Luftwaffe communications.

The intelligence report concluded with a section on the captured Gruppen-Kommandeur, Oberstleutnant Hans Hefele. During his final flight, he sat in the observer's position, he had dropped the bombs aimed at the minesweeper and fired the nose gun at an attacking Spitfire. He had served in the Spanish Civil War as a Staffel Kapitan and was awarded the Iron Cross First Class for operations over Poland, although he was not with KG26 at the time.

Contrary to other captured airmen, Hans Hefele did not believe the air war could be a deciding factor and did not believe in bombing towns, except to make soldiers surrender. He criticised the Nazi Party for concentrating too much on physical training at the expense of education. His final remark the interrogator found particularly illuminating when Hefele said, 'If Germany loses the war, there will be 100 years of peace in Europe.' (Author's note – how correct that appears to have been!)

Intelligence report No. 48/1940 dated 19 April 1940, gave details of the contents of a pocket notebook Hans Hefele had in his possession when detained. These were notes apparently made since he took command of the unit on 18 January 1940. The intelligence staff quickly deduced that the Luftwaffe were becoming more security conscious and aware that too many documents were being carried on aircraft and subsequently falling into the hands of British Intelligence.

Like previous prisoners, Hans Hafele and Rudolf Benisch would feature in the M-Room reports. Yet again, AI1(k) had received more valuable intelligence.

On 8 April 1940, two more Heinkel III's of 4/KG26 and 6/KG26 were brought down by Hurricane fighters. One machine 1H+FM fell into the sea near the Orkney Isles and the other, 1H+DP made a forced landing at RAF Wick in Caithness. Both aircraft had been briefed to attack the Fleet anchorage at Scapa Flow.

The crew of the Heinkel that came down in the sea, spent a day in their dinghy before they were rescued and detained. The aircraft at Wick had the wireless operator and air mechanic killed in the Hurricanes attack.

On 10 April, a Heinkel III (1H+-M) of 4/KG26 was attacked by Hurricanes and Spitfires of Nos. 603 and 605 Squadrons near Kinnairds Head, Aberdeenshire, while attacking a convoy. Bombs were dropped without success, but both engines were damaged and the air mechanic and wireless operator were killed.

The pilot, Oberleutnant Harold Vogel, although badly wounded, managed to bail out with his observer. Vogel made a successful descent into the sea, but the observer somehow fell from his fully deployed parachute canopy and was killed. HMS *Woolston* plucked the pilot from the sea and took him back to Rosyth.

On 26 April a parcel of documents was sent to AI1(k) from the Admiralty. These were recovered from the sea by HMS *Arethusa* which had returned home from Norway.

The documents appeared to refer to four German airmen who were believed to have been lost. The men were listed as Unteroffiziers Karl Eilert, Willi Bolz and two men named Ramming and Tammen. The last two names came from tabs cut from clothing and their origins were unknown. (It appears their bodies were probably recovered and then buried at sea by the Royal Navy.) No identity discs were included, but an envelope addressed to Unteroffizier Eilert and sent to Feldpost nummer L31074, Luftgaupostamt, Hamburg 1 was attached to the bundle.

Two documents were found in the parcel in connection with the issue of Very cartridges from Lubeck-Blankensee to the 9th Staffel of KG30 at Westerland. These sheets were dated 17 April 1940.

Some documents detailing wireless information were passed on to AI1(e). A wireless table did not follow the usual layout used by KG26 and was not dated. There was mention of Trondheim, Stavanger and Kristiansund which indicated the table to be a fairly recent one. The table mentioned only Staffeln 1, 2 and 3, but the number 1 had been crossed out and a number 7 inserted.

There was a reference to 'X Korps Wotan' and what that meant was unclear to the intelligence staff. One previous prisoner had previously said Wotan was probably a code name for a section of the 10th Fliegerkorps (i.e. KG26 and KG30), but in time, Wotan would take on a very different meaning for AI1(k).

A final assessment by Air Intelligence deduced that the documents were from a Junkers 88 of 9/KG30 operating from Westerland and probably lost on or shortly after 17 April.

The rest of April remained fairly quiet for AI1(k), but on the final day of the month, a Heinkel III (1T+EL) of 3/KGr126 crashed at Clacton-on-Sea in Essex, killing the crew of four and a number of civilian residents. The cause of the crash was unclear and there was little of intelligence value at the crash site. However, one crewman had *II/KG245* written inside a glove. By way of its expanding library and archives, AI1(k) were able to deduce the unit this aircraft belonged to.

This brought an end to the month of April 1940. Elsewhere across Europe, an invasion of Norway was underway and in time, there would be an invasion of the Low Countries and France.

AI1(k) was successfully deciphering and collating a great deal of enemy intelligence, but in the coming weeks and months, their work rate would increase dramatically.

Chapter 8

Norway, Blitzkrieg & Dunkirk

In early April 1940, Germany invaded Norway with the Luftwaffe playing a major part in the operation. Elements of the Royal Air Force, Royal Navy and the British Army went to assist and thwart the Nazi invasion, but within weeks this operation had failed with great loss of life and materiel.

AI1(k) was still primarily dealing with intelligence relating to airmen captured over the United Kingdom or near its shoreline, but reports and intelligence started to filter back from Norway.

According to their own records in 1940, only five enemy machines were recorded by AI1(k) as being brought down over the United Kingdom in April. The main reason for this apparent reduction, was the operation by Germany against Norway.

In late April, AI1(k) received reports (Nos. 51 & 58/1940) detailing the forced landing of a Junkers 88 of KG30 in Norway on the seventeenth day of that month. The aircraft was identified as being coded 4D+BL and the crew belonged to the 3rd Staffel of KG30.

The identify disc of one captured airman bore the number 62744, but when compared to previous intelligence, this indicated the identity disc numbers did not run consecutively. This was because the number 62750 had previously been found to belong to an airman from the 6th Staffel of KG30 (6/KG30).

The second report stated that it seemed likely KG26 and KG30 were operating in close co-operation, because the orders for this flight had come from Hermann Göring, transmitted to the crew by Hauptmann Vetter. He was known to have been the Staffel Kapitan of 1/KG26 and was now in command of the Second Gruppe of KG26 (II/KG26).

The crew had just landed at their home airfield at Westerland from Stavanger, when they received new orders. They repositioned to Aalborg in Denmark before receiving further orders. However, it was doubtful they had enough fuel to undertake their final flight and probably would have landed at Trondheim on their return journey.

Their orders were to attack an aircraft carrier reported to be off the north coast of Norway towards Narvik where British and French troops were operating (Author's note: probably HMS *Glorious*). The JU88 was to carry 1,000 kilo bombs for this mission and they were believed to have also carried smaller bombs which may have prevented the aircraft from carrying a larger and sufficient fuel load.

Despite searching for the aircraft carrier, the crew could only find a few islands and exceeded the limits of their fuel supply. For this reason, they made a forced landing and tried to destroy their aircraft with incendiary bombs. This failed, so they stuffed the cockpit with straw and lit this. This ignited and the aircraft was totally destroyed. Eventually, with no hope of a return to German lines they were captured.

In May 1940, just three German aircraft were reported as being downed over or around the United Kingdom.

The first was a Dornier 17, shot down by Hurricanes of No. 43 Squadron off the coast, East of Wick in Caithness. The aircraft was lost with its crew and was later identified as belonging to Wekusta Ob. d.L.

One airman, Oberfeldwebel Anton Fally, the wireless operator, managed to bail out and was later picked up by an RAF rescue launch, but he was already dead. Sadly, his parachute became entangled around his neck and strangled him. The only intelligence retrievable was on the deceased's body and included his uniform and insignia. His identity disc bore the number 71000 A, the letter being presumed by Air Intelligence to be the airman's blood group.

AI1(k) were informed by the Royal Navy of a Dornier 18 flying boat which was brought down by three Hudson aircraft over the North Sea on 10 May 1940. The Dornier (K6+CH) of 1/KuFIGr.406, was flying at low-level when it was hit by anti-aircraft fire and the guns of the three RAF Hudson aircraft. This caused significant damage, killing one of the crew and injuring another. The flying boat landed on the sea and after the crew were taken off by a Royal Navy vessel, the ship rammed and sank the flying boat. Few details were sent to AI1(k) and from their own records, it is unclear what happened to the surviving crewmen, although they had already noted that the men belonged to 2/KuFIGr.506.

The final Luftwaffe machine brought down, crashed into the North Sea between The Wash and Teschelling on 11 May. This was a Junkers 88 (F6+-M) of 4(F)/122 which was on a reconnaissance flight from Munster and tasked with looking for British shipping.

The Junkers 88 was attacked by three Spitfires of No. 19 Squadron. The Junkers crew claimed a Spitfire destroyed and another damaged, but British records reveal no losses of Spitfires that day.

The pilot, Unteroffizier Reinhold Krulich, was badly injured, the observer, Leutnant Freidrich Meyer, was unharmed and the wireless operator, Unteroffizier Walter Hobel, was injured. The air mechanic, Unteroffizier Hermann Kunze, was killed. The crew were plucked from the sea and during preliminary interrogations (report No. 104/1940), it was discovered they were an experienced crew who had flown over Poland and France. The intelligence report was dated 23 May, almost two weeks after the crew had been captured, and in many ways shows that events in April and May 1940 were beginning to swamp the usually efficient AI1(k) system for handling Luftwaffe prisoners.

The Royal Navy was very concerned about torpedo carrying enemy aircraft, especially after its battles off the coast of Norway. They therefore asked Air Intelligence for assistance and sent them a photograph of a German torpedo washed up on the Yorkshire coastline.

In intelligence log 61/1940, dated 3 May 1940, Felkin gave a summary of the unit's findings in relation to German torpedoes. Prisoner A68 (I cannot identify this man) was the first Luftwaffe prisoner able to give any information regarding the subject. The torpedoes dimensions were 17'5" long and about 18" diameter. A68 confirmed these dimensions without prompting and recognised them as being a type dropped from Heinkel 115 aircraft. (The last Heinkel 115 known to have resulted in prisoners in the UK was on 21 October 1939, however, A68 may have been a prisoner captured in Norway and conveyed back to the UK.)

A68 freely discussed the torpedo and it was noted that apart from its dimensions, the only difference between this and a U-Boat torpedo, was a pair of diametrically opposed vanes, roughly one third of the way back from the nose of the device. A68 explained that they acted like ailerons on an aircraft and kept the torpedo on an even keel when dropped from the aircraft before it entered the water.

A68 told the interrogators that the torpedo was held and connected to the aircraft in the middle, but chocks both fore and aft, stopped it from swinging in the slipstream. The prisoner thought torpedo dropping tactics were suicidal, except in darkness or in misty conditions. At the rear of the torpedo was a projecting spring-loaded flap. When the torpedo entered the water, the flap would be pushed backwards and the device's motor would start running.

A68 claimed the recovered torpedo had a range of about 3,000 to 4,500 yards. The nose had an ordinary percussion cap, but magnetic torpedoes had a plain, smooth nose cone.

In addition to his valuable information on torpedoes, A68 also gave a number of details about the laying of sea mines. He said that if a mine landed on land, it would explode and they were no use in water with a depth greater than 50 meters. The magnetic mines only became active once a salt plug had been washed out by the water and the device armed. After leaving the aircraft, mines deployed a parachute, held in a cone shaped tail unit. The smaller mines utilised one parachute, but larger devices needed a drogue chute to assist in deploying the larger parachute.

A68 claimed that Heinkel 115's could not carry mines or torpedoes further than the Firth of Forth when operating from the German Bight.

A report was sent to the Admiralty and various other departments, but there must have been a steady flow of prisoners from Norway, as an attached document states that due to the constant new arrivals, prisoners of war were not held long at the centre. If any of the recipients of the report had any questions, they should telephone as soon as possible and before noon on the 6 May 1940. It also noted that A68 was originally in the German Navy and seconded to the Luftwaffe for four years.

In Norway, the Luftwaffe used a force of paratroopers and aircraft for deploying land troops. This was advantageous due to the mountains and fjords which hindered ground movements. Intelligence in relation to both subjects was quickly transmitted back to Air Intelligence and Denys Felkin was quick to complete reports on his unit's findings.

Intelligence log 71/1940 dated 9 May 1940, covered the interrogation of a number of German paratroopers detained in Norway.

One prisoner was identified as a Gruppen-Fuhrer from the 2nd Company with an identity disc number of 62843. The first and second companies had been joined together for their mission and this officer stated three Gruppen normally formed a company, but on this occasion an extra unit was added to form four Gruppen, making what he called a 'Heavy company'.

The Gruppen-Fuhrer stated that seven of his men had jumped too soon from their aircraft and were not heard of again. Almost all their equipment was lost, as it was dropped into inaccessible places on the mountain sides.

The officer had been a member of the regiment for three years and took part in the occupation of Austria, where the unit was used as standard infantry and did not use their parachutes. He also went to Prague when the Nazis took control of Czechoslovakia.

During the Polish campaign, he was engaged collecting metals for delivery back to Germany for their industrial base, before the area was handed over to the Soviets.

German paratroopers were now equipped with a new type of automatic pistol, which was made of steel and had a bore of 8 or 9mm. The magazine held thirty rounds of ammunition and was fitted underneath the gun, it was about ten to twelve inches in length. It clipped into the weapon just in front of the trigger guard, forming a support when used in the prone position. There was also an extension to the butt, allowing it to be fired from the shoulder. (This is believed to have been the new MP40 which replaced the M18). A paratrooper armed with this weapon, usually carried six spare magazines, all of which could be reloaded, but they were normally discarded once used in action.

The prisoner stated that the sight range is 200 meters, but in reality, it is useless at anything over 75 meters. The prisoner, the report noted, gave the general impression the new weapon was inefficient and unreliable. He added that only one such weapon was provided to each Gruppe and that was used by the Gruppen-Fuhrer. Despite these claims, a previous prisoner had stated that the weapon was given to the 3rd section leader.

The Gruppen-Fuhrer said each company normally had two bicycles for use as dispatch riders, but they had not been included in the Norwegian operation.

Numerous other intelligence reports were completed regarding German paratroopers which at the time were something of a mystery to the British.

A final report by Felkin (No. 103/1940) provided a composite report of his general findings from the interrogation of a number of German paratroopers, however, the Nazi invasion of the Netherlands was now nearing completion and had seen further massed formations of German paratroopers dropped over a number of locations… It is unclear whether his report therefore included details and intelligence from the Netherlands, although, as we shall see later, he was receiving intelligence from that front.

Denys Felkin opened his summary by stating that no man was able or willing, to give a complete outline of the paratroop organisation. This led him to believe the regiment was by no means stable and companies and even battalions, may be altered in number.

Previously it was believed membership was voluntary, but it appears from interrogations, that may not have been the case. Many of those captured had been members of the *Feldherrenhalle Standarte* – the SA troops used for ceremonial occasions and guard duties. They had been disbanded in 1938 and given the choice of joining the new parachute regiment or being considered a coward!

At the start of the Norwegian campaign, there was one full regiment of paratroopers, a second was almost complete and a third was in training at Wittstock. This training establishment could allegedly accommodate five hundred men.

A paratroop regiment consisted of three battalions of about six hundred men, excluding non-jumping personnel such as cooks and drivers. The battalions were divided into four companies with an establishment of one hundred and forty-four active jumpers.

A table of paratroop losses in Norway was compiled from identity discs, as well as the names of commanders captured, wounded, or known to have died. In the 1st Regiment of paratroopers, the 1st battalion was believed to have suffered heavy losses with the 3rd and 4th companies having sixty men captured. However, the 2nd and 3rd Battalions did not appear to have had any men captured.

The 2nd Regiment's 1st Battalion had two hundred and eighty men captured, while the 2nd Battalion had another fourteen men captured. Thirty-two other men believed to have been from a 3rd Battalion were also detained. On face value, it appeared the Norwegian campaign was something of a failure for the new German paratroop force.

It is clear Denys Felkin did not have a high opinion of these new troops. A further assessment (intelligence report No. 105) followed on the 23 May 1940, detailing the unit's uniform and in particular their distinctive helmet, parachute, weapons and rations.

Intelligence log 85/1940 gave details of aircraft identified as being used in the transport of troops to Norway. Three Gruppen had been identified as being involved in the operation, belonging to the *Zur besonderen Verwendung Gruppe* or z.b.V. Their aircraft bore the following markings:

z.b.V. 1... 1Z+--
z.b.V. 2... 9P+--
z.b.V. 3... G6+--

The transport aircraft Gruppen were noted as being large, one Junkers 52 was noted as belonging to a 10th Staffel and the identification letter 'Z' was also reported, indicating a very large fleet of aircraft.

In the Netherlands, a number of paratroopers had been captured around The Hague and Rotterdam. Most were captured after about twelve hours on the ground. A number of other troops had been landed on the ground by JU 52 transport aircraft and a considerable number of those aircraft were shot down according to Felkin's report.

A number of airfield ground staff were also detained, possibly brought in to manage new arrivals once the aerodrome was captured. In addition, there were a number of captured ground personnel and aircrews from Heinkel and Messerschmitt 109 and 110 units.

Denys Felkin noted that the interrogation of Luftwaffe prisoners in the Netherlands was rushed and although a list was made and attached, it should not be considered completely accurate.

It is clear that after a quiet January to April, May 1940 was a very busy month for AI1(k). Their main problem was most prisoners were now captured on foreign soil and were not subject to the same rigorous security conditions as those detained in and around the UK. As a consequence, any intelligence gleaned from these men was possibly tainted and conflicted with other information. Some of the prisoners were transferred back to the United Kingdom, but many remained in the host nation. In time, many would be released by the advancing German Army and returned to their combat units.

Although Denys Felkin had an excellent intelligence system in place in the UK, he could not control events on foreign soil, where allied, yet foreign forces interrogated downed German airmen before the British officers could intervene. Some intelligence was disseminated back to the British intelligence services, but compared to that obtained through their own work, it was not as detailed and it was difficult to assess its value and provenance.

Intelligence log No. 107/1940 is a perfect example of how deficient intelligence reports were when sent from the continent back to AI1(k)...

The report, signed off by Felkin, gave some details about the crews of two Heinkel III's (B3+AM and B3+KM) brought down near Lille, France on the 19 May 1940.

The two aircraft had taken off at 0900 hours from E-hafen near Oldenberg on a reconnaissance flight ahead of another seven aircraft who awaited an escort of Messerschmitt 110 Zerstorer aircraft. Flying at 9,500 feet the two Heinkel's received heavy anti-aircraft fire before being attacked by three or four Spitfires. (This was clearly incorrect, as there were no Spitfires in France/Holland at that time.) Both aircraft came down and B3+AM burnt out on the ground, the crew of four being wounded. The other aircraft did not burn and the pilot, Unteroffizier

Wilhelm Seeck, was shot and killed by troops as he tried to set the Heinkel alight. The wireless operator of the aircraft was also killed and the air mechanic injured. The observer was not harmed.

Although very little other intelligence was gathered, the crew stating they had no Geschwader or Gruppe number, they did give an extensive list of names and ranks of senior officers, including the Geschwader Kommodore, Oberst Lackner. He was allegedly hurt while escaping an aircraft by parachute and was in hospital. The second Gruppen Kommandeur was said to be Oberleutnant Kostner and the 4th Staffel Kapitan was Hauptmann Michel.

Although the prisoners did not give numbers for their unit, their aircraft identity letters on the fuselage were in white. This, together with their identification of 4th Staffel and II Gruppe personnel made it clear their aircraft came from the 4th Staffel, II Gruppe, but the question was, to which Kampfgeschwader did they belong? In time the B3+-- code would be recognized as belonging to KG54, so these men belonged to 4/KG54, part of the 2nd Gruppe.

With the capture of the Netherlands and an end to intelligence from that region, Felkin signed-off another report on 25 May, detailing intelligence on miscellaneous Luftwaffe personnel in Holland (log No. 114/1940). The report was only two pages in length and probably indicative of the scarcity of detailed intelligence from that front.

The report opens by stating that a number of specialists had been detained around The Hague. These included anti-aircraft gunners, all of whom were to have operated 2cm (20mm) guns, which were to be delivered after their arrival by Junkers 52 aircraft. It was noted that the guns could also be used as anti-tank guns according to some of the prisoners.

One prisoner said that in his aircraft, all bar three of the gunners were killed. He was wounded and their guns never arrived. The prisoner gave details of his own service, unit and training. He was only experienced with the 20mm gun, but considered the 8.8cm (88mm) gun to be a poor weapon which would rarely bring down aeroplanes. He did consider the 3.7cm Skoda Czech gun as the best, although he had never even seen one.

This prisoner's comment about the 88mm gun, a weapon that would become feared by tank and aircrews alike, is astounding with hindsight. It is similar to the comments of the paratrooper officer, who claimed the MP40 machine pistol was no use. In retrospect, it is now clear that both men were probably trying to mislead their interrogators and both weapons had long successful 'careers' ahead of them, costing the lives of many Allied personnel.

Air Intelligence had ascertained that a Junkers 52 (9P+-L) had been flown to Holland with an officer engineer and two mechanics, as well as spare parts to repair any damaged Junkers 52's. Unfortunately, the aircraft was shot down and the only survivor was identified by his identity disc number as belonging to 3/z.b.V 9.

One aircraft AI1(k) were very interested in, was the Junkers 87 dive bomber – the legendary Stuka. The aircraft had been active throughout Poland and the Low Countries during the Blitzkreig campaigns with devasting results, but on 14 May, one made a forced landing south-east of Brussels in Belgium. For once, the intelligence sent back to AI1(k) was of a high quality.

The Junkers 87 (L1+HV) was initially identified as belonging to II/LG1. Feldpost numbers and crew identity disc details were available, as was an Ausweis which was issued at Dedelstorf on 23/1/40. It was typed on paper stuck with grey linen.

The dive-bomber crew had been on a reconnaissance flight and carried no bombs, when it received a direct hit from a light anti-aircraft gun and had to make a forced landing. The crew admitted making eight bombing flights previously and a second reconnaissance flight. The bombing operations had been primarily aimed at the fortress line at Utrecht, but also against communications and included ground strafing.

Neither the identity disc numbers or the Feldpost numbers tallied with those of a previous prisoner allegedly from the same unit. Despite this, it was assumed both machines came from IV/LG1 and the discrepancy was caused by the earlier prisoner, having just transferred from another unit and retaining his old numbers. Both members of this crew gave their aircrafts code letters willingly and independently.

The crew and their unit, IV/LG1, had been based at Barth before the war, but moved to Poland for the campaign. Their aircraft had no protective armour and the crew claimed to know nothing about armour being fitted to other JU 87 aircraft. The aircraft had two fixed forward firing machine guns and the point of convergence could be adjusted while in flight by the crew. There was one free moving machine gun firing backwards in the rear cockpit. Its arc of fire was to the rear of the wings and 30 degrees down and 80 degrees upwards.

Additional fuel tanks could be fitted for long range operations, either on the fuselage or more likely under the wings. With extra tanks the range could be increased to over 800 kilometers. Normal speed was said to be between 195 and 215 mph, but in the dive the velocity was 365 to 400 mph. The pilot claimed that on one occasion, diving without airbrake deployment, a velocity of 490 mph was reached.

On a long dive attack, the angle was usually 70 degrees, increasing to 80-90 degrees. The pull-out would be no lower than 500 feet above ground level. The Revi gunsight fitted slightly to the left on the instrument panel coving was used for bombing, while the ring and bead sight was to the right and used for the machine guns.

Whether Air Intelligence already possessed this intelligence from other sources is unknown, but it was clear this was some of the best intelligence they had received from the Low Countries in recent weeks.

AI1(k) continued to receive various documents for analysis, but some concerned matters other than Luftwaffe fighters and bombers. Intelligence report No. 127/1940 is a five-page report detailing the co-operation between the Wehrmacht and the Luftwaffe – in essence their Blitzkrieg tactics. The intelligence came from a leaflet dated 8/3/1940 and issued from the Commander in Chief of the German Army. It dealt with the signals to be used between troops on the ground and aircraft. In addition, a second typewritten sheet, dated 14/3/1940, gave a number of ground signals to be used by troops to Luftwaffe aircraft flying in support of the army.

The papers stated that for close and successful co-operation, immediate and unmistakable mutual recognition of each other as a friendly force was essential. The air superiority of the Luftwaffe over that of the enemy, allowed the German army to identify itself from below as German forces, by means of visible signals on the ground.

The reports stated that generally, both the army and the air force must mutually acquaint one another regularly and in advance, of ground and air movements in the operational zone. Officers of all ranks were responsible for exact adherence in all circumstances.

Swastika flags were the chief identity marks for all troops. According to the circumstances, they should be laid on the ground, waved or spread on top of vehicles and secured on tanks so that they can be visible to aircraft.

The designated operational zone should be marked on maps and mutually agreed between the air force and the army. Outside of the operational recognition zone, troops must identify themselves temporarily to aircraft when requested to do so, or when they believe it necessary and the aircraft are recognised as friendly.

Yellow towel signals and white squares were to exhibited as recognition signals at the rear of all tanks. Yellow towels are to be used when Swastika flags were not available. In snowy conditions, the white squares were to be replaced by dark-coloured squares.

At night, troops on the march and in positions must show their identity if requested by aircraft. This would be achieved by flashes of white light, providing their position was not endangered by such an act.

The Luftwaffe aircraft should display the 'German cross' national markings, but army recognition of German aircraft was required. Very light signals were an additional means of recognition and Very light signals could be ordered for a definite period of time.

Flying in certain formations (e.g. in a line astern or in line abreast) could be used for identification by troops, but the presence of enemy fighters could make this impossible.

One of the reports concluded with a large number of ground symbols to be used in communications between the ground and aircraft. Some of these are in the following table:

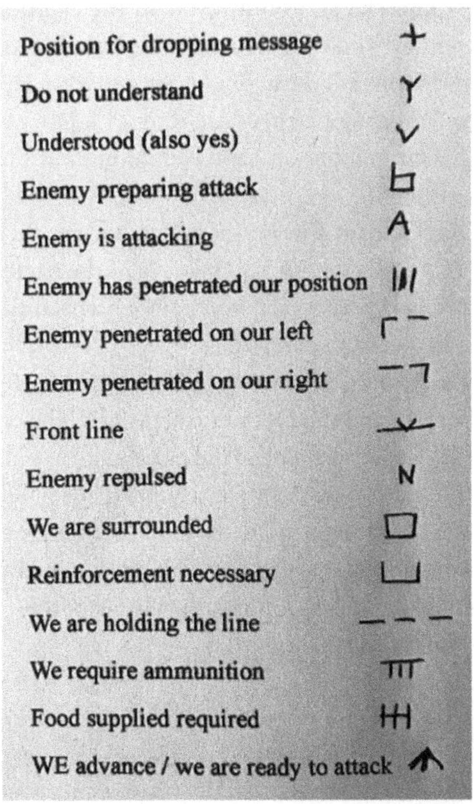

On 3 June 1940, Denys Felkin signed off intelligence report No. 129/1940. This was an unusual report, because it contained very little information regarding the aircraft concerned.

The report dealt with a Dornier 17 reported to have taken-off from Gutersloh with orders to ascertain the state of defences around the airfield at The Hague, preparatory to the landing of paratroopers and other soldiers. The aircraft was shot down at 0710 hours local time at Woerden, twenty-five kilometers north of Rotterdam. The names of the crew were not given, but the report stated the observer was the Staffel Kapitan and Gruppe Training Officer. He belonged either to the Ob.d.L. or a special Reconnaissance Staffel attached to the paratroop units. The officer had been in charge of photographic reproductions and preparing 1,500 copies of the plans for the Dutch and Belgian campaigns. Immediately before the war, he had been stationed with a Reconnaissance Staffel at Berlin-Tempelhof and previously as an instructor with the paratroops at Stendal for eighteen months.

The officer, who was not been named in the report, stated that it had been hoped an attack on The Hague would result in the capture of the Queen of Holland and the country would immediately capitulate. From examination of loss and crash reports, there is little doubt the observer in this machine was Oberleutnant Heinz-Wolfgang Florin of Aufkl.St.7 Fl. Div. His aircraft was shot down by a Dutch fighter and he was captured uninjured. The rest of the crew bailed out, but were injured.

According to Oberleutnant Florin, the orders for the flight had been given to him by General Kurt Student the commander of the parachute troops. They were to be given a strong fighter escort, but their fighters failed to arrive and they circled at 6,500 feet to await their arrival.

Without any fighter escort, they were attacked by enemy fighters, believed to have been Dutch Fokkers and the Dornier caught fire. The crew did not send a message back to their base and abandoned their aircraft to be immediately captured on the ground by Dutch troops. As a consequence, many of the paratrooper's aircraft (JU 52's) were badly shot-up by the anti-aircraft fire and armoured cars on the ground. The intelligence report concluded that the failure of the German operation at The Hague aerodrome, may be ascribed in part, to the shooting down of Oberleutnant Florin and his Dornier 17.

The Wehrmacht had all but defeated the French Army and the British Expedition Force (BEF) by the start of June 1940 and the Dunkirk evacuation was in its final days. Despite this, AI1(k) was still receiving intelligence regarding downed Luftwaffe aircraft in France.

On 3 June 1940, Denys Felkin signed off intelligence log No. 130/1940 which gave details of a new type of aircraft brought down near Lille on 20 May – a Dornier 215 of 3/LG2 (L2+MS).

The Dornier, similar to the older Do. 17 was on a reconnaissance flight from Cologne, when it was intercepted by six to eight French Morane fighters and shot down at 0745 hours. Two of the crew were killed and one seriously wounded, but the pilot, Unteroffizier Erich Luther, escaped without injury and was duly captured and interrogated – almost certainly by the French who passed details on to the RAF. The pilot's moral was deemed by the interrogator to be bad.

Unteroffizier Luther stated that he had previously belonged to 8/LG2, but at the end of 1939, there had been a reorganisation and he was transferred to the 3rd Staffel. In fact, it appears the entire 8th Staffel had become the 3rd Staffel of LG2.

Just prior to the start of the Norwegian campaign, Luther flew his aircraft to Hamburg civilian airfield where it became unairworthy. He therefore flew a Junkers 52 (L2+ZS) – which belonged to his Staffel – to Norway, ferrying troops there. In the second week of May, he flew the JU52 back to Hamburg and collected the Dornier 215 (L2+MS). He flew this machine to Cologne and two days later he was shot down near Lille.

Luther had low moral despite Germany's recent advances and victories. He was very talkative and told his interrogator that his unit was purely a reconnaissance unit, its aircraft scattered across various aerodromes. His Staffel Kapitan was Oberleutnant Schormeyer, a pilot who had previously commanded them as the 8th Staffel.

Luther said he had been warned against giving information about the Dornier 215, especially concerning its new engines, but despite this, he told the interrogator they were water cooled. The aircraft had a built-in camera and more than three machine guns, but no cannon was fitted.

Although the war was not going well for the British, intelligence was still being gathered and some of it was very important, including a number of secret documents passed on to AI1(k), (see intelligence log No. 131/40). These included extracts regarding directions to flak units on both day and night barrage fire and was dated 27 December 1939.

It noted that barrage fire had frequently been employed in – 'Quite hopeless circumstances with a resulting high waste of ammunition.' Accordingly, the Commander-in-Chief (Hermann Göring) had directed that daytime barrage fire shall not be directed against aircraft above clouds if they cannot be seen, as this might endanger Luftwaffe fighters. At night-time, barrage fire would not take place against enemy aircraft at 16,500 feet or more in altitude. When ordered to fire, only twelve shots were to be fired by each battery. Barrage fire must never give away the position of the flak unit or result in a waste of ammunition.

Although the wasting of ammunition was a valid point, it also clearly indicated that the flak units were running short of ammunition in late 1939. Had Germany been unprepared logistically for war in late 1939? In addition, the directive also stated that in some weather conditions, searchlights were of little use and in such circumstances the Gruppe will forbid their use.

These documents were invaluable and although six months out of date, the intelligence was passed on to RAF Bomber Command who would have been very interested to receive this information.

Another document dated 6 December 1939, concerned the Luftwaffe Aircraft Reporting Service. It stated that in order to obtain a true picture of aircraft movements, reports of take-offs and landings which are indispensable to the Air Watching Centre's known as *Flukos,* were to be passed-on quickly. However, reports sent long in advance of such movements caused unnecessary congestion of telephone lines. Therefore, 'Aircraft take-offs and the raising of balloon barrages are to be notified by the Air Observers 30 minutes beforehand.'

Similarly, all anti-aircraft gun practice firing, searchlight and target practice should be reported thirty minutes before hand. Landings of aircraft must also be reported immediately.

One specific directive gave an excellent example of how rigid and precise the Nazi regime was in relation to air traffic. It stated that in order to furnish a better survey of traffic in home territory, aircraft on courier and travel services must fly on specified routes, these were:

- Hannover-Stade-Gluckstadt-Westerland.
- Hannover-Marx-Jever (avoiding Bremen and Oldenburg).
- Jever-Varel (avoiding the closed areas of Wilhelmshaven) -Brake-Gluckstadt-Kiel.
- Stadt-Bremen (approach from the north).
- (Marine courier route) Berlin-Wilhelmshaven-Nordholz-Gluckstadt-Neumunster-Berlin.

The directive noted that after take-off, flying routes are to be approached in the quickest way possible with a direct course taken between the two named places.

When approaching the coastline in bad weather, aircraft should fire a Very light signal flare. When approaching well-known anti-aircraft positions, aircraft must simplify the recognition for the gunners by flying a slight 'serpentine course' which would allow the national (German) cross to be displayed. (i.e. a continuously changing banking course to allow the national insignia to be observed and identified.) If the gunners fire a warning shot, the aircraft must immediately fire a Very light flare signal.

When a unit ascertains the time and approximate course of a returning formation from overseas, they must communicate this immediately to the Air Observers.

The directive also gave a narrative on the bureaucratic manner in which forms had to be filled out. It included what columns had to be filled-in when reporting fighter movements and the various codes to be used for direction of flight. It also gave precise directions for the use of radio messages. It was in effect, a very rigid and bureaucratic system, although the intelligence was six months old, it was still very useful to AI1(k) and Bomber Command.

The third and final document was a Luftwaffe form titled: *Tactical Observations in Air Defence* and dated 27 December 1939. This was a very valuable document and gave an insight into the thinking of Luftwaffe High Command, their rigid and in some cases, almost 'nanny-like' systems. In addition, some of the recommendations seemed less than helpful. The report noted:

- Crews who had hitherto flown together, should not be separated as tactical experience was valuable.
- In formations of fighters constantly ready for immediate operation, the leader must appoint a deputy, even if he is absent for a short time to avoid delays.
- To avoid delays from reconnaissance flights, the wireless office should be in direct proximity of the Operations Room.
- It is imperative that bomber and reconnaissance aircraft both outward and returning, make use of the protection afforded by clouds.
- Operational instructions for individual aircraft must be given with consideration to the respective crews. Crews or formations making their first operational flight over the Western Front will require special instructions.
- The camouflage of ground organisations must be carefully watched. The results of such camouflage can only be visualised from the air. It should not be forgotten to camouflage the top and side identity markings of aircraft.

- Single bomber and reconnaissance aircraft when attacked by enemy fighters should endeavour to escape in clouds.
- Should an enemy fighter possess greater speed (than the Luftwaffe aircraft), it is recommended that at the moment he reaches a firing range, a steep dive to one side or the other should be made, this will frustrate the attack.
- It is usually advisable to open fire early (aircraft gunners, not fighter pilots). This however, is only effective if carefully aimed bursts are fired and the ammunition distributed so that the drum does not require changing at the critical moment. Fighters taking cover behind the bombers tail can be reached by the rear gunner moving his gun.
- French and English fighters always adopt a *Schwarm* formation (4 or 5 aircraft) of more. They adopt the *Rotte* (2 aircraft) formation when flying over home territory and fly patrols to prevent penetration by our reconnaissance aircraft. Attacks are made from above rear or below rear making use of blind spots.
- If *Direction Finding* fails when blind flying, it is only advisable to continue, if the necessary details for navigation with dead-reckoning are available and a change in conditions is not expected. Otherwise, the aircraft should return to base to avoid the danger of loss.
- To achieve the greatest distance with the given quantity of fuel, a twin-engine aircraft would economise by running both engines at a lower speed, and on no account, by the cutting of one engine or the other. This applies to all aircraft at all altitudes and irrespective of the load carried.
- 2 cm ammunition explodes with a bright flash, this should not lead to the immediate assumption that the target has not been set on fire.
- All crews have been instructed that aircraft are to be destroyed when landing in enemy or neutral territory. Disregarding this instruction is a most serious offence and will be heavily punished. Documents, maps etc. Together with secret aircraft accessories such as Lotfe bomb sights must in every case be destroyed.

These points are just a selection of the many listed in this secret document. The staff at AI1(k) must have read this document with a degree of incredulity. After many months of war and the processing of numerous prisoners, it was clear many airmen were not following these instructions, even though they were very precise and quite condescending for trained aircrews. The Nazi regime and Luftwaffe High Command clearly wanted a rigid and inflexible control system.

As the Dunkirk evacuation was completed and the RAF and Britain took stock of their situation, there was a late arrival from France. This was an intelligence report (No. 135/1940) relating to the downing of a Messerschmitt 109E, North of Lille on the 19 May 1940. The Messerschmitt was shot down by an RAF Hurricane and the unnamed pilot bailed out into captivity. Although the pilot was not named in the French report, examination of Luftwaffe loss records identified this man as Unteroffizier Hans-Joachim Hartwig of 5/JG2.

It is likely the pilot was interrogated by the French and this report was sent on to the RAF with the pilot's details redacted, but it is possible he was transferred back to Britain and dealt with by AI1(k). Why the report did not give his name is unclear and if he had remained in France, he may have been liberated by the advancing German forces.

The pilot told his interrogators that he belonged to 5/JG2 and had taken off from St Trond at 1145 hours that morning. He also claimed that both JG1 and JG2 were called the *Richthofen* Geschwader. He was flying with three other Messerschmitt 109's at 10,000 feet, when a single Hurricane was spotted below them. His three colleagues dived upon the British fighter, but he remained above as his engine was not working properly. He was making his way back towards the German lines, when he was attacked by three more Hurricanes and his windscreen was covered in oil and water. His back suddenly felt 'hot' so he bailed out, fearing his aircraft was on fire.

Hartwig said his Messerschmitt was fitted with a DB 601 engine, but he had heard of a new engine which had a take-off power of 2,000 hp. Other units were already re-equipped with the new type, but he could not say which units they were. This intelligence must have caused some concern for the RAF, who had already found that their Hawker Hurricanes were in most cases, outperformed by the ME109E's in France.

With the end of the evacuation, the Luftwaffe turned its attentions back to Britain. At 2330 hours on the 7 June, a Heinkel 115 (8L+EL) crashed into an apple orchard near Eyke Rectory, Woodbridge in Suffolk. A magnetic sea mine it was carrying exploded scattering wreckage over a wide area. Two of the crew were killed immediately, but the pilot, Feldwebel Paul Randorf, was seriously wounded and died two days later. Little intelligence could be gathered from the scene, apart from identity discs and a map with a flight path marked upon it. Despite this lack of evidence, AI1(k) eventually reported that the aircraft belonged to 3/ KuFIGr906.

On 12 June, a Heinkel III (4T+BH) of Wetterkundung Staffel 51, was brought down by Spitfires in the Thames Estuary off Margate. The aircraft had apparently been on a reconnaissance and weather flight when they were attacked and shot down. Two of the crew survived, being pulled out of the sea naked. Where their clothes went was a mystery. The dead observer was a meteorological expert commonly known as a 'Weather Frog'. He was distinguished by his uniform's green insignia on the collar (hence the name).

As activity started to gather pace, Kampfgeschwader 4 (KG4) were tasked with a raid on the bomber airfield at RAF Honington in Suffolk on the night of the 18-19 June. During the raid, five of their Heinkel IIIs were shot down across East Anglia, the North Sea and the English Channel. Eleven airmen were captured and taken to Air Intelligence for interrogation, although some were wounded and needed hospital treatment.

On 24 June, AI1(k) completed an intelligence report (No. 149/1940) detailing the findings of four of the Heinkel's brought down that night. A previous report, No. 146, had already covered these aircraft and crews, but this went into much more detail.

The report, signed off by Denys Felkin, stated that after further interrogation of the captured airmen and examination of their effects, it was deduced that the 4th, 6th and Stab Staffeln of KG4 were based at Merville on 18 June, and they started their mission from that location. From various crewmen's diaries, it was possible to build a detailed picture of the movements of various aircraft and the different Staffeln, which was reproduced in a table. The men's morale was deemed to be excellent and all the captured pilots had several years of experience with many war flights.

A Heinkel III (5J+GA) of Stab/KG4, came down in the garden of the Bishop of Chelmsford's home in Springfield Road, Chelmsford at 0030 hours on 19 June. The sole survivor from the crew of four, was Leutnant Erich Simon who was wounded. (Author's note: this aircraft is believed to have been shot down by the renowned fighter ace, 'Sailor' Malan of No. 74 Squadron).

Leutnant Simon told his interrogator that his mission was purely one of reconnaissance and to observe the results of the bombing. After crossing the coast, his Heinkel had been picked up by searchlights while at 16,000 feet and he flew on instruments to avoid being dazzled by the lights. The pilot told his interrogator that some pilots have dark glasses (goggles) to avoid glare from searchlights and some aircraft had curtains fitted at the side of the pilot to prevent them being dazzled, but these were optional.

The Heinkel was put into a series of flat turns, but the pilot could not avoid the searchlights. He was engaged by very accurate anti-aircraft fire which he believes caused damage, three bursts being within twenty feet. In addition, they were attacked by a fighter (Malan) and the controls were shot away, so Leutnant Simon bailed out. He did not say anything about his three deceased colleagues.

The second Heinkel III (5J+KP) of 6/KG4 was shot down by a fighter (a Spitfire of No. 19 Squadron flown by Flying Officer G.E. Ball), after being caught in searchlight beams at 0215 hours. It landed in the sea off Margate, Kent, the observer being killed when he bailed out and his parachute caught on the tail of the aircraft. The bombs were ditched before the pilot, Leutnant Hans-Jurgen Bachhaus, cooly ditched the aircraft near the darkened shoreline and the remaining crew paddled to shore in their dinghy. It appears very little was said by the three surviving crewmen, but a diary did give some details of aircraft and crew movements from January 1940 onwards.

In addition, a map was recovered from the aircraft, parts of which were brought ashore for examination. This showed a course of 307 degrees to the target at RAF Honington and a return course of 133 degrees.

Heinkel III (5J+DM) was originally believed to belong to Stab II/KG4. The crew initially claimed to have been caught in searchlight beams and intercepted by three Bristol Blenheim night-fighters. Whether this was correct or a figment of their imagination is unclear, but the air mechanic was wounded by gunfire and an engine stopped. Hoping to return home on one engine, they dropped their bombs, but the other engine failed and the pilot, Oberleutnant Ulrich Jordan, ditched the aircraft in the shallow waters off the beach at Cley in Norfolk. The crew scrambled ashore and were quickly captured, including the observer – Major Dietrich von Massenbach the Gruppen-Kommandeur.

After crew interrogations and examination of papers and identity discs, it was established the Heinkel belonged to 4/KG4 with the Gruppen-Kommandeur on board. Major von Massenbach had only just replaced Oberst Erdmann who had commanded the unit in Poland.

In reality, it appears the Heinkel was attacked by just one Blenheim, that flown by Pilot Officer J.D. Humphreys of No. 29 Squadron who claimed a Heinkel III off Norfolk at midnight.

Another Heinkel III (5J+AM) of 4/KG4 came down at Six Mile Bottom in Cambridgeshire at 0115 hours. They were an experienced crew, having been together for many months and undertaken as many as seventy war flights.

The Heinkel had crossed the Norfolk coastline at 16,000 feet and was quickly picked up by the searchlights, which the crew thought was very bright, even with the full moon. They dived to 3,000 feet and kept turning and climbing, but they could not escape the beams and there was no anti-aircraft fire. They claimed to have been attacked by three Spitfires, one of which had a landing or headlight on which seemed to be looking for them. The crew added that when one Spitfire entered the searchlight beam, their top rear gunner shot it down. The observer Oberleutnant Joachin von Arnim, told his interrogator that he held his own fire as the top rear gunner was a crack shot and had previously shot down a Hurricane over France.

Examination of RAF records finds that it is unlikely this crew was engaged by three Spitfires. It is more likely they were attacked by a Blenheim of No. 23 Squadron, flown by Squadron Leader J.S. O'Brien and his crew. He had an unconfirmed claim for a Heinkel III over Newmarket at 0115 hours, just a few miles north of the Heinkel's eventual crash site. Unfortunately, O'Brien's own aircraft was hit and although he bailed out successfully, Pilot Officer King-Clarke was killed when he bailed out and hit one of his aircrafts propellors. Corporal Little was also killed when the Blenheim crashed at Newmarket.

It is possible the Blenheim had its landing lights on in a bid to identify the Heinkel, but this seems unlikely, especially as searchlights were already illuminating the bomber. The bomber crew possibly tried to concoct a story to throw their interrogator off anything of intelligence value.

Examination of the wrecked Heinkel found armour plating behind the wireless operator's position, the pilots back, and several strips under the cockpit floor, protecting the pilot and observer from attacks from below. There was no armour for the under-fuselage gunner's position. The crew reported hearing many bullets striking the armour plating and believed this had saved their lives. The crew bailed out, but the air mechanic, who was not wearing his chest parachute at the time, was killed.

Although not covered in this report, the fifth Heinkel III that night came down off Felixstowe near the Cork lightship at 0115 hours. This also belonged to 4/KG4 and the crew were all killed. The body of Hauptmann Herman Prochnow, the Staffel Kapitan was recovered from the sea and buried with full military honours. This aircraft appears to have been shot down by Pilot Officer J.S. Barnwell of No. 29 Squadron who claimed a Heinkel III at this time off Felixstowe.

The night had been a very successful one for the RAF night-fighters and two other KG4 aircraft returned home with damage following fighter attacks over England. In addition, other machines were damaged by British anti-aircraft guns. It was a chastening experience for KG4.

The following week in June 1940 was fairly quiet, but the Luftwaffe returned to British skies on the night of the 25-26 June, when KG4 and KG26 attacked targets from Hull to Lothian in Scotland.

Two aircraft from 3/KG26 were brought down, one (1H+BL) by fighters in the Firth of Forth at 0100 hours, the other (1H+GL) by anti-aircraft fire off Turnhouse, Firth of Forth at 0105 hours. Hauptmann Schmilden, the Staffel Kapitan, was injured but captured. Four of the other airmen were killed and another three captured with varying degrees of injury. The crew of the second Heinkel, when interrogated, gave their aircraft code and their Feldpost number which identified them to Air Intelligence as belonging to 3/KG26.

The final aircraft (5J+BL) was shot down at the mouth of the River Humber at 0015 hours by a night fighter – almost certainly a Spitfire of No. 222 Squadron flown by Pilot Officer Morant. The crew were killed, but two of their bodies were picked up a week later by the crew of HMS *Brazen*. Their identity disc numbers soon identified them as belonging to 3/KG4.

One final enemy aircraft was brought down in June 1940 – a Heinkel III (5J+EK) of 2/KG4. The crew of four claimed to have been shot down by a twin-engine aircraft, but no claims matching this can be found in RAF records. The aircraft ditched in the sea and after taking to their dinghy, the crew were picked up and taken to Newcastle, before being handed over to the RAF interrogators.

The crew were quite talkative, explaining the three maps they carried, including a target map created from an aerial photograph of the target. They had been briefed by an intelligence officer about anti-aircraft gun positions and barrage balloons before take-off. The observer worked out a route and navigation using bearings obtained from the beacons at Borkum and Calais. Once over England, they used dead reckoning for their navigation.

After a very hectic springtime with defeats across Europe, AI1(k) was now fully established and ready for the expected assault upon Britain.

Over the next few months, their system and its efficiency, would be tested with a high number of prisoners to interrogate, not to mention the need to examine their aircraft and any documents. If AI1(k) could handle this surge, they could handle just about anything, but before we look at the summer of 1940, we must examine the M-Rooms and the tactics employed to covertly listen to the prisoners' 'private' conversations.

Chapter 9

M-Rooms – RAF Intelligence Tactics & Stool Pigeons

AI1(k) as an intelligence organisation, was not only interested in military matters, but morale, war crimes, Nazi propaganda and what the average German airman and others felt about their political masters.

The M-Rooms were an excellent source of intelligence regarding these subjects, as were the cozy little chats with the likes of psychologist C.H. Brooks and the various interrogating RAF officers. (See the later chapter on C.H. Brooks.)

Over time, the highly sensitive M-Room microphones, which were hidden in all manner of places, would record the deepest thoughts of many of the Luftwaffe airmen and later in the war, they would be used to listen in on SS and Gestapo men, as well as Generals, Field Marshals and Admirals. Although the Luftwaffe prisoners in 1939-1940 arguably did not provide information of the magnitude of those later in the war, they did provide a wide range of subjects which were of interest to people inside and outside the Air Intelligence community.

In 1939 and early 1940, many of the so-called *listeners* employed at Trent Park were British military personnel who were fluent in German. They were often graduates of Oxbridge or other red brick universities, while some had worked in Germany, but their spoken German was in many respects, far too perfect for their role as a *listener*. Even the interrogators themselves had operated in the higher echelons of German society and perfected a form of 'Kaiser's German' rather like the King's English. This was not a problem with captured personnel who spoke perfect high-societal German like a General, but when it came to listening to an Unteroffizier or a Flieger from the back streets of Hamburg, or a rural man from the Polish borders, the dialects were hard to understand. For this reason, in the second half of 1940, CSDIC and AI1(k) started to recruit a number of German refugees and others, who were now part of the British Army and the Pioneer Corps. These men, many of whom have never been named, played a vital part in the M-Room intelligence gathering business as *listeners*. They never saw the German prisoners and many of the other intelligence personnel did not know what they did or that M-Room tactics were even employed. The *listeners* sat in the basement or detached rooms away from the prisoners, translating and recording what was said in great detail. Their documents now housed in the UK National Archives and known as SRA records are a very detailed record of events.

As we have already seen, CSDIC and AI1(k) started to use codes for individual prisoners instead of names on their reports. As well as their code, the reports would often give a rank and occasionally the prisoner's role in a crew, such as pilot or observer etc. and even whether they belonged to a fighter or a bomber unit.

By examining these transcripts and the details they contain, such as the date an individual was shot down, his unit, a geographical location, together with their rank and position, if stated, it has been possible in a good number of cases to identify certain individuals when compared to Luftwaffe loss and prisoner records. Although in many cases, I believe the individual I name is almost certainly correct, some are a little more uncertain. This should be remembered with every named individual in this book.

Sometimes, the fireside chats with an interrogating officer over a cigarette and a glass of whisky or brandy, provoked discussion about life in Germany and politics. Many airmen like Franz von Werra would only discuss the state of world affairs and not military secrets. Little did they realise, their idle chatter was as useful as information on the next variant of the Messerschmitt 109 or the development of a new bomber.

Transcript SRA7, dated 22 November 1939, gives an early first impression of how concerned the German airmen were with their captivity. This conversation is believed to have taken place in the Tower of London and the transcript documents a conversation between the named individuals – Unteroffiziers Wilhelm Unger and Berhard Hochstuhl of 1(F)/122 and Hilmar Grimm of 2/KuFIGr.606. These two of the men had been wounded when captured and received medical attention. One of them (unclear which) stated: 'I had the wind up when they were going to cut me. I refused to be chloroformed, because they might perhaps use the opportunity to make me talk.'

Another man responded stating; 'They, (as in the British interrogators) know much more than we do.' One then responds; 'You can always see when Germany has had successes, because they are not so friendly to us then.'

Surprisingly, the next M-Room transcript (SRA8) took place over a month later in the Tower of London and is dated 24 December 1939. This time

Unteroffizier Bernhard Hochstuhl was placed in a room with Leutnant Wilhelm Meyer, an observer with 4(F)/122.

Meyer asked Hochstuhl how long he had been in the Tower. Hochstuhl explained that he had already been sent on to a prisoner of war camp, but had been returned to the Tower of London once more. Meyer asked him if he had been interrogated again and whether he was on a Junkers 88. Hochstuhl replied, 'Of course not – not even a 111.' (Author's note: this is an odd statement as Hochstuhl had been part of a Heinkel III crew).

Meyer said, he could not understand why the RAF would want Hochstuhl back at the Tower of London again and the young Unteroffizier replied nervously, 'I have had unpleasant experiences here, even though the treatment is not too bad, I don't trust these fellows anymore. I don't trust the quietness of it here. I have had my experiences in the Tower. They use all sorts of experiences to get information out of us. I think it is despicable when they put English officers into German Air Force uniforms.'

It would appear Hochstuhl had been subject to a stool-pigeon, but what exactly did he mean by, 'Unpleasant experiences and the quietness of the place?' Did he suspect hidden microphones and stool pigeons or was there something else?

There is one possible tactic at the Tower of London which you will not find in any official records… the allegation that the Tower and even more precisely, the Salt Tower, is haunted. For many decades even hundreds of years, there have been allegations about ghosts in the Tower. I had two great uncles in the Irish Guards and they maintained to the point of argument, that the Tower was haunted and they had witnessed things. Even putting aside, the question of whether the Tower of London is haunted, the mere planting of the thought in a young prisoner's mind and the quietness of the place, could play tricks with his mind. The Tower would have been subjected to blackout regulations and even today, many people state the interior is dark and quiet at night, even in the midst of modern twenty-first century London. The Salt Tower rooms are covered in graffiti from Tudor prisoners to back up any ghost stories and with the dark silence of the night, a prisoner would therefore say anything to get away to a cosy POW camp. Is this what Hochstuhl meant? We will never know.

With the relocation of AI1(k) to Trent Park, the forbidding Tower of London was left behind, but the prisoners were still very wary of their interrogators and surroundings.

Transcript SRA10 on 12 January 1940, gives details of a conversation between the re-located Leutnant Wilhelm Meyer and Unteroffizier Theodor Steyrer, his radio operator when they were shot down in late November 1939.

Theodor Steyrer was clearly very suspicious of the interrogation centre stating, 'This is the place where they try to pump you. I should not like to discuss anything important here – I don't trust these people. I've already examined the floor, but there's nothing there.' Despite his claims the two men continued talking and the covert microphones picked up everything for the listeners.

It was clear that many prisoners were keen to discuss what they had told their interrogating officer, unaware that they were now being listened to. In transcript SRA35, dated 23 February 1940, Unteroffizier Gerd Kahle (the same man from chapter six) and Obergefreiter Heinz Hegemann of KG26 chatted away, even laughing about telling the interrogating officer that they had been making practice flights. Hegemann even stated that a British policeman had pointed out RAF fighters when they drove past an airfield, this undoubtedly leading to a report to the local Chief Constable and new instructions on the handling of prisoners of war.

As we have seen, the interrogating officer would sometimes make a deliberate mistake to distract a prisoner or loosen their tongue. Hegemann appears in this transcript to have fallen foul of this simple tactic when he states:

> 'I had to laugh when he (the Interrogating Officer) said to me: "But you have the JU211 motor?" I said, "What do you mean?" He replied, "That isn't one?" 'No, that was a Jumo 211." "Never," he said… "The JU211 you had in it, had a compressor and a D motor." "Well," I said, "You are of course entitled to think what you like."'

Unteroffizier Gerd Kahle featured again in transcript SRA39 on 28 February. This time he talked with Leutnant Erich Grote (prisoner A36).

Kahle told his new companion that the officers there had a frightful wind-up (meaning the interrogators). Grote responded by saying that in his opinion, the British underestimated German industrial capacity. Kahle replied, 'Surely you mean they overestimate it?' He then went on to explain that his interrogation officer had said fifty to sixty aeroplanes were being turned out every day, but in reality, it was twenty to twenty-five bombers ready for active service. Erich Grote quickly added that they were not at that stage yet with the JU88, but such idle chatter was manner from heaven for the *listeners* and AI1(k).

While the M-Rooms often proved that prisoners had lied or avoided giving relevant information to their interrogators, the transcripts could also confirm that they had given correct information.

In transcript SRA61, dated 11 April 1940, one prisoner, A47, identified as Oberstleutnant Hans Hefele of Stab II/KG26 and A48, a Leutnant pilot believed to be his pilot, Rudolf Gustav-Adolf Benisch, discussed giving information to their interrogators:

> Benisch: 'This is only a temporary camp. We remain here until we have been squeezed dry. I tell fairy tales only when I am asked about anything…'
>
> Hefele: 'He (the interrogator) asked me what was the speed of our machine. I said 400 km. There is no harm in saying that, because he knew it before. I won't tell these fellows anything new. I told him that there was no such thing as a Stab Staffel as a formation on its own.'

As the months passed by, the number of prisoners increased and with the *listeners* using codes to identify the different airmen, it is hard to identify individuals. The *listeners* were still covertly listening to the prisoners' conversations and they continued to discuss their interactions with the AI1(k) interrogators. The intelligence staff were not only keen to obtain information about the Luftwaffe, its aircraft, men and tactics; they also sought information about Germany, its politics and even religion.

Transcript SRA200, dated 22 July 1940, briefly recorded a curious conversation between A278 – a Feldwebel and A249 an Oberfeldwebel. The Feldwebel said he had been asked by the interrogator if he had any religion in Germany. The prisoner – clearly an ardent Nazi – replied, 'If Hitler no longer lived, then I should not desire to live.'

The same man then added, 'The Englishman is always master when in the Colonies and lashes about with his whip. The German is too sentimental for that – he can't do it.'

Such conversations not only revealed the true sentiments of the prisoners, but also the manner in which the Nazi philosophy had brainwashed the young men of Germany since 1933.

The interrogators were still trying to identify various elements and parts found in the wrecked German aircraft.

Transcript SRA305, dated 10 August 1940, details a conversation between an Unteroffizier A320 and a Gefreiter (A312) identified as Heinz Morgenthal, an air mechanic on a Heinkel III of 8/KG55, which was brought down in the early hours of 29 July.

The unidentified Unteroffizier (A320) told Heinz Morgenthal that the interrogating officer wanted to know what the yellow drums in the aircraft were for. He said, he had told his interrogator that he did not know, but every fifth drum actually contained explosives and every third drum down ammunition.

Transcript SRA333, dated 15 August, at the height of the Battle of Britain, appears to show some dissent when asked about Nazi statements, while having a good impression of the Air Intelligence staff at Trent Park…

The two airmen are identified by their earlier comments in the transcript, as well as their ranks. A331 is believed to be Major Frederich-Karl Schlichting the Gruppen-Kommandeur of Stab II/KG2, brought down on 12 August 1940 and Leutnant Hans Werner Regenauer of 2/JG26, who was also shot down into the Channel on the same day:

> Regenauer: 'The day before yesterday we had our first war flight. My aircraft fell into the sea near Dover. I don't know how they fished me out. I only opened my eyes in the cabin. Here they knew all about my Geschwader. I have been treated very decently here.' (Regenauer in later years revealed he spent seven hours in the English Channel before being fished out and taken ashore. Before this action, he had not even seen an enemy aircraft).
>
> Schlichting: 'The people make a good impression on me. I am pleasantly surprised that I am so well treated.'
>
> Regenauer: 'I imagined being a prisoner of war to be quite different, I thought it was more or less what it was in Spain.'
>
> Later he added: 'The interrogating officer here says that Göring stated that no English airman would come to Germany. As far as I know this was never said.'
>
> Schlichting: 'Oh yes it was.'

Feeding information to prisoners in their interrogations then placing them with other detainees, often with conflicting attitudes and opinions, could cause a disagreement, the dropping of personal defences and lead to the disclosure of some very valuable information. One of the best examples of this is found in transcript SRA367, dated 21 August 1940.

Two Oberleutnants identified as A349 and 346 were in an M-Room and told they were about be joined by another Oberleutnant (A345). By a process of elimination and examining their stated facts, A345 is believed to be Gerhard Oszwald, an observer, and Staffel Kapitan of Stab/KG2, while A346 is believed to be his pilot, Heinz Schlegel. A349 is believed to be another pilot – Heinz Rosse of Stab II/KG54. All three men were shot down on the 13 August 1940 over Kent and Sussex:

> Schlegel: 'Oh, that will be Oszwald. Oh Lord! Now I wonder what he'll be like. How damnable.'
>
> Rosse: 'You're really enthusiastic, aren't you?'
>
> Schlegel: 'And how!'
>
> Rosse: 'You must just treat him with contempt.'
>
> Schlegel: 'You wouldn't be fool enough to bring down the Staffel Kapitan's enmity on your head!'
>
> Oszwald enters the room (having probably just been interrogated).
>
> Oszwald: 'Oh good morning Rosse. Oh, you're here too Schlegel, how are you?'
>
> Schlegel: 'Rotten. As one must expect here.'
>
> Oszwald: 'He (the interrogation officer) told me that they had shot down 175 of our aircraft the day before yesterday. I only said that I placed great faith in the German reports. When I told him that I would be home for Christmas he was astonished. Our losses were without doubt, very heavy. A first heavy blow was to have been carried out against England, then there was to be a pause and then it was to start again unexpectedly. But everything did not go quite right. They underestimated the power of the fighters here, there is no doubt about that. The first attack went wrong.'
>
> Schlegel: 'That is right, I have the impression also that the attack failed.'

The three Oberleutnants were shot down on 13 August – 'Adler Tag or Eagle Day'. This was the day when the Luftwaffe planned to destroy the RAF fighter force on the ground. Unfortunately, it failed because of the weather. A recall order was transmitted, but many formations, including KG2, which contained the aircraft of Oszwald and Schlegel, carried on. Some fighters tried to communicate that the mission had been cancelled without success and the bombers continued to be met by RAF fighters. In this transcript, the annoyance of the three men is clear:

Oszwald: 'The losses are very heavy without a doubt. Yesterday Eastbourne was bombed.'

Schlegel: 'Eastbourne?'

Oszwald: 'Yes, the interrogating officer told me. I said, "If that is true and if there were no military targets, it is only a reprisal for the numerous night attacks made by the English on our towns" and then he said no more.'

Oszwald and Schlegel then explained to Rosse how their attack had failed and the 1st Gruppe failed to turn up. They were carrying extra fuel and flying above the clouds. They found a gap and dived towards their target, but the weather was poor with mist and the fighters attacked them. Oszwald then left the room and the other two men continued talking:

Rosse: 'Now you are together with your Staffel Kapitan you are very pleased, aren't you?'

Schlegel: 'Yes, it's lovely! What a fool he is!'

Rosse: 'But you appear to love him!'

Schlegel: 'He is a cowardly swine.'

Oszwald returned to the room:

Rosse: 'One of the intelligence officers here told me that the German Air Force had once been the best in the world. But that was no longer the case. There upon I said to him, that we were the first crew in our Staffel not to return… We've lost a whole lot of aircraft, eight of them.'

Oszwald: 'We lost eleven aircraft in Poland, but no crews. The interrogating officer could not understand why there were two officers in some aircraft and not at all in others. That I can't understand either. He's quite right, but we often made that mistake.'

Schlegel: 'It was not my fault that we flew together.'

Oszwald: 'Better preparations were made as a rule.'

Schlegel: 'With us everything was rottenly arranged. All that telephoning in the evening! Dreadfully slovenly.'

The two colleagues carried on discussing the poor performance and at one point, Oszwald said he even considered retiring once the war was over. The long transcript must have made pleasant reading for Denys Felkin and his team at Trent Park.

Transcript SRA390, dated 24 August 1940, continued in a similar vein. Two unidentified Feldwebels were in conversation when one said: 'He (the interrogating officer) said that the English have shot down 2,000 machines, I don't believe that.'

His friend clearly overstating what he had seen responded: 'I don't either. If it were true it wouldn't matter, I have seen 1,000 machines in Paris.'

Major Frederich-Karl Schlichting of Stab II/KG2 was still at Trent Park in late August and featured in another transcript – SRA395 – on the twenty-sixth of that month. This time he was in conversation with A383 – a Hauptmann believed to have possibly been Heinz Loncier of 9/KG53, although this cannot be confirmed. The two men quickly turned to what they had been asked by the interrogating officers. They were less than impressed by the interrogator's efforts:

> Schlichting: 'One or two big questions interested him here. Firstly, is there going to be an invasion or not? None of us can answer that. The second question is what is the reason for all these attacks? None of us can answer that either. Of course, each one of us knows his objective, but the whole object?... And the third is our disposition and they know a great deal about that.'
>
> Loncier: 'In my case he was interested to know the effect of their night attacks on us. I didn't say much. I explained to him that there was a lot of open spaces, gardens, parks etc. in a big town. Yes, he said, but don't windows get broken? Yes, I replied, that is true, but it is only glass. Yes, he said, but then the people will get cold. It is ridiculous that they are pleased when their bombs splinter the window panes and that thereby, they hope to engender a revolution!'

The excellent record system and database AI1(k) had created by September 1940, can be seen in transcript SRA445 on the second day of that month. Two Gefreiters, A404 – believed from the transcript and other records to be possibly Gunther Fleischmann of 3/KG51, who was wounded when he was shot down on 12 August over Sussex, and an unidentified A407. Gunther Fleischmann told A407 with some amusement: 'He (the interrogator) told me I was from KG51. I said "Yes, that is so." I thought it was so funny that he knew.'

Another example can be found in SRA495 from 10 September 1940. This time, A427, an unidentified Leutnant and A426, an unidentified Oberleutnant, sat discussing the merits of different bomber aircraft, their lack of armour and the need for the crew to wear steel helmets. A427 stated that in the week of 26-31 August, the casualties in his Gruppe were so high, because they did not remain in formation when ordered to do so. He then added that only five out of eight aircraft come back as a general rule before stating: *A427:* 'The interrogation officer tells me that you belong to 7/KG51 (note by transcriber: actually KG53?). Kommandeur is Major von Paul... I can't think how they know all that.'

A426 appears to be Oberleutnant F. Zipse the pilot of a 7/KG53 aircraft brought down on 18 August and the only man of this rank brought down in the weeks leading up to the date of this M-Room transcript.

A427 appears to be Leutnant Johann Kernbach. This deduction is made as he appears from the transcript to be a bomber pilot and must have been shot down after 31 August, but before the M-Room text was completed on 10 September. Adding to this, the fact transcripts were not always completed on the day of the recorded conversation, we are looking for a Leutnant from a bomber brought down between 1 and 9 September 1940. Looking at AI1(k) records, there are only two men that fit those parameters and one of those from KG30, came down in Sussex at 1740 hours on the ninth. Therefore, it is unlikely to be him, as it would be very rare for someone to be transported to Trent Park and interrogated so quickly. This leaves just Leutnant Johann Kernbach of 6/KG76. Although he appears to be *our man,* his unit's losses both in AI1(k) and Luftwaffe records do not corroborate the claim he made in the transcript about his Gruppe's losses. This might have been a deliberate misleading statement and it is likely A427 was Johann Kernbach, but it cannot be confirmed.

Oberleutnant Helmut Rau, the Staffel Kapitan of 3/JG3 was shot down on 31 August and soon arrived at Trent Park, where he was given the code A433. He was recorded in an M-Room in conversation (SRA496 on 10 September) with another unidentified Oberleutnant known as A395.

Rau was somewhat concerned about the amount of information the RAF interrogator already knew about him and his unit, stating: 'I got command of the 3rd Staffel on the twentieth, but they know everything here anyway, who are the Kommandeurs and so on. I wonder whether this is due to treason or what?'

The unidentified Oberleutnant (A395) believed their telephones were listened to in France, but Rau was concerned the British knew everything: 'Yesterday, I asked the young Lieutenant whether he knew anything of Tiedmann (Author's comment: Oberleutnant. Helmut Tiedmann of 2/JG3 shot down and captured on 18 August), for he asked me if there was anyone I knew, whom I would like to meet. First, I told him Rotenknecht, whom I know has been shot down too, because he had been hit in the radiator; I could see it, he was flying near me. And, besides… I asked for Tiedmann. He enquired and said, "Helmut Tiedmann?" He even knew his Dienstelle, 6th Staffel JG3 – not quite right, he isn't 6th Staffel, but JG3 all the same and he said to me, "Yes, he is in prison."'

Sadly, his friend Rotenknecht was not a prisoner of war.

These are just a few of the many occasions in which M-Room *listeners* recorded information about the prisoners' experience of AI1(k) and their tactics. The Trent Park system was clearly very effective and somewhat disturbing for the new arrivals.

In the next chapter we shall examine what the M-Room *listeners* heard about aircraft, losses and tactics.

Chapter 10

M-Rooms – Aircraft, losses and tactics

The M-Room *listeners* soon started to hear all manner of conversations between the Luftwaffe prisoners and naturally, the main subject matter was that of aircraft, losses and tactics.

The RAF and AI1(k) had an excellent intelligence system, supported by the other agencies before the war started. They knew a good deal about the Luftwaffe fleet of aircraft and its tactics, having observed the Kondor Legion in action during the Spanish Civil War. They also had information about new aircraft projects and when their 'guests' started to discuss these new developments, they were keen to note the views of the airmen, some of whom professed to having first-hand knowledge and experience of these new machines.

Transcript SRA2, dated 3 November 1939, noted a conversation between two unidentified prisoners (they were neither named or given a code reference to identify them). The two men discussed the new Dornier 215 as a decent machine, one man claiming he had not seen another machine that could touch it. They also discussed the Heinkel 112 which was described as 'Not bad', while they claimed the Junkers 52 transport plane was now obsolete.

On 22 November 1939, SRA7 detailed a short conversation between Unteroffiziers Unger, Grimm and Hochstuhl in the Tower of London M-Rooms – possibly the Salt Tower. The three men discussed and described the destructive power of the 500-kilogram bomb. Unger told the others that if dropped where the flag was (referring to the flag on top of the White Tower in the Tower of London), 'It would burst the walls right down to the ground.'

Grimm added that the device was like a torpedo with any amount of stuff in it, iron, steel etc.

By January 1940, AI1(k) had moved to Trent Park and the intelligence continued to flow, but at a greater rate.

Transcript SRA9, dated 12 January 1940, documented a discussion between Leutnant Wilhelm Meyer and his crewman Unteroffizier Theodor Streyer. The two men discussed the fact both the Messerschmitt 109E and the Messerschmitt

110, made too big a circle when turning. SAR10 on the same day, noted the same two men discussing a recent RAF Wellington bomber raid, which ended in disaster for the British…

> 'The English machines are better armed, in particular they have the rear machine-gun mounting, for there, the enemy chasers cannot hit so easily. The forward position can also fire to the rear, he had a dual machine gun. Apparently, not much damage was done in Heligoland, they are said to have attacked with one hundred machines. The 110's apparently did good work there…'

The so-called Battle of Heligoland took place on 18 December 1939. Twenty-two Wellington's from three squadrons were tasked with attacking German Navy battleships and cruisers at anchor in Wilhelmshaven. The daylight raid was attacked by Messerschmitt 109s and 110s, twelve of the Wellingtons were shot down, two damaged and fifty-six airmen killed. The German Propaganda Ministry overclaimed, stating the Luftwaffe had destroyed thirty-eight out of forty-four bombers (clearly twice the size of the actual formation). The Wellington gunners also overclaimed, believing they had destroyed over sixty enemy fighters! The real German losses amounted to just two Messerschmitt 109s destroyed, although a number of other ME109s and 110s were damaged.

The interesting point is that Meyer and Streyer were shot down in mid-November 1939 – were they talking about an event a month after their capture? How did they know about this?

Previous attacks had been made on the German fleet to a much lesser extent, but it appears they were talking about the specific 18 December incident. This is an interesting conundrum when one considers no Luftwaffe prisoners arrived from aircraft shot down over the UK and its surrounding waters between the end of October and 13 January 1940, a day after the airmen's conversation was recorded.

The two German airmen discussed the Junkers 88, noting that a formation of the aircraft had made a successful attack on Scapa Flow. Streyer added that the aircraft is very slim and not easy to hit, but he then qualified this by saying he had not seen one yet.

Meyer said the Messerschmitt 110 is said to be easier to maneuver than the Messerschmitt 109. Both were said to be as fast as a Spitfire – clearly with hindsight, rumour control had got the better of these men.

The same two men were still being recorded on 14 January in transcript SRA13. This time they were discussing the fact German industry would be manufacturing 1,000 kilo bombs to drop on the Maginot Line.

As we have seen, rumour control and speculation was rife among the German airman, rather like that between British and Allied airmen. Unteroffizier Gerd Kahle of 1(F)/122, shot down on the 13 January 1940, as we have already seen, was a very productive individual for the *listeners* and AI1(k).

In transcript SRA19, dated 27 January, Kahle chatted with Leutnant Ernst Korner and Unteroffizier Walter Heckt, telling them that the Luftwaffe now had a new dive-bomber – the four engine Heinkel 177 which was being built. This, he claimed could carry two 1,000 kilo bombs. As already mentioned, the Heinkel 177 did not reach production until 1942, having been initially conceived as a large dive-bomber, but was really a long-range heavy bomber. It is clear AI1(k), like all good intelligence agencies and departments, needed to corroborate the claims they were hearing, rather than basing any assessments on one piece of information.

Two days later, transcript SRA20 recorded the same three airmen still chatting about new aircraft and operations. Gerd Kahle was keen to talk about new aircraft, such as the Heinkel 112, an aircraft which actually lost out to the Messerschmitt 109 for Reich contracts. Kahle claimed that the Heinkel 112 had a landing speed of 170 kph and a top speed of 650–700 kph In reality, the prototypes could only achieve a maximum speed of 488 kph at 11,500 feet – was he bragging or trying to deceive anyone who was listening?

It is interesting to note that Gerd Kahle, allegedly being a Heinkel test pilot, must have had some inside knowledge about the Heinkel 112 and the Heinkel 113. The Heinkel 113 was a wholly fictitious development of the Heinkel 112, created by the Reich propaganda machine in early 1940. The aircraft was said to have a top speed of 670 kph at 16,000 feet – a speed similar to that which Kahle claimed the Heinkel 112 could attain. The Nazi Propaganda Ministry certainly worked wonders and British intelligence believed the machine not only existed, but entered operational service. This intelligence was passed to front line squadrons and in 1940, a number of RAF pilots claimed to have not only encountered the Heinkel 113 in combat, but to have shot one down. (In all probability they were Messerschmitt 109E's.)

In addition to these misleading statements, Kahle also stated that the Messerschmitt 109R was not fully introduced yet. Bearing in mind the Messerschmitt 109E was the current active operational type in early 1940, what

Kahle was talking about is unclear. The ME109F entered service towards the end of the Battle of Britain and the ME109G much later. There was a high-altitude ME109H, a ME109K in late 1944 and even an aircraft carrier version – the ME109T – which was designed, but never used. What, in January 1940, Kahle was referring to with the Messerschmitt 109R is unknown and he may have been talking nonsense for the sake of talking. Was this because he thought he was being listened to? Or was he trying to provoke comment from the other prisoners?

Transcript SRA50, dated 28 March 1940, had two Feldwebels, a pilot and an observer chatting away in an M-Room. The two men A44 – identified as Franz Schnee of KG26 and A46 – Ernst Breiler of 1/Auf.Gr. Ob. d. L., discussed how they were shot down before Franz Schnee and Brieler made the following remarkable claims:

> Schnee: 'Our AA guns fetched down three machines of the first Staffel and one of the third Staffel.'
>
> Breiler: 'They have shot down more of our own machines than enemies.'

The two men soon changed direction and talked about other matters:

> Schnee: 'A U-boat had got stuck on the Goodwin Sands, we were detailed to sink it. Destroyers were hanging around. We were there with three machines and dropped our bombs, but did not hit. The next day the boat was gone. Probably they had towed it away. Now they are building U-boats at high pressure.'
>
> Schnee: 'I know from a worker in the aeroplane factory at Wittenberg, that they were building JU 88's there, but later this was stopped and they started on other machines.'
>
> Breiler: 'Possibly it was the 217 (?). We had two 88's, but they were always out of commission – there were too many gadgets.'
>
> Schnee: 'I wonder what they will do with the Dornier 215?'
>
> Breiler: 'They are to be used for laying mines.'

The U-boat was probably U16 which ran aground on the Goodwin Sands on 25 October 1939. It is believed to have struck a sea mine, before being attacked by destroyers with depth charges. There is no other note of the Luftwaffe attempting to bomb it, but it is possible.

The M-Room information was vital to Air Intelligence and its partner agencies, but it always required corroboration. The Junkers 88 and the Dornier 215 would soon be seen in the skies of France and Britain.

On the 3 April 1940, in SRA56, Brieler and Schnee were still being recorded in deep conversation, but this time they were joined by A45, identified as being possibly Unteroffizier Alfred Dietrich, a member of Schnee's own crew from 2/KG26.

Once again, the comments of the airmen were apparently misleading and deceptive, whether by deliberate design or confusion is unknown:

> Schnee: 'The H 112 is single engine. I saw it at Brandenburg, quite new… The new Geschwader, the new Gruppen are going to Schwerin. Those present at Schwerin are going to Borkum. "27" they are in Wurttemberg. The Taifun was the first plane with "Maschinenkanonen"' (aerial cannon? – this latter question was added by the listener).

Schnee, an observer Feldwebel, appears to have been completely discombobulated with his facts. As we have seen the Heinkel 112 was not in service, although he might have seen a test aircraft. Jagdgeschwader 27 (JG27) if that is the unit he meant, was equipped with Messerschmitt 109E's and were operating in Germany in early 1940. The confusion is exacerbated when one considers the Taifun was the Messerschmitt 108 – a single engine sports aircraft, developed in the mid-1930s and utilised by the Luftwaffe for liaison flights; it certainly was not armed with a cannon!

By May 1940, a number of prisoners from Norway and the Continent were arriving at AI1(k). Transcript SRA116, dated 10 June 1940, detailed a conversation between A201, an Oberleutnant reconnaissance pilot, A187 a Leutnant fighter pilot – believed to be Leutnant Hans Strehl of 1/JG51, shot down by a Hurricane off Dunkirk on the 23 May and A139, another unidentified Oberleutnant.

A201 was clearly a member of KG30, as he mentions flying in formation with A25, a fellow prisoner believed to be Hauptmann Helmet Pohle of 2/KG30. A201 said he was on a weather reconnaissance at zero hour for the paratroop attack on Holland (on 10 May), when he was shot down by the Dutch and his 'right engine' gave out. By a process of elimination and checking loss reports, A201 appears to be Oberleutnant Theodor Beermann of 4/KG30, although reports state he was attacking a flak post at 0615 hours. Although he seems to be A201, we cannot confirm this 100%, but we shall refer to this man as Beermann in this account…

Hans Strehl stated: 'I belong to our 1st Staffel. Our machines are all "109 Emils." Before we had "109 Doras." My machine has only four machine guns, it has no cannon… In my machine, the machine guns are set at 150 meters. On other machines in my Staffel, they are set at 250 meters.'

A139 added, 'A138 told me that in his machine, the machine guns were set at 200 meters. He also had a 109 and it had two cannon and two machine guns.'

Such information was invaluable when assessing the firepower of the Messerschmitt 109 and the general abilities of its pilots.

Hans Strehl added the following facts which Air Intelligence gratefully received:

> 'The 111 only carry 500 kilo bombs. The JU88 is as fast as the 110. The 110 carries two cannon and three machine guns, that is the normal destroyer amount. The armour is behind the tank, to hit the tank in an attack on a 109 is exceedingly difficult… A Spitfire is very like a 109, You have to approach to within at least 100 meters before you can spot that it is not a 109… The JU88 does 430 kph, I flew in one on reconnaissance.'

On 12 June, the same men were still being recorded in conversation (see transcript SRA117). Part of the transcript states:

> Beermann: 'That is the successor of the HE which was finished at the same time as the ME109, but was much too expensive.'
>
> Strehl: 'No, it was not too expensive…'
>
> Beermann: 'Oh yes, it was. Considerably dearer in comparison.'
>
> A139: 'Yes it was pushed off on other countries.'
>
> Beerman: 'It was pushed off abroad and this new Heinkel – that is said to be the "Zero" series. It appears there are fifty of them in existence.'
>
> Strehl: 'It appears to be easier to maneuver, but it is said to be not such a good dive-bomber. But, otherwise, from the flying point of view, it is better.'
>
> Beerman: 'The Focke Wulf is said to be really good.'
>
> Strehl: 'Apparently, it is quite marvellous.'
>
> Beerman: 'It is said to take off better, although it is heavier and to be considerably faster. It has a radial engine.'

This appears to have been the first mention of the Focke Wulf 190 fighter which would come into service in August 1941, with dramatic results. AI1(k) not only had German airmen discussing Heinkel fighters that did not enter service or were a figment of propaganda, they had imaginary versions of the Messerschmitt 109 and now had a new fighter in the form of a Focke Wulf (190).

These were worrying times for Denys Felkin and his team. The German forces had swept across Europe and the British Army had been evacuated from Dunkirk. The Battle of Britain was about to begin and it was clear the Nazi aircraft industry was in full swing building new advanced models.

Transcript SRA148, on 6 July 1940, added further concern for Air Intelligence. This time an unidentified Unteroffizier and a Feldwebel were recorded discussing dive-bombing before moving on to two more new aircraft. This time they discussed the Focke Wulf 175 or 187 which one man called a 'Measly little gnat.' They also discussed the Junkers 86 which they claimed was so shiny, it looked like silver. It also had an endurance of seven and a half hours and consumed fuel at 700 litres per hour.

We now know that the Focke Wulf 187 Falke (Falcon) was a twin-engine fighter, but only a few were built and sent to a front line unit for evaluation. They did not enter production and service. The Junkers 86 was a high-altitude reconnaissance and bomber aircraft with a pressurized cockpit, it was often seen over the skies of England in 1940 at altitudes of up to 46,000 feet.

M-Room transcripts could also identify some unusual information, but the problem was the *listeners* and the interrogation officers, had no way of interfering and could not direct a conversation. Consequently, something of real interest could lead to an abrupt end in the chatter, much to the angst of the intelligence staff. One such event is recorded in SRA222 on 26 July 1940.

Prisoner A285 – an Obergefreiter, possibly Walter Plock of 4(F)/122 and A289 – a Feldwebel, possibly Willi Baden of 4(F)/14, were in conversation when Willi Baden stated:

> 'In the attacks we ignite large smoke developers (*Rauchkorper*), they are electrically ignited and they develop thick red smoke clouds.'

Unfortunately, the other prisoner did not respond and went off in another direction talking about Junkers transport aircraft. Baden did not return to the subject and this must have been very frustrating for the intelligence staff.

The Luftwaffe prisoners were not always so enthusiastic about their aircraft. Transcript SRA297, dated 8 August 1940, features A302, a Gefreiter believed to be Gefreiter Hohmann of 1/KG40 (Focke Wulf 200 Kondor) and A315, an

Unteroffizier believed to be either Justus Kehres or Gerhard Lehm of 2(F)/122 (JU88). Both men were brought down in the final week of July 1940 having technical problems with their aircraft.

The men discussed how well they had been treated by their captors, before moving on to their aircraft and how they were brought down:

> Kehres or Lehm: 'The devil knows what was wrong with it. Anyway, it suddenly broke down.'
>
> Hohmann: 'Without being fired at?'
>
> Kehres or Lehm: 'Yes.'
>
> Hohmann: 'Exactly the same happened to us. We were not hit at all, we had carried out our task, flew off and the mechanic forgot the petrol.'
>
> Kehres or Lehm: 'Forgot what?'
>
> Hohmann: 'To change the petrol lever.' (Author's note - to change the fuel tanks over.)
>
> Kehres or Lehm: 'Surely the pilot should do that in my opinion. Well, don't let us talk about it, there's no point in doing so.'

Transcript SRA305, on 10 August, also appears to mention the same incident. This time, A312 Gefreiter Heinz Morgenthal of 8/KG55, tells his colleague that Hauptmann (name deleted in the report), was on a Kondor when all four engines stopped. This appears to be Hauptmann Zenker, the pilot of Hohmann's Fw. 200.

On 20 August, two Obergefreiters (A368 and A372) were recorded in conversation discussing their recent combat and the loss of Hermann Göring's nephew, Oberleutnant Hans-Joachim Göring, a Messerschmitt 110 pilot with 9/ZG76.

A372 has been identified as Franz Obser, a member of the same unit and brought down at Clapham, West Sussex on 16 August. Obser not only gave details of the demise of the head of the Luftwaffe's nephew, but also some discord in the Staffel, when he stated:

> 'During this attack, Göring, nephew of the Field Marshal was killed. In the distance, we saw how two aircraft were trying to stand up to a whole swarm of Spitfires. One of them must have been Göring. There was no point in our going to his help alone. Graf von Castell still tried to help him, but what's the use of that with one aircraft? Then Thiele and Schlagenfuss… They got back to Germany. Thiele was wounded in the leg and said he

could not fly anymore, that his leg was too weak. He always hobbled around with a stick. But when he heard he was to return to Germany, you should have seen him run! His leg was not too weak for that. Well, now he's home he's had a special uniform made and struts around playing the hero…'

On the 11 September, two fighter pilots (an Oberleutnant, A430 and a Leutnant, A445) were recorded in transcript SRA498 discussing the merits of various aircraft and tactics. From evaluating the text details and dates, A445 appears to be Leutnant Karl Stix, an ME110 pilot of 4/ZG2, shot down over Essex on 7 September 1940.

The two pilots discussed how well they had been treated by the British, before Stix described how, with the ME110, one has to climb up to great heights in order to get away from the Spitfires. That was why the aircraft had been remodelled and now climbed beautifully, but it is fearfully sensitive. Stix described a new Focke Wulf which was in construction at Ofenheim. This was a Zerstorer with three engines and a fuselage that looked somewhat smaller than the ME110. He claimed it was much faster than the ME110 with quite small wings and nose, but the secret, he claimed, lay in its elliptical wings. It would be ready for service in 1942.

This account from Karl Stix appears to corroborate the earlier claims made in transcript SRA148 on 6 July, when two non-commissioned officers discussed the Focke Wulf 175 or 187, one man calling it 'a measly little gnat.' It was clear to Air Intelligence that an upgrade on the Messerschmitt 110 was certainly under construction.

As the Luftwaffe tactics changed in September 1940, so too did the outlook of the prisoners. Mounting heavy losses led to a dip in morale, which was evident in transcript SRA535 on 14 September. Prisoners A469, believed to be Feldwebel Willi Schutel, a wireless-operator gunner in a Messerschmitt 110 of Stab I/ZG2 and A473, believed to be Unteroffizier Kurt Koch, an ME109 pilot of 9/JG51 had both been shot down on Saturday 7 September. After discussing how they had taken off and were shot down, their mood changed:

Koch: 'These war flights are a curse.'

Schutel: 'In these big attacks, a whole lot of aircraft were smashed-up.'

Koch: 'I'm afraid that our fighter escorts are considerably weakened. One notices that now. With us 30-40 English were there immediately and we were 20-25 "109s." They simply must start the attack before winter, or we'll have no fighters left.'

> Schutel: 'This wretched water is the hell of a nuisance.' (i.e. English Channel.)

A short time later:

> Schutel: 'How many prisoners belonging to the Luftwaffe have they got here?'
>
> Koch: 'A thousand I should say. If the landing does not come soon – before this winter – they'll keep getting stronger here and we shall keep getting weaker. As far as clothing, food and those things are concerned, the Englishmen as yet feels nothing of the war.'

It was clear the Luftwaffe was suffering and the morale of some men was falling. Air Intelligence knew of aircraft losses that came down on British soil and near the coastline, but it was clear the enemy losses were much higher and having a significant impact upon morale and their ability to continue the scale of their air attacks.

The morale of airmen continued to fall, as did their expectations of the Luftwaffe's abilities. In transcript SRA591, recorded on the 20 September 1940, two Leutnant fighter pilots were recorded having a lengthy discussion. The two men, A519, believed to be Leutnant Karl Westerhoff of 6/JG3, an associate of Franz von Werra, shot down on 31 August and A509, Leutnant Kurt Bildau of 7/JG51, shot down on the 15 September; discussed the frailties of Messerschmitt's radiators and the fact a whole ME110 Zerstorer-Geschwader had been disbanded because of their losses.

One airman stated that once a Messerschmitt was hit in a radiator, the engine fails and the Spitfire wins. They also discussed the fact the Luftwaffe had 'finished with the Stukas quite quickly.' He said he had escorted them against a convoy, but when the Spitfires arrived, they did what they could, but three or four (Stukas) were shot down and the remainder fled.

As Autumn arrived in October, the Battle of Britain was virtually over and so too was the high morale of the Luftwaffe. In SRA695, recorded on 5 October, A504, a Major and a bomber and Gruppen-Kommandeur spoke with A520, an Oberleutnant fighter pilot. These men are believed by examining the text of their transcript and Luftwaffe loss records, to be Major Max Gruber, a Heinkel III crewman of Stab II/KG53, brought down on 15 September; and Oberleutnant Karl Fischer, a Messerschmitt 109 pilot of 7/JG27, shot down on 30 September.

The two men discussed why Germany had delayed attacking Britain and should have attacked immediately. The Oberleutnant ridiculed the British pillbox construction, saying they would not withstand a single shot. While the two men talked, anti-aircraft guns could he heard outside. Major Gruber said all the shooting was quite pointless, especially in the fog outside. He added that they nearly always found their targets because the anti-aircraft guns and searchlights pin-pointed them.

The two men soon discussed fighter escorts for bombers and how difficult it was to manage. Major Gruber said he had once reached London and the whole fighter Geschwader had gone, leaving them alone and defenceless. He then asked his companion:

Gruber: 'Did you notice what was smashed up in London?'

Oberleutnant: 'Yes, and I must admit that I was greatly disappointed.'

Their conversation, mostly directed by Gruber, considered the numbers of aircraft they were losing each flight, the human casualties and that in a bomber you could do nothing against a fighter. It was very clear the Battle of Britain was nearly over.

Despite the fact Luftwaffe losses were up and their morale was evidently down, some airmen persisted and maintained that the battle was not yet over.

In transcript SRA770, recorded on 17 October 1940, two airmen, A593, believed to be Oberleutnant Karl Sauer of 2/JG52 and A594, Leutnant Bernhardt Malischewski of 4/JG54, both shot down on 12 October; discussed how they were brought down, Malischewski stating that Spitfires were now arriving in ever increasing numbers.

Karl Sauer stated that he was very nearly lynched by civilians in London, even though he had come down near Ashford. He then added, the Luftwaffe had bombers which had not been brought into action yet, and there was still Bomber Geschwader which have not been at the front.

Leutnant Malischewski said he could not believe the bombing of London was continuing and there must be a reason for it, adding he would not be surprised if a revolution started in England. The two men clearly thought the fight for air supremacy was to continue, but the RAF's strength was increasing not decreasing. Similar comments would continue to be recorded from other airmen captured and interrogated at Trent Park during October 1940.

Chapter 11

M-Rooms – Morale & Propaganda

In the last chapter it was clear that by the end of the Battle of Britain, German morale had taken a pounding. This contrasted markedly when compared to the words gathered from M-Room prisoners in 1939 and the first half of 1940.

The first prisoners of war, those who went to CSDIC and Air Intelligence at the Tower of London in early November 1939, were recorded as having high morale. In one transcript (SRA2) on the 3 November, two unidentified prisoners were recorded in conversation. One said they could not make an escape from there (the Tower of London), but must try when they were in a POW camp. However, the other man refused as he was married and believed that if they got away, they could in certain circumstances be shot. In reply, the first prisoner told his compatriot to keep his chin up, he was going to ask for cigarettes, a razor, books and newspapers – the German government could pay for it afterwards.

By the end of the month of November, transcript SRA7 recorded a group of non-commissioned officers who had already been recorded in the M-Room over previous days. Hilmar Grimm, shot down off Hoy on the 17 October in a Dornier 18 of 2/KuFIGr 606, Wilhelm Unger the rear gunner from a Heinkel III on the 22 October and Berhard Hochstuhl of 1(F)/122 chatted away, hypothesising about events:

> Grimm: 'The King said yesterday in his reply, that he was ready to negotiate.' (Noted by the listener to refer to the King's letter to King Leopold and Queen Wilhelmine – the King of Belgium and the Queen of the Netherlands.)
>
> Unger: 'If the King were only so crafty as to make peace.'
>
> Grimm: 'An international conference is to decide what he (Hitler) has to give back.'
>
> Unger: 'We must stick to Russia. Perhaps Poland would remain like the former Congress Poland.'

It was clear that they believed peace was possible and very likely with negotiation, but clearly their understanding of recent events and the political situation was somewhat misinformed and naive.

As the war entered a very cold winter, it seemed to grind to a halt, mainly due to the cold weather and heavy snow falls. Despite this, the morale of most prisoners remained high and SRA10, dated 12 January 1940, recorded a conversation between Leutnant Wilhelm Meyer and Unteroffizier Theodor Streyrer. Clearly believing victory and a wider European war was inevitable Meyer stated:

> Meyer: 'Once we are in France, then things will move as quickly as in Poland and they will quickly give in. We shall not lose the war – that would be too ridiculous.'
>
> Streyrer replied: 'The Finnish war is also influenced by Hitler, we are sending consignments through the Gulf of Finland, that is simpler than by rail.'
>
> Meyer: 'Perhaps the Italians will pass through Switzerland?'
>
> Streyrer: 'If we win the war, we shall split up France and England. The Irish are also National-Socialists.'

While AI1(k) could clearly listen to the high morale of their prisoners, it must have concerned them these men expected a much wider conflict in the coming months and with what was thought to be an inevitable victory, the destruction and break-up of the United Kingdom.

In transcript SRA20, at the end of January 1940, Leutnant Ernst Korner, a Dornier 18 observer, was recorded stating that if the English were wise, they would return the colonies to Germany and make peace. He did not believe India would hold together and English ships were being sunk every day. Korner then ventured further, saying he did not believe England had any interest in 'Smashing up Germany' and the war was not good for either nation.

It was clear that many sensible airmen did not want war and believed peace and negotiation was the way forward. However, with the war continuing and more prisoners starting to arrive at Trent Park, the M-Room *listeners* continued to add to their collection of transcripts.

In transcript SRA50, dated 28 March 1940, Feldwebel Ernst Breiler, a pilot with 1/Auf.Gr.Ob.d.l gave a long detailed, somewhat comical and clearly propaganda induced commentary on events:

> 'The English and Americans are counting on a revolution breaking out in Germany. The English know absolutely nothing about politics. They don't realise that their freedom is a weakness. In the democratic countries, everything is discussed publicly. Now they are surprised that it should have been possible for the German planes to reach Scapa (Scapa Flow).
>
> 'Every fourth German disagrees with Hitler. In spite of not agreeing, he thinks to himself, the war is upon us, we must see it through. I'm not pessimistic about Germany, but I don't believe in an absolute victory. Germany and England are both greatly interested in peace. Through the war, Germany may get communism and England may lose her colonies. But it is possible that, unless peace is made within six months, England's chances will improve. England is getting 2,000 machines from America now. That is not much, but these machines have a certain significance.'

A psychologist could write a thesis on Ernst Breiler's comments. It is clear his words were the product of Nazi propaganda and some personal experiences. He seemed like a number of other prisoners, to be somewhat confused about where events were heading and the general political situation. However, some might think he was more than a little clairvoyant in terms of his comments on communism in Germany and the dismantling of Britain's colonies.

In May 1940, with the invasion of Denmark and Norway, prisoner attitudes appear to have hardened. In transcript SRA86, dated 9 May 1940, A57 – an unidentified Leutnant pilot, from 3/KG30, spoke with A70 an Oberleutnant pilot – possibly Harold Vogel of 4/KG26, who was shot down on the 10 April 1940. The two men showed contrasting opinions and some bombast...

> Vogel: 'It's not in our interest that Italy should enter the war, for if she did, we should have to supply her with iron. It is better for us that Italy should not join in the war, but should keep our enemies permanently on tenterhooks while we make our big moves in Europe.
>
> 'I hope the Norwegian campaign will be over by 20 May. Trondheim is too small as a jumping off station for the air force, but I hope that we can transport troops from Trondheim to Narvik. Narvik is very hard to attack. Our men will hold out there till help comes from Trondheim. Narvik itself is of no interest to us. The main thing is that the transport of iron ore to Germany is assured.'

A57: 'The present situation is that the English have no influence on events. They only wait to see what Germany does. They got a smack in the eye in Czechoslovakia, in Austria and in Poland; in Norway they'll get another one. Norway was their last trump card and now they've lost it. I would not be surprised if everything in England were laid in ashes before long. Always, Blitzkrieg, that is the motto! We can use the Norwegian coast as a jumping off spot and basis for our air force and U-boats. We are now in a position to bomb the English ships on the east and west coasts continuously.

'I hope that one day, Holland and Belgium will be occupied in one lightning move. Clean up the "Channels" and then comes the landing of troops in the South of England. From there, the troops can gradually roll northward. In the meantime, we can take France in an easy detour and that will be the end of the war criminals.'

The considered words of the Oberleutnant were very different to those of the bombastic Leutnant, but while Vogel's views were clearly measured and sensible, those of the other prisoner must have been quite alarming for AI1(k). A57 was clearly another hardened product of National Socialism and on the same day he was placed in an M-Room with another Oberleutnant pilot (A67). This man cannot be identified and may have been captured in Norway before being transferred back to Trent Park.

A57 continued with his diatribe, but this time his attitude changed. A67 was somewhat more considered and clearly perturbed by the Leutnant:

A57: 'The English are vile beasts. They have destroyed our fleet and smashed up a lot of planes. Out of twenty-two crews, we lost four through AA fire. Most of my comrades have already gone west… I could cry at how much has been smashed up in Norway. I had many friends in the navy, now they're all done in. It hurts me to think of our losses…

'The people at home know nothing about our losses. It is wrong that they are not told about them and that one tries to magnify the English losses through untrue reports.'

A67: 'I can't imagine how much the war is costing us daily. Such stupidity! I've already had suspicions that we will lose the war.'

A57: 'We must not lose the war, or Germany will be split up again.'

While Feldwebel Ernst Breiler's earlier comments would have provided excellent essay material for a psychologist, the change in attitude of A57 in two separate transcripts on the same day, must have given the *listeners* and Air Intelligence food for thought. Which was his genuine thought pattern?

After listening to Oberleutnant Vogel's considered views on the invasion of Norway, the *listeners* soon heard further concerns about the campaign. This time the comments came from two officer pilots: A70 – KG26's Oberleutnant Harold Vogel again and A84, a Hauptmann also apparently a member of KG26 and possibly captured in Norway. The *listeners* noted the following comments in transcript SRA92, dated 14 May 1940: The two airmen criticised the conduct of operations in Norway. They complained about the snow, cold weather and the lack of suitable landing places. They believed members of the Luftwaffe were overworked and had not been granted leave for a considerable time. Vogel stated that before operations started in Norway, two crews in each Staffel of his Gruppe received permission to go on leave, but at the beginning of operations, the leave was suddenly cancelled. Vogel was granted leave as a special favour, spending his leave in Berlin from 17-20 April.

The Hauptmann's leave was due on 13 April, but it was cancelled. He complained that Oberst Fuchs did not talk to his officers in Norway and he had not seen Fuchs during the whole period he was in the country.

With reference to the invasion of Holland and Belgium, the opinion was expressed that the German troops would complete their operations in the two countries within a fortnight; the war would be over by September, then England would be attacked immediately after the occupation of the Dutch and Belgian aerodromes.

In the forthcoming attack upon England, large formations of the Luftwaffe would drop bombs on strategically important points, while parachute troops dropped in lonely spots would destroy bridges and railway tracks. The British government would move its seat to Canada from where it would be unable to conduct military operations against Germany. A new government for England would be set up by the Germans.

When the *listeners* sent the transcripts on for analysis, it was clear there was a military objective through Norway, the Low-Countries and on to Britain. How much of this was propaganda and sheer bluster was unclear, but the morale of the airmen was clearly very high even after their capture.

After Norway and the invasion of the Low-Countries and France, German morale appeared to remain sky-high, this despite the Luftwaffe sustaining a high number of casualties.

In transcript SRA20, dated 14 June 1940, an Oberfeldwebel and an Unteroffizier were recorded in conversation. The Unteroffizier said the Luftwaffe had incurred heavy losses, but the Oberfeldwebel dismissed this, adding that they still had machines. Not to be dismissed, the Unteroffizier then said, 'Yes, but what about the crews? I think there must be 1,500 German prisoners in England.' The Oberfeldwebel replied, 'More than that. I estimate that of aviators alone, they must have at least 2,000 prisoners.'

These comments were amazing when one considers that only sixty to seventy Luftwaffe prisoners had been detained from aircraft shot down over and around the UK coastline at that time. We know a large amount of JU52 aircraft were shot down over the Netherlands and there were losses over Norway, Belgium and France, but it is clear the morale of these men was suffering with their over estimation of Luftwaffe losses. As with any airman or soldier's level of morale, it is dependent upon the propaganda they receive and their own combat experiences. Deciphering these comments and corroborating them with other information was the work of the intelligence analysts at Trent Park. They would pass their findings on in general reports which are covered later in this book.

The M-Room *listeners* continued to record the statements of the chattering prisoners at Trent Park…

On 22 June 1940, transcript SRA124 recorded a conversation between two unidentified Oberleutnants (A212 and A232). One man speculated that Germany must have lost 50,000 men at Dunkirk, before adding that he estimated 90% of the active Luftwaffe roll had been used up in the fighting. The same officer continued with a confused dialogue stating:

> A212: 'In Germany there are some optimists who think England will put an end to the war. I don't think the English will do that. The English are our natural allies against Russia. The Russians have now occupied Lithuania.'

However, his companion in the M-Room thought differently:

> A232: 'I cannot believe that the Russians want to leave our side. They only want to dominate the Baltic coast. I expect the Russians will move against India. It is important that Churchill should be removed and that England should get a decent government. Lloyd-George, or some other reasonable man, could take over the government. England would now give up half

> its world empire to undo 3 September. The English are counting on our using up our petrol supplies quickly and that we shall be finished. So far, we've not felt any lack of petrol. In Belgium we used only the finest English petrol. We looked out for any odd stores and took as much petrol as we needed, until the distribution of the captured petrol had been organised. In my Staffel, every officer had a car of his own and besides this, the Staffel itself had four cars.'

In July the Battle of Britain began, the Luftwaffe was on a high and expected an easy victory.

On 19 July 1940, transcript SRA188 recorded a conversation between two officers believed to have been Leutnant Albert Striberny (prisoner A269) of 3/LG2, shot down on 8 July and Leutnant Joachim Schroeder (A275) of 9/ZG76 brought down on 11 July.

The two men discussed the use of Messerschmitt 109s by Switzerland and the possibility that once the war was over, they would make the Swiss join the German Reich. Leutnant Joachim Schroeder then made a very interesting comment:

> 'I have on several occasions said to English soldiers, "Hitler is a very fine man" and they have always answered, "Yes, he's a very fine man." So, one sees that the people do not agree with their government, not even the army!'

It is clear with over eighty years of hindsight, that Schroeder possibly did not understand the British sense of humour and that the soldiers may have been taking the proverbial with the young airman. The fact he believed this, underlines the effect Nazi propaganda had on impressionable young Luftwaffe personnel and their morale.

When the Battle of Britain started, it was clear from new prisoners of war that their morale remained high. On 29 July, a transcript (SRA245) detailed a conversation between A294 – believed to be Hauptmann Dieter von Malpitz of 3/LG1, shot down on 24 July and another Hauptmann (A296). This is believed to have been Hauptmann von Zenker of 1/KG40, a Focke Wulf 200 Kondor pilot.

In the transcript von Zenker describes his final flight near Belfast, but he appears to claim he was in a Heinkel III not a Kondor. After discussing aircraft and being shot down, they moved on to their own opinions of the British and the war:

> Malpitz: 'The people here (in Britain) have no conception of what is going to happen. In Holland too, they took all these precautions, but it was no good. The French refugees did more to harm the French than our guns.'
>
> Zenker: 'If the British Empire breaks up, we should not benefit. I think it very probable that Japan will take over Australia. After the war, the Fuhrer will reconstruct England as he is doing in France.'

By mid-August, the first cracks were beginning to appear in the morale of the German airmen. Transcript SRA326 detailed a conversation between two non-commissioned airmen. One man said all the prisoners in the establishment (Trent Park) were airmen adding, 'They are shooting down a great many of us.' The other man replied, stating that the previous day, it appeared sixty aircraft were shot down, but this was reportedly halved in reports at home to keep the German people quiet.

Transcript SRA375 recorded the conversation of three unidentified Oberleutnants on 22 August 1940. One stated that Germany was only friends with Italy, because Germany had no other friends! After being told to shut up, another officer stated:

> 'The soldiers here are really decent. We would have been treated differently by the French. Our propaganda says the English have no food left. They have more than we have, it was exactly the same in France.'

Although the prisoners mostly talked about tactics, losses and aircraft, as well as politics, occasionally they did discuss National Socialism. Their comments attracted a great deal of attention from the *listeners* and the intelligence staff, as it was an insight into life under the Nazis.

SRA393 on 25 August 1940, recorded a conversation between another three unidentified Oberleutnants, this time discussing the relationship between National Socialism and the Roman Catholic Church in Germany, again it must have been very enlightening:

> A346: 'The opposition of the Catholic priests to National Socialism is appalling.'
>
> A345: 'These people (the Catholics) consider themselves better than we, they consider themselves intellectually superior to the armed forces. I think it will slowly get better – with the people who have been through the Hitler Youth.'

> A346: 'If it doesn't get better, then it will get worse for them (the Catholics).'
>
> A349: 'You can't obliterate Christianity which has existed for centuries at one stroke.'
>
> A345: The New Idea (*Neugeisterei*) will not achieve more than has already been achieved by the Christian church.'
>
> A346: 'A priest once tried to influence my parents against National Socialism. In consequence, my father did not want to go to church any more, not a single one of the peasants went any more, the church was empty.'

Sometimes the comments from the prisoners must have been taken with the proverbial pinch of salt. It was clear, men of lower ranks were only regurgitating Nazi propaganda and rumours.

On 27 August, SRA 412 recorded two unidentified non-commissioned officers discussing the Italian armed forces, Egypt and Palestine. They clearly had a low opinion of the Italian armed forces and especially the air force. They believed the Italian armed forces were unlikely to be successful on their own, but the British were entirely unaware of the extent to which German agents had poured into Egypt, Turkey and Palestine. Many had occupied important civilian posts in government offices, railways and waterworks etc. It was certainly clear to AI1(k) and its affiliate intelligence departments, that it was unlikely these men would possess such intelligence. However, it was indicative of high morale, rumour control, propaganda and an expectation of victory.

Although prisoners still mostly believed a German victory was likely, some of the men were clearly softening in their estimation of the British – a nation that appeared in contrast to that portrayed by the Nazi propaganda machine.

Transcript SRA445, recorded on 2 September 1940, a chat between two Gefreiters, one of whom may have been G. Fleischmann of 3/KG51 (shot down on 12 August). The conversation covered a number of subjects, but one man suddenly stated:

> 'I had imagined captivity in England to be quite different. I had thought they would treat airmen badly, but the people are so friendly.'

The two airmen agreed that it was pure propaganda in the German newspapers and one said that if he returned home, he would say he was treated very decently by the British.

This attitude appears to have continued throughout September 1940, as Luftwaffe losses increased and more prisoners arrived.

On 14 September, SRA535 recorded two men, believed to have been Feldwebel Willi Schutel of Stab I/ZG2 and Unteroffizier Kurt Koch of 9/JG51:

> Koch: 'There's no point in escaping, for the whole thing won't last much longer anyway… One must admit that they do themselves well here, they've got cigarettes, coffee, tea, even cocoa. They still have everything, even butter and stuff like that. Well, if the landing does not materialise and we have to wait here till next year, it will be damnable,' he added sarcastically.

By the 20 September 1940, German losses were rising and the number of prisoners continued to increase, but the *listeners* and Air Intelligence started to detect a lowering of morale and some pessimism amongst some men.

Transcript SRA576 noted a conversation the previous day (19) when two unidentified Oberleutnants discussed recent events. One stated that Hitler should have started the battle against England at once, after the occupation of France. He was convinced of a German victory, but why was there a delay? The other officer cited the need to make preparations, but it was clear there was some consternation in the men's minds.

Although some airmen were concerned, others continued with high morale and the repeating of Nazi propaganda. Two airmen A493 – believed to have been Feldwebel August-Wilhelm Muller of 4/JG3 and A488 – Feldwebel Hermann Koops of 9/ZG76, discussed matters:

> Muller: 'For us the war is won. There is no other possibility. I can't believe that Adolf would go into a war which he could not win.' (The listener noted that this last sentence was said in a different tone of voice and perhaps the prisoner was reassuring himself.)
>
> Koops: 'I'd like to know how much longer it will last.'
>
> Muller: 'Yes I'd like to know that too.'
>
> Koops: 'It won't develop into a proper war. As soon as we get a footing here, it will be over.'
>
> Muller: 'No, not with the English.'
>
> Koops: 'But it is so senseless!'
>
> Muller: 'There won't be an easy peace, if the real Englishman by himself had to decide, then perhaps…'

> Koops: 'But here where I would say there is 80% Jewish capitalism behind it… The whole English resistance is being sustained by two men. That is Churchill, who has the power and the King, because he – how shall I express it – because he still has a lot of influence on Conservative Englishmen through his person. You do think that Churchill is for peace, Churchill is playing a role. I'm sure of it. The fellow is tough, he's a good man, Churchill. My conviction is that of General Field-Marshal Milch. When he said goodbye to our lot at Doblitz, he remarked "That fellow is tough, he's a good man. Our press naturally abuses him, doesn't it? And the English abuse Hitler. But if they knew him as a man, they would not pull him to pieces so much."'

On 23 September, SRA591 recorded a lengthy conversation between two pilots, A509 – Leutnant Kurt Bildau of JG51 and A519 – Leutnant Karl Westerhoff of 6/JG3. As seen in the last chapter, the two men talked at length in the M-Room, this despite Westerhoff's best efforts not to talk to the interrogators and his alleged attempts with von Werra to make up stories for any covert microphones and the *listeners:*

> Bildau: 'They know already that we are assembling troops on the French coast, also about the Geschwarden and everything else, the French tell them anyway.'

The *listeners* noted that the two pilots agreed an invasion would be difficult, but that the present state of affairs was intolerable and the invasion would be carried out successfully in spite of all difficulties. The two men were not clear how this could be achieved, but imagined a series of diversionary attacks, simultaneous to the main attack. They agreed that Stukas and transport aircraft would play an important part in the assault. Contrary to the views of some previous prisoners, the two Leutnants thought it stupid to invade England via Ireland, as the Irish liked the Germans as little as the English.

Kurt Bildau suddenly relapsed into some depression and stated that he had read in a newspaper, the Fuhrer might not invade at all, but the sea blockade and aerial bombardment would suffice.

Karl Westerhoff took a different tone:

> Westerhoff: 'You won't get these people down by the blockade and aerial attacks. If he tries to do it that way, the English are right and the war may continue for years. I am of the opinion that we should have attacked the

> English immediately after Dunkirk, when they had lost all their material. But we can't do it without an invasion. Otherwise, the losses with which we won our victories in France would be in vain. Somehow, we will do it. Norway appeared to be absolutely impossible and yet the plan succeeded.'

Both airmen had recently spent time in Jersey and Guernsey. They agreed that relations were good with the islanders, but what else could the people do? The locals had shown hesitation in attending dances given by the occupiers, but the adjutant invited the Lady of Sark and 'her beautiful daughter', so the islanders soon accepted. 'This also dispersed the misgivings of the 'Channel Island maidens' one man recounted.

The comments of Westerhoff and Bildau were very interesting for the intelligence staff. On one hand they expected an invasion, everything was ready, but they clearly had some misgivings about their leadership. They seemed to agree that the British knew a lot about the German forces and their plans, but whatever the difficulties, they expected the Wehrmacht to overcome them.

The comments about the Channel Islands must have also been very interesting for Air Intelligence. The islands were hastily evacuated in mid-1940, but a large number of civilians had remained. What conditions were like was of interest to the British government and its intelligence agencies.

There is no doubt that German morale had changed over the preceding year. Apart from a few die-hard Nazis, they now held an honest respect for the British people and the Royal Air Force. Many men wanted the war to end so they could return home. The thought of an elongated war with increasing casualties and a strengthening England was a major concern for many of them. Such misgivings and other accounts were readily accepted by the *listeners*, providing a positive intelligence picture for the British authorities.

The Air Intelligence staff had to be careful to check accounts and where possible corroborate them. Sometimes there were allegations of war crimes by the British and in transcript SRA675, on 4 October 1940, an unknown Gefreiter from a bomber crew (A557) told his colleague:

> 'Near Calais a Spitfire shot down a German bomber and when one of the crew bailed out with his parachute, the Englishman shot him with his machine guns. That is a clear proof that they are swine. A German would never do a thing like that. The Englishman was afterwards shot down by a 109. I don't know what they did with him.'

It is clear over eighty years later, that there were so-called war crimes committed by both sides. However, careful analysis of the RAF and Luftwaffe records fails to find a possible match to this story and it appears to have been yet more Nazi propaganda, or rumour control at its worst. Either way, the Air Intelligence staff had to sort the intelligence wheat from the chaff.

Chapter 12

M-Rooms – Promotions, Medals, Senior Officers & War Crimes

In the past three chapters, we have seen a variety of attitudes and opinions gathered from Luftwaffe prisoners by the M-Room *listeners*. In this final section on the intelligence gathered via the covert microphones, we will see the rigid discipline of the Luftwaffe was not that successful and bred a degree of contempt. The M-Rooms are remembered today for their discovery of the development of Nazi wonder-weapons and the Holocaust, not to forget other war crimes; but in 1940 the M-Room *listeners* were already recording details of apparent war crimes as well as SS and Gestapo activities.

On 29 January 1940, transcript SRA20 recorded a discussion between Unteroffizier Gerd Kahle (the man who was alleged a test pilot and provided a wide range of information to AI1(k), most of it apparently inadvertently), Unteroffizier Walter Heckt and Leutnant Ernst Korner.

It was clear the three men were less than content with the promotion system in the Luftwaffe and the lack of experience. Kahle said he believed you must serve six months before being promoted, but Korner said a number of men were promoted to Feldwebel the previous year, despite only having served since the outbreak of war in September 1939.

In transcript SRA26, a couple of weeks later, two non-commissioned airmen were recorded talking about their officers. The various names they reeled off were an important source of intelligence and very useful in building files on the different Geschwader and Staffeln. They also detailed the behaviour and attitudes of some officers, stating that the Waffenmeister – a man called Mueller, had cursed an airman called Sievert who was helpless with laughter when he was abused.

Oberleutnant Kuschke had reportedly shouted at a man called Petri for being absent from roll call, but Hauptmann Pohle later deleted the charge. Helmut Pohle of KG30 was clearly a very well-respected man. As we have seen, he was captured earlier in the war in October 1939 and was said to be an associate of Hermann Göring.

The airmen of KG30 seem to have been very talkative when it came to their officers and in SRA85 on 6 May 1940, A57 – who cannot be identified even though he said he belonged to the 3rd Staffel of KG30, was quite talkative. This was despite showing in transcript SRA86 (examined in the last chapter), that he was quite a hardened Nazi. He spoke about Oberst Fuchs of KG26. Fuchs would be later described in transcript SRA92 by two KG26 officers, as someone who didn't speak to his junior officers much. A57 said of Oberst Fuchs:

> 'Oberst Fuchs is very nervous so many machines are being smashed up…'

The two transcripts certainly described Oberst Fuchs, the Kommodore of KG26 as a nervous man, who did not talk to his junior officers while his Geschwader was sustaining heavy losses – a claim that was corroborated by the number of losses recorded by AI1(k).

Sometimes, personnel could not stop themselves from talking, bragging about their own personal standing in a unit.

On 10 June 1940, transcript SRA116 recorded an unidentified Oberleutnant (A139), possibly a paratroop officer, claiming to be related to senior officers. He gave details of events in Holland and General Kurt Student, the head of the Fallschrimjager (Parachute units):

> 'A day before my departure for Holland, I read a round robin in which it was stated that at zero hour, all Dutch and Belgian ships were to be attacked. My uncle – Oberst Schwaber, is a personal friend of Göring. Oberst Schwaber tried to occupy Rotterdam with General Student. A138 told me that General Student had asked for help after his landing in Rotterdam. In the meantime he tried to negotiate with the Dutch. Before that, bombs had already been dropped on the town. General Student told the Dutch these were by way of a warning and that if they did not surrender, the attack on the town would start in earnest. During the negotiations, General Student was wounded by a Dutch officer with a revolver. Student was taken off to Berlin seriously wounded. It appears that Rotterdam has now been more knocked about than Warsaw. We must now build up our ground organisation to attack England.'

Later he added…

> 'Oberleutnant Schaefer piloted General Student's machine, I was with General Student for two years. After the Polish war, I went back to him and in the middle of November went to the Luftlandetruppen. In the Luftlandedivision there is a reconnaissance Gruppe. It is divided into two Luftflotten. They have a certain number of JU88's, but they do not go in for diving (dive bombing).'

This information gave AI1(k) an insight into the invasion of the Netherlands, the aerial attack, the heavy bombing of Rotterdam and General Student. However, it is now widely believed Student received a serious head wound from a stray German bullet, rather than the account given above.

The conversation continued and A187 – Leutnant Hans Strehl of 1/JG51, shot down on 23 May and A201 – Oberleutnant Theodor Beermann of KG30, added further comments regarding Oberst Fuchs of KG26:

> Beermann: 'Oberst Fuchs the Kommodore is dreadfully unpopular. I have exchanged words with him.'
>
> Strehl: 'Fuchs is just as unpopular as General Richthofen. Richthofen now has the "Flieger Korps."'
>
> Beermann: 'Admiral Raeder has been dismissed.'

Despite this comment from Oberleutnant Beerman, Admiral Raeder had not been dismissed as Commander of the German Navy, although he is known to have had some disagreements with Hitler. Where Beermann received this information is unknown, but it is clear such a comment could easily lead the Air Intelligence staff astray and everything needed to be corroborated.

The three men were still in the M-Room two days later on 12 June and still talking about their senior high command, but in more derogatory terms:

> Beermann: 'He is the greatest ass we have, Student – the biggest fat-head.'
>
> Strehl: 'Just like Dr Raeder. He is not liked at all in the Navy.'
>
> Beermann: 'Raeder?'
>
> Strehl: 'Yes.'
>
> Beermann: 'Well, is he any good?'
>
> Strehl: 'Well yes, but he has no influence at all – he has nothing to say.'
>
> A139: 'Otherwise the Fuhrer always chooses the right men.'

> Strehl: 'As a matter of fact, General Student is really the man who built up the whole thing (parachute unit). That is certainly his work, but otherwise, in the Polish war and then again when we were in Norway, it was a big flop… The Dutch and the Belgians had become suspicious and had made fantastic preparations. The Dutch captain said to me, "We knew beforehand that you were coming down here."'
>
> Beermann: 'And above all, the English wireless reported three days beforehand that we intended to send airborne troops to Holland. We denied this of course.'

Soon they returned to the subject of General Richthofen:

> Beermann: 'This general, General Richthofen, was stationed at Ramdohm with his Fliegerfuhrung z.b.V. He was in Poland too. They nearly wiped out the Poles…'
>
> Strehl: 'Yes, but Richthofen he'll fight like the devil! Just as in Spain. There he made those low-flying attacks.'
>
> Beermann: 'Yes, but Spain was quite another matter, those were merely training flights!'

At the conclusion of the transcript Beermann told the others that everyone involved in the capture of Liege was promoted to the next rank. When Leutnant Strehl asked if that included everyone, he replied, 'Well, the principal participants, they also got the Ritterkruze (Knights Cross).'

This was probably one of the most enlightening transcripts received by the M-Room *listeners* up to that point.

The subject of promotions and the award of decorations was a constant gripe for the Luftwaffe men. On 26 July 1940, an unidentified Oberfeldwebel (A283) was heard complaining:

> 'At Rotterdam all parachutists got the Iron Cross First or Second Class, although they only fought for three days. I've been an aviator since the beginning of the war and have got nothing. An aviator who has no Iron Cross after the war will be looked down upon.'

On 1 August, two more non-commissioned officers were heard griping about medals. One stated:

> 'I can surely put in for the Iron Cross First Class after thirty-three active service flights? The officers get one after three flights and what do we get? We don't get the Iron Cross.'

It was clear all was not well in the Luftwaffe at the height of the Battle of Britain. At the height of the summer on 20 August, an unidentified Oberleutnant and A346, believed to be Oberleutnant Heinz Schlegel of Stab/KG2, were recorded on transcript SRA364 discussing Field Marshal Herman Göring:

> Schegel: 'Hermann came to the aerodrome and they said it would be a good occasion for handing out Iron Crosses. He was very friendly and easy to talk to, but he did not have much knowledge of the situation; he has an assistant for that, a very able little fellow.'
>
> A349: 'What does Hermann look like?'
>
> Schegel: 'Oh, he has a fat corporation, looks rather unhealthy, wears brown boots, a knobbly stick and an enormous pistol; on top of that he wears a white cap, so altogether he looks rather ridiculous.'
>
> A349: 'Steady on!'

Oberleutnant Heinz Schlegel of Stab/KG2 and A349 started to talk about Staffel Kapitans and one in particular (noted by the listeners as possibly being A345 – Oberleutnant Gerhard Oszwald of Stab/KG2, a man we met in a previous chapter), who called his men swine and other things. The other officers were fed up with his attitude, especially when he was pleased when an officer he could not stand, failed to return from a flight. Heinz Schegel stated, probably reflecting on the fact Oszwald had himself now been shot down and captured:

> 'I'm certain the Staffel has now sighed with relief, because he always treated the people so badly, they lost all confidence. If the war had gone on for a couple of years with him in command, the men would have mutinied and when once in a while he did something for them, he did it not for them, but in order to boast about it to the others.'

The comments about various officers continued throughout August 1940 and in transcript SRA393 on the twenty-fifth of that month, three Oberleutnants reeled off a number of names with a number of barbed comments…

Hauptmann Blunck or Plunck was declared to be a good officer, but he could never make a decision without consulting his wife they said. He once gave his wife some important papers to read, but she lost them!

One officer called Lanz could never get on with the Unteroffiziers who made complaints about the way he treated them.

Hauptmann Huber or Hubner at the Military Academy, had no idea how to lecture, while one called Bauer couldn't distinguish one aircraft from another.

Such information was invaluable for the file builders at AI1(k). A name linked to a unit or an airfield with a small amount of comment about his attitude or his wife, could be used in the future to 'open up' the most reluctant of prisoners.

Medals and promotions were an issue for many of the prisoners, but one element that did create some discussion was the alleged dishonesty of some senior, supposedly successful fighter pilots. Just like the victory claims of Franz von Werra, other well-known pilots were allegedly manipulating their own scores.

In transcript SRA591, dated 20 September 1940, A519 – Leutnant Karl Westerhoff of 6/JG3, a fellow member of von Werra's Geschwader and A509 – Leutnant Karl Bildau of 7/JG51 discussed over claiming by fellow fighter pilots. Westerhoff claimed to have personally shot down three aircraft, while Bidau claimed four confirmed and two unconfirmed victories:

> Bildau: 'Do you know Oseau who is with us? (Author's note: probably Walter Oseau of JG51.) Of the twenty he claims to have shot down, I should say half was the truth at most and incidentally he was a thief.'
>
> Westerhoff: 'Do you know Hauptmann von Hahn who is with us? Once when he was flying, a Spitfire was reported. He went up, but did not fire a shot and then believe me, he reported, "Shot down a Spitfire."'

Karl Westerhoff continued explaining that when von Hahn landed and made the victory claim, it was gently pointed out to him that his magazines were practically full of ammunition. However, the Hauptmann told them to mind their own business and made his claim:

> Bildau: '…flew to London, Suddenly the Schwarmfuhrer reported that his engine was smashed and that the whole Schwarm would have to turn around. Then over the Channel near Gris Nez they saw two Hurricanes and he shot them down. Suddenly he had forgotten his damaged engine…'

> Westerhoff: 'At the beginning we were amazingly honest in the Staffel. We said we would only report victories when doubly corroborated.'
>
> Bildau: 'Then they started the unfortunate practice of giving the Iron Cross Second Class for the first aircraft down, Iron Cross First Class for four aircraft down! It happened over and over again that our Staffel Kapitan shot down an aircraft and then slunk off home. He did not care what happened to us afterwards, Just, ran away and left us in the lurch!'
>
> Westerhoff: 'I cannot understand how German officers can give such a display of morbid ambition. Surely it is of no consequence how many "kills" you have made. But they are quite unscrupulous.'
>
> Bildau: 'Gruppen-Kommandeur Wick…' (Author's note: believed to be Helmut Wick of JG2.)
>
> Westerhoff: 'Is a bluffer and Mobius and Fritz Wolcke…'
>
> Bildau: 'They are Staffel Kapitane who count everything that falls down and it is clearly proven by a number of witnesses to be a direct victory of someone else, to their own bag,'
>
> Westerhoff: 'It makes a lot of bad blood and spoils the tone of the unit.'
>
> Bildau: 'Molders (Author's note: Werner Molders the JG51 Kommodore) told the Feldmarshal that this system of counting victories should not continue…'

The two Messerschmitt pilots continued their discussion claiming there was a belief, that men with high victory scores would get the best 'fat' peacetime jobs, while the efficient conscientious fellows would be left out in the cold. They added that their own units held a belief, those who held the rank of Oberfeldwebel were unlucky and were always shot down.

While Werner Molders was clearly respected by the two pilots, Helmut Wick of JG2, who claimed fifty-six kills before being killed on 28 November 1940, was not. He was described as a 'Bluffer' having claimed nearly thirty kills between 11 August and 15 October 1940.

Hauptmann von Hahn of JG3 claimed six victories during the Battle of Britain, taking his total to eleven. He was given command of I/JG3 and went to Russia with the unit in 1941. He made a string of claims reaching a total of thirty-one victories and was awarded the Knights Cross. He survived the war and died aged forty-three in 1957.

Hauptmann Walter Oseau of JG51 had claimed twenty victories by the time of the prisoners conversation and this corroborates the claims of Bildau. Oseau claimed thirty-one kills during the Battle of Britain, taking his total to thirty-eight victories. He remained operational with various Geschwader until 1944 and took his score to 118, before he was shot down and killed on 11 May 1944. At the time of his death, he held the rank of Oberst.

While it was clear all was not perfect in the Luftwaffe, the *listeners* started to pick up the first reports of war crimes and poor treatment of people in the occupied territories.

In transcript of SRA86, dated 9 May 1940, the *listeners* overheard A70 – believed to be Oberleutnant Harold Vogel of KG26 tell a comrade:

> 'The English have no organization. After the landing of our troops, the SA and the Gestapo must at once get busy to see that they don't start organising. They only make grandiloquent speeches and take votes, but they can't make a decision on anything. When our troops march in here, they'll at least learn to respect us.'

While some of the prisoners clearly respected or feared the Nazi apparatus, others were quick to denounce it. In the transcript SRA116 on 10 June 1940, an unidentified Oberleutnant (A139) who was possibly a paratrooper captured in Holland stated:

> 'M30 (Author's note: a naval prisoner) says that so far, only the first half of the armoured division has been in action. At the end of three weeks the tanks which had been in action must be replaced in order to be overhauled… M35 says that the SS troops had heavy losses. The SS troops fight so stupidly that he would sooner fight with the worst infantryman than with the SS troops.'

As the Blitzkrieg moved across Europe, many people on both sides of the divide speculated about the use of poison gas, like that used in the First World War. Gas masks had been issued to the British population and those in Germany. In SRA124 on 22 June, two unidentified Oberleutnants (A212 and A232) discussed poison gas:

> A232: 'Has gas been used yet in France or Belgium?'
>
> A212: 'We ourselves do not want the beastly thing. Certainly, we have prepared for gas, but the Fuhrer is so humane that he does not use it. Every fighting soldier is against gas.'

A few weeks later, other prisoners were recorded saying every man, woman and child in Germany was now equipped with a gas mask. Two unidentified prisoners (A265 and A267 – two Unteroffiziers) in transcript SRA178 were recorded talking about 'nerve gas'. One man appeared to have been asked about this by his interrogating officer, but neither man knew anything about it; the two finding the idea of a paralysing gas quite amusing according to the transcript.

The interrogating officers clearly had a brief to continually assess the threat and risk of an aerial gas attack upon Britain. In late July 1940, transcript SRA245 recorded a conversation between two Hauptmanns', one A296 who is believed to possibly be either H. Schmilden of 3/KG26 or von Zenker of 1/KG40 stated:

> 'We won't start with gas. If the English start, then we'll do it too. We are prepared for it. I have so far seen no gas bombs and I know the artillery carry no gas shells yet.'

Hearing such language from a Hauptmann must have steadied the nerves of Air Intelligence. By 1 August 1940, Denys Felkin signed off a General Report (Intelligence report 213/1940) which concluded with his observations on the possible use of gas. He noted:

> 'Regarding gas, all prisoners of war say that the Germans will not be the first to use this, particularly as the Fuhrer is an old infantryman and is such "a kind humane man." There is no doubt that this attitude would easily change if Germany decided to use gas. One man spoke of bacteria bombs, which would be the reply if we were to use gas; but it is improbable that this man had any real information on the subject.'

Despite Felkin's positive report, more evidence of gas was soon heard by the *listeners*, when on 14 August, two unidentified Oberleutnants, A318 and A286, were talking in whispers. Despite whispering, the high-quality RCA microphones heard A286 say:

> '3 months… everything completely over. In France we have all the documents (unterlagen)… I saw those cases myself. On them was written "Only by the special order of the Fuhrer." They were sealed and tightly packed. In the meantime, it will come as a complete surprise. We have gas bombs and then all the heavy industry…'

A number of prisoners were also recorded discussing what they believed was illegal and prohibited ammunition. In transcript SRA318, on 14 August, a Leutnant (A314), an Oberleutnant (A286) and a Hauptmann (A294) – possibly Dieter von Malpitz Staffel Kapitan of 3/LG1 (JU88s), but this cannot be confirmed, were heard discussing their ammunition:

> A294: 'That is our trouble, for instance I always said, "how shall we do that with the B ammunition?" I said to the Gruppen-Kommandeur, I cannot take responsibility of having my men shot by drumhead court martial afterwards, should they be taken prisoner and caught with B ammunition. Then we got something signed by Göring that we were all to get the certificate that the B ammunition was only for air defence etc. But that was no good, so on 10 May, I told my Gruppen-Kommandeur, please give me a decision on this point. Then he again did nothing. And then when no decision was given again, I gave orders in the Staffel that all aircraft which had ammunition for forward machine guns, which are for the W/T operator and which might be used for fighting, should not get any B ammunition.'
>
> A314: 'We did exactly the same. The drums which don't contain B ammunition are marked with a white chalk line and only these drums are to be placed in front. Every alternate shot we used a tracer and then alternating we used SS, SMK and B ammunition…'
>
> A286: 'I threw away a whole drum of B ammunition in a wood.'
>
> A294: 'That is not necessary.'
>
> A286: 'It is.'
>
> A294: 'It is not forbidden. It is permitted in aerial warfare. It is only forbidden against human targets.'

Clearly the ammunition was causing some consternation among the bomber crews, but also for fighter pilots as indicated by intelligence log Nos. 360 and 386.

Oberleutnant Hans-Jorgen Ehrig the Staffel Kapitan of 1/JG77 was involved in a dogfight on the 31 August and made a forced landing near Tenterden in Kent. An experienced pilot who had fought in Spain, Poland and France, he held the Iron Cross First and Second Class and had previously belonged to JG51. In his possession, interrogators found a certificate authorising him to use 'special ammunition', which was specified as 'explosive and incendiary ammunition.'

On the same day, Leutnant Rudolf Ziegler of Stab II/JG54 was also shot down. According to intelligence report No. 355, he refused to answer all questions, but was found in possession of a similar certificate dated 'Battle HQ 29.4.40.' it stated:

> 'He was specifically ordered only to use the belt ammunition against aircraft and balloons.'

The intelligence report signed by Flight Lieutenant Guy Jepson, Felkin's deputy, added that this information was interesting in view of the ground strafing of troops in both Holland and France.

Leutnant Ziegler was clearly questioned about this and although he refused all information, he did talk about his certificate, stating that this was because the belts contained incendiary ammunition known as 'P.m.K'; but more recent papers referred to this as explosive ammunition. The AI1(k) report concluded that these certificates were probably issued in case of trouble when a pilot was captured.

There were other concerning comments overheard by the *listeners* and on 26 August, A383 a Hauptmann, possibly Hauptmann Loncier of 9/KG53 was in discussion with A331, a Major – believed to be Major Fredrich-Karl Schlichtling of Stab II/KG27:

> Loncier: 'How are the French behaving?'
>
> Schlichtling: 'They are starting sabotage. They stretched a cable across the road and a car was smashed up against it. Then the Naval Commander in Chief in Paris was shot at in his car. At our aerodrome, they lighted four fires to show the English the way. It is really dreadful in Paris… How long will these Freemasons and Jews manage to hold the people? They know for certain that one day, there must be German-English reproachment and then they will be completely finished. As far as I can see, the people have already had enough of war. How long they can hold out is really only a question of food…"

In mid-September, transcript SRA543 recorded two unidentified Oberleutnants (A430 and A480) discussing the Home Guard in Britain and Poland. They discussed the arming of civilians in case of an invasion and the moral justification for this. A480 said the Luftwaffe would drop leaflets warning the British Home Guard they would be shot if captured with arms in their possession.

In response, A430 described the shooting of a Pole, an educated man captured with a revolver in his pocket. He had taken part in anti-German riots in Silesia in 1919-1923. A430 admitted being in command of the firing squad and this left a great impression upon him. He also added that due to frequent attacks on German troops with razors, all Poles, civilian and military found in possession of a razor were shot without trial. Another Pole who denied carrying weapons had grenades in his haversack, he too was immediately shot. The same two men continued in conversation and in transcript SRA555, A480 stated:

> 'I was in a café in France. There were ten SS officers there. They behaved like swine. The policy which Churchill has followed will be bitterly avenged. Once our troops get a foothold, then England is done for within a few days. Churchill said, "I want to pulverise Germany," and the Fuhrer replied, "I want to eradicate England from the map."'

It was clear there was a lot to fear from Nazi Germany in 1940, but it was also clear there were a good number of Luftwaffe airmen who did not like the war, the Nazi philosophy or some of their senior officers. They wanted peace and to return to their homes and families.

Chapter 13

Knickebein & X-Gerät (X-Device/Apparatus)

One of AI1(k)'s greatest successes concerned the identification of the German blind bombing system known as *X-Gerät* (translated as X-Device or X-Apparatus). Prior to the start of the war, British Intelligence had received information that indicated the Luftwaffe was developing a series of electronic aids for its aircraft.

It was widely known at the start of the war, that a blind-approach landing system called *Lorenz* was in operation and a similar system was developed by the Allies.

Simply put, the *Lorenz* system used a radio mast which sent out an electronic beam from the end of the runway. An approaching aircraft would receive the beam on apparatus installed in the cockpit and the pilot would hear in his headset a series of morse code like dots if he was to one side of the centre line of the runway; and a series of dashes if he was on the other side of the correct line of approach. If the pilot was on the correct heading and approach line, he would hear a continuous tone in his headset until he landed.

It was because of this development and other known attempts by German scientists to develop radar or radio direction finding (RDF) equipment, that the British intelligence services took the threat of other electronic navigational devices very seriously.

The German scientists were quick to adapt the *Lorenz* system with larger, more powerful transmitters. Tests found the specially adapted beams, sent out over a longer distance, did not spread in bandwidth like the original *Lorenz* beam. This allowed the new beam to travel many, many miles, only widening to a beam width over a distant target of just a few tens of yards.

The new system had one projected beam, which would guide the bombers to a city e.g. Liverpool, where another beam, sent out from another transmitter at a different geographical location, would intersect the first beam over the target. Flying along the first radio beam, the observer or wireless operator would listen to a tone in their headset to keep the bomber on course – rather like the

Lorenz landing system. Once the intersecting radio beam was encountered, this changed the tone in the operator's headset and the bombs were dropped on the target. Although it was not as accurate as later electronic aids, it allowed bombing accuracy which was far superior to the efforts of Royal Air Force bombers, who often missed their targets, in many cases by miles.

This new blind bombing system was called *Knickebein* and its transmitters were disguised to look like the familiar blind landing system. The first transmitters were set up inside the German border, but after the invasion of France and the Low Countries, extra aerials and stations were set up to increase the range and accuracy of *Knickebein*.

British intelligence and the Air Ministry were keen to counteract the blind bombing system and an eminent scientist – Reginald Victor Jones, more often known as just R.V. Jones was tasked with leading the team investigating this issue.

Information had already been received before the fall of France and the French had passed some of their initial findings on to the British.

Enigma coded messages were being deciphered and R.V. Jones was beginning to understand what the system may entail, but during the first few months of the war, the British scientists were struggling. What made them more concerned, was fresh intelligence that indicated another new system, another *X-Gerät* (X-apparatus) was being developed in Germany. The British, while still grappling to understand the earlier *Knickebein* system, now knew a more advanced system of some kind was already in development.

The British scientists would soon discover that the later *X-Gerät* system used several intersecting radio beams to locate a target, each beam being named after a German river. In time they would discover that the main beam, which was called *Weser*, was similar to the intersecting beam used with *Knickebein*, but it operated at a much longer radio frequency. Other transmitted beams named *Rhine*, *Oder* and *Elbe*, indicated precise stand-by points and a release point for the bombs.

Flying along the main beam, the wireless operator or observer would hear a brief signal (the *Rhine* beam) in his headset and set up his bombing equipment (rather like with *Knickebein*). The equipment consisted of a stop-clock with two hands. When the *Oder* beam was crossed, the clock automatically started its own operation and the two hands started to move. When the final *Elbe* beam signal was encountered, one hand stopped at zero and the other reversed, moving back towards zero. When the moving hand finally reached the hand indicating zero the bombs were automatically released.

There were not very many *Knickebein* systems in operational use in the winter of 1939-1940, but their number increased in the spring of 1940. The *Knickebein* system was initially referred to by a number of German prisoners of war and intelligence reports as *X-Gerät*, but there were only a limited number of aircraft deployed with the *Knickebein* apparatus.

The later system, as we shall see, did not become operational until later in 1940. It was therefore imperative during early 1940, that AI1(k) identify intelligence regarding both systems to assist R.V. Jones and his team of scientists.

R.V. Jones wrote an autobiography which was published in 1978, called *Most Secret War.* The book gives a fascinating insight, not only into his work, but the assistance given to him by Denys Felkin and his team at AI1(k) Cockfosters. The book deals with the electronic intelligence war in great detail and it is well worth a read, but we shall concentrate on the assistance Trent Park gave to R.V. Jones.

In October 1939, R.V. Jones was working at Bletchley Park when, as he describes him, 'Josh, an outstanding cryptographer' was sent to take part in the interrogation of a Luftwaffe leutnant shot down attacking British shipping in the Firth of Forth. According to Jones, the interrogation party was led by Flying Officer Denys Felkin, but as this was an early inquisition, it was decided he should be joined by some technical experts to assist him.

To support Felkin, Josh (his name was clearly still secret when the book was written), an unnamed officer from the German Section of Air Intelligence and Flight Lieutenant Maggs from the Y-Service (AI1(e)) were called in to assist.

The aircraft concerned was one of two Junkers 88's of KG30 brought down on 16 October 1939. One aircraft coded 4D+DH piloted by Oberleutnant Hans Storp and his crew of Feldwebels Hugo Kohnke and Hans Hielschar and Obergefreiter Kramer, were attacked by Spitfires and shot down. As we have already seen in an earlier chapter, Kramer was killed before Storp ditched the aircraft in the sea. The three survivors scrambled out into a dinghy before being captured and taken into captivity.

Jones states that before the interrogation took place, the group of interrogators held a preliminary meeting to discuss their tactics. It was decided they must establish moral superiority over the prisoner. To do this, a long table was placed in a room with the interrogators sat behind one side of it. The interview with the prisoner took place on 20 October and the AI1(k) record can still be found in the UK National Archives as an interrogation report.

According to Jones, the prisoner was marched in between two guardsmen and made to stand to attention before the board. Despite this disciplined regime, the interrogation of Oberleutnant Hans Storp appears to have been quite comical, but the official records naturally omit the joviality…

Jones noted in his book that Hans Storp was marched in, 'Giving a good impression of a Nazi airman with his gleaming black boots, straight back, his head held high and smart drill.' He clicked his heels together and gave a Nazi salute to the board while simultaneously giving a verbal, 'Heil Hitler'. Josh, according to Jones, was quite surprised and instantly stood up, responded with his own Nazi salute and a curt 'Heil Hitler' of his own. Having quickly realised what he had done, he tried to sit back down, but missed his chair and fell under the long table. What Oberleutnant Hans Storp, Denys Felkin, Flight Lieutenant Maggs, or the other unidentified member of the panel must have thought is not known, but any moral superiority must have disappeared very quickly!

The reports in the UK National Archives do not detail this hilarity, but state Storp and his crew did not receive any navigational assistance from home stations. This was possibly a misleading statement and the prisoners were not telling the truth, especially as they had also told their interrogators that if they flew in cloud, they believed they could not be picked up by the British RDF (radar) chain. What was mentioned by the crew was that the bombs were released by the Observer and not the pilot. This comment seems to have surprised the interrogation team, little did they know, how close this comment was to the elusive prize they sought.

Although the reports do not mention *Knickebein* or *X-Gerät* specifically, it is clear the interrogators were looking for information on the subject and must have asked about navigational assistance from the home stations in Germany. The intelligence reports in The National Archives are not signed, but appear to have been completed by a flying officer who was the Chief RAF Interrogation Officer – in other words by Denys Felkin.

The pilot of the other Junkers 88 of KG30, Hauptman Helmut Pohle, was also interrogated the same day as the first crew. The three members of his crew had sadly been killed and he was the only survivor. The intelligence report stated somewhat bizarrely, that Pohle was unwounded, but had facial injuries and a fractured jaw! He did not mention anything about *Knickebein* or *X-Gerät,* but did say he was a personal acquaintance of Field Marshal Hermann Göring and General Bodenshatz. Still suffering from his injuries, he asked that a telephone call be made to Berlin to have a specialist doctor flown over in a Red Cross aeroplane to treat him.

As we have seen in an earlier chapter, there were numerous interrogations of airmen captured in 1939, but those from KG30 appear to have been the main target for questions about *Knickebein* or *X-Gerät*. It is therefore probably safe to assume, that intelligence had already been informed or suspected that aircraft from KG30 were already carrying the secret equipment.

On 17 October 1939, a Junkers 88 from 2/KG30 (4D+EK) was hit by anti-aircraft fire over Hoy in the Orkney Islands, while trying to attack the Royal Navy anchorage at Scapa Flow. Three of the four-man crew were killed, but the wireless operator, Unteroffizier Fritz Ambrosius, managed to bail out of his burning aircraft, receiving some injuries in the process. As a wireless operator from an aircraft of KG30, he was extensively interrogated and a lengthy intelligence report was produced – indicative of him being a very communicative prisoner.

As we have seen, Fritz Ambrosius gave extensive details about his unit and its officers, including Hauptmann Helmut Pohle, corroborating the statement that he was a personal friend of Hermann Göring and if he had not been shot down, would have been transferred to the Air Ministry in Berlin. Fritz Ambrosius gave a great deal of information about the war flights of KG30, especially the attacks in the Firth of Forth over the preceding days and even their losses.

His interrogation continued and the prisoner was asked about his own aircraft and its engines. He was keen to discuss the aircraft, it's performance and the production time for new machines. He even discussed take-off weights, airspeed, further developments and was clearly a great asset to Air Intelligence, but there was no mention in the intelligence reports of the *Knickebein* or *X-Gerät* systems.

On 28 October 1939, another machine from KG26 made a forced landing near Edinburgh after being damaged by anti-aircraft fire and Spitfires. This time the aircraft was a Heinkel III of Stab/KG26 (1H+JA). As mentioned in an earlier chapter, two of the crewmen were killed and the pilot Unteroffizier Kurt Lehmkuhl was badly injured. The observer, Leutnant Rolf Niehoff, escaped injury and was interrogated by intelligence officers two days later. Their intelligence report discussed in an earlier chapter is quite lengthy and gives details of how the Heinkel was lost.

Rolf Niehoff had quickly vacated the aircraft which was relatively intact, but he did not remove or destroy any of his maps or papers. Local civilians quickly surrounded him and he gave his pocketknife to one of them, before receiving a penny in exchange for an autograph from another person. Niehoff provided AI1(k) with information about KG26 and the Polish campaign, as well as giving the names of a number of senior officers, but no information appears to have been obtained about the *Knickebein* or *X-Gerät* equipment.

AI1(k) must have been desperate by this time to obtain some detailed information about the electronic equipment, but despite having a number of crewmen from both KG26 and KG30, very little information appears to have been obtained. However, there is always the possibility this information was held in separate secret files that have never been released.

On 2 November 1939, a conversation was recorded in one of the M-Rooms at the Tower of London. Recorded as transcript SRA/1, it recorded Leutnant Arndt Fischer and Oberleutnant Gustav Atwater of F (1)/122 speaking about the range of German radio. (They were the pilot and observer from a Heinkel III F6+DH, brought down 22/10/39.) Whether their discussion concerned German civilian radio or the beams for *Knickebein* or *X-Gerät* is unclear and must have been very frustrating for the *listeners*:

Atwater: 'Does German Radio work here?'
Fischer: 'With damped vibrations?'
Atwater: 'Yes, they can't do it with undamped vibrations.'

Unfortunately for the secret *listeners*, the conversation ended as the two men arranged their bedding for the night and it was unclear what exactly they were talking about. However, as the men did not come from KG26 or KG30, it is likely they were talking about the range of simple civilian German Radio stations.

On 7 November 1939, a three-page report titled: Report No. 1 Interrogation of Prisoners, gave details of Oberleutnant Wilhelm Ohmsen and Unteroffizier Wilhem Jung. Their Heinkel III had been shot down at Hazebrouck near Dunkirk, France, five days previously.

According to the report, Oberleutnant Ohmsen said he knew of a new and secret apparatus referred to in the Luftwaffe as *X-Gerät*. He claimed this device was used for the detection of aircraft which were out of sight and hearing, by means of an electrical or wireless process. This, he claimed, was a development based on the British invention (clearly referring to RDF/radar) and not related to any x-rays. The term *X-Gerät* merely denoted the secrecy of the apparatus.

The intelligence officers now had someone specially mentioning the device, but little did they know he was giving them something of a proverbial red-herring.

On 8 November 1939, the M-Rooms at the Tower of London recorded a discussion between Petty Officer Hilmar Grimm, shot down off Hoy on 17 October in a Dornier 18 (8L+DK) of 2/KuFIGr 606 and Unteroffizier Wilhelm Ungar, the rear gunner from Atwater and Fischer's Heinkel III on 22 October.

The two men discussed various matters before one man stated without reply: 'Wireless apparatus, if it gets under water, is rendered completely useless.' Why the airman said this and why there was no response is unclear, but the comment once again must have caused some frustration to the *listeners*. However, like the chat between Atwater and Fischer, it is unlikely to have concerned *Knickebein or X-Great,* as neither man served in a unit deployed with those systems in late 1939.

In his book *Most Secret War,* R.V. Jones states that in early 1940, he received from AI1(k), a secretly recorded conversation between two German airmen, discussing something called *X-Gerät or X-Apparatus.*

By this time, the SRA transcripts detailing the M-Room conversations no longer stated which airmen were involved and merely gave their coded identification, their rank and position in a crew; e.g. A28, Feldwebel, Pilot.

From late February 1940, there are a number of SRA records which contain discussions relating to *X-Gerät or X-Apparatus.*

On 21 February, report SRA 31 gave details of a brief chat between A29, an Unteroffizier pilot – now known to be Gerd Kahle of 1(F)/122 shot down on 13 January 1940; and A35, an Obergefreiter air mechanic of 5/KG26 – Heinz Hegemann – brought down on 9 February. In the report, Kahle tells Hegemann:

> 'He (Interrogating officer) came again about X-apparatus this morning, three months ago he heard something about it – a report from France.'
>
> Hegemann replied, 'Did you tell him that you knew something about it?'
>
> Kahle stated, 'No, I naturally did not let him know that I had heard about it.'

SRA33 dated 23 February, details a conversation between A30, a Feldwebel pilot and A34, an Unteroffizier pilot. By a process of elimination, A30 is believed to be Feldwebel Hermann Wilms, the pilot of a 4/KG26 Heinkel III (1H+FM) brought down at Sneaton near Whitby, Yorkshire, on 3 February 1940. A34 is believed to be Unteroffizier Helmut Meyer, pilot of a 5/KG26 Heinkel III shot down on 9 February 1940:

> Wilms states: 'He (the interrogating officer) asked me about X-Apparatus.'
> Meyer replied: 'Yes, a machine came down in France, which had the secret X-Apparatus on board. I said, why didn't they send it… (indistinct) Yes,

perhaps the X-Apparatus is unknown, perhaps they are only for those who made raids on the UK, built in later….'

On the same day, SRA35 recorded that Wilms joined A29, an Unteroffizier pilot and A35 a Obergefreiter mechanic or flight engineer. These men are believed to be Unteroffizier Gerd Kahle of 1(F)/122 and Obergefreiter Heinz Hegemann of 5/KG26. The men discussed various matters before Hermann Wilms stated:

Wilms: 'Didn't you know about the new X-Apparatus?'

Kahle: 'I thought you didn't know anything about it yet, as I had to do with all these new things.'

Later that day, Kahle and Hegemann were joined by A34 – Unteroffizier Helmut Meyer the pilot of Hegemann's Heinkel. The three men continued chatting and SRA36 records that Meyer said:

'They seem to be bothering their heads a lot about the *X-Gerät*.'

The discussion quickly changed direction and there was no further mention of the new apparatus.

From SRA35 and 36, it appears prisoners were being interrogated by Denys Felkin and his team and asked about *X-Gerät,* before being placed in an M-Room with the others to try and establish what the system was. However, it appears the airmen were reluctant to talk about it, even when the recently interrogated man mentioned the interrogating officer was interested in the secret device.

On 27 February 1940, AI1(k) finally received a breakthrough and it is very likely this was the transcript R.V. Jones reported being sent to him in early 1940.

SRA37 details a conversation between Heinz Hegemann of 5/KG26 and A38, an Unteroffizier wireless operator. This latter man is believed to be Wilhelm Berger of Aufkir.Gr.Ob.d.l, his Heinkel III (T5+OH) was shot down near St. Abbs Head, Berwickshire on 22 February. The two airmen's conversation was the most open yet and noted by the M-Room *listeners* as follows:

Berger: 'He (the interrogating officer) also enquired about the bombing apparatus.'

Hegemann: 'Only you mustn't give it away that it is something for the bombs. Otherwise, they might still want to photograph it… They have just shot down a machine in which *X-Gerät* is installed, and they can try it out as much as they like, for it is so secret that only he knows about it or the crew knows it and if the crew keep their mouths shut, they'll never find it out. They can try it out and examine it as much as they like. It is a sort of apparatus that they will never find out.'

Berger: 'Is it an aiming apparatus?'

Hegemann: 'No, it is not an aiming apparatus, it is an apparatus in which the bombs are hung, that is the bombs hang in it and it's a contraption which hangs behind the wireless operator and the wireless operator switches it on. When the aviator has started and on flying away … there are several transmitters in Germany and you fly according to the landscape left and right, only in bad weather. It is in fact, a bad weather apparatus. And Peilanlage (*listeners* comment: a direction-finding installation?) is made – and so a current is sent down from a machine, downwards, then you know whether you are over a village or a town, or towards the objective which you are trying to reach. And when you are over this, the order comes from over – over this 'guiding ray' (*Leitstrahl*) to the *X-Gerät* and so the bombs drop quite automatic.'

Berger: 'I have never heard anything about this.'

Hegemann: 'A grand thing. In peace time we flew round about Brunn often enough with this damned apparatus. You have to do nothing, only first you have to set your course. That is one to do, they drop out on their own. Over there they press the key, then the bombs drop out. Well, when this comes over here, there's a lovely lot of fog about, their eyes will pop out of their heads with astonishment.'

It is clear now with hindsight, that Hegemann was talking about the link between the new *Knickebein* and the *Lorenz* landing system. He was clearly alluding to the fact that the system was well hidden and was not an aiming device for the aircrew, but an automatic all-weather system for dropping bombs controlled by radio transmissions in Germany.

This is almost certainly the information provided by Denys Felkin to R.V. Jones in early 1940. AI1(k) and Jones clearly had a breakthrough and they were starting to understand the *Knickebein* bombing system, but more information was needed, especially with regard to *X-Gerät*. Therefore, the RAF interrogators continued to question further new arrivals at Trent Park and Jones met with Denys Felkin at a club in Bath, where the two men quietly discussed the problem and the need for further intelligence from the Luftwaffe prisoners.

On 4 March 1940, Jones reported that in his opinion, the Luftwaffe had a new bombing apparatus involving the application of pulse radio technology, but there appeared to be confusion in the minds of Luftwaffe prisoners, who were confusing two separate systems – the *Knickebein* system and the *Lorenz* blind-landing apparatus. Some even confused the system with a form of radio altimeter, scanning the ground and giving a position from reflected obstacles with enough accuracy for bombing.

The first *X-Gerät* system with the intersecting radio beams, was, in the mind of R.V. Jones, probably an automatic bomb release system and the significance of the X in *X-Gerät,* indicated a targeting system (i.e. X marks the spot). *X-Gerät* translated to X-Device or X-Apparatus and this caused some confusion when the later newer system was also referred to in the same manner.

AI1(k) Intelligence report No. 28/1940 signed by Felkin and dated 7 March 1940, describes the information given by the crew of a Heinkel III (1H+AK) of 2/KG26. It was shot down on 27 February and the crew of four were detained.

The very lengthy report gives a lot of information, but it notes that the observer of the aircraft – Unteroffizier Hermann Jonas, stated that he relied on dead reckoning for his navigation, backed up by checking with radio beacons and on his last flight, he used the beacon at Hornum. He gave details of another beacon at Norden, but his wireless operator (A41) – Feldwebel Karl Henrici – said it was not a satisfactory beacon for taking bearings.

Another wireless operator from a separate crew, the report noted, (A24 Unteroffizier Heckt of 2/KuFIGr506) stated there were two UKW transmitters at Borkum, one with a beam direction of 267 degrees and one of about 20 degrees. On one occasion, he said they flew from Lubuck over the Bay of Helgoland until at 3,000 feet and thirty miles out, the northerly beam from Borkum was picked-up. They flew along this to Borkum, then instead of landing, they flew along the westerly radio beam (on 267 degrees) which was the stronger of the two. They continued along this beam for about ninety miles. The northerly beam (20 degrees), he declared, was about six miles wide at a distance of forty miles and quite easy to find.

Another UKW transmitter was identified by Feldwebel Henrici, who confirmed all of the information given by Unteroffizier Walter Heckt. This second one was at Rantum and this also had a beam that pointed westwards, but Henrici said the Borkum beams were to define the German frontier and prevent their own aircraft landing on foreign territory.

It is clear Denys Felkin believed this was very important information and his report amounted to seven pages of A4 paper.

R.V. Jones heard nothing new for some days, but he did see an interesting entry on a piece of paper recovered from debris taken from the Heinkel III (1H+AC) of Stab II/KG26. That machine had been shot down on 3 April 1940, coming down in the sea off Whitby. The crew of five were very experienced and included the Gruppenkommandeur Oberstleutnant Hans Hefele, Leutnant Rudolf Behnisch (pilot), Leutnant Georg Kemper (observer), Unteroffiziers Albert Weber (wireless operator) and Alfred Bachle (mechanic – flight engineer).

The recovered paperwork had been passed to AI1(k) and Felkin showed it to R.V. Jones. The translated paper stated:

> Navigational aid: Radio beacons working on Beacon Plan A. Additionally from 0600 hours Beacon Duhnen. Light Beacon after dark. Radio Beacon *Knickebein* from 0600 hours on 315 degrees.

In his post-war book, R.V. Jones states that ordinary radio beams were used as standard navigational aids for observers, but if attacking a target in England, the bearings for the beams would lie somewhere to the east, between 45 and 135 degrees. The stated *Knickebein* beacon in this intelligence was different and 315 degrees pointing north-west. Jones deduced the 315 degrees was some kind of a beacon beam, set to transmit in that direction for that day. The question was why?

On 5 March 1940, transcript SRA44 detailed a chat between a number of crewmen. One man believed to be Feldwebel Karl Henrici, referred to *X-Gerät* and stated:

> 'Only those above know all about it, one merely knows how to handle it. Berketsch – I know him, that is the second man on the machine. We were told most particularly to be careful about anything we said, should we be taken prisoner, as the smallest thing may betray something!'

As we have already seen in an earlier chapter, on 12 March 1940, AI1(k) intelligence report No. 31/1940 gave intelligence relating to a Heinkel III of 1/KG30 which crashed into the sea off Wick in Scotland on 8 March. The crew were sadly killed, but a satchel was found floating in the sea and recovered by HMS *Griffin*. This contained various interesting papers, with some relating to wireless and direction finding. These were sent to AI1(e) for evaluation, but in the words of the report:

'Most interesting of which is a description of the Ultra short-wave landing apparatus and gives particulars for connecting this up and tuning it in, and shows photos of the apparatus, including the visual indicator.'

Another piece of paper gave frequencies for radio beacons at Jever, Hornum and Borken.

SRA50, dated 28 March, detailed a discussion in an M-Room between airman A44, believed to be Feldwebel Franz Schnee, a wounded observer of a 2/KG26 Heinkel III (1H+GK) shot down by fighters off Tynemouth on 3 February 1940; and A46 – Feldwebel Ernst Brieler, the wounded pilot of a Heinkel III from 1/Aufkir. Gr. Ob. d.l., also shot down by fighters on 7 March off Aberdeen. The two men discussed how they were shot down before Schnee asked Brieler:

Schnee: 'Did he tell you about the *X-Gerät*?' (Meaning the interrogating officer…)
Brieler: 'Here they know more than I do. I know nothing about it.'
Schnee: 'I knew nothing about it either.'

It is clear that by a process of elimination, Felkin and his AI1(k) team were reducing the number of Geschwader and Staffeln likely to be operating with this secret equipment. It was also possible that only selected machines in KG26 were using the *X-Gerät* system and not every member of that unit knew about its existence and operation.

The crew of the Stab II/KG26 Heinkel from which the piece of paper detailing the beacon information originated, were less than forthcoming with information. On 11 April, SRA61 notes that A47, an Oberstleutnant Gruppen-Kommandeur – almost certainly Hans Hefele from this crew and A48, a Leutnant pilot (the machines pilot Rudolf Benisch), were recorded discussing their recent interrogations:

Benisch: 'This is only a temporary camp. We remain here until we have been squeezed dry. I tell them fairy tales when I am asked about anything.'

Hefele: 'He (the interrogating officer) asked me what was the speed of our machine. I said 400 kph There is no harm in saying that, because they knew it before. I won't tell these fellows anything new here. I told him there was no such thing as a Stab Staffel as a formation on its own.'

> Benisch: 'Here they have got a complete Heinkel from the Stab Staffel. He told me that they got the machine intact. The FuG 10 was in it too.'

The FuG 10 was a radio transceiver used by the *Lorenz* blind-landing system among other things. The aircraft alluded to was that of Stab/KG26 (1H+JA) which came down intact at Humbie near Edinburgh, on 28 October 1939. Leutnant Rolf Niehoff had been the observer in this crew, but as already stated, he does not appear to have given any information about the bombing or navigational systems on board the aircraft.

AI1(k) continued to press the airmen for information while listening in on their conversations. According to transcript SRA65, dated 17 April 1940, Hefele and Benisch were joined by another leutnant pilot, this one believed to have been Kurt Weigel of 6/KG26. Weigel had made a forced landing in his Heinkel III at RAF Wick on 8 April, with a dead wireless operator and mechanic. They had been subjected to a fighter attack. The recorded conversation stated:

> Weigel: 'He (the interrogation officer) went for a walk with me this morning. He asked me why we use the calculation tables and what is an *X-Gerät*. I said, I knew nothing about the calculation tables and that the *X-Gerät* is FuG 10. He also asked me about Gamma *Gerät*.'
>
> Hefele: 'Gamma-*Gerät* is a sound detector for U-boats.'

Oberstleutnant Hefele appears to have still been trying to divert the interrogators, as Gamma-*Gerät* was actually a large artillery piece. However, it is clear that Weigel had linked *X-Gerät* to the FuG 10 radio and thereby to the *Lorenz* system. This was an important advance for Air Intelligence.

R.V. Jones continued to investigate and speculate on *X-Gerät,* believing it was linked to intersecting radio beams. His hypothesis gained traction when he had lunch with Aeronautical Engineer Arthur Edgar Woodward-Nutt (in charge of Air Defence Research Section).

Woodward-Nutt told Jones that there had been a rumour from the French, that the Germans had been setting up some kind of a radio beam station on their frontier. Radio specialists at Farnborough had been very surprised by the narrow width of the beam they thought could be broadcast by these new transmitters. If correct, the beams would require only a short wavelength, but this meant they would not bend sufficiently with the earth's curvature. After speaking to

Woodward-Nutt, Jones spoke to a number of radio specialists about radio wave propagation (the bending of radio waves in the earth's atmosphere) and it was soon deduced, that this was possible and there might be a way to counteract the German radio beams.

As we have already seen in an earlier chapter, Intelligence report No. 54/1940, on 28 April 1940, noted that there had been a reference in some recovered documents to something called 'X Korps Wotan'. An unidentified prisoner said Wotan was probably a code name for a section of 10th Fliegerkorps, but this would soon prove to be something very different.

Another AI1(k) Intelligence report No. 109/1940, dated 24 May 1940, raised the issue of radio beacons and *Knickebein*. The report cited a number of documents recovered by a Royal Navy vessel and apparently belonging to a Heinkel III (1H+AC) of II/KG26. The papers contained a log and a diary which contained an entry:

> '5/3/40 Two thirds of Staffel on leave. In afternoon studied about *Knickebein*, collapsible boats etc.'

The log highlighted the word *Knickebein*, which had been encountered before in relation to radio beacons, but no radio beacon with this name had ever been identified and therefore, AI1(k) deduced this could be the code name for a special type of beacon or device.

Work continued to interrogate newly arrived prisoners of war, but only three aircraft were shot down over or around Britain's coastline in May 1940 and these were not aircraft likely to carry the new system. The lack of prisoners and aircraft to examine was due to the invasion of Norway and then the Blitzkrieg assault across the Low Countries.

In June the situation was exacerbated by the retreat from France and Dunkirk, but that changed on the night of 18/19 June, when a number of Heinkel's from KG4 were shot down over Britain.

R.V. Jones says he received information that the Heinkel III's of KG4 and KG27 (actually KG26?) were almost certainly fitted with the *X-Gerät* apparatus. This information almost certainly came from a decrypted Enigma message intercepted on 5 June 1940. That message when decoded a week later stated:

> Chief Signals Officer Fliegerkorps IV at 1455 hours: Knickebein Kleve ist auf punkt 53 Grad. 24 minuten nord und ein grad west ein Gerichtet.

(Translated as Kniekenbein Kleve is 53 degrees and 24 minutes north and 1 degree west).

The decrypted and translated Enigma message which could not be shared with anyone else, not even Denys Felkin, was one of the final pieces of the jigsaw Jones needed. It also appears to have been connected to the paperwork recovered from the Stab II/KG26 Heinkel in early April. This was confirming Jones's suspicions about German radio beams.

R.V. Jones contacted Felkin at Trent Park and asked him to check with any recent bomber crew prisoners on this subject, while closer examinations were made of captured enemy equipment. A full reassessment of the results of the technical examination of the earlier captured Heinkel III (brought down during one of the Firth of Forth raids in October 1939), found the *Lorenz* blind-landing system, to be much more sensitive than required for just a blind-landing approach. In addition, Jones now knew the radio frequencies of the system.

On 20 June, another unidentified prisoner of war told Denys Felkin that *Knickebein* was a bomb-dropping device involving two intersecting radio beams. The prisoner claimed to be anti-war and drew diagrams and sketches of the equipment for the interrogator. This man almost certainly came from one of the five KG4 aircraft brought down on the night of 18/19 June. Eleven prisoners were detained, three were wounded, one severely, but those fit and eligible for interrogation included Oberleutnant Ulrich Jordan (pilot), 38-year-old Major Dietrich Freiherr von Massenbach (an observer and the Gruppen-Kommandeur), Oberleutnant Joachim von Arnim (observer); Leutnants Hans-Jurgen Bachhaus and Erich Simon (both pilots) and wireless operators Oberfeldwebel Leimer and Unteroffizier Kuhn.

On 21 June, R.V. Jones was summoned to Downing Street to present his findings and theories to Winston Churchill and a distinguished panel. Scientist Henry Tizard had reservations that the Germans were using radio beams and believed it was all a hoax to divert British attention. Others members of the panel even doubted the need for such electronics, although if they knew the accuracy of RAF bombing at the time, they would surely have been converted to the electronic theory.

R.V. Jones gave a lengthy presentation detailing the fact they knew of two transmitting stations and had found evidence in a wrecked aircraft, together with the very precise *Lorenz* equipment.

Churchill was so impressed with the young scientist he ordered the use of an aircraft to try and identify these *X-Gerät* radio signals. Over the coming days, an Avro Anson detected a number of beams and one appeared to be directed at the Rolls-Royce engine works in Derby.

Further Enigma encrypted messages identified new transmitters being set-up at Brest and Cherbourg. The code names *Knickebein* and *Wotan* were used in the messages indicating the transmitters use. (Wotan was a one-eyed god, associated with Freya, a name linked to German radar. These links were not lost on Jones, especially after the previous intelligence report cited the name X-Wotan.)

On 27 July 1940, Denys Felkin circulated a diagram recovered from a German bomber which stated that for long-range raids, the *Knickebein* had to be tuned by specialist teams of engineers. On the same day, another Enigma signal was decoded at Bletchley Park and found to be a request from KG54 for such a specialist team to attend their airfields. KG54 operated mainly over the south-west of Britain from airfields in the Normandy peninsula and coupled together with the information on the transmitters at Brest and Cherbourg, it appeared the unit was preparing for beam operations over Britain.

In early September, the Luftwaffe started a series of night-time raids. On the night of the seventh, Jones recalls being woken by a telephone call from Bletchley Park. They had a new decoded Enigma report which mentioned beams and one which had a width of eight to ten seconds of arc. This meant the beam was no wider than twenty yards at a range of 200 miles. Then there was a tantilising comment that *X-Gerät* was being fitted to a Heinkel call sign 6N+LK of KG100. It was now clear to Jones that *Knickebein* and *X-Gerät* were two different systems and he needed to develop a method to counteract these beams.

During the height of the Battle of Britain, the information continued to arrive via the prisoners at AI1(k).

On 15 September, Intelligence log No. 526 gave further details of documents recovered from five Heinkel III's of KG26, shot down on 11 September. One aircraft had a signals table for the day, similar to previous W/T Signals tables recovered from other KG26 aircraft. The new table gave the KG26 radio frequency, the Geschwader Kommodore's call sign and those of the other Stab-Staffel aircraft. A notable omission in this table from previous documents, was the exclusion of all III/KG26 and I/KG100 aircraft – this was possibly due to their work as *X-Gerät* aircraft.

Intelligence log No. 615, dated 27 September 1940, discussed a wide number of Luftwaffe matters, but on page three there was a section titled 'Seeing in the dark.' This report stated a very senior in rank prisoner, had discussed an apparatus for seeing in the blackout from an aircraft over Berlin. He claimed that despite the blackout, they could see the city as if it were illuminated. He went on to claim that the equipment had been fitted to certain reconnaissance aircraft for testing.

AI1(k) noted that this story reflected an earlier German Propaganda Ministry account about a secret weapon called *Cloud X-ray*. This was allegedly fitted next to the pilot's seat so he could see through fog and cloud. It was pointed out to the prisoner by the interrogator, that it was curious why German propaganda would discuss details of such an important weapon which must have been secret. The unnamed officer agreed with his interrogator.

The *Knickebein* radio beams were given the very apt code name 'Headache' by British intelligence, and attempts to block them were naturally given the codename 'Aspirin'. The small twin engine Avro Anson aircraft was fitted with receivers and flew around the United Kingdom in a bid to identify the beams and their bearings. After identifying the beams, a deceptive false beam far away from the actual target was broadcast from a British transmitter, in a bid to deceive the bombers and make them drop their bombs upon open countryside.

On the afternoon of 30 October 1940, AI1(k) obtained another piece of the *Knickebein* jigsaw puzzle when a JU88 (L1+GS) of 8/LG1 was shot down by Spitfires and made a forced landing near Ely in Cambridgeshire. The four-man crew was captured, but one of them had a personal diary which contained the longitude and latitude positions and frequencies of a number of *Knickebein* transmitters across France and Germany. The reports did not disclose the name of the diary owner – but it was likely to have been either the wireless operator Obergefreiter Paul Fliger, who was wounded, or the observer – Unteroffizier Anton Brommer.

Although unclear, it appears documents and maps in the aircraft showed possible directional beacon beams to London and possible targets. Other information led AI1(k) to deduce that the beams from the *Knickebein* transmitters at Dieppe and Cherbourg, had a width of between 200 and 300 meters over London.

The newer *X-Gerät* proved to be much more difficult to counter than *Knickebein*. Initial attempts were not so successful, but the final mystery was identified on 6 November 1940 at 0449 hours, when a Heinkel III of 1/KG100 became hopelessly lost and made a forced landing on the foreshore at West Bay, Bridport, Dorset. Three of the crew survived and waded ashore to captivity, although they thought they were in France. One crewman – Feldwebel Paul was killed.

When it was realised that this was an aircraft from an elite pathfinder unit, efforts were made to pull the Heinkel ashore, but this nearly became an abject failure. The attending local Army officer was outranked by a Royal Navy captain on an attendant ship. The naval officer decided to pull the aircraft off the beach and tie it onto the ship for transport to a facility. Unfortunately, the ropes broke and the Heinkel sank in deeper water offshore. Suitably chastised, the Royal Navy gave up and the Army eventually brought the aircraft ashore at low-tide.

The aircraft, as expected by Air Intelligence, was found to be equipped with the new *X-Gerät* system which was quickly salvaged and sent for scientific examination. As a result, new jamming equipment was developed and future raids were affected, but not before the terrible raid on Coventry on 14 November 1940. Eventually the electronic system was defeated with an extra misleading beam.

In his autobiography, R.V. Jones lamented what he saw as a failure by other intelligence sections to link the information, his theories and the information provided by Felkin's AI1(k) team. In the autumn of 1940, Denys Felkin's team identified a series of code words given by the Luftwaffe to various targets, but they failed to prevent the terrible bombing of Coventry in November 1940.

The German scientists soon created a new system called *Y- Gerät* and in time, this too was counteracted by R.V. Jones and his team of scientists. There has, however, been debate over the decades, with some Luftwaffe crews claiming the British efforts to counteract them were not as successful as the British claimed.

Although the scientists must take credit for a good share of the work against *X-Gerät*, Denys Felkin and his team at Air Intelligence were instrumental in identifying the background and obtaining the initial human intelligence to defeat the Luftwaffe's bombers.

Chapter 14

The Start of the Battle of Britain

The Battle of Britain brought large numbers of enemy aircraft and consequently, increasing numbers of prisoners of war.

In the early hours of 1 July, a Heinkel 115 (M2+CL) of 3/106 was operating off the North Yorkshire coast on a minelaying operation, when both engines failed for unknown reasons. The pilot successfully landed the seaplane on the North Sea and the crew evacuated the machine for their dinghy. It is believed the crew managed to send an emergency radio call because a Heinkel 59 'Red Cross' aeroplane (D-ASAM) of Seenoflug.Kdo.3 was scrambled from Germany to look for the crew.

The three-man crew of the Heinkel 115 were picked up by a British ship and taken to Grimsby with the rescue crew completely unaware of this.

During the early morning light, the rescue aircraft flew back and forth near a passing British convoy off the North Yorkshire coastline and three Spitfires of No. 72 Squadron based at Acklington intercepted the Heinkel 59. The Spitfires shot the float plane down despite its Red Cross markings and the crew of four were picked up from the sea by an escorting naval vessel.

The crew are reported to have vehemently protested the alleged breach of Red Cross neutrality, but it was all in vain and they were taken ashore into captivity. Two of the crew were found in possession of Red Cross Ausweis passes, claiming the protection of the Geneva Convention, but they were still led into captivity.

The shooting down of Red Cross marked aircraft was a delicate issue for the RAF, but Air Intelligence had for some time considered the aircraft to be rescue aircraft which spied upon shipping and reported convoy movements for follow-up attacks. This, if correct, was a breach of the Convention and therefore the aircraft could not claim immunity (rather like hiding ammunition in a hospital).

The intelligence report noted that the identity disks of two of the four airmen, corresponded with those known to fly aircraft from 1/106 and 3/906; the assumption therefore being this machine was at least, partly crewed by combat airmen.

The Luftwaffe activity around Britain started to increase and at 1700 hours on 2 July, a Heinkel III (5J+EL) of 3/KG4 attracted intense anti-aircraft fire over Newcastle. The aircraft was then intercepted by a flight of Spitfires, but escaped into the cloud layer with an injured air mechanic – Feldwebel Alfred Weber. The crew headed south and attacked the oil tanks near Hull, but three more Spitfires attacked them and the pilot, Oberfeldwebel Hermann Raisbach, was forced to ditch the aircraft in the sea off Hull. The four-man crew were rescued, with the wireless operator Oberfeldwebel Rudolf Ernst being wounded. The pilot and the observer, Oberleutnant Friedrich Koch, had escaped injury thanks to the armour plating fitted behind the pilot's seat. Air Intelligence noted that the crewmen were experienced, with the pilot and observer having seen action in Spain, Poland, Norway and France.

On the afternoon of 3 July, 8/KG30 sent a number of Junkers 88's to north-east Scotland. One aircraft (4D+IS) was attacked by British fighters and crashed into the sea off Dyce in Aberdeenshire. Three of the crew were killed, but the observer – Unteroffizier Rupert Herlinehner survived, although his condition is unclear.

A second Junkers 88 (4D+NS) was also shot down by fighters off the Aberdeenshire coastline, the crew being killed. One body was picked up from the North Sea, but various documents allowed the intelligence officers to identify the parent unit of both aircraft.

Further south on the same day, a Dornier 17 (3Z+GS) of 8/KG77 conducted a lone attack on the fighter base at RAF Kenley, before it was intercepted a short distance away over Tonbridge by Hurricanes. The preliminary interrogation report No. 161/1940, states the aircraft was attacked by the three Hurricanes at 8,000 feet and headed for the clouds. The air mechanic, Unteroffizier Waldermar Theilig, was killed in the attack, while follow-up attacks injured the pilot, Unteroffizier Richard Brandes, and seriously wounded the observer, Oberleutnant Hans-Georg Gallion. The pilot made a forced landing in a hop field at Paddock Wood, Kent and the wireless operator, Obergefreiter Erich Hofmann, was killed.

An assessment of the wreckage, the cockpit area, the personal effects of the crew and their documents by the preliminary interrogator, found a good number of important items.

One of the crew had a hotel bill for a stay in Dusseldorf dated 22 June 1940, while a map had a track marked on it from Berck. A scrap of blood-stained paper had a list of place names which seemed to correspond with the track marked on the map.

The Dornier 17 was noted as having six machine guns in various locations and was somewhat better defended than other similar models. The pilot's seat was armoured and there was a semi-circle of armour placed behind the wireless operator's position.

In a detailed report, the preliminary interrogator noted that eight 50-kilogram bombs had been jettisoned just before the aircraft crashed. The radial engines were in good condition and almost certainly thoroughly inspected by staff from AI1(g). The unit markings were noted as a white shield bearing a black eagle on both sides of the aircrafts nose.

Six days later, at the end of the report, signed by Flight Lieutenant Guy Jepson on behalf of Felkin, there was an additional comment noting that the aircraft had dropped six live 50 kilo bombs in the neighbourhood of RAF Kenley. Nine other bombs had in fact been jettisoned just before it crashed, therefore the complete bomb load was fifteen 50-kilogram bombs. Why the full load had not been dropped on Kenley was not speculated upon by the officer.

On 4-5 July, two more Heinkel III's from 4/KG54 (B3+DM) and 8/KG1 were brought down in Dorset and near Folkestone. Three of the crew in Dorset were killed and the fourth man – wireless operator Unteroffizier Heinz Karwelat was wounded and hospitalised. Various documents were found to assist the AI1(k) interrogators, including a KG54 logbook found on the body of the observer.

Three of the 8/KG1 crew from V4+GS died when they were shot down by a Spitfire and came down in the English Channel off Folkestone. The pilot, Oberfeldwebel Hermann Frischmuth, and the observer, Unteroffizier Gottfried Wagner, were wounded and captured. They disclosed that this was the crews first war flight over England.

On 8 July, the first Messerschmitt 109E to come down on English soil arrived at Blabdean Hill, Elham in East Kent. The event resulted in a report No. 169/1940, once again signed by Flight Lieutenant Guy Jepson in place of Denys Felkin.

According to the report, the pilot, Leutnant Johann Bohm, of 4/JG51, was very talkative from the start and told the interrogator his Messerschmitt had a complete circle of armour plating built into the fuselage behind his seat. This had yet to be confirmed by the inspectors from AI1(g) at the time the report was written.

Johann Bohm told his interrogator that he was in a formation of four ME109's flying in line astern and chasing a Spitfire, but other Spitfires were climbing towards them from below. He was hit in the engine by one of these fighters and went into a dive, reaching speeds of 700 kph (435 mph). The Spitfires followed him down, firing continually until he eventually pulled out at 1,500 feet.

Bohm freely discussed his air fighting tactics. He said he normally only used his four machine guns against fighters, but with bombers, he started with machine guns and when in close, used his cannon. He said this was not a standard practice and other Staffel pilots used the complete opposite tactic.

The document analysis team would have been very happy, with a diary taken from Johann Bohm which contained a full list of his Staffel including aircraft works numbers, fuselage numbers and pilot names and ranks. This included his Staffel Kapitan Oberleutnant Fozo. (Josef Fozo, who would claim fifteen victories by the end of the Battle of Britain and twenty-four by the time he was grounded due to injuries in 1942. He survived the war.) Twelve aircraft and pilots were listed, leading the Air Intelligence staff to conclude there were three reserve aircraft from the standard nine aircraft Staffel. Two types of Messerschmitt 109's listed the E1 and E3 types.

Leutnant Bohm had been a member of the air force for two years and at the outbreak of the war he had been with the fighter training school at Schliesheim. He was posted to his current unit on 6 December 1939 and had since completed ninety-five war flights. The emblem of the 4th Staffel JG51 – a raven with a red umbrella under its wing was noted on the fuselage – tail side of the German cross.

This amount of intelligence from one aircraft and its pilot was unusual, especially as the Luftwaffe and the Wehrmacht fully expected to win the war within a few weeks or months!

Within a few hours of Leutnant Johann Bohm's arrival with his ME109, another Messerschmitt 109 arrived at Sandwich in Kent. This machine belonging to 3/LG2 was piloted by Leutnant Albert Striberny and shot down by RAF fighters. He bailed out as the aircraft plunged into the ground and disintegrated. Unlike Bohm, Striberny refused to give any information other than his own details and that he was quartered at St. Etienne near his base near Boulogne. Very little was left of the aircraft and there was little of intelligence value, but the units yellow Mickey Mouse motif was found on parts of what remained of the rear fuselage.

On 9 July, yet another Red Cross marked Heinkel 59 (D-ASUO), this one from Seenotflu.Kdo.1 was brought down. This Heinkel 59 was subject to a very detailed three-page intelligence report No. 189/1940 signed by Denys Felkin. Like most intelligence reports, this was also marked 'Secret', but its contents were somewhat contentious and would not make happy reading for some parties.

Above left and above right: Late Second World War images of Group Captain Samuel Denys Felkin, commanding officer of AI1(k) Trent Park & Chief RAF Interrogator. (Images courtesy of Nigel Parker)

The Salt Tower, Tower of London. Three to four rooms were used to house POWs with hidden microphones wired back to a main M-Room. The exact location of the M-Room is unknown, but the prisoner's rooms were on top of one another. The lowest floor, a Tudor dungeon may have housed the M-Room and was accessible via its own door. The prisoner's rooms still contain the graffiti of Tudor prisoners, but nothing from the Luftwaffe. (Author's Own)

Salt Tower was in the south-east corner of the inner curtain wall. The Broad Arrow Tower with its own microphoned rooms, (unfortunately covered in scaffolding in this image) was just along the wall. The block between them is the New Royal Armouries, used to house POWs. (Author's Own)

A view from outside the White Tower looking at, from left to right: The Old Hospital Block and the New Royal Armouries. The two towers were part of the wall behind these barrack blocks. The Salt Tower is behind the trees in the distance. (Author's Own)

An image of Trent Park in the 1930s. (Copyright holder untraceable)

Trent Park in 1960, similar to how it looked in 1940–1945, but without the sentries & fencing. (Courtesy of Trent Park Museum Trust)

A Feldwebel detained in the week prior to 21 September 1940 is helped from an Army HQ probably heading for Trent Park and AI1(k), assuming he is not wounded. Although the identity of the Feldwebel is unknown, the only uninjured captured man of that rank between 16–20 September 1940 was Erich Kalowski the radio operator of a Heinkel 115 of KuFIGr 506; shot down off the Northumberland coast on the sixteenth. (Courtesy of Historic Military Press)

Oberleutnant Werner Voigt of 4/JG 3, captured on 8 October 1940. (Courtesy of Historic Military Press)

Intelligence Officer Flight Lieutenant Michael Golovine MBE examines the wreckage of a Junkers 88 which crashed at Stocks Lane, East Wittering, on 20 November 1940. Although after the end of the Battle of Britain it is a perfect example of a crash site assessment by an intelligence officer. (Courtesy of Historic Military Press)

Summer 1940: Oberleutnant Franz von Werra of JG 3 in the cockpit of his Me 109 and his pet lion cub Simba, which caused him so many problems when confronted by Squadron Leader Denys Felkin at Trent Park. (Courtesy of the Andy Saunders Collection)

A post escape publicity shot of von Werra. (Courtesy of the Andy Saunders Collection)

Above and below: Two images of Franz von Werra's Messerschmitt 109E at Winchet Hill, south of Marden in Kent. The aircraft has been partly camouflaged to protect it from enemy fighters and placed under guard, while AI1(g) examine it. (Images courtesy of the Andy Saunders Collection)

Airmen examine Heinkel III G1+DM of 4/KG 55 on East Wittering Beach, Sussex. The aircraft was brought down by Spitfires of No. 602 Squadron, killing four of the crew. The pilot, Leutnant Albert Metzger, made a successful forced landing despite his injuries. (Wing-leader photo archive)

He III G1+BH of 1/KG 55 brought down on 25 September at Ballard Down, Dorset. Four of the crew survived. The preliminary interrogator or site assessor appears to have missed the white lion on their report which was sent to AI1(k). (Wing-leader photo archive)

Feldwebel Theodor Metzner (2nd left) a pilot with 8/KG 55. His Heinkel III (G1+CS) came down near Newbury, Berkshire on 29 July 1940. Metzner and his air mechanic, Unteroffizier Kurt Bocker were captured soon after landing, but two of his crew, Gefreiters Morgenthal & Ostheimer, evaded capture for two days. His observer, Feldwebel Josef Markl, evaded for a mammoth nine days. (Wing-leader photo archive)

Hauptmann Walter Kienzle was attached to Stab/JG 26 and flying as Geschwader Kommandeur Adolf Galland's wingman on 30 September 1940. He was being evaluated as a possible Gruppen Kommandeur when he was shot down by a Hurricane of No. 303 (Polish) Squadron and seriously wounded. He was treated in hospital and had a leg amputated. He was later sent to a POW camp where he met up with von Werra and Steinhilper. (Wing-leader photo archive)

Above left: Oberleutnant Anton Stangl, Staffel Kapitan of 5/JG54. He is believed to have collided with another Messerschmitt 109E flown by Leutnant Herbert Strasser of 7/JG52 on 1 September 1940. Stangl's 109 came down at Ruckinge near Ashford, Kent. (Wing-leader photo archive)

Above right: Leutnant Herbert Strasser of 7/JG 52 casually sitting on the wheel of his Messerschmitt 109E in France. He is the man believed to have collided with Anton Stangl of 5/JG 54 on 1 September 1940 while in combat with Hurricanes. Both men survived and Strasser's Me 109 crashed to earth at Winchelsea Bridge, Rye, East Sussex. (Wing-leader photo archive)

Below: The stranded Me 109E of Oberleutnant Paul Temme, Grupp Adjutant of 1/JG 2, brought down on New Salts Farm, Shoreham, East Sussex on 13 August 1940. Note the Gruppe Adjutant chevron. The aircraft bears three victory bars on the upper rudder next to the swastika. Temme was one of the first recognised 'Aces' brought down and interrogated. When captured, he had five confirmed victories. (Wing-leader photo archive)

Above: Me 109E of Leutnant Werner Bartels, Technical Officer of Stab III/JG 26, on North Down, Margate, Kent. He was shot down by a Spitfire on 24 July 1940 and seriously wounded. He spent time at the Royal Herbert Hospital in Woolwich before being interrogated. In the image RAF technical personnel inspect the aircraft, while the censor has chosen to remove the Technical Officer insignia from any published image. (Wing leader photo archive)

Below: Oberfeldwebel Artur Dau of 7/JG 51 is given a drink and a cigarette by his captors. He was brought down by a combination of AA fire and Hurricanes, coming to earth at Poulton Farm, South Alkham, Kent on 28 August 1940. Dau was a 'difficult' prisoner and did not give much to his interrogators at Trent Park. (Wing leader photo archive)

Oberleutnant Hasso von Wedel of Stab/JG 3 was a very interesting character. Shot down at Ruckinge, Kent on 15 September 1940, he was 47-years-old and a former First World War pilot. He should not have been on the front line, but was allowed to fly operationally to gain experience of combat conditions in the Second World War. Interviewed by C.H. Brooks at Trent Park, he formed part of a lengthy report concerning the attitudes of captured Luftwaffe airmen. (Wing leader photo archive)

Unteroffizier Gerhard (Gerd) Kemen of 1/JG 26, shot down on 14 August 1940 near Dover. He was very badly wounded according to the preliminary interrogation report and not expected to recover, but despite this, he was interrogated. He did recover, but his injuries necessitated his repatriation in 1943. This image shows him in a Feldwebel's uniform upon return to Germany. (Wing leader photo archive)

Werner Molders and his brother Viktor (3rd and 6th from the left), both of JG 51. AI1(k) are alleged to have believed they had captured the Kommodore of JG 51 before they realised it was his 'little' brother. (Courtesy of Chris Goss)

Above left and above right: Haupt Joachim Schlichting Stab III/JG 27 and Haupt Joachim Roth 9/KG 76. Both men were seriously injured and treated at the Royal Herbert Military Hospital, Woolwich. (Courtesy of Chris Goss)

Left and below: Leutnant Heinz Schnabel of 1/JG 3 & his Me 109E. He was treated at the Royal Herbert Hospital before his attempted escape in November 1941 with Harry Wappler. (Both courtesy of Chris Goss)

Above left: Leutnant Wolf Münschmeyer, pilot of Messerschmitt Me 110 C-4, (2S+-H), of 1/ZG2, which crashed at Beaties Farm, North Baddesley, Hampshire, at 1600 hours on 13 August 1940. Wolf Münschmeyer was seriously wounded and captured. (Courtesy of M. Mace)

Above right: A young Ulrich Steinhilper poses on a motorcycle in front of his Messerschmitt 109, probably in early 1940. As an Oberleutnant he was brought down at the end of the Battle of Britain and gives an account of his interrogation which is different to that of von Werra. (Wing leader photo archive)

Trent Park is currently undergoing an extensive renovation via The Trent Park Museum Trust. By 2026, the house will have a museum featuring the work undertaken during the Second World War. This recent image of one of the main ground floor rooms under renovation gives an idea of the scale and opulence of the house. (Courtesy of Trent Park Museum Trust)

Above left: At Trent Park, AI1(k) had a network of tunnels under the house which held a variety of store rooms, archives, offices and the M-Room listening positions. (Courtesy of Trent Park Museum Trust)

Above right: The main underground M-Room listening position photographed recently and undergoing renovation, prior to being re-furnished as it looked in 1940–1945 as a listening position. (Courtesy of Trent Park Museum Trust)

Trent Park in 2013 prior to its restoration project. The exterior has changed very little but by 2026 it will have a museum detailing the work of the Intelligence Services and Listeners during the Second World War. (Courtesy of Trent Park Museum Trust)

The Heinkel 59 had been looking for the pilot of a Messerschmitt 109E missing over the English Channel (Leutnant Hermann Striebel of II/JG51), when it was attacked at 2000 hours by Spitfires of No. 54 Squadron. The Heinkel being unarmed immediately alighted upon the water by the Goodwin Sands off Deal in Kent. The Walmer lifeboat was soon on the scene and towed the Heinkel away, beaching it near the lifeboat station on the shingle beach. The four-man crew were all registered as members of the Red Cross and immediately claimed immunity from detention and demanded release.

An AI1(k) preliminary interrogator's inspection found a detailed logbook on board the beached aircraft. This referred to a different Red Cross aircraft (D-AGUI) based at Trondheim in Norway. The entries in the logbook confirmed that the Seenostaffel was genuinely engaged in air-sea rescue work, although two entries in May and June indicated work carrying senior staff officers or supplies.

Two other entries detailed efforts to rescue RAF airmen, the rescue of Squadron Leader Doran on 30 April 1940 and a search off Stavanger for the crew of a downed Hudson the following day.

The logbook entry for Squadron Leader Doran, gave details of the search and location of the airman who was sighted in his dinghy with a second man seen swimming next to him. Having landed on the water, a rescue was attempted, but the man in the water had drowned. According to the log, artificial respiration in the Heinkel was unsuccessful. The man in the dinghy (Doran), had a chin wound, but refused first aid from his rescuers. (Doran had been flying a Bristol Blenheim from RAF Lossiemouth when he was shot down.)

The log entry for the 4 May, gave details of an unnamed, rescued '*English Staffel Fuhrer*' who had thanked the crew.

Various other flight details were recorded, including the transport of General Major Tittel and his adjutant from Bergen to Kristiansund on 5 June 1940. They had been bound for Trondheim, but due to fog they had diverted and the senior officer continued onwards by car.

The log indicated the 9 June was a very hectic day, with the crew making a number of flights and the next few days were also busy with the aircraft still being located in Norway. Their last flight, according to the logbook, was 15 June, when they transported wounded men to Mosjoen to the north of Trondheim.

On face value, this aircraft did appear to be a genuine Red Cross machine which had even rescued RAF airmen. The aircraft may well have had a secondary covert role as a reconnaissance machine, but the logbook, Red Cross documentation and the named RAF squadron leader all provided powerful evidence this Heinkel 59 was undertaking rescue work. While the RAF had brought down a number of these aircraft (and would do so in the future), it did not provide, on face value, a positive media message. Despite Denys Felkin's intelligence report, the RAF and the British government would continue to claim these aircraft were spying on convoys.

In early July 1940, the British continued to push merchant convoys through the English Channel and the Straits of Dover. The Luftwaffe continually tried to destroy and disrupt these convoys and on 10 July, a number of Dornier 17's, escorted by Messerschmitt 110's, tried to attack them. The result was the loss of a Messerschmitt 110 and a Dornier, three airmen being captured and three killed.

At lunch time on 11 July, three Messerschmitt 110's of 9/ZG76 were brought down in combat with RAF fighters over the sea off Portland, Dorset. One aircraft (M8+-T) crashed at Verne – its crew, which included Field Marshal Hermann Göring's nephew, were killed. A second ME110 came down in the sea off the Ney Breakwater at Portland and Leutnant Joachim Schroder was captured, but his gunner Gefreiter Franz Sorokoput was killed. The third aircraft (2N+EP) made a forced landing at Grange Heath near Lulworth. The crew tried to burn their papers and a soldier shot the pilot, Oberleutnant Gerhard Kadow, causing him serious injuries.

On the evening of 11 July, a Heinkel III of 2/KG55 (G1+LK) was shot down by fighters and made a forced landing on the east beach at Selsey in Sussex. The rear gunner and the air mechanic were killed, but the observer, wireless operator and pilot were detained with injuries. The pilot, Oberfeldwebel Erich Slotosch, was taken to hospital and a preliminary intelligence report submitted the following day. Slotosch would later be transferred upon recovery, not to Trent Park, but for unknown reasons to the London Cage (see later chapter).

Over the next few days, there was an increase in enemy aerial activity and this resulted in a number of downed aircraft and new prisoner arrivals.

According to Intelligence log No. 181/1940, on 13 July, a Dornier 17 of 2(F)/123 on a reconnaissance flight to Dorset was shot down by Hurricanes. The aircraft came down in the sea with the loss of the pilot and wireless operator, but the observer, Oberleutnant Max Graf Kesselstadt, was wounded and captured. According to the AI1(k) preliminary report signed off by Felkin, the observer had to undergo emergency surgery, but there was ample evidence in the papers recovered that the aircraft was based on Jersey in the Channel Islands.

The observers pay book showed him to belong to the 3rd Company of Fliegerrausbildungs-Regiment 41 at Frankort-Oder on 2 September 1939. From

3 to 14 June 1940, he was with the Erganzungs Aufklarrungs-staffel Ob.d.L and on 15 June posted to 2(F)/123.

The observer's diary began on 15 June 1940 and detailed his operational service to date with the unit. Continually flying Dornier 17's, the entry for 26 June, states JU88's had been promised. He arrived in Jersey on 1 July, making his first war flight on the third and his second flight the following day. He had been shopping in St Helier on the fifth, but reported two of their aircraft missing on 7 July.

Kesselstadt also listed a number of items he was going to send home to his parents and girlfriend. His parents were to receive tea, coffee, cigarettes, cigars, stockings, food and soap; while his girlfriend would receive similar items, as well as alcohol and cutlery knives.

Although we do not have details of Kesselstadt's subsequent interrogation post his hospital treatment, AI1(k) now had a firm foundation for their pre-interview preparations. Added to other information about this type of aircraft, the man's unit and even knowledge of the island of Jersey, it meant they stood a very good chance of getting this man to talk.

On 15 July, a Heinkel III (1H+EK) of 2/KG26 was shot down by a Spitfire whilst on a mission to bomb RAF Leuchars in Fife. The aircraft crashed into the sea off Peterhead and the four surviving crewmen (the air mechanic was killed), were picked up and taken into the fishing port of Fraserburgh two days later.

It appears the wireless operator, Obergefreiter Henrich Probst, was very talkative and intelligence report No. 192/1940 gives details of the information he supplied.

The report, signed by Felkin on 20 July, states that the wireless operator had a number of documents on him, which with 'judicious interrogation revealed his service career'. The prisoner admitted serving in the Luftwaffe for three years and gave details of his training. On 15 March 1940, he was sent to Konigsberg where he undertook blind-flying training until 20 April, then he joined KG26. Initially he was posted to the 4th Staffel and made five to six daylight raids on Norway, operating from the airfield at Fornebu.

Around the end of June 1940 or early July 1940, the whole 2nd Gruppe of KG26 – or rather what remained of it – was withdrawn from active operations for a period of rest, and may possibly have been disbanded. Certainly, the Gruppe had been on continuous operations since its mobilisation in August 1939 and it had suffered a good number of losses.

The prisoner was a newcomer to KG26 and told his interrogator that 1/KG26 were stationed at Kristiansund in southern Norway, while the whole of KG30 were based at Aalborg in Denmark. He also added that the airfield at Aalborg was covered in 'Stacks of "Satan" 1,800 kilo bombs', information that was gratefully received and certainly passed on for possible action; although prisoners over the winter of 1939-40 had mentioned a shortage of such large bombs.

The wireless operator was also in possession of a Shooting Record Book (air gunnery log). This detailed the tests he had undertaken at Tutow, which indicate five main groups, similar to tests undertaken by RAF air gunners during their training, with fixed machine guns at fixed targets, as well as moving targets and gun turrets set on a small railway like system. There was no apparent air-to-air training mentioned:

Group 1: Fixed stand to fixed target.
Group 2: Fixed stand to moving target.
Group 3: Moving stand to fixed target.
Group 4: Moving stand to moving target.
Group 5: Aircraft to fixed ground target.

The intelligence report also noted there was provision for training using clay pigeons, but this element had not been encountered by Air Intelligence before.

As usual, this information was analysed and assessed by AI1(k), before disseminating it to the relevant organisations and adding it to their growing library of information held by Trent Park.

Although the Luftwaffe were making a number of raids, these in many cases, were probing attacks and reconnaissance flights which were still gathering vital intelligence for the German planners.

On 21 July 1940, a Messerschmitt 110 (5F+CM) was shot down by Hurricanes from No. 238 Squadron and made a forced landing at Goodwood Home Farm near Chichester. The Messerschmitt had been tasked with taking photographs of southern England after leaving its base at Cherbourg.

Intelligence log No. 195/1940 noted that the two crewmen pilot, Oberleutnant Friedrich Karl Runde and his wireless operator, Feldwebel Willi Baden, had been injured in the action. Initial assessment and interrogation failed to establish the aircraft's unit straight away, although one of the crew had been a member of 1(F)/124.

Intelligence also ascertained from at least one of the airmen, that they recently had a good meal at Fouquet's restaurant in Paris which cost the princely sum of 425 Fr. for two.

The crew had completed at least one previous reconnaissance flight over England, tracks being visible on two large-scale maps found in the aircraft. One was noted as being directed chiefly towards railway junctions and the other, towards airfields and other military installations. There were a number of symbols and markings on the maps which were sent to AI3(b) for assessment. The main symbols were circles, squares and equilateral triangles, but other more obscure markings included two conjoined triangles with an arrowhead, a cross, an object that looked like a musical note and a treble clef from a sheet music.

The pilot, Oberleutnant Runde, held the Iron Cross First Class, having received this while on operations in Poland in September 1939. He admitted being with the same Gruppe throughout the war, although he had converted to Messerschmitt 110s. AI1(k) deduced with this information and other factors, that this aircraft therefore belonged to 4(F)/124.

A further intelligence report for this aircraft (No. 196/1940) provided some new information to AI1(k). This detailed the contents of a diary belonging to the wireless operator Feldwebel Baden and contained a series of notes and dates regarding German parachute flares. It noted that the flares were carried, one in each quarter of a standard Heinkel bomb chute.

The notes stated the flares burn during the time taken to fall 1,500 meters and therefore the fuse is set to go off above that height. The rate of fall in seconds, depends according to the type of flare – a LC50 type A or C. These weighed 32 kilos and consisted of a cylinder, a fuse, the flare and its parachute.

The notes contained a set of instructions translated as follows:

> ‘4 LC 50’s are hung in the flare carrier ETC 50, the cable of the Zeit Zunder Zusatzgerat (ZZG) – i.e. Time fuse auxiliary mechanism.
>
> 1. Switch on ZZG, 5 to 10 minutes before release.
> 2. Select delay, If the lamp lights up then the apparatus is not in order, switch off.
> 3. Release switch gear, put main switch to ‘on’ and ‘arm’ the bomb release.
> 4. Press release knob. The live bombs will fall immediately.
>
> Bombs which have been made safe again are not live, but not (merely) if the switch gear has been switched off.’

The table in the diary also gave the LC50’s power as 600,000 candle power with a burn time of five to six minutes. It’s rate of fall was five meters per second. The information was distributed to the usual organisations plus the arms department.

Messerschmitt 109's protected any attacking aircraft over the Channel convoys, but at this time, they rarely ventured too far in land over southern England. That changed on 24 July, when aircraft of JG26 ventured over the tip of Kent and lost two of their number – Intelligence log No. 202/1940 gave details.

The third Gruppe of JG26 had consisted of about forty Messerschmitt 109's when they were alerted to a dogfight over Dover. As they sped towards the action, III/JG26 were attacked by Spitfires of No. 54 Squadron and Leutnant Josef Schauff of 8/JG26 was hit and bailed out over the town of Margate, but his parachute failed and he fell to his death. His machine disintegrated as it landed in Byron Avenue, Margate.

The second machine was flown by Leutnant Werner Bartels who was older than the average fighter pilot. When interrogated, he claimed that as they headed for Dover, he was caught 'beautifully' with a deflection shot by a Spitfire. Bartels's aircraft had only flown ten hours and had little damage, bullet strikes being found upon inspection on the wing and fuselage. Bartels does not appear to have suffered any injuries when he made a forced landing at North Down near Margate, but he may have received some bullet wounds. The report says he was transferred to hospital with 'serious injuries', but whether that was to the underground hospital at Dover Castle or to a local civilian establishment is unknown. He was then later moved to the Royal Herbert Military Hospital in Woolwich.

Werner Bartels was the Technical Officer of the Gruppe. Although severely wounded, Bartels was given a preliminary interrogation and said he had only been called-up three months before, having been the director of an aircraft factory. He told his interrogator that there were some Heinkel 113 fighters based in Norway and possibly in Holland, but none in France. (Author's note: this as we have already seen, was totally incorrect.)

Two days after the preliminary interrogation report (No. 202/1940), a second report (No. 204/1940) was signed off by Felkin. This noted that Bartels had been 'Re-interrogated in hospital where he was seriously ill.' Despite being very ill, the interrogator managed to obtain from Bartels that he had spent five years in Brazil, working there training and re-organising the nation's army under a French Mission. He had spent so long in South America he had married a Brazilian woman.

When he returned to Germany from Brazil, Bartels worked in the Messerschmitt factory and was quite convinced the Messerschmitt 109 could not carry bombs without considerable structural alterations.

Bartels said the 3rd Gruppe of JG26 were the only aircraft based at Calais. They had been at Orleans at the time of the French armistice, returning to

Monchengladbach to re-equip. He also told the interrogator that the chevron (< |) on his aircraft fuselage indicated a Gruppe Stab aircraft, although as we have seen, in reality this meant it was the Adjutant's aircraft. Bartels was clearly trying to mislead his interrogators.

The report concluded, stating that a piece of paper found in the second aircraft (that of Leutnant Josef Schauff which crashed in Margate), contained details of the call signs for the third Gruppe Staffeln as well as the Geschwader. These were:

> Geschwader – Adler, Stab – Condor, 7th Staffel – Tiger, 8th Staffel – Panther, 9th Staffel – Lowen.

Werner Bartels ended up in the Royal Herbet hospital at Woolwich, staying there until some-time in December 1940.

On 25 July, another Messerschmitt 109 pilot (fuselage marked 6 + ~) came into custody and was just as talkative as Bartels. This aircraft from 8/JG52 came down at Elvington Court, twelve miles West of Deal, Kent.

The unwounded pilot, Unteroffizier Max Reiss, told the initial interrogator, that he was part of a flight of six aircraft from his Staffel, two others having become detached and engaged. It was his second flight of the day when they were attacked by Spitfires and his radiator was damaged. Reiss managed to land his ME109 which was still in good condition and something of a prize for Air Intelligence.

During questioning, Max Reiss stated the horizontal snake line (~) on the fuselage was the marking of the III Gruppe of JG52. The 1st and 2nd Gruppen used vertical lines or at an angle, but he was unsure which.

His entire Gruppe were based at an emergency landing field, used because others in the area had been unsatisfactory. His own Staffel Kapitan was Oberleutnant Ehrlich who held the Iron Cross, both First and Second Class. The Kommandeur of the III Gruppe was Major Fermer and the JG52 Kommodore was Major Meherhardt.

Reiss's comments about his Staffel Kapitan are interesting, as Oberleutnant Lothar Ehrlich of 8/JG52 was posted missing the day before Reiss was captured. In addition, his comment about the Kommandeur of the III/JG52 being Major Fermer is also misleading. Oberleutnant Herbert Fermer was the Staffel Kapitan of 7/JG52 and was also killed in action the day before Reiss was captured. Major Meherhardt appears to be fictitious and was not the JG52 Kommodore. Clearly,

Max Reiss was being less than truthful and AI1(k) probably knew this from their own records.

Reiss claimed the III Gruppe had only been at Calais two or three days, having had three weeks leave after many combats with French Curtis fighters. Reiss had been in the Luftwaffe for three years and his morale was deemed to be good by the interrogator. His Ausweis was grey in colour and issued at Fliegerhorst Kommandantur Mannheim-Sandhofen on 2 February 1940. It was signed by Hauptmann Binderler.

Bartels and Reiss had provided quite a bit of intelligence for AI1(k), although some of it was very misleading and it was disseminated through the usual channels, while being used to update the records at Trent Park.

On 28 July 1940, a Junkers 88 (9K+HL) of 3/KG51 made a forced landing on Buckholt Farm near Bexhill in Sussex at 0514 hours. Intelligence reports No. 210 & 224 of 1940 gave details of this aircraft and its crew.

The aircraft had been on a night raid, but became completely lost. The crew had problems with their Direction-Finding equipment and after flying back and forth across England and possibly Ireland, they managed to obtain a bearing for home. However, running short of fuel, they ditched their bombs in the English Channel and flew back to England where the pilot made a wheel's-up forced landing. As they came into land, they started to receive gunfire, one shot passing through one of the pilots' boots without harming him. For some reason, the crew did not set fire to their Junkers and they were detained unharmed.

Inside the aircraft the wireless operator's papers provided a treasure trove of intelligence, listing various codes:

F.w.F. till midnight...................... .... bfh
F.w.F. after midnight... ....wzm
Main frequency and call sign, 4969 kcs................7aj.
Emergency frequency and call sign, 5192 kcs.........osx.

A number of beacons and their codes was also given, as well as the following codes for the day:

46 – Middle English Channel, 47 – Northern English Channel, 48 – Southern English Channel, 49 – Enemy fighters, 50 – Attack carried out, 51 – Attack possible without blind flying, 52 – Switch on beacons, 53 – Southampton and 54 – Birmingham.

The crew consisting of Oberfeldwebel Josef Bier, Leutnant Willi Ruckdeschel and Unteroffiziers Heinz Ohls and Martin Multhammer were unharmed and in fair to good spirits.

Their aircraft, which displayed the unit's emblem of a white edelweiss on a blue shield below the cockpit, was salvaged and repaired. It later flew in RAF colours with No. 1426 Enemy Aircraft Flight, familiarising pilots with the JU88.

On 27 July 1940, one of the oddest episodes started when a Heinkel III of 8/KG55 was shot down and crashed at East Woodhay near Newbury, Berkshire in the early hours. The exploits of the crew featured in intelligence reports Nos. 211 and 225/1940.

The crew of five: pilot Feldwebel Theodor Metzner, observer Feldwebel Josef Markl, wireless operator Unteroffizier Kurt Bocker, air mechanic Gefreiter Heinz Morgenthal and gunner Gefreiter Ernst Ostheimer, bailed out after being hit by anti-aircraft fire over Bristol.

The aircraft hit the ground and disintegrated, the pilot and wireless operator being captured soon after landing by parachute. The three other crewmen remained at large, two for forty-eight hours and one – the observer Josef Markl for an unbelievable nine days.

Preliminary Intelligence log No. 211 completed two days after they arrived and signed off by Denys Felkin, is very interesting and shows that even the meticulous work of AI1(k) could be fallible.

The report noted the Heinkel III of KG55 had been flying south when it was caught in searchlights which the captured pilot (Metzner) and wireless operator (Boker) stated were very good. Although they heard no anti-aircraft fire, the aircraft was buffeted and the left engine caught fire. When Metzner shut the engine down, the other one started to fail and the crew decided to bail out. The Heinkel crashed and was consumed by fire.

At the time of the report (29 July), only the two airmen had been accounted for and were not wounded. The report however, noted that there was one dead airman in the wreckage of the aircraft.

Metzner and Boker would not give very much information to the interrogators, but the part aircraft's code (+ CS) and the first two letters were deduced from one of the prisoner's identity discs and a Brown Ausweis issued at Neudorf on 5.2.40. The identity disc number normally belonged to the 7th Staffel of KG55. In addition, markings in the clothing of Metzner, indicated he once belonged to III/KG355 – the pre-war designation of KG55.

Their flight plan was identified as possibly originating at Villacoublay and their objective being Severn Beach to the north of Avonmouth. This was deduced from one of two maps recovered from the wrecked aircraft. No other documents or papers were recovered from the two prisoners, but it was noted that the two men were at large for some time and may have thrown them away.

Although, the first report indicated there was a body or a believed body in the wreckage, it soon became clear other crew members had escaped and were at large. Two days after the aircraft was brought down, on 29 July, the air mechanic Heinz Morgenthal and the gunner Ernsy Ostheimer were eventually captured. The observer Feldwebel Josef Markl was, however, still on the run.

After nine days on the run, Josef Markl was captured. A report signed by Felkin, dated the 7 August (log No. 225/1940) was completed as he said, 'The details are given for the general interest and to put on record, that it is possible for an enemy airman to remain at large for a long period in the neighbourhood of quite a large town.'

The report noted that the first two prisoners had told the interrogators that the crew consisted of five men and they had all bailed out. The first two prisoners gave the names of their three colleagues. A search found the third and fourth airmen, but there was still some doubt about the fate of the final man, as what had been thought to be a charred human hand in the aircraft's wreckage, turned out to be just a charred leather glove!

Eventually, a flying helmet and other items, folded up and hidden some distance from the crash site, proved conclusively that a fifth man was on the run.

Josef Markl eventually gave himself up and gave a full account of his adventures.

Markl had been the third man to jump, exiting the Heinkel from the front hatch of the aircraft, but he caught his foot and another man had to release him. Unfortunately, his parachute haversack was blown out from his body and he had great difficulty in clutching on to it, finding and eventually pulling the ripcord.

Once the parachute was deployed, he swung heavily in the high winds and ended up entangled up a pine tree. He managed to extract himself and sat on a branch destroying everything he had of military value. He eventually climbed down with his flying helmet and walked towards what he thought was Newbury to surrender.

After entering the town, Markl decided he did not want to be captured and turned around and walked to the outskirts, where he hid in some bracken and nettles. He had a small bar of chocolate which he ate and gathered water from the dew on his handkerchief. This was then wrung into his mouth to drink. Markl stayed in his hide for a few days, eating edible roots and eventually finding a source of water. He then decided to walk up a neighbouring ridge to examine the local landscape. Upon reaching the top he stayed in a wood, but later returned to his initial bracken and nettles hide.

Markl recounted hiding and two men passing within thirty yards of him to examine a hay field. Another man, out pigeon shooting with his spaniel passed underneath the tree in which he was hiding, but they did not see him. He also reported hearing several couples in the woods, although the report did not explain what they were doing!

Eventually, Markl was becoming weak through lack of food and said he was 'indifferent' to capture. He spent another night in an unlocked shanty at a clay pigeon shooting butt, recalling there was no rain and he never saw anyone searching for him.

Wanting to surrender through lack of food and water, he encountered a man and a woman on bicycles, but when they saw him, they rode off as fast as they could. A man in a car also saw him and did not stop.

Eventually, a car passed him and pulled-up. It reversed and he told the chauffer that he wanted to go to the nearest Military Commander. The car belonged to Lady Buckland who was in the rear of the car. Markl, the report noted, seemed to be astonished that the lady in the car was not surprised or even agitated at the sight of a German airman.

Lady Buckland and her driver took Markl to the police station where he surrendered his pistol and sixteen rounds of ammunition. He told his RAF interrogators that he was agreeably surprised at the way in which he was treated as a prisoner of war.

Despite having destroyed his documents, Markl had kept his Ausweis which he also surrendered. Felkin noted that personal consideration aside, it would indeed have been to his own advantage to give himself up and have news of his safety sent to his wife, who was about to have a baby. Markl's morale was very high and he had suffered remarkably little from his experience.

The Battle of Britain had only just started, but the coming months would not only lead to a high incidence of prisoners and aircraft wreckage, but also an increase in some valuable intelligence for AI1(k).

Chapter 15

The Fight for Survival (August 1940)

After the increase in Luftwaffe activity in July 1940 and a corresponding number of new prisoners of war, Air Intelligence was faced with a probable invasion of the United Kingdom. Many of their new prisoners were full of bravado and fully expected to be repatriated in due course, once the invasion was completed. Surely, it was only a matter of time, before the Wehrmacht landed on the south coast of England and British Army, which left most of its heavy equipment in France would be overrun.

In late July and early August 1940, the JU87 Stukas which spread fear among the Allied forces and civilians alike in France and Belgium, were tasked with destroying the convoys Britain persisted in sending through the Dover Straights. However, unlike the skies of France and Belgium, the sky above the English Channel and England was a deadly place for the dive-bombers and a large number were shot down.

In the early hours of 12 August, a Heinkel III (1G+AC) of Stab II/KG27 was shot down by a night-fighter near Wimbourne and its five-man crew bailed out.

The bomber crew were soon captured and provided RAF Air Intelligence with a prized crew which consisted of not one, but two Majors – Frederick Karl Schlichting and Hans-Jurgen Brehmer. To have two high-ranking officers on one aircraft was unusual and detracted somewhat from the other three crewmen – Oberfeldwebels Herbert Frey, Gunter Lohneng and Willi Bendrich.

The intelligence log No. 240/1940, states that the crew had been tasked with bombing the (Bristol Aircraft) Blenheim factory in Bristol. They dropped their bombs and claimed to have hit the harbour area and were on their way home, when they were attacked from below, by either a Hurricane or a Defiant. Why two Majors were on the aircraft was not covered or explained in the preliminary interrogation report, but it was sure to have been covered in subsequent interrogation reports which do not appear to have survived.

Later, on the afternoon of the twelfth at 1:00pm, a Messerschmitt 109E of 5/JG53 made a forced landing near the Berwick Railway crossing, near Lewes in Sussex. The pilot, Unteroffizier Leo Zaunbrecher, told his initial Field Interrogator that he had been attacked by a Spitfire at 19,500 feet and his controls were shot away. His main fuel tank was punctured and he was injured, before being taken to hospital in an ambulance.

This particular prisoner of war and crash site are an excellent example of the obstacles and confusion Air Intelligence often found when trying to maintain the integrity of the wreckage, the prisoner and any documents they held.

On page 107 of Nigel Parker's *Luftwaffe Crash Archive Volume 1*, there is a report by Police Constable 768 William Laker of Sussex Constabulary. He reported being off-duty and staying with his parents at Berwick, when a German Messerschmitt with its engine shut-off, made a forced landing. He ran to the crash site and found the injured pilot lying against a wheatsheaf, surrounded by railway workers. His parachute and tunic had been removed and Laker observed a bullet wound in the pilot's right shoulder. He gave the pilot first aid and arranged for the local Home Guard to provide a sentry. In time, a contingent of Royal Engineers arrived and PC Laker handed the pilot's belongings to their sergeant. When the ambulance arrived, the 23-year-old pilot was taken to the Princess Alice Hospital in Eastbourne.

A second report I obtained, comes from East Sussex Constabulary records and was written by an Inspector Morris.

The Inspector noted that the aircraft had come down, the pilot was injured and an ambulance had been summoned. Inspector Morris attended with two uniformed constables and a detective constable, arriving at the same time as the ambulance at 1:25pm.

Inspector Morris claimed a Sergeant Major Moule of 326 Battery, Royal Artillery was in charge of the aircraft and the prisoner, having posted armed sentries and claiming that he was detailed to act for the military at all aeroplane landings in the district. He had reportedly searched the pilot and taken possession of his papers etc. No mention was made of PC Laker.

Inspector Morris noted that the pilot had a bullet wound to his left (not his right) scapula and other minor injuries. His name was Leo Zourbrecher, born 14-2-1917 and his number was L37120. At 2:00pm Flying Officer Eales from RAF Biggin Hill (the local AI1(k) initial interrogation officer), telephoned to say he was attending and directed that if there was more than one prisoner, they should be kept apart and people should be kept away from the aircraft.

Morris concluded his report, noting that the aircraft had a very large number 14 on its side. On the tail was the smaller number 11 and a still smaller number

3367 beside it. Clearly, the police inspector did not realise the number 3367 was the aircraft works number and the number 11 was in fact two victory bars for aircraft shot down by this aircraft (assuming they were not achieved by different pilots).

The AI1(k) intelligence report No. 245/1940, signed by Denys Felkin, states that in preliminary interrogation, the pilot said he was from the 5th Staffel and all their aircraft had a badge consisting of a red devil with a bow and arrow. However, another POW had stated this was the marking of JG53, when based at Cambrai in June 1940. This Messerschmitt 109 was also noted as having an armoured bulkhead behind the pilot's seat.

With so many people attending the crash site, it is not surprising that the report concluded by stating that the pilot's identity disc was missing, having been removed by a civilian and had yet to be recovered. The report also noted that the pilot's Feldpost number was L21535.

Clearly there was a lot of confusion in terms of the Feldpost number and the numbers noted by Inspector Morris, the latter apparently not being reported to Flying Officer Eales when he arrived. There was also confusion about the pilot's injuries and although Morris reported, but mistook the victory bars as a number 11 on the tail, the intelligence report failed to mention them at all. Even the pilot's name was different in the two official reports, given as Zaunbrecher and Zourbrecher.

In the earliest chapters of this book, we saw the efforts Felkin and his colleagues went to, to develop a system that maintained the security and provenance around arriving aircraft and prisoners. This also detailed the fact the army would provide escorts and when necessary, POWs would be housed in police cells before being escorted to the Tower of London and later to Trent Park. Despite these instructions, it is clear that at times, things went wrong as in the case with Leo Zaunbrecher in August 1940.

In the UK National Archives, there is a report dated 22 August 1940, from an unidentified Major from MI5, a Regional Security Liaison Officer. He had recently attended a CID Special Branch Conference and was somewhat concerned about Police-RAF POW activities, sending a report to Group Captain J.O. Archer at AI1(d):

> Arising out of Minute 5 on the Minutes of the CID Special Branch Conference, No. 7 Region on 15 August 1940, which I am sending to you forthwith, I would like to make the following suggestion through you to the Air Ministry.

Already during the war certain enemy airmen who have landed in this country, either by crashing or baling out, have been at large for sufficient time for them possibly to have made contacts with residents in this country before they passed into the hands of the police or other forces of the Crown.

All enemy airmen are at some time or other, interrogated by an Air Force officer who speaks German.

It is extremely desirable that the local police should have an opportunity of putting to the enemy airman, all such questions as they consider necessary, covering the movements of and contacts made by the enemy airman since landing.

It is my experience that it is rare to find a policeman who speaks German.

It would be of the greatest assistance to the civil power, if the Air Ministry would issue instructions extending to the police by courtesy, the services of the RAF interrogating officer.

I do not think it at all desirable that any police officer should be present during an interrogation of an enemy airman by a Royal Air Force interrogating officer, and I am not in any way suggesting this course.

What I do suggest, and I want to put the point strongly, is that before an interview takes place, the Royal Air Force interrogating officer should have a short talk with a police officer sent for the purpose, in order that the police may indicate those questions which they particularly wish to have cleared up; and moreover, that when the Royal Air Force officer considers that the interrogation, so far as he is concerned is at an end, he should then talk with the police officer to tell him the answers to the police questions and to see whether there is any further matter which the police would wish to have put to the enemy airman.

I should be obliged if you should inform me what arrangements are made for interrogating enemy airmen by Royal Air Force officers from this influencing point of view.

Are the enemy airmen brought to some centre or centres which have already been decided upon and interrogated there, or does the interrogating officer go to carry out his interrogation at whatsoever place may be found to be convenient?

The report was eventually passed to Squadron Leader Denys Felkin at Trent Park as it was clear the Major was asking questions about a top-secret intelligence system and classified locations. Denys Felkin replied in writing to Group Captain Archer on 3 September 1940, enclosing a list of AI1(k) Field Interrogation officers, who he stated, were working constantly and in close contact with the police interviewing prisoners at Police Stations. He added for onward transmission to the Major:

> 'Every Interrogation Officer gets a large number of details as to where aircraft have come down from the police, who are a most reliable source of information; at the same time the police are getting a great deal of information from our local Interrogation Officers and they are only too willing to help the police in the type of questions you have suggested in your letter.
>
> 'I am certain, I am correct in saying that there is very good co-operation between our people and the police.'

The response was very clear, 'we already have an efficient service in place which assists and liaises with the local police… and I am not telling you anything about our interrogation centre!' Although Felkin had been diplomatic and reassuring, another report to Group Captain Archer from the same Major on 11 September, was less than complimentary of Denys Felkin and AI1(k):

> 'I attach hereto a copy of minutes from Squadron Leader Felkin. I can hardly describe how unsatisfactory I feel these minutes to be and I am quite certain that you will realise how irritating this is! It was just because the thing was not working in the manner in which Squadron Leader Felkin seems to imagine it to be working that the matter was put to me by the whole of the Special Branch organization for the whole of No. 7 Region.
>
> 'I hardly think it is worth my while bothering you any further with the point, as in spite of the desire of the police that they should be assured that directions have been given on the lines set out in my minute, it is only too abundantly clear that the officer at the Air Ministry was not prepared to see that such instructions were sent to the Interrogation Officers. Accordingly, I have written to each of the Interrogation Officers at Filton, Mount Wise and Warmwell.'

Group Captain Archer passed these comments on to Denys Felkin, together with a copy of the letter the Major had sent to the three local RAF Interrogation Officers in the West Country. Archer added that Felkin may wish to address some of the

Major's points in a letter to ALL Interrogation Officers, although to date, he had no reason to believe this was necessary. Whether Felkin sent a letter is unclear, but as he was running such a secret and very busy operation, it is very likely he did not send his Field Interrogation officers some form of a reminder. Either way, the politics around AI1(k) and their work could be very delicate, while there were clearly continuing issues with the processes of prisoner and evidence preservation.

Intelligence log No. 247/1940 would become an important report. The log detailed the downing of a Junkers 88 (9K+AA) of Stab/KG51 on 12 August, at Godshill Park on the Isle of Wight. The four-man crew unusually comprised of an all-officer crew; the pilot and Geschwader Kommodore Oberst Johann Fisser; the observer, Leutnant Franz Schad; the wireless operator, Oberleutnant Werner Luderitz and the air mechanic, Leutnant Adam Nothelfer.

Sadly, Oberst Fisser was killed, while Leutnant Nothelfer was badly burned and the other two slightly wounded. Schad and Nothelfer were admitted to Royal Herbert Military Hospital in Woolwich and that shall be discussed in a later chapter.

The fact four officers, including the Geschwader Kommodore were all on board the same aircraft, was very unusual. In time, it has been alleged, this particular loss caused Hermann Göring to order that a crew should only have one officer on board, as too many officers were being lost.

On 13 August, in the early morning light, the Luftwaffe launched what was supposed to be Adler Tag (Eagle Day). Massed formations of bombers were to attack a number of airfields and RDF stations, with the Dornier 17's of KG2 briefed to bomb Eastchurch on the Isle of Sheppey in Kent. Unfortunately, the raid ran into trouble with the weather and was cancelled, but KG2 and several other units continued with the mission due to communication issues. As a consequence, a number of aircraft were shot down, including five from KG2.

While the Luftwaffe were in some confusion, so too it would appear, were the RAF and AI1(k) that day.

Dornier 17 (U5+DS) of 8/KG2 came down on the mudflats at Seasalter in Kent, the pilot, Oberleutnant Muller, the observer, Staffel Kapitan Oberleutnant Morich, and wireless operator Oberfeldwebel Langer being killed. The air mechanic, Feldwebel Rudolf Hansten, survived although he was badly wounded.

So many enemy aircraft were being shot down, it appears the Field Intelligence Officers were getting confused and inadvertently mixing up their reports. The Intelligence log No. 249/1940 covering this particular Dornier 17, clearly states that three of the crew, including the pilot, were killed, but the mechanic,

Feldwebel Hansten, was badly wounded. Despite being badly wounded, Hansten was interrogated and gave details of his unit and the Third Gruppe of KG2. He also noted that his observer, Oberleutnant Morich, was the Staffel Kapitan.

The report did not mention that Morich was in fact missing at the time of the report and adds to the confusion by stating, 'The pilot stated that the whole of his Staffel took off from Douai at 07:00.' Sadly, the pilot (Muller) was deceased and it is likely that information was provided by the badly wounded Rudolf Hansten.

The report concluded by stating that the body of an Oberleutnant Horst von der Groeben had also been recovered from the sea, he had a grey Ausweis marked '*Fliegerhorstkommandtur 9/11*', but it had up to that point, been impossible to positively identify the body. In reality, this was the body of Oberleutnant Horst von der Groben part of a crew from a Dornier of 7/KG2 lost on the same raid.

Oberleutnant Morich is still missing to this day, but Oberleutnant Muller (Hansten's pilot) and Oberleutnant von der Groeben from the other Dornier were buried in Whitstable Cemetery. The original burial location of Oberfeldwebel Langer's body is unclear, although he is now buried in the German Military Cemetery at Cannock Chase.

Three days later, another Dornier 17 of 3/KG2 was shot down and burnt out on Whitstable Beach. The remains of the four-man crew were buried in one coffin on top of the coffins of Oberleutnants Muller and von der Groben in Whitstable Cemetery. After the war, the remains of the latter crew were exhumed from their unmarked grave and interred at the German Military cemetery at Cannock Chase in Staffordshire.

For many years the confusion of August 1940 continued and the remains of the two forgotten officers (Oberleutnant Muller and Oberleutnant von der Groeben) remained interred in Whitstable Cemetery.

In 2012, local historians attempted to get the two men exhumed and interred at Cannock Chase with their countrymen. I cannot confirm the exact date they were moved to Cannock Chase, but both men now lie with their comrades in Staffordshire. Thankfully, the confusion of August 1940 has now been concluded.

So many aircraft were shot down in August 1940, it is clear from examining the available records held at the UK National Archives there was considerable confusion, and many prisoners and aircraft wreck reports appear to be missing from the preliminary interrogation records between 18-26 August.

Although there was confusion surrounding the Dornier 17 of Feldwebel Hansten at Whitstable, an examination of the wreckage did uncover one prized piece of intelligence. According to additional log No. 280/1940, a report was found detailing the experiences of bomber attacks carried out by Flieger Division 9.

This lengthy report gave details of preparations for a flight, night-time navigation, W/T navigation skills and the use of radio beacons and ranges. It also noted that W/T transmissions should be strictly curtailed and messages only sent in exceptional circumstances. Warning messages regarding barrage balloons and heavy anti-aircraft fire were permissible with their precise location. Tactical weather reports should only be transmitted when 100 kms from the enemy coastline, but damage to the aircraft could be sent, including in the message, the aircraft's home base. In addition, if a flight is delayed and the return journey was likely to include a late arrival over a friendly coastline, a message should be sent an hour before crossing the coastline to alert friendly fighters and flak.

Such a document should not have been carried on an operation by the crew and once again, this was evidence of lax operational security by Luftwaffe aircrews at the height of the Battle of Britain.

The number of aircraft coming down and their related prisoners was overburdening the Field Interrogation Officers of AI1(k). It appears they missed some very valuable intelligence from their preliminary reports and No. 252/1940 is an excellent example of this…

On 13 August 1940, a Messerschmitt 109E with the fuselage markings < + and a capital *R* in black, made a forced landing at New Salts Farm, Shoreham in Sussex. The tail also displayed three victory bars on the tip of the fin. The pilot, who was not wounded or injured, was Oberleutnant Paul Temme, the Gruppe Adjutant of Stab I/JG2. He was in fact a five-victory ace, but the preliminary report dated 14 August, failed to mention any of these details.

The intelligence report failed to mention the victory bars and it does not appear the Field Interrogator identified Temme as a possible ace.

The German pilot told his initial interrogator that he had a poor engine and had been shot down by two to three Spitfires. He currently flew one operation a day, but during the invasion of France, he flew five a day. The field interrogator noted that he carried a tin of chocolate with 2% caffeine, but this pilot also had eight Pervitin pills for use if he ditched in the English Channel. These would strengthen him while in the sea, as the aircraft did not carry a rubber dinghy. He said, one pill should be taken every half hour, but all eight could be taken at once if necessary.

The preliminary report noted that a report from AI3(b) had previously noted the fact Pervitin pills had been used by the German Army and this sample was sent to Wing Commander Kilpatrick for analysis. While this was important intelligence, the report appears to have missed another opportunity with an ace pilot coming into their custody. Whether this error was ever identified and later corrected with a secondary interrogation is unknown. He was eventually sent to a POW Camp in Canada and returned home to Germany after the war.

On 24 August, log No. 282/1930 recorded the loss of another Messerschmitt 109, this time at East Langdon near St Margaret's Bay, Kent, but this report was much more detailed.

The aircraft was noted as being marked with a yellow number 10 outlined in black next to the fuselage crosses. In addition, there was a unit badge consisting of a weeping raven wearing spectacles and holding an umbrella. The aircraft and its parent unit were soon identified as 6/JG51. The aircraft was noted as having three yellow stripes on the tail (victory bars) with each having the dates 7.7.40, 29.7.40 and 15.8.40.

The pilot was Oberfeldwebel Fritz Beeck, aged twenty-nine with a total service length of nine years, including over a year in the artillery. He held the Iron Cross Second Class. Fritz Beeck was very talkative and had good morale according to the AI1(k) report.

Fritz Beeck told his interrogator that he had been on his second flight that day, the first being at 0800 hours when his unit escorted about twenty bombers attacking an aerodrome near Canterbury. After a quick lunch, they set off again with eight aircraft from his own Staffel and some from 2/JG51 to escort bombers to another airfield near Margate (Manston).

During this second flight, Beeck got into a scrap with Hurricanes and a few Spitfires, he did not think he received any hits, but on the way home his oil duct broke and with a faltering engine, he made a forced landing. Examination of the aircraft found a number of bullet holes, including one in the engine.

Fritz Beeck admitted escorting bombers the previous week to an attack on an airfield south-east of London, but it was not Croydon. The pilot was so talkative he was re-interrogated and a further report was submitted (No. 311/1940 on 27 August).

In the second report, Beeck had stated that his Messerschmitt was equipped with the standard armament of two cannon and two machine guns. He said he preferred to use the cannon if he could move into a suitable position, but weighing everything up, he thought more machine guns might be better.

Beeck said he had been flying operationally in Belgium and France since 20 May 1940. There was no definite system of rest days, usually unfavourable weather restricted flying and this counted as a rest day for the fighter pilots. No official days of leave had been granted.

Beeck told the interrogators his Staffel had escorted both Heinkel IIIs and Junkers 88's during the summer, but they were not really given much of a briefing, only being told the number and type of aircraft and where to rendezvous with them. In a clear sky, the bombers liked to fly at 13,000 feet with the fighters above them at 19,000 feet up to 22,000 feet. At whatever height the bombers are operating, the fighters liked to fly 8,000 to 9,500 feet above them.

Fritz Beeck also told his interrogator that damaged or destroyed aircraft were replaced by ferry pilots flying them in immediately. The interrogator was clearly still asking about the Heinkel 113 fighter aircraft, but Beeck said he had never flown one, but from hearsay, he had heard they were not very satisfactory and not likely to be adopted. He could give no more specific information.

In late August 1940, AI1(k) started to gather intelligence that the once much-vaunted Messerschmitt 110 heavy fighter, was being made into a fighter-bomber. On 15 August, six of the Messerschmitt's were shot down across Surrey and Sussex. These aircraft belonging to a new Geschwader – Erpr. Gr. 210.

One survivor was Unteroffizier Johann Werner, a wireless operator/gunner from an aircraft (S9+BB) of Stab/Erpr.Gr.210, brought down at Redhill airfield after a bombing attack on RAF Croydon. His pilot, Oberleutnant Horst Fiedler, the Gruppe Adjutant, was seriously injured and died on 18 August, but Johann Werner was unharmed.

AI1(k) were keen to obtain evidence from a crewman from one of these 'new' fighter-bombers and Werner appears to have been keen to talk to them.

In intelligence report No. 321/1940, Werner explained that he had completed his radio training in May 1940 and was sent to Copenhagen where he trained with an Erganzungs Staffel comprising of fourteen pilots and fourteen wireless operators. They had been told to climb to 13,000 feet before diving without bombs, pulling out of their dives at 1,500 feet. The angle of the bombing dive was forty-five degrees, estimated by a red line drawn on the aircraft's windscreen. (Clearly, when the red line was level with the horizon the angle of the dive was correct.) When they pulled out of the dive, their speed was about 420 mph and a further 600 feet was lost in altitude as the pilot pulled the aircraft out of the dive. The crews made ten practice dives per day, with no perceived ill effects upon the crews or the aircraft.

The new crews went on to make practice bombing attacks with cement filled bombs, using the 'Revi' gunsight which is usually used for the aircrafts forward armament.

Johann Werner advised the interrogators that aircraft, when possible, dived out of the sun and against the wind. If attacking a ship, they would dive along the length of the vessel. If they had to bomb across the wind, the pilot would have to use his judgement and aim purely by experience, taking the wind into account. The release of the bombs was not automatic and carried out by the pilot.

In June 1940, Werner had been posted to Erpr. Gr. 210 at Denain. He said he was one of the last to be posted to this new unit, but none of the other students went with him. AI1(k) therefore assumed correctly that other ME110 fighter-bomber units were being formed.

Intelligence log No. 325/1940 is quite an extensive report, detailing the loss of a Heinkel III of Stab III/KG1 on 27 August, at Caterham in Surrey. The aircraft was piloted by Major Willibald Fanelsa, the Gruppen-Kommandeur and someone who would come into contact with Oberleutnant Franz von Werra, as he became the senior German officer at the POW Camp at Grizedale Hall in Cumbria.

Fanelsa and his crew of four non-commissioned officers, were shot down by anti-aircraft fire on a night-time raid to Coventry and bailed out over Caterham, Surrey.

A two-page report, dated 29 August and signed by Flight Lieutenant Guy Jepson at AI1(k), gave quite a few details about this aircraft and the major's interrogation, with a map being found which had their flight plan clearly marked upon it.

The crew, when interrogated, stated that their starboard engine was not running well, even before they had left the ground. Once over their target, factories in Coventry, their port engine stopped, although they believed this was due to anti-aircraft fire. With the starboard engine starting to falter they lost altitude. Coned by searchlights, they blindly dropped their twenty 50 kg bombs from an altitude of about 4,800 feet. The interrogators noted that the crew's attitude was that they were perfectly good bombs and although they could not identify a suitable target, they dropped them thinking they might as well do some damage somewhere! When challenged about this blasé attitude, Major Fanelsa maintained there were strict instructions against bombing London and if any bombs were dropped on the capital city, it was by accident.

As the aircraft continued to lose height, the crew bailed out at 2,300 feet. As they dropped below the clouds searchlights picked them out in the night sky and heavy anti-aircraft fire made their parachute descent very uncomfortable. The crew, during interrogation, stated that when flying above clouds, searchlights always helped them identify London by the terrific concentration of their beams on the underside of the clouds.

One recovered map had what appeared to be a very large number of operational aerodromes marked on it in France. Another map had British airfields marked on it, as well as a series of red circles at Selsey Bill, Dungeness, Beachy Head and Shoreham.

Four target maps of Coventry were also recovered with aerial photographs dated 8 June 1940. The images appeared to be factory targets and were each given a number/code. The maps also had a number and a letter. The targets were:

- GB7311bc – Armstrong-Siddeley Aircraft engine works.
- GB7312bc – Rover aero-engine works with an additional target GB803 – Morris Motor works.
- GB7412bc – Daimler Co. Ltd. Aircraft and engine works with the following subsidiary targets:
    - GB206 – 'C' Maintenance unit.
    - GB523 – Gasometers.
    - GB673 – Explosive and raw material works.
    - GB739 – Subsidiary aircraft engine works.
    - GB7314 – Alvis Ltd. Aircraft-engine works.
    - GB7321 – Aero-Engine accessory works.
    - GB7912 – Engine works.
    - GB8011 – Body builders.
- GB738bc – Humber-Hillman engine works, subsidiary target Humber-Rootes shadow factory. Second target on map GB1050 – Whitley Abbey airfield.

The target maps and images were forwarded on to AI3(b).

Another document found in the wreckage of the aircraft, was a loading plan dated 28/3/1940 and detailed a Heinkel III H3 loading. This document was forwarded to AI1(g). The document allowed for a crew of four (not five as in this case) and an all-up weight of 11,600 kg. One column was the bomb-load and the other full fuel tanks:

Full Bombs: Full Tanks:

Bomb load...........2,000 kg............................970 kg.
Oil.........................165 kg.............................180 kg.
Petrol inner tanks.....1,040 kg..........................1,040 kg.
Petrol outer tanks.......500 kg..........................1,515 kg.

Perhaps Major Fanelsa and his crew thought invasion was inevitable and there was no problem with telling the RAF interrogators this information. Why they thought this is strange, as surely, they would be in serious trouble if their own authorities found they had been so happy to talk. This conundrum is one that regularly appeared over the summer of 1940, why were so many enemy airmen happy to talk to the RAF interrogators?

Not every Luftwaffe airman was keen to talk, and on 28 August, AI1(k) received into their custody another Messerschmitt 109 pilot. This one was Oberfeldwebel Artur Dau of 7/JG51.

The 29-year-old pilot, holder of both the Iron Cross First and Second Class, came down by parachute at South Alkham near Folkestone at 1655 hours. Little did the people on the ground who immediately captured him realise, but he had seven confirmed aerial victories to his name, making him an ace and one of the highest scoring prisoners to date. A series of photographs were taken of him with the Home Guard, local police and civilians, one of which is included in the plate section of this book.

Artur Dau was taken away and according to intelligence log No. 334, gave few details and refused to discuss his unit. His Messerschmitt 109 was totally destroyed, but his identity disc number was noted as bearing the number 53528, while his Feldpost number was L29620. His Ausweis was made of white paper, numbered FPN L29620 and it was dated 11.7.40. He was soon identified from these details as a member of 7/JG51 by Air Intelligence.

Dau did discuss being shot down and claimed that he was about to attack some Hurricanes over the coast, when he received an anti-aircraft hit in his own engine. He bailed out into captivity. Although he did not give his unit, his Gruppen-Kommandeur was said to be Hauptmann Trautloft. His own unnamed Staffel Kapitan was said to have twenty aerial victories to his name. This information appears to have been correct as Hannes Trautloft was the Gruppen-Kommandeur and his Staffel Kapitan was Walter Oseau, a pilot previously discussed in this book.

Dau stated that his Staffel had three previous losses. (This appears to have been correct, although the unit would suffer increased losses in the coming weeks.)

Whether AI1(k) ever realised that this man was a seven-victory ace is unknown from the available records, but it appears they had no idea from this first preliminary interrogation report.

Author Chris Goss in his book *Luftwaffe Aces in the Battle of Britain* states that Dau later said:

> 'Suddenly I had two Hurricanes in my sights and my Rottenflieger attacked them. I opened fire on the second aircraft when I was hit by flak from Dover and had to bail out. After my landing, I was taken into custody by Coastguards. Then a "Bobby" arrived and took down my particulars. I was then taken to Folkestone and locked up in a cell. Shortly after an RAF officer with a bandaged head appeared in my cell. We shook hands and he asked me if I was the pilot of the Bf 109. I said, I was and he pointed to his head and said, "You did that." I answered him, "I am sorry." Then he left.'

Chris Goss identifies the RAF pilot as probably being Squadron Leader Don Finlay of 54 Squadron who received a scalp wound that day. Whether Dau was visited by Finlay before the arrival of a Field Interrogation Officer is unknown, but it appears there was quite a bit of fraternization between Dau, the Coastguard, Kent Police officers, the Home Guard and an RAF pilot before full details could be obtained from him.

The threat of invasion continued into September 1940 and the number of enemy aircraft brought down continued to increase. At the same time, the numbers of prisoners also continued to climb and AI1(k) and the other Air Intelligence sections were under severe strain.

Chapter 16

The Turning Tide (September 1940)

On the late afternoon of 1 September, a Messerschmitt 109 made a forced landing at Newbridge, four miles north of Rye in East Sussex. The aircraft marked with a white '11' next to the fuselage cross belonged to JG26.

The pilot, Leutnant Josef Burschegens, was slightly wounded in a dogfight, but he claimed his injuries were probably from anti-aircraft fire rather than a British fighter. His morale was not described as high or low as in other reports, but noted simply as a 'Heil Hitler', probably indicating the man to be an ardent Nazi who gave the salute and held the Iron Cross First and Second Class. He claimed to be a member of 3/JG26, but it was clear to Air Intelligence this was incorrect.

The preliminary intelligence log No. 393/1940 once again appears to have inconsistencies and omissions. The report states the aircraft and prisoner belonged to 3/JG26 not 7/JG26. It noted the pilot's identity disc number and his Feldpost number, as well as a small slip of paper that gave the call signs for his Geschwader, the Stabs kette, the 7th, 8th and 9th Staffeln, plus the Gruppe Battle HQ and Reserve. This correctly led the interrogating officers to assume this indicated a pilot from III/JG26 and not I/JG26 or 3/JG26 as stated by the pilot himself.

Whoever filled in this intelligence report did not give any detail of unit markings apart from the number 11 on the fuselage. Neither was there any mention of any victory markings on the tail. A later report noted some changes to the aircraft's construction, but again no specific markings were mentioned. In reality, Josef Burschegens was a ten victory ace and certainly one of the leading pilots in arguably the Luftwaffe's premier Geschwader. Whether AI1(k) later recognised this man is unclear, as any later reports are no longer available.

Chris Goss, in his book *Luftwaffe Aces in the Battle of Britain*, states that Burschegens later reported being shot down by the rear gunner of a Messerschmitt 110 when he went to its aid. Whatever the truth, the Luftwaffe had lost another top fighter pilot and it is possible, but not confirmed, that Air Intelligence missed an opportunity.

The battle seemed to still be going well for the Luftwaffe and on 3 September 1940, a Messerschmitt 110 of 2/ZG2 (3M+BK) was shot down by a Hurricane and the crew bailed out into the sea off Herne Bay, Kent. (See intelligence log No. 401/1940).

The pilot Oberleutnant Siegfried Gottschalt and his wireless operator, Unteroffizier Max Hoffmann, were pulled from the sea and brought ashore. The two men appear to have been quite talkative, even Gottschalt, the Staffel Kapitan who had a fractured ankle.

The crew had been on a freelance patrol when they were shot down and living in tents at their airfield near Paris. Gottschalt was noted as having high morale, but the wireless operator, who held the Iron Cross Second Class had reportedly poor morale. He had been in the Luftwaffe for three years, but most of that time had been spent in training.

Oberleutnant Siegfried Gottschalt was later transferred to the Royal Herbert Military Hospital at Woolwich and he was still there in the officers' ward, in early December 1940.

Despite Denys Felkin and AI1(k)'s clearest instructions on how to handle prisoners and to keep them away from other POWs, there were still problems.

Intelligence log No. 402/1940, cites the incident with Unteroffizier Heinrich Elbers of 8/JG54 on 2 September. Elbers was shot down by RAF fighters, force-landing his Messerschmitt 109 at Finns Far, Kingsnorth near Ashford in Kent. He received wounds to a foot and was taken to a local hospital. Unfortunately, the intelligence report noted that he was placed with another prisoner of war, who had already been interrogated and therefore his future interrogation was deemed to be useless.

On 3 September, a man we have already met in the chapter of Franz von Werra, came into British custody (see intelligence log No. 404.1940). Leutnant Walther Manhart was the pilot of a Messerschmitt 110 (3U+EP) shot down in combat and force-landing at Maldon in Essex. His wireless operator, Unteroffizier Werner Drews, was severely wounded and taken to hospital, but Manhart, a member of 6/ZG26, was taken into custody 'refusing to say a word' to the interrogator.

The crewmen's identity discs and their Ausweis papers were seized, while the aircraft was noted as having distinctive markings of a red and white curved-sided diamond, with a red diamond inside it; as well as a yellow Dutch clog on the fuselage. The unit was quickly identified by Air Intelligence staff as belonging to 6/ZG26, despite the lack of verbal information from the crewmen.

Walther Manhart was deemed to have good morale and like previous prisoners, clearly believed to be a Nazi, the report noting the words 'Horst Wessel' and 'Heil Hitler'. From this we can assume he gave a verbal 'Heil Hitler' and perhaps sang or whistled the infamous Horst Wessel (Horst Wessel Lied) song.

As we have already seen, Walther Manhart was the man who had left the graffiti comment in Franz von Werra's cell, 'You'll laugh Tommies, but you will still lose the war!'

This initial intelligence report did not note whether there were any victory bars on the ME110, but what it missed was the detail that Manhart had achieved seven aerial victories, making one of the highest-scoring ME110 aces of the battle. Like the other missed 'aces', whether AI1(k) ever recognised the man as an ace is unknown from surviving records.

Despite the apparent bravado of many of the newly arriving enemy prisoners, a report from a Royal Army Medical Corps Major and doctor, dated 4 September, gave Felkin and his team some hope.

The report stated that while the morale of Luftwaffe prisoners remained very good, there had been a few exceptions. Some prisoners examined at the centre (i.e. Trent Park), showed evidence of a certain amount of strain, probably caused by the tension of waiting for the 'great attack to begin' and in certain cases, by the amount of hard work which the air crews have had to do.

The medical officer in the previous ten days had noted that POWs arriving, 'Show evidence of nervous exhaustion. All reflexes were +++, pupils were dilated. There is marked tremor and motor restlessness.'

Many men were living on their nerve ends. Such intelligence, together with the use of Pervitin pills, showed the Luftwaffe to be overstretching its resources.

On 5 September 1940, AI1(k) received a very strange prisoner in the form of Hauptmann Wilhelm Meyerweissflog of Stab/JG53. The aircraft made a forced landing near RAF Manston in Kent and the pilot was quickly detained.

This Messerschmitt 109E had very distinctive fuselage markings with the standard coding for the Geschwader Adjutant: < | - + -

Hauptmann Wilhelm Meyerweissflog turned out to be an 'elderly' 50-year-old pilot, born in 1889, who had learned to drive a car in 1911. He had served as an observer in the First World War and was a pre-war reservist in 1939.

Happy to converse with his RAF interrogators, the middle-aged pilot had until recently been at a Technical Bureau before being called-up. He initially became an Administration Officer attached to the Staff of JG3, before joining

JG53. He had been on leave and returned late on the evening of 4 September, the day before his capture.

The next day shortly after lunch, he said he was looking out of his window and saw 'A lot of the boys going off and thought he would like a flip too.' He jumped into his Messerschmitt and flew vaguely in the direction of England, nearly being shot down by a British fighter. He then made a forced landing, which more by luck than judgement, he came out of safely and was detained. When apprehended, he had not the slightest idea where he was. Whether he made a forced landing because of combat damage is unclear in the report.

Wilhelm Meyerweissflog was unharmed and his morale was noted as being 'Good under trying circumstances'. The report noted that his mission was a 'Very freelance patrol!' It seems very little intelligence was gleaned from this man, who was seen as something of an oddity by staff at Trent Park.

Intelligence log No. 483/1940 detailed the shooting down of JU88 (4D+AD) of Stab III/KG30 into the English Channel off Pagham, Sussex on 9 September, at 1750 hours. Two of the four-man crew were killed and the other two were seriously injured, being taken to hospital. The report noted that 'So delirious were the injured men, that few details could be obtained from them'. They were found to be in possession of Danish and Belgian currency in their pockets and no documents were recovered from the aircraft.

Various Ausweis passes, identity discs and a Feldpost number were recovered and the unit was quickly identified. One of the two survivors was a Major Johann Hackbarth. At what point Air Intelligence identified that he was the son-in-law of General Kesselring is unknown, but Hackbarth was admitted to the Royal Herbert Military Hospital at Woolwich and was still on the officers' ward in mid-December 1940.

Intelligence log No. 495/1940, detailed another prisoner who was badly injured, yet he was apparently interrogated regardless of his severe burns.

Feldwebel Heinrich Honisch was shot down in his Messerschmitt 109E of 1/JG53 on the evening of 9 September by Spitfires. His aircraft caught fire and he bailed out suffering severe burns in the process. The Messerschmitt fell to earth near the Old Jail Inn, Jail Lane on the south-eastern perimeter of RAF Biggin Hill and was wrecked.

It is clear that at the height of the Battle of Britain, Air Intelligence staff would interrogate injured airmen, perhaps even before they received any required medical treatment. The 23-year-old Heinrich Honisch was clearly interrogated by an RAF Field Interrogation Officer (almost certainly from Biggin Hill), as the report states:

> 'This pilot, although in very great pain from burns, would give away absolutely no information regarding his unit, and said that he knew all about our aerodromes, because English prisoners in Germany gave away such a lot of information of this sort when interrogated.'

It would appear the damage to his Messerschmitt was not too great, as the log referred to two small discs, about the size of a penny, on the underside of one of the wings towards the trailing edge. These were painted like RAF roundels with a date 13.8.40. These, the report added, appeared to be bullet hole patches inscribed with the date they were inflicted.

Even if a prisoner was sent to a hospital for treatment, there was a continuing risk of him coming into contact with other prisoners of war who had already been interrogated.

On 8 September, the crew of a Dornier 17 (U5+BN) of 5/KG2 were shot down by anti-aircraft fire near Farningham Road railway station, south of Dartford in Kent. The four-man crew of this aircraft were wounded and taken to a local hospital, but there were so many German prisoners there, they soon came into contact with them and compromised the intelligence and interrogation situation.

Not every prisoner was interrogated soon after capture. On 6 September, Leutnant Max Himmelheber of Stab/JG2 was shot down and bailed out, fracturing his femur when he landed at Plumtree Farm, Headcorn, Kent. Intelligence log No. 504/1940 notes that he was too severely injured to be interrogated and was taken directly to hospital. He was still in the officers' ward at the Royal Herbert Military Hospital in Woolwich in mid-December 1940.

While prisoners were arriving in continually increasing commodities, there were the occasional oddities. Log No. 514/1940 dated 12 September, details the capture of a pilot from a Heinkel III of 1/KG26 at Uckfield in Sussex the previous day.

Three of the crew were missing when the first report was completed, but the pilot, Feldwebel Wilhelm Jabusch, who was wounded, was clearly less than pleased with the RAF fighter pilots. He claimed that after being hit by '15 Spitfires' and having lost an engine, his crew fired a red Very flare to indicate they had been hit. Despite this, they were attacked again and the controls hit, forcing Jabusch to bail out at 6,000 feet.

Various bits of aircraft and even a compete dress uniform, with an Iron Cross and other decorations on a hanger, as well as a ceremonial dagger, floated down to earth near Tunbridge Wells. The uniform had name tags bearing the name Unteroffizier Gerhardt Schilling, who it transpired was the wireless operator in Jabusch's crew.

Feldwebel Jabusch must have been quite talkative, as the Heinkel was identified as belonging to 1/KG26 coded 1H+KM and his identity disc and Ausweis all helped in confirming his unit. Despite their best efforts, the British failed to locate the wreckage of the aircraft. The reason for this was simple, it later transpired that the other crewmen had managed to control the aircraft, ditched their bombs and various items of unwanted equipment (including Schilling's best dress uniform) and flown the Heinkel home. Whether Feldwebel Jabusch was ever informed of this is not known, but it must have been very embarrassing for him.

The 15 September 1940 is remembered today as Battle of Britain Day. Although the number of Luftwaffe losses that day were not the highest during that summer, the massed aerial armadas crossing back and forth towards London resulted in a high number of downed aircraft and airmen. The numbers contributed to the high number of losses throughout August and early September, which in turn caused a very high work rate for AI1(k) and the wider Air Intelligence community. In some cases, this led to confusion and possibly some missed intelligence opportunities.

On 15 September, a Dornier 17 was damaged by anti-aircraft fire, before a Spitfire finished it off over Kent at 1445 hours. The aircraft which was badly damaged, was flown by 22-year-old and slightly wounded Leutnant Herbert Michaelis. The crew bailed out before it crash-landed onto Barnehurst Golf Course near Dartford.

Leutnant Michaelis was captured and taken to a hospital in Dartford (probably Joyce Green), while his wireless operator, Unteroffizier Willi Burbulla, was badly injured and taken to another hospital (possibly the Royal Herbert in Woolwich).

The intelligence log No. 530/1940 states that the mechanic, Flieger Hermann Bormann was killed, it was believed due to his parachute failing to open. He came down somewhere in the Maidstone area, where his body was 'quietly buried by a Maintenance Unit and his effects have not yet been located'. In fact, Bormann not only survived, but passed through Trent Park and was interviewed and assessed by the psychologist C.H. Brooks (see the later chapter on C.H. Brooks). What caused this confusion is unknown.

The observer, Unteroffizier Kurt Haufberg, was missing, but later reports state that his parachute failed and in fact he was the man buried by the Maintenance

Unit near Maidstone; such was the confusion surrounding this aircraft and its unfortunate crew.

Leutnant Michaelis was later transported to the Royal Herbert hospital in Woolwich and remained there until at least December 1940. He had been through the Polish and French campaigns, but claimed this was his first war flight to England and their target was to have been the London docks.

A recovered identity disc indicated that this machine and its crew belonged to 5/KG53, although the coding of the aircraft (+IM) indicated a 4th Staffel machine. The extensive AI1(k) records had not previously recorded any Dornier 17's serving with KG53 and this caused some confusion. It appears other prisoners from KG53 were asked about these crewmen, but none could confirm these man as being members of that Geschwader. Eventually, by a process of elimination, AI1(k) identified that this machine belonged to 4/KG3. It is likely the misleading identify disc was from a crew member who had previously served with KG53.

Sadly, control of the crash site appears to have been very poor, not only from an intelligence point of view, but public safety. The preliminary report states that three quarters of an hour after the crash landing, souvenir hunters were picking over the wreckage when a bomb exploded killing at least one civilian.

On the same day that Michaelis and his crew came down, another Dornier 17 (F1+FH) of 1/KG76 was brought down over central London, in one of the most famous cases of the Battle of Britain. The incident was used by British propaganda to highlight the bravery of the RAF fighter pilots, but there was a darker side to the incident which went unreported in 1940…

Intelligence log No. 543/1940 states that the Dornier crashed at the corner of Wilton Road and Victoria Station Yard, London SW1 at 1150 hours. It also starts by unusually stating that this aircraft had engaged the attention of three Interrogation Officers, straining the entire resources of AI1(k).

The report stated that the rear gunner and his part of the aircraft landed in Fulham and the tail unit ended up on the roof top of a house in Vauxhall Bridge Road. The pilot bailed out and came down in Kennington, where he was fiercely attacked by a crowd of people who tore his parachute and harness to shreds. It noted that the pilot, 27-year-old Oberleutnant Robert Zehbe had been severely wounded – in fact, we now know he died of his injuries, almost certainly from the civilian assaults.

The wireless operator, Obergefreiter Ludwig Armbruster, landed at Sydenham Wells Park without harm, while the air mechanic, Unteroffizier Leo Hammermeister, landed in Dulwich with some wounds. The observer,

Unteroffizier Hans Goschenhofer and the gunner, Unteroffizier Gustav Hubel, were both killed.

The aircraft had apparently disintegrated over the Victoria area of London and various documents fluttered down to be collected by the public. The surviving crew members told the interrogators that they had departed an airfield near Beauvais and flown at 15,000 feet. They were hit by anti-aircraft fire, causing one engine to 'pull badly' and the aircraft lagged behind the formation. It was then attacked by four to six Spitfires and the Dornier caught fire.

Fragments of a recovered diary, gave details of the Staffel movements since July 1940, including operations against various RAF airfields. The report which was signed off by Flight Lieutenant Guy Jepson, rather unfairly concluded, that the survivors (Armbruster and Hammermeister) had good morale, but 'were rather unintelligent'. No further mention was made about the terrible fate of the pilot Robert Zehbe.

Subsequent evidence found that Hurricanes of No. 504 Squadron had attacked the aircraft and one flown by Sergeant Ray Holmes appears to have struck the tail of the Dornier, causing it to detach and both aircraft fell to earth. Ray Holmes managed to bail out and was hailed a hero by the British media for saving Buckingham Palace. The same media not surprisingly, made no mention of the incident with Robert Zehbe.

Some subsequent researchers and historians have claimed that Zehbe was already injured by the time he landed by parachute, but the attack by the civilians appears to have been so severe, it was noted by the intelligence report as a fierce attack which shredded his parachute and harness.

There were surely further reports from Air Intelligence on this case and the death of Zehbe, but they appear to have been lost or destroyed.

While undertaking research for this book, I found the following account on www.getsurrey.co.uk. This was an interview with Ron McGill who was 10-years-old in 1940 and published on the 75th anniversary of the event in 2015. Ron told the reporter:

> 'The most vivid moment of my young life arrived in the late morning of the following Sunday, September 15, when my mother and I had been visiting relatives near Kennington Park and the sirens sounded. As we hurried along we began to hear the noise of the 'ack-ack' barrage and the sound of engines and then the formation passing overhead and turning eastwards again towards Dockland. To our astonishment we realised a

> green parachute was coming down on us and he skimmed the Oval cricket ground wall and dropped by the doorway of a community centre by the Oval underground. Unbelievably, the German airman had come down by a centre, packed out with the survivors of the East End bombing of the previous Saturday. A frenzied crowd came rushing out with as many weapons and knives they could grab to deal with this enemy, who had suddenly arrived at their door, although badly wounded and no obvious threat to anybody. The parachutist died. We found out later, that this German airman was Oberleutnant Robert Zehbe, the pilot of a Dorner 17.'

Ron McGill was also quoted by Alfred Price in his 1990 book: *Battle of Britain Day,* as well as another witness to the event at the Oval tube station named Walter Chesney.

Chesney had been on a bus with his wife by Oval tube station, when the air raid siren sounded and the passengers had to get off and take cover. The couple sought refuge in an archway opposite the station when suddenly:

> 'The German airman appeared beside them a few yards away, as if from nowhere. His parachute was caught over electric power cables and he ended up dangling just above the ground. People came from all directions shouting, "Kill him, kill him." They pulled him down, they went crazy. Some women arrived carrying knives and pokers and they went straight in and attacked him. In the end, an army truck arrived and half a dozen soldiers had to fight their way through the crowd to get him. They put him in the back of the truck and drove off.'

The intelligence report, together with the comments from Ron McGill and Walter Chesney in 1990 and 2015, leave little doubt that Oberleutnant Robert Zehbe was killed by an angry civilian crowd, although records give his date of death as 16 September 1940. These facts undoubtedly highlight the manner in which it strained the resources of AI1(k) and required the work of three Intelligence Officers.

Naturally the media reported the efforts of Sergeant Ray Holmes and not the apparent murder of the German pilot. Robert Zehbe was buried at Brookwood Cemetery in Surrey.

In a bid to ascertain exactly what occurred and what investigation had taken place, as well as the involvement of Air Intelligence staff, I wrote to the Metropolitan Police, the Surrey Historical Services in Woking (which holds old

Coroners records) and the Surrey Coroner's Courts to see if they held any details for this incident and death. Unfortunately, the Metropolitan Police did not have any records relating to this incident.

Coroner's records do not appear to have recorded any details, but I was informed this was unlikely, due to the fact it was deemed to be a death from wartime action and therefore did not sit within the realm of the Coroner. This appears to be the case, as the death of an RAF pilot from enemy action, would result in the issuing of a death certificate by his commanding officer. Although this was a death caused by an angry civilian mob, it is possible this was 'hushed-up' and the man's death was deemed to be due to action.

The intelligence officers of Air Intelligence and AI1(k) were very busy on 15 September 1940, with sixty-three prisoners arriving, while yet another airmen appeared to try and mislead them.

Leutnant Hans Bertel bailed out of a Messerschmitt 109E and landed near Maidstone in Kent. It appears he said very little, as the intelligence report (No. 548/1940), dated 17 September, gives little detail and states the aircraft had not been located, even two days after his arrival.

Hans Bertel told the initial interrogator, that he had been flying at 19,000 feet and thought he had collided with another Messerschmitt 109 and entered a spin, leading him to bail out. He had his identity disc and an Ausweis issued to him on 2.2.40 at Mannhein-Sandhofen, but Bertel claimed to be the Gruppe Adjutant of I/JG53.

The preliminary intelligence form gave his aircraft markings as < | +, but these may have been added without seeing the wreckage, as such markings referred to a Geschwader Adjutant and not a Gruppe Adjutant.

Hans Bertel was clearly a very experienced pilot and the holder of the Iron Cross First Class. The Air Intelligence files quickly identified that the number on Bertel's identity disc (65162), belonged to someone from 2/JG52 and this was confirmed when a prisoner from I/JG53 said they did not know Bertel.

The Air Intelligence system had worked once again in identifying Bertel and his unit, but what happened to his Messerschmitt 109E and whether he had collided with another aircraft is unclear to this day.

On the final day of September 1940, three Messerschmitt 109's came down with apparently very communicative non-commissioned officer pilots, as noted by their respective intelligence logs Nos. 656, 657 and 666/1940 which were signed off by Flight Lieutenant Guy Jepson.

The first two came down at 1400 hours, one at RAF Detling near Maidstone and the other on Clayton Farm, Peasmarsh, Sussex.

The Detling Messerschmitt 109 was flown by 20-year-old Gefreiter Erich Mummert of 4/JG52. The aircraft White 2+ also bore a unit shield of a red cat with an arched back. Full details of the pilot, including his identity disc, his Feldpost number and Ausweis were obtained, and he said he had departed his airfield at Calais at 1230 hours to escort bombers to London.

Erich Mummert, who was not injured, was one of six Messerschmitt's flying at 27,000 feet when they noticed Spitfires 1,500 feet below them. They immediately tried to form a defensive circle, but this was difficult to achieve with just six aircraft. The 109s had to head for home (presumably because they were low on fuel) when they were bounced by a Spitfire from above. Mummert dived to 20,000 feet, throwing off the Spitfire, but as he climbed again towards a formation of six to eight ME109's, he claimed he was mistaken for a British fighter and they attacked him. The attacking 109 hit his radiator, but his armour plating saved him from personal harm.

Mummert put the fighter into another dive down to 4,500 feet, but this time his engine overheated and he tried to make a forced landing on an airfield. He missed this airfield and found another (Detling) where he made a wheels-up landing on the edge of the landing area.

Mummert said he had one and a half years flying experience and had completed about forty war flights, some in the past two weeks after his Staffel had returned to France. Although he claimed to have completed one flight in France and four to five over England, he had not achieved one aerial victory. He claimed he was about to be promoted and would also have received the Iron Cross.

The young pilot also told the interrogator that his Staffel had lost four aircraft on 27 September. He had flown from an airfield, one of twelve in the Calais, Colombert, Boulogne area. He claimed they were well camouflaged and he could land at St. Inglevert, if he could not locate his own airfield. A recovered map showing all these airfields was sent to AI3(b).

The aircraft which came down at Peasmarsh belonged to 3/JG52 and was flown by Unteroffizier Kurt Wolff, aged twenty-three, who received some minor injuries.

Like Mummert, Wolff had taken off from the Calais area to escort bombers to London. His Staffel formation comprised of twelve aircraft and were at 29,000 feet when they were attacked by about twenty-five Spitfires. Wolff claims to have put his ME109 into a steep bank, but lost control, he thinks due to the high altitude. He was then attacked by a Spitfire and shot through the controls and engine which suddenly stopped. Wolff circled downwards and bailed out before being captured.

Kurt Wolff admitted to flying throughout the French campaign before going to Zerbst and then on to Bonninghart near Krefeld. At the beginning of August, he moved to Brussels. He claimed to have flown on operations from Calais and on one to RAF Kenley when his engine stopped, but he managed to get home from 19,000 feet.

Interestingly, Kurt Wolff claimed to have been a gunner on a JU87 Stuka in 1938, before training to become a pilot.

In terms of Gruppe losses, Wolff claimed these were made good by pilots and aircraft from the fighter training schools. All new pilots were fully trained and ready to go into action. The report ended by noting his morale to be good and he was friendly and pleased with his treatment at the hands of his interrogators.

Unteroffizier Horst Perez of 4/JG26 came down at Eastdean, west of Eastbourne at 1730 hours. He made a wheels-up landing, presenting Air Intelligence with another example of a Messerschmitt 109E, which was noted to be in good condition. The aircraft was coded 4 + - with a white figure 4 outlined in black. The '*S*' Schlageter Geschwader crest and a Tigers head Staffel emblem were also noted on the fuselage.

Horst Perez stated his unit had taken off to escort bombers, flying at between 16-18,000 feet via Eastbourne to London. Unfortunately, the bomber formation never arrived and the ME 109's circled over Eastbourne at 28,000 feet, only to be attacked by British fighters. A second attack followed and Perez's engine failed.

Unfortunately, as Perez exited his cockpit, he was shot and wounded in the hand and jaw. Given immediate first aid, he asked the RAF interrogator about a number of friends who had been recently reported missing. One was known by AI1(k) to belong to 4/JG26 and the other two were from I/LG2.

Despite his injuries, he was interrogated and told the officer he had only recently arrived in France, but had been making at least one sortie a day – weather permitting. Prior to arriving in France, he had been in Vienna.

The report concluded that his morale was fair, but he was not very sure of himself – which was probably due to the circumstances of his wounding!

Air Intelligence also started to see a number of Austrian airmen coming to the attention of AI1(k).

On 30 September, Gefreiter Gustav Strasser of 6/JG52 arrived, having been shot and seriously wounded near Dorking in Surrey. His injuries were so bad, there was only a short interrogation of the pilot, before he was sent off for treatment. Despite his situation, the pilot managed to tell the primary interrogator that he had not been attacked by British fighters and his engine caught fire, causing him to take to his parachute.

Despite his injuries, the pilot's spirits were deemed to be very high. He was an Austrian who announced that he had been a member of the Nazi Party in its 'illegal days'.

It was clear that he had only just completed his flying training, as a letter in his possession stated he had been at *4 Erganzungsjagdgruppe* (Fighter school) at Merseberg on 9 August 1940.

Another Austrian who arrived into the custody of Air Intelligence on the last day of September was Oberleutnant Freidrich Oeser, the 22-year-old pilot of a Junkers 88 (3Z+DK) of 2/KG77, which made a forced landing on Gatwick racecourse in East Sussex after a fighter attack. Upon preliminary interrogation, Oeser freely admitted to having served three years in the Austrian Air Force, before being transferred to the Luftwaffe. He was admitted to the officers' ward of the Royal Herbert Military Hospital at Woolwich for treatment and was still a patient in December 1940.

Air Intelligence and the wider Intelligence community, now knew that the German military was taking military personnel from Austria into its own forces. They also knew the Luftwaffe had tried to recruit personnel from the Czechoslovakian air force, but with much poorer results.

It was clear to the staff at AI1(k) that for most men, their morale was beginning to dip. If they were not like Horst Perez or the Austrians, they seemed content to have been captured alive and in one piece. In the past, it was assumed this was because airmen believed victory was assured and they would soon return home; now it appeared, stressed airmen were just glad to be alive and out of the fight.

With the recent heavy losses, the Luftwaffe started to reduce the intensity and number of daylight attacks on Britain. Heinkel's, JU88's and Dornier's started to make night-time raids, using the cover of darkness to try and evade the Spitfires and Hurricanes of Fighter Command. The JU87 Stuka dive-bombers were almost completely withdrawn from operations over England and the once much vaunted ME110 was relegated to fighter-bomber missions. This left the ME109's to continue their fighter sweeps across south-east England, often escorting 'Jabo' or bomb-carrying ME109's.

As the autumn approached, it brought with it thicker clouds, heavy rain, fog, mist and later some frost.

Most German airmen knew the planned invasion was over, whether it would happen in 1941 was immaterial, aerial operations would continue and those already captive, would have a winter in a prisoner of war camp to look forward to.

Chapter 17

The General Reports

AI1(k) over the summer of 1940, collected a vast amount of information. The registry and document sections continually added to their binders and filing cabinets, listing pilots, observers, aircraft, units, Staffel and Geschwader emblems etc.

AI1(k) completed a large number of reports from these files which would be disseminated to various other intelligence departments. In this chapter, we shall take a look at some of those composite general reports, many of them signed off by Squadron Leader Denys Felkin, as well as the reports completed on various German Geschwader during the summer of 1940.

Air Intelligence had been compiling general intelligence reports since the start of 1940 and we have already seen examples concerning the German paratroop force, its structure and weapons in May 1940.

On 1 August 1940, Air Intelligence report No. 213/1940 discussed some of their recent findings concerning the Luftwaffe. They identified that wireless operators had started to be equipped with a steel helmet, made of a thin pliable steel and covered in leather. In addition, it had been reported that some rubber dinghies were being equipped with a wireless transmitter, which on a fixed frequency of 5,000 kilocycles, would automatically send out a continuous distress signal, possibly with the aircrafts call sign. A morse key was also included to send messages. In effect, this was a 1940 style emergency distress beacon, an antiquated version, but similar to those equipping modern aircraft and pilots today. The interrogators later found that the new equipment was not in the dinghy, but would float and start to transmit once in contact with the water. It was a very innovative idea for 1940.

The raids on Britain were naturally a concern for Air Intelligence, especially the tactics employed. Night bombing was of particular concern and although AI1(k) was well on the way to identifying the *X-Gerät* systems, the report on bombing, appears to have deliberately misled and mis-reported any knowledge they had of the system in August 1940.

The report stated that night bombing was almost universally considered by airmen of the Luftwaffe to be unsatisfactory, as it was often impossible to aim accurately. German airmen it added, relied to a large extent, on direction-finding for navigation. This resulted in them being unable to locate a target easily at night. Luftwaffe bomber crews without exception, said they were trained for daylight precision bombing, maintaining that no matter how well trained they are, night-bombing cannot really be accurate. Despite this, numerous crews claimed to have been sent out at night to gain experience.

The report continued and with the hindsight of over eighty years, it is clear the prisoners were trying to mislead their interrogators or telling them what they believed they wanted to hear. The report states:

> 'Whilst admitting that the RAF raids have caused quite a lot of material damage, they say that, in spite of the ease in picking up the coast, owing to the climate, night bombing is more difficult against this country than against Germany...
>
> Many prisoners of war admit that considerable damage has been caused by our raids in Germany, and the Ruhr and Rhineland at least, regard daily air raids as inevitable with disturbing effects upon the population.'

We now know the RAF in 1940 was hardly inflicting a scratch upon German targets, with many bombs missing their targets by many miles.

This intelligence report continued, stating that there were various reasons for the 'half-hearted ineffectual daylight raids against this country'. Small bomb loads were carried, as the French airfields were inferior and sub-standard for German bomber operations. In August 1940, it was claimed that many units were still re-equipping and reorganising following the battle for France.

Night raids on Britain, according to the report, were nuisance raids, necessary as a sop to the German people and because of the expected effect upon British arms production. Bomber crews said they were under strict orders not to bomb, unless they could identify the target and they often returned home with their bombs. This was contrary to the situation in France, where 250 kg bombs were dropped indiscriminately on towns.

While it was known German airmen sought cloud cover for protection, at night they wanted clear moonlit operational conditions. Often an experienced crew would be sent out to check the weather and report back by wireless. If the sky was clear, a main raid would go-ahead. Many prisoners reported being given vague instructions on what targets to bomb, such as oil tanks in a certain area or a coastline, rather than a precise target.

Almost without exception, Luftwaffe prisoners stated that the German people and in particular the Fuhrer, hoped for peace and to avoid 'total warfare'. They seemed to pity the British, because they claimed they do not realise the full-scale of the attack when it comes. Many prisoners believed that raids of 1,000 aircraft a time would be sent over and with their new Lofte bombsights, they would pulverise their targets.

While prisoners appeared to either mislead the interrogators or were perhaps not aware of the special navigational-bombing aids on some aircraft, it is clear AI1(k) were not disclosing what they knew about *X-Gerät* and *Knickebein* in their general report – a report that could end up in anyone's hands.

All prisoners who spoke about the subject, stated the German forces would not be the first to use poison gas, this they claimed, was due to the Fuhrer being an old infantryman and 'Such a humane man'. One prisoner spoke about bacteria bombs which would be used if the British used poison gas. However, the report added that this man probably had no real information on this matter.

A month later, on 1 September, another General report was submitted (No. 369/1940). This time it noted:

> 'Recent arrivals have been interrogated regarding their views on the present period of activity. While the majority, either have no idea what is going on or believe that at last, the great attack is about to commence, a few have given a different explanation. The present attacks will probably be intensified for a short period, if weather conditions permit and are designed with three main objects:
>
> 1. To reduce our fighter strength and
> 2. To undermine and destroy civilian morale,
> 3. To put our defences to the test.
>
> In connection with point 3, several prisoners mentioned that the correct tactics would be to send over two large attacks. The first could be entirely shot-down and the fighters will have to come down to refuel and re-arm. While the fighters are grounded, the second attack would develop and destroy all our fighters on the ground.'

Again, with eighty years of hindsight, we now know this was only partly correct. The Luftwaffe was keen at this time to destroy the RAF airfields and Fighter

Command, but it is obvious the detailed strategy had not totally filtered down to the grass roots airmen. The comment about destroying civilian morale, certainly marked a shift away from earlier claims of returning home with bombs and not hitting towns.

The prisoners were noted as showing increased signs of strain, being on a constant state of high preparedness, but they still believed in a German victory, simply because this 'Must happen'.

The intelligence report noted that a Junkers 88 coded B3+BM, of 4/KG54, the crew led by Hauptmann Lothar Maiwald being captured, was brought down in a forced landing on 21 August, at Kings Sombourne, Sussex. An interesting sheet of paper was recovered with some written notes on it, probably added during a lecture or briefing. There was a clear inconsistency in the typed document and the handwritten notes.

The typed words stated that bombs must not be brought back to base, but only targets were to be bombed. Houses are not to be struck. Bombs were not to be dropped on the outskirts of London or Liverpool. However, the added handwritten notes stated there were exceptions when the bombs had to be jettisoned or there was an attack by fighters.

The document also stated that trained crews could only undertake single aircraft flights and cloud cover must be available. No Unteroffizier crews were to be used (i.e. a crew without an officer or a senior NCO on board).

It was also clear there were concerns about sabotage on the airfields in France, as the document included instructions to check for sabotage. These checks included fuel filters which had to be tested daily, fuel tested for water and all acts of sabotage discovered were to be reported immediately.

A further general report dated 27 September, noted that various prisoners had told their interrogators about a new Focke Wulf fighter, although no pilot prisoner had actually flown one. The various statements allowed AI1(k) to put together a very good description of this new fighter:

> 'The fuselage is very high and fairly substantial, and there is apparently a very high tail wheel, so that entry into the fuselage has to be made by a ladder. The wings are narrow, very short and have a pronounced taper. They are set rather lower in the fuselage than in the case of the ME109. The tail unit is more rounded than that of the ME109. The aircraft is reputed to have a better all-round performance than the ME109, having a superior take-off, steeper rate of climb, and a landing speed said to be in

> the neighbourhood of 180/190 kph. The maximum speed is approximately 70 kph higher than that of the ME109. The armament consists of one cannon and four machine guns.'

In September, prisoners started to report that the Messerschmitt 109 was being used as a fighter-bomber, but this hindered performance and the general opinion was against this new tactic.

It was noted that a large number of Messerschmitt 109's brought down over the past month had damage to their radiators. Many pilots of these aircraft complained about this vulnerability and added that armour was needed, even if it reduced the aircrafts performance.

Messerschmitt 109 pilots had varying opinions on the merits of their aircraft and those of the Spitfire. However, the general opinion was that the Spitfire was superior. One pilot stated that the best way to avoid a Spitfire, was to bank away sharply and enter into a shallow dive, endeavouring at the same time to turn without letting the nose drop further and turn back onto the Spitfire. The pilot did however state, that in a tight turn the Spitfire was superior.

These comments are interesting as historians know that the fuel injected engine of the ME109 allowed it to enter a negative-g dive, whereas the Spitfire's 'float' carburetor would cut out momentarily due to fuel starvation. It is likely the ME109 pilots knew this by late September 1940, but it does not appear to have been mentioned or discussed in the various interrogations. Did the 109 pilots try to mislead their interrogators?

Although the issue of Spitfire vs ME109 performance was not discussed in greater detail, there were paragraphs detailing cold start procedures for the ME109 and even the Dornier 17 bombers.

The general report moved on to the use of smoke producing units on some German bombers.

On 15 September 1940, a Dornier 17 (F1+FS) of 8/KG76 made a forced landing at Lullingstone Castle Farm near Eynsford, Kent. The crew of four were captured, three being wounded, one of whom died shortly afterwards.

Examination of the aircraft by AI1(g) identified a previously unknown smoke producing unit. The surviving crewmen in interrogation, stated this had never been used by them, but they thought it was to make any attacking fighters think the aircraft was on fire.

AI1(g) noted that the apparatus was set up externally on the tail, with a jet pointing to the rear. In the rear fuselage were bottles of hydrogen, nitrogen and oil. The technical experts surmised that the nitrogen ejected the oil, which was ignited by a pilot light type device using the hydrogen. This would cause the smoke and possibly some flame to extend from the rear of the Dornier.

The AI1(k) general report stated that in addition to this aircraft, Oberleutnant Hans Kauter, the observer of a JU88 (4U+BL) of 3(F)/123, brought down at Machynlleth, South Wales on 7 September; had a diary in his possession with an entry saying he had been engaged in special work in connection with smoke apparatus. His diary noted that he had interviews with officials at the German Air Ministry and on one occasion with a Field-Marshal.

Hans Kauter was interrogated and said he had, 'Tried out a smoke producing system on a Dornier 17'. This he was told, was to produce a smoke screen for troops while flying at just 120 feet. Kauter gave a detailed technical description and eventually admitted that he had carried out experiments in connection with the use of mustard gas, but no further information was given. He did add, that Germany would not be the first to use the poison gas and the Fuhrer was absolutely against this.

The report added a few paragraphs regarding a device for seeing in the night sky (see the chapter on *X-Gerät* and *Knickebein*), before moving on to the possibility of an invasion.

One prisoner, an unidentified Major in a bomber unit, identified as A504, but believed to be Max Gruber of Stab II/KG53, stated that General Oberst Busch of the 16th Army was to command the invasion force. (Author's note: this was likely as he commanded the 16th Army in France and later took it into Russia in 1941.) The prisoner added that the war could not end without an invasion and that it would be attempted with tanks landing at several places. He also stated the German General Staff believed the RAF only had 700 front line aircraft left.

With the Battle of Britain changing, another General report was issued on 7 October (Log No. 710/1940). This one noted Luftwaffe prisoners of war say the British searchlights are more numerous than German lights and much more powerful. They also stated that British AA fire was more accurate. The high-quality of defences around Dover had also been mentioned. How and what the German airmen were comparing the British guns to is curious, unless they had come under fire from their own anti-aircraft guns or were just comparing it to French, Belgian, Dutch and Polish guns?

The prisoners also commented on the fact that British searchlights and gun batteries were located around targets and therefore it was easy to locate a target. Another airman said the guns on the Essex coast pointed towards Orfordness and this was an aid to their navigation.

One unidentified prisoner stated that the JU88 can be fitted with an iron cutting device called a *Blechschneide* for cutting barrage balloon cables. Another prisoner, somewhat oddly reported that ME109's can be fitted with an iron bar to push aside balloon cables, but he had no personal knowledge of this (and his comments were almost certainly meant to deceive). The same man also said Heinkel IIIs were being tested with a triangular wire frame for similar reasons.

It is clear that many prisoners tried to divert and mislead their interrogator, probably having a good laugh with their comrades in the M-Room. However, whatever the truth, the report noted that it was indicative of the fact the balloons were a real concern to the airmen.

Poison gas was never far away in these general reports and this one concluded with some worrying comments to go with the issue of the gas-laying aircraft mentioned in the last general report.

Two unidentified Messerschmitt 109 pilots claimed that if the stalemate continued, Germany would use every weapon which might give them an advantage. This included chemical warfare and specifically poison gas.

In addition to the general reports, AI1(k) completed regular reports detailing all manner of information and intelligence.

A lengthy report (No. 214/1940) on 2 August, highlighted the training and length of service for prisoners of war. It even detailed the daily regime at the wireless operators' school in Halle, before examining ten servicemen's careers in some detail.

Log No. 216/1940 gave details of how to set up and test the new Lofte C7a bombsight before a mission. This included details of sighting, angles and ground speeds, before adding the aiming procedure on approach to the target. Who gave this information is unknown, but a slip of paper was found in JU88 (9K+HL) of 3/KG51 which crashed in Sussex on 28 July. The crew, which consisted of Oberfeldwebel Josef Bier, Leutnant Willi Ruckdeschel and Unteroffiziers Heinz Ohls and Martin Multhammer, were all unharmed and in fair to good spirits. It is possible, but not confirmed that the observer, Leutnant Ruckdeschel, may have provided this information to the interrogator. The information gave precise details on how to set-up the bombsight with a certain ground speed at various altitudes – the information was very interesting to the RAF and its associated scientists.

Security in the Luftwaffe continued to be slack during the first year of the war. The interrogators and various other Air Intelligence departments were inundated with information, maps and documents that should never have been taken on operations.

By September 1940, numerous prisoners were being detained with personal notebooks, that not only contained many helpful details, but comments from lectures they had attended. AI1(k) reports state the various captured notebooks complied with a definite scheme showing that the lectures had been ordered by a higher authority. The lectures appeared to fall into two headings, firstly how much or how little should be taken on board an aircraft and what information should be given to any interrogating officer upon capture. In summary, security lectures had told them that only identity discs and Ausweis papers should be taken on board the aircraft, while pay books and flying certificates should be left at home. Clearly, this was not always adhered to.

Although prisoners showed a general reluctance to divulge their own unit details, fighter pilots in particular, were happy to ask about missing colleagues from their own Staffel. This naturally gave away their own Staffel, Gruppe and Geschwader. Added to the knowledge of identity discs, Ausweis papers and Feldpost number details, it was simple to work out the airman's unit. This was so prevalent, AI1(k) recommended this be pointed out to British airmen in case they were captured and they fell into this trap.

The second area of the lectures dealt with 'Field Security' and encompassed the civilian population in France and sabotage. One prisoner from KG53, said his Staffel had three aircraft maliciously damaged on their airfield and crashed just after take-off.

One airman's notebook contained instructions regarding the drawing of tracks on maps. The planned track should never be drawn right up to the target and their return airfield. However, AI1(k) noted that these instructions did not seem to be carried out and drawn tracks often led to a precise target and all the way home to their airfield.

Other reports by AI1(k), covered technical details on bombs and their ballistic properties, as well as Luftwaffe fighter tactics and escorting bombers. They even discussed the issue of 500 kg bombs with cavities for gas contained in glass containers (Log No. 145/1940).

The losses on 15 September, led to a single report for that day, No. 568/1940. The report signed off by Denys Felkin on the eighteenth, stated that thirty-two enemy aircraft had been identified by AI1(k) as being shot down on the afternoon of 15 September. The total comprised of twenty bombers (Dornier 17's and Heinkel III's), eleven ME109's and a single Messerschmitt 110. Although the report could not state an exact number, it appears there were two to three distinct raids.

AI1(k) had identified the first raid between noon and 1240 hours, with five ME109's from JG27 and JG53 being brought down, as well as five Dornier 17's from KG76. The report states that a senior officer who was flying as a Rottehund and not in command of the operation, said in interrogation that more than one fighter Geschwader was operating on freelance patrols to create a diversion. This officer appears to be Oberleutnant Hasso von Wedel of Stab JG3. He was not in a position of command and on a freelance patrol when brought down near Ruckinge, Kent at 1215 hours that day.

The only other Messerschmitt 109 pilot of a comparable or senior rank captured that day, was Oberleutnant Helmut Reumschussel of 2/JG3, but he was the Staffel Kapitan. It therefore appears Hasso von Wedel was the prisoner providing this information, especially as we know from his initial interrogation and later interview with the psychologist C.H. Brooks at Trent Park, that he was very communicative and happy to talk to his interrogators. (See the later chapter on C.H. Brooks.)

Enemy aircraft brought down during the second and possibly third raids between 1430 hours and 1630 hours according to AI1(k), comprised of fifteen bombers from KG2, KG3, KG26 and KG53. Only six Messerschmitt 109E's was shot down.

A Major shot down leading one of the bomber formations (Max Gruber of Stab II/KG53), stated that the formation formed up over France and the escorting fighters joined them. As soon as everyone was in place, the Fighter Leader 'waggled' his wings and they set course. The fighter escort took position to the sides, above and behind the Heinkel bombers which were in a *Kette Kolonne* formation of nine *Ketten* in vics in line astern.

The Major added that the weather conditions had been difficult for a large-scale formation with clouds and poor visibility. On at least one occasion, they lost sight of the escorting fighters on the right of their formation. Fighters from the left side, therefore moved to the right of the formation and the Major assumed the initial formation had gone off to engage some Spitfires. (As already mentioned, the German aircrews nearly always referred to the British fighters as Spitfires, even though they were outnumbered by the Hurricanes – aircraft many of the POWs had encountered in France. It was therefore clear the Spitfire had taken on some form of legendary persona among the prisoners.)

It appears the Major, referred to as a Gruppen-Kommandeur later in the same report, states that the proportion of fighters to bombers, was less than two fighters to one bomber.

The morale of the German airmen when interrogated apparently did not show any marked deterioration since the start of the battle, although there were, as there had been on previous interrogations, isolated instances of limited training, especially amongst air gunners with poor morale. (This may also have been linked to the inadequate protection for the gunners when compared to that given to pilots, observers and wireless operators.)

The general report noted that documents from one aircraft of KG26, showed the crew to have been on operational service throughout the war and to have made nearly forty war flights. Only one aircraft from KG26 was listed as being shot down that day, a Heinkel III (1H+IH) of 1/KG26, which crashed at Foulness in Essex. The crew were well-known from other intelligence that AI1(k) had stored away in their library, including the mechanic, Feldwebel Karl Potenberg, who had previously featured in the German media.

The AI1(k) report added that there did not appear to be a shortage of aircrew and the fact some older men like Oberleutnant Hasso von Wedel were flying, was attributed to their want to take part, rather than any shortage of personnel.

A number of prisoners, especially bomber crewmen, described British fighter attacks as 'furious'. One crew had seen another member of their formation brought down after being rammed by a British fighter (this may have been Oberleutnant Robert Zehbe's Dornier struck by Sergeant Ray Holmes over Victoria). German bomber crews also believed that once an aircraft had been split from the main formation, all was lost and they would be shot down.

It was now apparent to AI1(k), that Luftwaffe losses were rising and probably unsustainable in the long term. In addition to the losses identified by Air Intelligence, various other pieces of evidence were being submitted to AI1(k) which identified other losses they had not recorded.

Intelligence log No. 605/1940 dated 25 September, states that during the previous month, a considerable quantity of miscellaneous effects had been delivered to the section. These had not been put through 'proper channels' and came from the most unlikely of sources. Despite this, considerable work by AI1(k) staff had identified that most items came from aircraft already recorded as being brought down, but other previously unidentified aircraft and crewmen were identified. The report contained an index detailing another seventeen aircraft shot down between 13 August and 15 September…

The first deduced that a body washed ashore at Portland, belonged to a crewman from a Messerschmitt 110 of 13/LG1. In many cases there was very little left of the aircraft or the unfortunate pilot or crewman. They could only be identified by piecing together bits of charred or sodden paperwork, identity discs or other documents. Although this work was valuable intelligence for the RAF, post-war this work also ensured that the relatives of German airmen could identify their relatives' graves.

The intelligence report also highlighted once again, that the Air Intelligence system was not infallible. Unteroffizier Albert Buschmeyer of 2/LG2 had suddenly turned up in a permanent POW Camp and no one seemed to know how he got there. Clearly too late for interrogation, his unit was assumed from his identity disc. Where his Messerschmitt 109 had crashed was also unresolved.

Similarly, Gefreiter Horst Liebeck of 7/JG26 was found in a hospital bed without the knowledge of AI1(k). His aircraft had come down at West Kingsdown, Kent after breaking-up under a fighter attack. He was initially identified as belonging to III/JG26, having an order in his personnel effects to collect 'ME109 werks No. 6309' which was stamped III/JG26.

Another deceased Messerschmitt 109 pilot was discovered and identified, when his decomposed body was washed-up at Dover on 15 September. A prisoner asked about this man and a document on the body was stamped 4th Staffel, leading to the deduction this was Leutnant Richard Larisch of 4/JG3.

Towards the end of the Battle of Britain in late October 1940, AI1(k) had a detailed understanding of not only Luftwaffe aircraft, personnel and structure, but also its training and morale.

Intelligence log No. 687/1940 noted that there had been no depreciation in the training and experience of Luftwaffe personnel over the summer. A number of recently arrived prisoners had only just joined their operational units, but in many of those cases, they had already completed a number of war flights in other theatres of war.

In relatively few cases, interrogators found that some prisoners seemed to be perhaps undertrained when judged against previous standards, but this was not the case with KG26. Their crews were very experienced and on operations for the past year. In fact, some of the Geschwader pilots had completed so many operations, they allegedly no longer counted their flying hours.

Some prisoners were very experienced and one prisoner had nine years military service and kept a complete journal of his career from 1931 to 1940. The airman identified as an Oberleutnant with 5/KG53 was shot down on 7 September and has now been positively identified as Oberleutnant Heinz Bauer, an observer on a Heinkel III brought down on the Isle of Grain in Kent.

Air gunners were considered by AI1(k) as the worst trained prisoners, although many of them had served previously and for some time as ground staff, usually as mechanics, before becoming gunners.

AI1(k) noted that there were some signs of a shortage of experienced Luftwaffe officers. As we have seen, Hermann Göring was said to have forbidden two officers from flying together in one aircraft and Air Intelligence linked this to the loss of an aircraft (G1+AA) on 14 August. On that occasion two officers, Oberste Alois Stoeckl the Geschwader Kommodore and Walter Frank together with an Oberleutnant Bruno Bossler were killed.

In addition, another prisoner stated during interrogation that many Feldwebels were being granted commissions. The prisoner somewhat pompously added that although they were admirable Feldwebels, they were hardly suited to an officer's role!

Morale was deemed in most cases to be very high despite the losses, but the nervous strain previously noted had disappeared according to the general report. It appeared losses were now being felt and a more fatalistic attitude had over taken the men. The number of prisoners recounting at length what would happen to Britian had become fewer in number and there was a growing realisation, the war against England was not going to be such an easy matter.

It was alleged that each day, two sets of German losses were prepared, one for Josef Goebbels and press publication, the other for the Air Ministry and circulation within the Luftwaffe.

As previously noted in discussions between prisoners in the M-Rooms, the awarding of the Iron Cross seemed to be made on a fairly wide basis. Ground personnel had reportedly been awarded the Iron Cross Second Class for being bombed, but one fighter pilot had completed two hundred war flights without a single victory. He then had a scrap with a Spitfire and saw it dive away leaving a trail of white smoke which turned black. His claim was confirmed and he was awarded the Iron Cross First Class.

The AI1(k) report took great delight in talking about supplies and resources. German airmen believed Britain to be short of food and petrol, being on the verge of starvation. Three Luftwaffe officers were so convinced of this, they decided to call the interrogators bluff. They saved up their prisoners 'pocket money' (given to them under the Geneva Convention), until they had £1 and then boldly asked for chocolate to that value. They were surprised when they received their pounds worth of chocolate which was a vast quantity in 1940.

AI1(k) took particular interest in the letters many prisoners had in their possession when captured. Many of the letters from relatives contained mention of British air raids on Germany, but there was no specific mention of damage, the general report stating the letters often merely echoed German radio and media accounts of the bombing. Many letters contained only family matters. One thing Air Intelligence did note, was an increase in the number of lucky-charms, as well as religious and sentimental items, often sent by female relatives to the prisoners. This it was believed was a reflection of the fact losses were beginning to mount and relatives and girlfriends were seeking solace in such items.

Letters from experienced prisoners who had been in camps for some time, were noted as becoming dispirited, this was because newly arriving prisoners were not telling them all the news from home. The first prisoners were very guarded with their information when writing home, but as time passed, they started to make errors and included some facts. These included the fact the castle at Langenbielau in Silesia held British POWs and details of the wireless operators intensive course at Halle and the Night Flying School at Pillau.

The AI1(k) report stated it was too early to make any sound judgement about the morale of individual units, but some were beginning to become recognisable. For example, airmen from KG77 were almost churlish in refusing to answer questions during interrogation. In contrast, pilots from JG3 although reluctant to give anything away, were very pleasant (see the final chapter on JG3). KG2 crewmen were noted for their snobbery and there was a large gulf between officers and NCOs across all units.

It is clear Denys Felkin's team at Trent Park had an excellent understanding of the Luftwaffe and its personnel. In fact, by the end of the Battle of Britain they were even reporting on rumours they had overheard from prisoners of war.

In one report, dated 1 November 1940, Denys Felkin stated there were a number of rumours amongst prisoners from different units and although there was nothing to indicate any credence to these rumours, it would be interesting to trace the source of such rumours.

Many prisoners boasted about the number of British aircraft captured intact, in many cases the crew having allegedly made a perfect landing and walked away, making no attempt to destroy their aircraft.

One account mentioned a Whitley bomber brought down intact near Oldenburg airfield in August 1940. When it was examined, it was said to contain eighty cannisters of microbes, thereby proving the British were planning to use chemical and bacterial warfare against Germany.

Other rumours from the prisoners were just ridiculous, including one that so many British fighters had been lost (about 3,000 it was said), the RAF was short of aircraft and machine guns. In fact, it was claimed fighters were taking off without any armament. Another claim was that the British anti-aircraft guns were so short of ammunition, they were firing blanks.

The claims continued, with one stating a formation of Spitfires had outnumbered a German formation, but refused to attack and turned away. It was always impossible to identify a link and origin to these rumours, but it was not hard to believe many of them emanated from the German Propaganda offices in Berlin.

Chapter 18

The Geschwader Reports

AI1(k) completed a number of reports on the various fighter and bomber Geschwader and some of these are examined in this chapter.

A report was submitted on 3 September 1940, detailing Kampfgeschwader 1 (KG1). It appears the report was submitted after five aircraft from this unit were shot down on 30 August. The objective of that raid, established after the interrogation of prisoners, was to have been an attack on the aerodrome and factories at Brooklands in Surrey and Farnborough.

The raid, according to one prisoner, contained 200-250 aircraft with an escort of Messerschmitt 110's. Five aircraft joined the attack from 5/KG1, but all five were shot down. (Seventeen airmen were captured, many of them injured and five were killed.)

Two maps were recovered from one aircraft with a number of triangles drawn upon them indicating various airfields. In addition, the observer, Feldwebel Richard Keter, had a diary in his possession which noted previous attacks on Rochester, Biggin Hill (x2) and Canterbury during August 1940.

Another aircraft (V4+MV) had a card found in its wreckage with courses calculated from Fecamp to Weybridge and Gravelines to Chatham and Harwich. The place of take-off for these aircraft had previously been given as Arvillers between Rosieres and Montdidier. It was also established by AI1(k), that on 17 August, the Staffel was at Dormfront near Montdidier and still located there on 22 August. However, one prisoner stated that on this final flight, they had started out from Nijmegen in Holland.

Although the five aircraft were from the same Staffel, they were classed as belonging to IV/KG1 because two of the prisoners had said they belonged to 10/KG1. Lettering on the aircraft which were badly damaged may have confirmed this, as they had a fourth letter which was a 'V' (e.g. V4+BV, V4+MV etc.). However, a later POW and documents proved that in spite of the lettering, the aircraft were from 5/KG1.

These deductions were confirmed by AI1(k) when they interrogated another POW and the Gruppen-Kommandeur of KG1 who stated there were only three Gruppen not four in KG1. This information almost certainly came from Major Willibald Fanelsa who was shot down on the 27 August in an aircraft of Stab III/KG1.

The report identified that the crew of aircraft V4+GV appeared to have only received a short period of training and the wireless operator Gefreiter Wilhelm Hofer, had only been in the Luftwaffe for twenty months. He had spent six months doing infantry training and nine months as a cook, before spending three to four months on wireless training at Halle. He then drifted from airfield to airfield for three months doing drill, before joining 5/KG1 in August 1940. He had been shot down on his first war flight and the interrogator noted that he did not like flying and had low morale!

The gunner from the same aircraft, believed to be Obergefreiter Walter Monninghoff was wounded, but his personal diary showed that in January 1940, he underwent training at Horsching near Linz and was then sent to *Ausbildungsgruppe 22* at Wels. At the end of March 1940, he commenced flying training at Gmunden and on 30 April, he was posted on to II/JG26.

What exactly happened to this man is unclear, he was with the 2nd Gruppe of the famous JG26 and its Messerschmitt 109's, but he appears to have been used as labour and eventually ended up at 5/KG1 as an air gunner on 16 August. He made his first war flight on 24 August and a second on the twenty-seventh. It was noted that there was also a complaint of 'no flying' in his diary while he was treated as labour. Could he have failed his flying training or committed some sort of discipline offence before being dispatched away as a gunner? It was certainly an unusual account, but he was shot down on just his third war flight against Britain.

As we have seen, AI1(k) were somewhat curious about the use of Messerschmitt 110's during the summer of 1940. By September, they started to put together quite a comprehensive history of the various units using this once much-trumpeted heavy fighter and presented it in intelligence log No. 447/1940.

Through detailed interrogation of prisoners, AI1(k) identified that prisoners from ZG26 had previously belonged to 3/JG142 'Horst Wessel' between January 1938 and September 1939. Therefore, ZG26 had been formed from a nucleus of men from that unit. This was confirmed when some recently arrived ZG26 prisoners had papers in their possession bearing the stamp of 1/ZG Horst Wessel 142.

Since May 1940, three Messerschmitt 110's from the First Gruppe had been identified as being shot down and associated preliminary intelligence reports were completed. A fourth loss had not resulted in an intelligence report – presumably because the crew had been killed.

Five preliminary intelligence reports were completed for aircraft from the Second Gruppe, but nine aircraft were identified as being shot down. The Third Gruppe had two reports relating to its losses, but a third machine had also been brought down.

There was some confusion at first about the fuselage coding U8+-- on the aircraft, as some prisoners from those machines had identity discs and papers indicating the aircraft were part of the First Gruppe of ZG26. One prisoner even possessed a photograph of his own aircraft marked U8+EK, but after interrogation, it was confirmed these markings referred to aircraft from I/ZG26, while somewhat confusingly, the 2nd and 3rd Gruppen aircraft were marked 3U+--.

The AI1(k) report could give no reason for the differing aircraft codes for aircraft from the same Geschwader, but thought it may indicate the possibility of a new unit being formed from elements of the First Gruppe ZG26.

Wireless code tables salvaged from various ME110 wrecks and dated 20 and 26 June 1940, show that at that time, I/ZG1, II/ZG26 and III/ZG26 were working together, but there was no mention of I/ZG26.

Various airfields and Feldpost numbers were identified from prisoners and various documents, while papers recovered from 3U+EP, referred to the *Verbindungsstelle Generalluftzeugmeister* at La Hulpe south of Brussels. This, AI1(k) surmised, may have been a maintenance unit for the ME110's.

On 16 September, another report was completed (No. 541/1940). This one detailed the Messerschmitt 110 Geschwader – ZG2. This one followed the structure of the first report and once again it was established that the aircraft in the First Gruppe were marked with a different fuselage coding when compared to those in the Second Gruppe; these being 3M+-- and A2+-- respectively.

One prisoner had told his interrogator there was no Third Gruppe in ZG2. Like the issue with aircraft codes on ME110's, this caused some confusion. AI1(k) surmised again, that either another ME110 Geschwader was to be formed and the crews from III/ZG2 were to form the nucleus of this new unit; or this was done to create the impression that far more Geschwader were operating than was actually the case.

AI1(k) was able to report that proven losses amounted to twenty-one aircraft or about 25% of ZG2 since 16 August 1940. However, a further six previously unidentified losses had been admitted by prisoners during interrogation and via the personal notebook of the Technical Officer of I/ZG2. This man being Oberleutnant Reinhold Messner of Stab I/ZG2, who was shot down on 3 September, in 3M+CB at Woodham Ferrers in Essex.

It was established that Major Ott, the Gruppen-Kommandeur of I/ZG2, was killed on the 11 August and his successor Hauptmann Kuelbel was killed the following day. The new Gruppen-Kommandeur was reported to be Hauptmann Heinlein, who had been Staffel Kapitan of 6/ZG2.

The Technical Officer's notebook, which should have been left on the ground, was a major source of intelligence for AI1(k). It noted that repairs were carried out at Guyancourt and Le Bourget, and that during 23 August to 5 September, aircraft of I/ZG2 were fitted with DB 601N engines; as were aircraft from II/ZG26 and III/ZG26. Armour plating was also being fitted to these aircraft.

The report concluded by stating that in the case of new aircraft being delivered, these would have an *Abwurfgerat* ('an ejector') fitted. Current Messerschmitt 110's, were not being converted, but AI1(k) suspected this was for the carriage of bombs, even though the unit had not been known to carry them. In time, this would prove to be a correct assumption and the aircraft would fly fighter-bomber missions.

KG26 had long featured in the intelligence reports of AI1(k) with their raids on the northern part of Britain. Although Air Intelligence built up quite a library of intelligence on this Geschwader, they needed to keep this up to date and on 23 September 1940, a further updated report was completed (log No. 598/1940).

In the weeks prior to the completion of the report, a large quantity of various documents had been recovered and the report's author, noted somewhat sarcastically, 'KG26's propensity in this direction (for taking documents on board their aircraft) are already well known.'

One aircraft 1H+ML of 3/KG26, came down on 11 September in Surrey. From logbooks found inside the wreckage, a full aircraft history could be traced, including when and where it was built, how many hours it had flown and when its engines had been replaced. By 11 September, various small parts had been replaced and the aircraft had completed approximately 300 hours flying time.

Another notebook belonging to the aircraft's air mechanic, gave lists of various aircraft work numbers and their unit codes, as well as lists of other air mechanics and ground crew with the Stab section and the 1st Staffel of KG26.

A new type of First Aid canvas satchel was recovered from one aircraft with a zip fastener. AI1(k) soon identified that the Medical Officer of KG26, seeing so many men returning with injuries, realised the standard First Aid kits were inadequate. He therefore placed three of his own improved kits in each aircraft.

It was established that the officer had given First Aid lectures and his kits had been well received, especially as one aircraft contained a report dated 24 July, when a crew returned with injured men. The report praised these new kits which were used to save the men's lives.

Two target photographs were also recovered from the crashed aircraft 1H+ML of 3/KG26. These depicted Barking Power Station and the Leven Road Gas works, both images were pre-war and dated 24 May 1939. They were probably taken by a passing Lufthansa aircraft which was suspected of taking images, while flying into Croydon airport on a regular route.

Like other airmen in different units, many prisoners from KG26 kept personnel diaries and notebooks which contained records of their own movements and war flights. One man had completed thirty-five war flights which AI1(k) described as more or less average for the 'old-stagers' of KG26.

The intelligence report ended by stating that a very cleverly written piece of anti-Hitler propaganda had been found in the aircraft 1H+BC (although no corresponding intelligence report for this aircraft can be found in the files). Despite it clearly being anti-Nazi in tone, AI1(k) did not attach much importance to it, noting that KG26 personnel had good morale and had shown a liking for dramatic and humorous writings of this type – clearly Air Intelligence did not understand the general lack of Nazi humour and this would almost certainly have been deemed treasonous in 1940. It is likely this was from a Heinkel III with the same coding 1H+BC of Stab II/KG26, reported as missing off the east coast of England on 5 September – the crew of four non-commissioned officers still being missing to this day.

The Messerschmitt 109E equipped fighter Geschwader were a source of curiosity for the staff at AI1(k), especially as the German media, rather like those in the First World War, had been keen to portray these knights of the air as Teutonic heroes. As we have already seen, the exploits of men like Franz von Werra were reported with photographs and diagrams, material that was happily catalogued for future reference at Trent Park. The careers and aerial victories of men like Adolph Galland and Werner Molders were reported incessantly, as were those of many other aces in the German media. As time wore on in 1940, AI1(k) established quite a database of the various JagdGeschwader (JG), although sometimes spellings and ranks left a lot to be desired...

Air Intelligence log No. 591/1940 gave a summary of JG27, starting with its commander, Oberst Ibels (Authors note: actually, Max Ibel). The report stated he lacked the colourful personality of a Galland or Molders, but appeared to be a sound commander. He had been awarded the Knights Cross in August 1940 for the unit's attacks upon French armoured columns near Montcornet and Poperinghe.

The *Frankfurter Zeitung* (newspaper) on 31 August 1940, had reported that JG27 had shot down 300 enemy aircraft and destroyed another 175 on the ground.

The report noted that the Gruppe-Kommandeur of I/JG27 had been, according to one prisoner, Major Riedel (Author's note: actually, Hauptmann Helmut Reigel), but he had been shot down and was posted as missing over the Channel. The Gruppe Adjutant was Oberleutnant Gunter Bode, but he was shot down and captured on 9 September and was the subject of intelligence log No. 497/1940. His ME109 was in good condition and recovered to go on display in various towns and cities.

The Gruppe-Kommandeur of II/JG27 was identified as Hauptmann (Walter) Andres, a man who enjoyed the confidence of his men and was regarded as a bit of a dare devil.

Other AI1(k) intelligence had identified the Staffel Kapitan of 5/JG27 as being Oberleutnant Dillberg (Author's note: actually Ernst Dullberg), but they were apparently short on intelligence regarding lower ranks individuals. They had little information about the movements of the First Gruppe, but the story of the Second and Third Gruppen was more complete.

Shortly after the outbreak of war, III/JG26 (Schlageter) was based at Dusseldorf and received additional pilots and aircraft taking them over their normal strength. Some of the more experienced men were posted to Doberitz to form the *Erganzungsgruppe 27,* which later became II/JG27. The unit was primarily used in defence of the Reich and was based in January 1940 at Jever. On a number of occasions, they intercepted British Wellington bomber daylight raids over the German Bight with many successes. In July 1940, they moved to the Calais area and with part of JG51 were attached to JG2 'Richthofen' Geschwader at Leewarden in Holland. The JG26 Gruppe took part in the Belgium, Dutch and French campaigns.

III/JG27 had been traced across various airfields in France from June to July 1940. They were based around Cherbourg and spent time escorting the *Seenotdienst* air-sea rescue aircraft over the English Channel. They also escorted JU87 Stuka attacks on Portland and the Channel convoys.

The morale of JG27 was deemed to be very high and the Geschwader had a number of well-known personalities, one man being the son-in-law of General

Eduard Milch. He was Oberleutnant Joachim Schlichting and would be granted the Knights Cross in 1941 and promoted to Major, even though he was a prisoner of war.

JG3 is a unit we shall concentrate on in a separate chapter at the end of this book, but suffice to say, AI1(k) held them in very high regard, despite the fact some rather mischievous characters like Franz von Werra belonged to this Geschwader.

JG54 gave AI1(k) some problems when identifying pilots and its various Staffeln. Eventually, according to intelligence log No. 707, in early October 1940, an unwounded prisoner with an identity disc number of 51575 allowed AI1(k) to identify him as belonging to II/JG54. This therefore enabled them to confirm a number of previous identifications from other prisoner interrogations. AI1(k) had by 7 October, identified thirteen JG54 aircraft shot down and another two men whom prisoners mentioned as being missing in action.

Interrogation of JG54 prisoners established that JG54, JG76 and JG21 had only one Gruppe each. They were amalgamated into the three Gruppen of JG54, so that JG76 and JG21 no longer existed as separate units. This intelligence was further enhanced and corroborated, when a prisoner from 7/JG54 had a paybook showing him to have been transferred from 1/JG21 on 5 July 1940.

The Geschwader Kommodore was identified as Major Hannes Trauloft and two months before the report, he had been the commander of III/JG54. It was also noted that in 1937, Hannes Trautloft, while an Oberleutnant, gave a display in an ME109, flying with two other pilots at the International Flying Exhibition in Zurich.

The II/JG54 in October 1940, had been in existence as a separate unit at Wien-Aspern before the war. It remained in Vienna for some time and its personnel still referred to themselves as the 'Wiener Gruppe'. After operating with JG51 during the French campaign, it became the I/JG76 and then II/JG54 in late July or early August 1940.

The AI1(k) interrogators identified that First Gruppe pilots never tired of the old political arguments. The Second Gruppe pilots appeared to have a much more easy-going Austrian attitude and were courteous and well-mannered. However, they were very security conscious and give very little information to their RAF interrogators.

The intelligence report noted that in July 1940, the Third Gruppe of JG54 had been formed from I/JG21. The Gruppe Kommandeur, Hauptmann Fritz Ultsch, was shot down and killed on 5 September at Bowers Gifford in Essex.

As a result, Oberleutnant Gunther Scholtz, the Staffel Kapitan of 7/JG54 was now the acting Gruppe-Kommandeur. According to intelligence received from JG54 prisoners, Scholtz was deemed to be a capable and popular leader, his confirmation as the new commander was believed to be a foregone conclusion and he has been credited with nine aerial victories against RAF aircraft.

In relation to III/JG54, the report noted that it was based in Holland at Bergen-op-zoom and some recovered documents bore the stamp *'Kdo Jagdgruppe Bergen'*. One unidentified prisoner of war told AI1(k) the Gruppe no longer used the name Bergen, but there is a reserve pool of JG54 personnel at Bergen, using the name *'Rest Kommando Bergen'*.

On 14 October 1940, intelligence log No. 746 reported on Jagdgeschwader 53. The report noted that JG53 had been formed by General Klein as a 'crack' fighter wing with special uniforms and either the Ace of Spades or the Tarot 'Card of Death' as their unit emblem.

The report added that JG53 had produced some notable officers including Werner Molders and Major Balthasar who had commanded Gruppen. Major Balthasar, it stated, is, 'Now commandant of the Fighter Training School at Werneuchen.' A number of other experienced pilots are also known to have flown in the Spanish Civil War.

These comments regarding Major Balthasar appear to be incorrect and an intelligence error. There was no known Gruppen-Kommandear at JG54 in 1940 named Balthasar, but there was Wilhelm Balthasar, who, having started with JG1, became Gruppe-Kommandeur of III/JG3 in September 1940. He became commander of JG2 in early 1941, before being killed in action in July 1941 – there is record of him being commander of a Fighter Training School at Werneuchen, but that was pre-war. Such inconsistencies were rare in the AI1(k) files, but when they were relying on prisoners for intelligence, mistakes could occur.

The intelligence report noted that the pre-war special uniforms and the Ace of Spades motif were suppressed by Hermann Göring. The Geschwader was now known as the 'Red Ring Geschwader' because of the red ring painted around the engine cowlings on their Messerschmitt 109s.

After the war, this comment has drawn the attention of historians and researchers who have questioned the reasons for this change, especially as the Geschwader later returned to their Ace of Spades emblem in late 1940.

Some sources claim that Hans-Jurgen von Cramon-Taubadel, the Kommodore of JG53, married a girl with family links to Judaism, Göring therefore punished the unit collectively by ordering them to overpaint their 'Ace of Spades' insignia with a simple red band around their engine cowlings. Cramon-Taubadel left the Geschwader in early October and the Ace of Spades emblem was allowed to return. However, some believe Göring allowed its return once the Geschwader had scored its 500th victory in mid-November 1940. Either way, it appears AI1(k) was not aware of these political shenanigans at the time.

The report also noted that with 453 victories at the time of the report, the Geschwader looked down upon other units and were, 'Particularly scornful of the much-boosted Richthofen Geschwader' (JG2). This comment is interesting, as we have already seen a conversation recorded in an M-Room of fighter pilots claiming the Kommodore of JG2 Helmut Wick was a 'Bluffer' and an overclaiming pilot.

The AI1(k) report noted that JG53 had developed a number of specialised formations and tactics, their favourite being a twelve aircraft formation divided into three *Schwarme* (flights). The leading *schwarm* would fly in echelon port and was called the *Angriffs Schwarm* (attack flight). The second or support *schwarm* flies echelon starboard, with the leading aircraft above and almost directly behind the lead aircraft of the *Angriffs Schwarm.* The remaining four aircraft of the third *schwarm* split into two Rotten (sections), flying in line abreast, the outside aircraft flying between 50–100 meters behind and in line with the outside aircraft of the first two *schwarme*.

The unit, by October 1940, was specialising in the escort of a Messerschmitt 109 (Jabo) bomber Gruppe, whose aircraft usually carried a single 500 kg bomb.

Pilots from JG53 reported undertaking two flights a day and rest days only occurred due to poor weather conditions.

Numerous prisoners from this Geshwader, stated that tests had been made with a captured Spitfire and the unit had devised attacking and defensive tactics. Their standard instructions when they have a Spitfire on their tail, was to climb or immediately dive at an angle of about forty-five degrees. Clearly, they had discovered the problem of the float carburetor in the Rolls-Royce Merlin engine and the intelligence had changed since the General Report issued on 27 September. In that report, one ME109 pilot allegedly stated the best way to avoid a Spitfire, was to bank away sharply and dive into a shallow dive.

The intelligence report continued, adding that contrary to comments from other POWs, some pilots from JG53 considered the Spitfire to be first rate in a dive, or climb steeper than forty-five degrees. One unnamed prisoner who had a fair amount of experience, was impressed by the Spitfires superiority in tight turns. He thought the only safe tactic for an ME109 to escape a Spitfire, was for the 109 to enter a steep bank and follow it with a shallow dive or climb. The report added that it was stated by prisoners, that in a one-v-one between an ME109 and a Spitfire below 21,000 feet, the Spitfire would be on the tail of the 109 after two to three tight turns. Above this height it was better for the Messerschmitt, the report claimed this probably accounted for the highly specialised formations used by JG53.

AI1(k) had noted a loss of thirty-five aircraft from JG53, six in August, seventeen in September and six in the first two weeks of October 1940. Another six were probably lost in September, but the intelligence team could not confirm this. The Geschwader Stab flight had lost one machine, while the First Gruppe had lost fifteen aircraft, the Second Gruppe eight and the Third Gruppe eleven aircraft.

This is just a small sample of the reports AI1(k) were compiling from the gathered intelligence, whether it be from prisoner interrogations, M-Room conversations, or documents and other media sources. The intelligence was not always perfect and there were some errors, but it certainly assisted the RAF and the Air Ministry.

Chapter 19

Leutnant Heinz Schnabel & Oberleutnant Harry Wappler

This is a very short chapter, but covers two very imaginative young German officers who were captured and passed through the intelligence system in 1940, before making an infamous escape attempt in 1941.

We have already looked at the behaviour and escape of Oberleutnant Franz von Werra, but there were other renowned escapers and two such men were Leutnant Heinz Schnabel and Oberleutnant Harry Wappler.

Leutnant Heinz Schnabel of 1/JG3 was an associate of Franz von Werra and had destroyed a number of British aircraft, when he was shot down on the same operation as von Werra, on 5 September 1940. Schnabel received some spinal injuries when he force-landed his Messerschmitt 109E on farmland at Handen near Aldington in East Kent at 1010 hours – the same time von Werra came down near Marden.

Heinz Schnabel when given an initial interrogation, admitted to being a pre-war civil flying instructor and was called-up at the start of the war. He had been wounded at Lille during the French campaign and would need further treatment for this and the injuries he sustained in his forced landing in a British hospital. He held the Iron Cross Second Class, but appeared to try and mislead his interrogators by stating he had made an escort mission to Manchester – a location well-beyond the range of a Messerschmitt 109E.

Rather than being sent to Trent Park, Heinz Schnabel was sent to the Royal Herbert Military Hospital in Woolwich. He was treated for his injuries and the old pre-existing chest injury from the campaign over France which caused him an issue.

After recovering from his injuries, Schnabel appears to have missed interrogation by AI1(k) at Trent Park and was sent to the London Cage in early 1941. This interrogation is covered in more detail in the chapter on the London Cage, but it appears Heinz Schnabel refused to discuss any military operations and tactics, but like his fellow JG3 pilot Franz von Werra, he was only too happy to give his political opinion!

After completing his interrogation at the London Cage, Schnabel was sent by train to join his old JG3 colleague Franz von Werra at No. 1 Prisoner of War Camp at Grizedale Hall in Cumbria. He was later moved on to the camp at Shap Wells Hotel in Cumbria, which was being used as Prisoner of War Camp No. 15 and it was there, he would meet fellow escaper – Harry Wappler.

Oberleutnant Harry Wappler was the pilot of a Heinkel III of 8/KG27, which was brought down on 13 September 1940. The aircraft had been on a night-time raid to Ellesmere Port near Liverpool and had bombed their target, when they headed for home via a secondary target in Newport, South Wales.

Over South Wales the aircraft struck what is believed to have been a barrage balloon cable and the Heinkel became uncontrollable. Wappler had decided to fly low to ensure they identified the target and for bombing accuracy. They were reportedly at 6,500 feet when they struck the cable above Tredegar Park. Wappler ordered the rest of the four-man crew to bail out, before he abandoned the aircraft and deployed his parachute.

Subsequent reports claim the bomber flew on, before hitting another balloon cable which brought it down on No. 32, Stow Park Avenue in Newport, killing two children in the house. The other three crewmen also died in the crash and do not appear to have heard Wappler's order to bail out.

Harry Wappler received some injuries, but he was subject of a preliminary intelligence report (No. 517/1940). Despite the loss of his crew and the dead children, his morale was deemed to be good and this had been his fourteenth war flight since the start of August 1940. The target, however, was deduced from the observer's map, which had a track to a position near Stanlow Point and a railway line (near Ellesmere Port).

Two other documents found in the wreck, gave details of a so-called 'Dislocation attack' on 7 September 1940. These attacks called for aircraft to take off at forty-five minutes intervals and each crew was given a choice of four targets depending on conditions. The other document was dated 8 September 1940, and gave details of nine aircraft, their identity codes, work numbers, flying hours on each aircraft's separate engines, their number of landings and assorted comments. Once again it provided AI1(k) with a major intelligence coup.

Like Schnabel, Harry Wappler was sent to the Royal Herbert Military Hospital in Woolwich for treatment of his injuries. He was eventually interrogated, like Heinz Schnabel, at the London Cage on 22 February 1941 and not at Trent Park.

Like Schabel's interrogation, this will be covered in more detail in the chapter on the London Cage, but we know he also gave very little information to his interrogators.

Once his interrogation was completed, Wappler was sent by train to the Shap Wells hotel prison where he joined up with Heinz Schnabel.

The two men soon started to plot their escape, especially as invasion was looking more and more less likely.

Schnabel and Wappler settled on a plan to use their Luftwaffe piloting skills. They secretly, with the assistance of other prisoners, made Dutch Air Force uniforms from their own clothing. The buttons were fashioned from plaster of Paris and they created false Dutch identity papers, but oddly with the rather English sounding names of Pilot Officer George Harry David and Flight Lieutenant Harry Graven.

On 23 November 1941, the two airmen hid in a pile of logs used for fuel in the prison camp. After dark and roll call had been concluded satisfactorily, the men forced their way through the camp fencing and headed towards the nearby railway line.

The two men had identified that the steep gradient at Shap Bank, made trains slow down and they waited for a passing train. Eventually, a north-bound goods train approached and slowed down enough for the men to scramble aboard one of its wagons.

In no time at all, the train pulled into the sidings at Carlisle and the two escapees went into the town and allegedly went to a cinema! After watching the movie, they mingled with the exiting crowds which co-incidentally included airmen from the nearby airfield of Kingstown. They quickly decided to go to the airfield, gaining entry at the gate with their false Dutch papers and hid behind a hangar.

The two pilots were fortunate enough to have stumbled upon an airfield which housed No. 15 Elementary Flying Training School (No. 15 EFTS). The airfield had numerous pilots passing through its gates and two new faces were not out of the ordinary.

The following morning (24 November 1941) Schnabel and Wappler managed to get an airman to start up a Miles Magister training aircraft for them and they took off. The two men had originally hoped to fly across to neutral Ireland, but the weather over the Irish Sea was not very pleasant and so they headed south hoping to cross to Europe.

Unfortunately for the daring duo, the Magister only had half a tank of fuel when they took off and as they reached the East Anglian coast, they realised they would not be able to fly to Holland. They landed the aircraft in a field near Scratby, just outside Great Yarmouth and discussed their options.

They were approached by a passing Police Sergeant, Clifford Fisk, to whom they showed their fake identity papers. Still keeping up appearances, Harry Wappler asked the officer if they could call the local airfield and request some fuel for their aircraft. Wanting to assist, Sergeant Fisk took Wappler to Caister Police Station while Schnabel stayed with the Magister with a second policeman.

It was now late afternoon and becoming dark, so a car was sent to pick up the two airmen and transport them back to RAF Horsham St Faith for the night.

The two men were questioned by a senior officer, but their act was co convincing, they were given rooms in the Officers Mess for the night. Eventually, news of their escape and the missing Miles Magister filtered through to Horsham St. Faith and the two men were quickly arrested in their rooms. Legend has it one was soaking in the bath when he was arrested.

The two airmen were taken back under guard to Shap Wells and sentenced to twenty-eight days solitary confinement. Like Franz von Werra, they were soon transferred to a camp in Canada, where they spent the remainder of their internment.

Yet again, Luftwaffe officers had shown their ability to escape and show great imagination and ingenuity.

Chapter 20

The C.H. Brooks POW Interviews (September-October 1940)

AI1(k) and various other elements of the intelligence network, were naturally very keen to obtain military information from the Luftwaffe prisoners held at Trent Park in 1940. Although some prisoners did divulge military information, most were reluctant to talk, but many of these prisoners were only too happy to chat about politics and life in Germany. Clearly, they believed this would not assist the interrogators or the British war effort, but in reality, this information was very valuable. It allowed the British to examine the political scene in Germany and the occupied countries, as well as farming, factory output, workers' rights in the Fatherland and the indoctrination of military personnel and civilians.

To examine the more talkative individuals, Cyrus Harry Brooks, a 50-year-old eminent psychologist was recruited to interview the prisoners. C.H. Brooks had written a number of books on the subject of 'suggestion' before the war and would later examine many leading German Generals and politicians in 1944-45.

In the UK National Archives, there is a small file (reference FO898/320) titled *Reports on interviews with PoWs – C.H. Brooks.* This file is logged under the Political Warfare Executive and Political Intelligence Department of the Foreign Office. The file contains summaries by Brooks of his interviews with prisoners of war between 1940 and 1942. Three papers give details of his interviews with Luftwaffe personnel at Trent Park in September and October 1940, and many of the facts he uncovered are very interesting and even surprising. He clearly enjoyed his chats with one man in particular – Oberleutnant Franz von Werra.

C.H. Brooks interviewed up to eight prisoners between the 16-19 September 1940 at Trent Park. Franz von Werra was in custody at that time and although he would not talk about military matters and information, as we have seen, he clearly was very happy to discuss National Socialism and politics. In many ways, C.H. Brooks discovered the real Franz von Werra missing from the 1950s books and the movie.

Brooks noted specifically that the most optimistic of believers in Hitler's victory, was Oberleutnant Von Werra, an ex-SA and SS man, aged twenty-six years, 'Who has a faith in Hitler that transcends the rational.'

Born in 1914, to Swiss aristocratic parents at Luek in Switzerland, von Werra was adopted by a German couple when he was a baby and his father was declared bankrupt. By 1925, Franz von Werra and the family were living in Cologne, but they too became impoverished by 1930. Clearly driven by circumstances, in 1933, Franz von Werra joined the SA – 'The Storm Division' of the Nazi Party, before joining the infant Luftwaffe in 1935. Commissioned to the rank of Leutnant in 1938, Franz von Werra was clearly an ardent Nazi, something omitted from the books and the movie *The one that got away.*

Brooks noted that von Werra believed consideration of the British naval and air strength, even the weather to be irrelevant. Hitler would decide when to invade and that would be the end of British resistance. Von Werra told his interviewer that everything that had happened so far was '*lacherlich*' (ridiculous) and in just twenty-four hours everything would be over…

Von Werra claimed that of the British defences, only the bare cliffs would remain. The German infantry having been landed in 'some miraculous fashion' would sweep over the country, blotting out the resistance of the 'ridiculous Home Guard'. He did however, say that no gas bombs would be used.

Brooks was quick to declare that von Werra was a successful product of Nazi education. With the possible exception of the Spitfire which brought him down, everything in Britain was 'ridiculous'.

Franz Von Werra claimed to have met Hitler several times and considered him to be a genius of colossal personal courage, who had proved this by visiting the front lines. Von Werra also laughably claimed that all active officers on leaving the Kriegsschule (War school), spent an afternoon and evening with the Fuhrer in Berlin.

The political chat soon turned to concentration camps and von Werra claimed that any officer can visit one of these camps if he so wishes. Brooks noted laconically, that he had never met an officer who had visited a concentration camp, none except this man Franz von Werra.

Von Werra openly supported pogroms and the beating of prisoners in concentration camps, although he claimed these were not so bad and are necessary for the rebirth of the nation. He declared his opinion that Germany was a modern Sparta and this would be a war to the death. When England loses, it will be '*Ausgeloscht*' (extinguished) he added.

Von Werra denied knowing anything of Fifth Column activities, although he admitted to hearing some rumours.

C.H. Brooks stated that he had specifically noted the opinions of von Werra for their psychological interest. His supreme confidence was exceptional when compared to the other Luftwaffe prisoners he had interviewed.

Von Werra was happy to disclose the fact he had visited aristocratic French connections in Paris and they had told him France's mistake was being dragged along by England; and they should never have entered the war. England had left France in the lurch and was sure to be beaten. His French connections now supported the government of Petain and were all for an understanding with Germany.

The German pilot told Brooks that French girls had been invited to the mess and treated in a '*Ritterlich*' manner (knightly or chivalrous). The girls believed their own nation had fought on the wrong side.

It is clear Franz von Werra left quite an impression on C.H. Brooks, but perhaps the most surprising element in today's twenty-first century, is his previously unreported ardent Nazi attitudes. One wonders whether Hardy Kruger knew the full facts when he played von Werra in the movie?

C.H. Brooks reported in this first report that as well as interviewing von Werra, he had interviewed a number of others who he did not name.

Brooks reported that when asked about reports of aeroplane losses, only two airmen accepted the German figures unconditionally. Two thought the reported figures from both sides were inflated by propaganda, while four others thought it impossible with the speed of air fighting in 1940 to make accurate reports – although despite saying this, one thought the German figures were correct!

Six of the prisoners (including von Werra) expressed an opinion on the outcome of the war. Three believed Germany would win, one thinking that victory would come before Christmas that year, while the others thought it would be in the autumn or spring the following year. Three airmen were uncertain of a victory, stating:

> '*Das kann keener Wissen*' (No one can know that)...
> '*Das muss man dem schicksal uberlassen*' (You have to leave that to destiny)...
> '*Das zu beurteilen bin ich ein zu Kleiner mann*' (I'm too small a man to judge that)...

One Gefreiter who had seen the ruins of Rotterdam after the Luftwaffe bombing stated:

> '*Sinnlos kaputt gemacht! Warum?*' (Senselessly destroyed! Why?)

The airmen stated that they lived in deserted houses in France and could not speak French, having little contact with the local population. Three men agreed there was no sign of hostility from the French civilian population and they were well cared for by the National Socialist People's Welfare group.

One airman said he believed the French were intimidated by their occupiers, but they hoped the British would win. Many French shops were closed and people queued for milk. The prisoner said he had heard of German soldiers being attacked at night, but knew nothing about sabotage. He added that German troops did not like being in France and wanted to go home.

Three of the younger prisoners interviewed had not been in the Hitler Youth, one because he came from a very rural area in which the Nazi Party was not really represented. Two other airmen had learned to fly gliders via the *Luftsportverein* which later became the *Fliegerkorps* of the Hitler Youth organisation.

The prisoners reported that farmers seemed to keep a surplus of products after quotas had been cancelled earlier in the war. People did not generally hoard food and goods because they did not dare, or they were too conscientious.

Apart from Franz von Werra, none of the airmen interviewed had been a member of the Nazi Party or admitted knowing anything about a party organization set up to look after POWs wives. Airmen prisoner wages they claimed, were paid to their wives at home in Germany.

At home, German children had not been evacuated. Most prisoners said they had no interest in religion, but some referred to themselves as Evangelist or Roman Catholic according to their baptism prior to the Nazi Party taking control. None of the men attended church in the Luftwaffe, but one man said he attended when on leave to keep his mother happy. The airman added that he had never heard of Pastor Niemoller (the imprisoned anti-Nazi who penned the poem '*First they came for...*'). He said sermons in Germany did not contain anything even indirectly political and although there were padres in the Luftwaffe, they were never seen except at a funeral.

Surprisingly, only von Werra claimed to know anything about the Gestapo or oppression. 'One intelligent Oberleutnant' even claimed that he did not know the Gestapo officials were drawn from the SS or that Himmler was head of the

Gestapo. One Feldwebel said, he had never seen a Gestapo man and asked if they wore uniform or civilian clothes. He added that he had no opinion on Jewish persecutions and had heard no lectures on the subject in the Luftwaffe.

These interviews were very illuminating for the British Intelligence Services and C.H. Brooks continued to talk to a wide range of airmen at Trent Park.

On 26 September 1940, Brooks interviewed Oberleutnant Rudolf Moller-Friedrichs, a Messerschmitt 109 pilot of 6/JG52, brought down over the Isle of Wight on 18 August. The German, who lost a thumb in the action, was happy to discuss matters with Brooks, having spoken at length to Flight Lieutenant Derek Rownsley of RAF Intelligence, when he was hospitalised at Netley near Portsmouth, before being finally transferred to Trent Park.

Moller-Friedrichs had been the head of Ideological and Physical Education of the Hitler Youth in 1935, visiting London to study the Scout Movement in the United Kingdom. He left the Hitler Youth, claiming he was dissatisfied with its aims and methods, joining the Luftwaffe and becoming a pilot and an officer.

Moller-Friedrichs claimed there was a movement in German political circles in favour of ending the war with Britain by means of a compensation. The movement he claimed had many influential supporters, including Party leaders and high-ranking military officers. No approach had yet been made via diplomatic channels, because it was believed, they would receive no response from the British.

The pilot told Brooks that the people in Germany believed continuance of the war was madness and would lead to the mutual annihilation of the two leading peoples of Europe. In his opinion, the Germans would be content with the re-establishment of the pre-Versailles frontiers and they would evacuate all the newly occupied territories. Germany would like its former colonies returned and to recreate a peaceful co-operation between the two nations. However, he believed that for this to succeed, the current German government needed considerable changes and Joachim von Ribbentrop for example, would need to go.

Moller-Friedrichs initially told Brooks that Hitler was amenable to influence and advice, but, if necessary, Hitler would not be allowed to stand in the way. He added that the German people were attached to Hitler, but what they wanted most of all was peace and freedom.

C.H. Brooks must have wondered whether this man was talking about a genuine section of the German society or was suffering a mental illness, especially when he stated that the object of the movement was the removal of the dictatorship. He believed the dictatorship had lost its justification and they needed the formation of an elected Peoples Government with power. He added that there were no monarchist tendencies in the movement, but if the British government were in favour of such an arrangement, he should be allowed to return to Germany to further a possible agreement with this new movement.

Moller-Friedrichs said he had considerable influence at home and implied that a certain member of the German government, would be ready to work in getting an agreement. He asked if he could meet with a person of authority and Flight Lieutenant Rownsley could be allowed to interpret for him.

Brooks was clearly unsure about this German pilot and his intentions. He noted at the end of his report:

> 'He is obviously by no means an orthodox Nazi and in so far as can be judged in a few hours talk, combines a certain naivete with shrewdness and for a Nazi, exception objectivity. He appears sincerely to believe the story and does not give the impression of a charlatan or a "plant." If such a movement exists, it is obviously to our advantage to know as much as possible about it, and on the face of it, the matter seems to be worth further investigation.'

Whether the matter was taken any further is unclear and I have been unable to identify what happened to the 26-year-old German pilot.

On 8 October 1940, C.H. Brooks submitted another detailed report concerning another four airmen he interviewed at Trent Park, three days before. Once again, they covered a wide range of views and concerns.

Oberleutnant Hasso von Wedel of Stab/JG3 was a man we have already examined earlier in the book. He was brought down, uninjured in his Messerschmitt 109E on 15 September at Ruckinge, Kent. The pilot was much older than his contemporaries, being forty-seven years of age and having fought with the German Air Force during the First World War.

Prior to the Second World War, von Wedel had been employed in the *Kriegswissenschaftliche Abteiling, Kriegsministerium* (War Science Department at the War Ministry), conducting research on the subject of German fighters in the 1914–18 war. He re-entered the Luftwaffe as a fighter pilot, partly because he wanted to compare present fighter tactics with those of the earlier war.

Oberleutnant Hasso von Wedel claimed to have made twenty-four war flights over England, considering the RAF to be an equal opponent, while fair and chivalrous.

He was sorry to have seen the German monarchy end and was sorry to give up his own monarchist ideas, but the monarchy in his homeland was finished.

Von Wedel considered Hitler a genius, who had proved himself by combining the idea of social equality with nationalism, for without nationalism, many Germans would not have supported him. Despite this claim, von Wedel claimed the big land owners in Germany were not wholly behind the Nazis, some rejecting National Socialism completely. Others accepted it because of the war, but only as long as the war continued.

The prisoner claimed the big land owners had gained much from the Nazis and there were no more labour and industrial troubles. Many land owners had given up land to rid themselves of heavy debts with interest rates of twelve per cent. The big industrialists still held considerable influence in Germany, but this was unofficial, through personal contacts with ministers and party officials.

Von Wedel also discussed their Italian allies, stating that he thought the organisation of the Italian Army had improved since 1918, but not the quality of individual soldiers. He believed a clash with Russia was likely, that nation's leaders being nationalists and realists, but the regime could not survive. Germany was not interested in Ukraine or the Black Sea, Hitler having changed his mind about this issue.

Hitler still wanted an understanding with England and the people of Germany were practically unanimously behind their leader on that issue. However, any peace must not be like that of 1918. Hitler did not want to see the break-up of the British Empire, as no other European power could hold it together and its survival was necessary for world order.

Despite these conciliatory claims, von Wedel claimed that a German invasion would occupy the whole of England in a month, this was because the British had no organisation or tradition of mobile warfare (blitzkrieg). Von Wedel was quick to add, that it was necessary to defeat the RAF, but the Royal Navy was a great obstacle. The German veteran then changed tact and stated that if the war was not over by Christmas, it would go on indefinitely.

Brooks summed up von Wedel by stating that he did not seem to have any close contacts in the Nazi Party and was unlikely to be in their confidence. He did however give the impression of representing a body of opinion among the landowning elite and the armed forces. Clearly, Brooks thought this information was interesting, but nothing more than that.

The next airman of interest to Brooks was Unteroffizier Karl-Heinz Feldmann of 3/JG53. He was shot down on 15 September, his Messerschmitt 109 coming down to earth near the Grand Redoubt at Dymchurch, Kent – he was unharmed making a belly-landing.

Feldmann, 22-years-old, came from the Ruhr Valley and was the son of a Social Democrat. He admitted to also having similar political views, but kept them secret from the German authorities. Feldmann told Brooks that he could not make any political comment, as he had heard practically nothing of anything, but the German case which he knew was pure propaganda. He did admit to occasionally listening to the BBC German news, as did many people he knows at home in Germany. This was because they wanted an objective picture of the situation, however the contradictions between the BBC and German news were often confusing.

The young pilot said he believed the 'Much trumpeted Nazi schemes for a New Order' were impracticable and just a camouflage. Although he was at heart an opponent of the Nazis, he had heard nothing but rumours about the brutalities in the concentration camps, while any released prisoners take care never to breathe a word about their experiences.

Feldmann claimed the coal mines of the Ruhr Valley were in full operation and production was increasing, as pressure was applied to the miners. The men were working extra-long hours, but when he was on leave recently, he found them to be standing up well to the pressure of work and air raids by the RAF. Feldmann reported that the small farmers of Germany were satisfied with the Nazi system.

Catholic districts such as the Black Forest are apparently not very loyal and sympathetic to the Nazi cause. There is no open opposition to the Party, but the oppression of the (Catholic) Church has produced a lukewarm attitude when compared to more Protestant areas of Germany.

In the Luftwaffe, everyone was assumed to be a National Socialist and therefore there was no political pressure upon them. Feldmann believed there were some senior officers who were non-Nazis, but no names were mentioned.

Feldmann believed there was a marked difference between the feelings of Frenchmen in Brittany and Normandy. In early August, he had gone to a restaurant with Staffel colleagues just outside Dinard. In what he called the social room, local separatists were having a meeting. They sang songs and made a number of speeches, leading Feldmann to the conclusion that the locals were friendly towards Germany and Britain was their enemy. Those attending the meeting gave a Nazi salute and shouted '*Salut Bretagne*'.

In Normandy, Feldmann believed the populace to be pro-British. He had recently had to bail out and landed in Normandy, where he was surrounded by civilians. Unable to speak French, he spoke broken English – much to the joy of the people who slapped him on the back thinking he was an Englishman.

Karl-Heinz Feldmann believed both British and German aerial victory claims were exaggerated, however, he stated Luftwaffe losses were considerable, but bearable. His own Staffel (3/JG53) had made forty attacks on England before he was shot down on 15 September. He claimed they had lost five out of twelve Messerschmitt 109s, but had destroyed seven Spitfires, three Hurricanes and thirty barrage balloons. The Staffel claims were all made by their experienced pilots. In terms of losses, Feldmann believed the young inexperienced pilots were no good, two being shot down within a week of joining the unit. He believed the Spitfire was superior to the ME109, equal in speed, but the British machine was more maneuverable.

Brooks summed up the young pilot as someone who did not care who won the war, even stating that he thought it might be better for Germany if Britain won. He did however, believe Germany would fight to the bitter end. Feldmann said, there was a feeling in Germany, that they could not win a drawn-out war, but the propaganda will dispel that idea.

Feldmann was surprised the invasion of Britain had been postponed, but he believed Hitler would invade, 'Even if it cost him his life.' He had seen lots of small boats on the coast of France near Etaples before being shot down. There were lots of men training, but he did not see any tanks.

Brooks was interviewing a wide range of airmen from Oberleutnants to Gerfrieters and pilots to wireless operators, each had their own opinions and information to give to this middle-aged psychologist. It is clear, over eighty years after the events, that they must have found his calm, friendly manner very comforting, but this allowed him to gather a plethora of intelligence.

One man who was apparently very shaken by his experiences before he spoke with Brooks was Flieger Hermann Bormann, a 22-year-old flight engineer from Gelsenkirchen. He was a crew member of a Dornier 17 (5K+JM) of 4/KG3, shot down by anti-aircraft fire and a Spitfire on the afternoon of 15 September. The aircraft, as already mentioned in the chapter on September 1940, crashed at Barnehurst Golf Course near Dartford. The pilot, Leutnant Herbert Michaelis, was injured and conveyed to the Herbert Military Hospital in Woolwich, but the observer, Unteroffizier Hausburg, was killed when his parachute failed to open correctly. The wireless operator, Unteroffizier Burbulla, was seriously wounded and died two days later. Hermann Bormann was initially believed to have been killed and this was stated on the initial AI1(k) report. In reality, Bormann, who was on his first operational war flight, was wounded and bailed out successfully, before being detained and hospitalised.

When Brooks spoke with Hermann Bormann at Trent Park in the first few days of October, he found him to be something of a physical wreck. The young airman cried and wept bitterly for two reasons – first his mother was seriously ill at home in Gelsenkirchen and his treatment in hospital had been so unexpectedly humane.

Although Bormann admitted passing through the ranks of the Hitler Youth and the *Arbeitsdienst* (Labour service) which he enjoyed, he seemed to have no political ideals or views on the result of the war. He did think it would be best if Germany and England made an alliance as everyone wanted peace.

Bormann said he was a carpenter by trade and wanted to return to his work, he even said he would not mind undertaking war work in England. He was a Roman Catholic and attended mass, but he had never heard the war or the politics of the Nazis mentioned in a sermon. Despite this, he thought the priests were all for Hitler.

The final airman in Brooks's report was 26-year-old Gefreiter Stephan Weinlich (actually spelt Weinlig), a wireless operator from a Heinkel III (1H+GP) of 6/KG26, brought down by anti-aircraft fire at 0135 hours on 24 September at Chobham, Surrey. Weinlich/Weinlig and his three colleagues survived unharmed and were quickly captured.

Weinlich was an Austrian from Vienna and in the words of his interviewer, 'Another depressing example of easy-going Austrian acceptance of Nazism, lock, stock and barrel.'

The prisoner's father owned a small varnish factory and although trade was restricted, they were quite satisfied with life. Life in Vienna was continuing as normal and workmen all have work. He spoke happily about work salaries and what goods were for sale in Austria.

Weinlich said he was a Roman Catholic, but knew nothing of Nazi oppression of the church or that Cardinal Innitzer had been 'molested' in Vienna for contesting the Nazis. Despite this, Weinlich thought the Austrian culture remained and everything, 'Is for the best.' He thought the war would be over soon and will end in a German victory by invasion or a blockade.

It was clear from these reports, that there was a very wide range of views and opinions among the German prisoners of war. Although they had not given away military secrets in their conversations with Brooks, it is clear he managed to gain a good understanding of the psyche of the Luftwaffe airmen and those connected to them.

It is interesting to note and wonder what other accounts were held in files compiled by Denys Felkin and his team at Trent Park. The vast majority of the intelligence reports held at the UK National Archives attributed to Felkin's team are the initial reports from the preliminary interrogations. Others contained a compilation of facts from other interrogations, but sadly the transcripts from those secondary interviews are no longer available. What is very clear, is that many German airmen were very happy to talk and even those who would not discuss military matters, happily spoke of politics, home life, religion, propaganda and other matters.

Chapter 21

Victory (October 1940)

With the start of October 1940, it was becoming clear, the anticipated German invasion of Britain was unlikely. Even the prisoners were beginning to believe the invasion was less likely.

The Luftwaffe had sustained a large number of losses, many of them experienced airmen and there was a clear erosion in the Luftwaffe's ability to keep up the large-scale daylight raids. Many of the medium bombers (Heinkel III's, Dornier 17's and Junkers 88's), changed tactics and started night-time raids against Britain's cities. At the same time, the number of Messerschmitt 109 fighters carrying single bombs was increasing. The formations comprising of these 'Jabos' were escorted by standard versions of the fighter, as they swept across the south-east of England as far as London.

During the early stages of the Battle of Britain, RAF Fighter Command Controllers endeavoured to keep their own fighters away from massed formations of Messerschmitt 109's on free-hunt sweeps. They directed the Spitfires and Hurricanes on to the German bomber formations, but now, bomb-equipped 109s were venturing across the south-east of England and they had to react. This resulted in large scale dogfights and an increased number of Messerschmitt pilots being brought down and into captivity.

On 1 October, Unteroffizier Edward Gerneth was flying a Messerschmitt 109 of 2/JG51, when he was brought down five miles south-west of Ashford in Kent (see intelligence log No. 676). The 24-year-old pilot was the holder of the Iron Cross Second Class and was engaged on an operation to escort a single Dornier 17 reconnaissance aircraft when they were attacked by a squadron of Spitfires. Gerneth claimed that he was cut off from the rest of his unit, which comprised of six ME109's, before he was hit in the engine which caught fire.

Gerneth told his preliminary interrogator that the Dornier escaped in the cloud layer and he bailed out, unwounded, landing by parachute near the wreckage of his own aircraft.

Edward Gerneth, whose morale was deemed to be fairly good, claimed to have completed four years of military service and this had been his second mission of the day. The first mission that morning, was an escort flight of ME 109 'Jabo' bombers to south and south-west London. Although he had escorted the Jabos, he had no actual experience of flying a bomb-equipped Messerschmitt 109 himself.

The pilot told his interrogator, that in the previous three to four weeks, he had made twenty operational flights, sometimes three or even four a day. Every fourth day was a rest day. It was clear the Messerschmitt 109 pilots were being tasked with a greater number of operations, perhaps more than in the first months of the battle and its peak during the summer months.

Gerneth was an experienced pilot. He did not fly in the Polish campaign, but played a part in France, where he was shot down and wounded at Calais, four days before the French armistice. After recovering, he rejoined his Staffel at St Omer where the whole First Gruppe had been based since his return to operations.

Although the war was now entering a difficult period for the Luftwaffe, Gerneth was happy to chat and told his interrogator (possibly Flight Lieutenant Guy Jepson who signed the log), that there were about twelve reserve aircraft and pilots at St. Omer.

Intelligence log No. 680/40 gave details of Oberleutnant Walther Fiel of 8/JG53 who was shot down on 2 October at East Peckham, near RAF West Malling in Kent. The unwounded pilot held the Iron Cross First Class and was very communicative with his preliminary interrogator, even if it was only to boast that he believed 'England was about to get the biggest hiding in history'. Clearly some hardened Nazis still believed the propaganda…

A great deal of information allowed AI1(k) to identify this pilot's unit. This comprised of his identity disk number, his Feldpost number and his white Ausweis which was issued at Koln-Ostheim on 17 March 1940. Walter Fiel actually refused to give any military information to his interrogator, but the talkative 26-year-old pilot, added that he had made several war flights over England.

Fiel did say that he had been at 16,000 feet when he was attacked by sixteen Spitfires and hit in the radiator. He dived away into a cloud layer and tried to head home to France, but his engine seized-up and he made a forced landing. The Messerschmitt 109 was not badly damaged and was yet another gift for the Air Intelligence inspectors.

The pilot's paybook showed that he had previously served with JG3, while a letter dated 14 September 1940 was also found in his possession. This informed

Fiel that Leutnant Landry of 2/JG3 was a prisoner of war in England having been shot down on 28 August. (Clearly the two men had been colleagues on JG3.) Sadly, Hans Herbert Landry had died in hospital the following month, whether this was disclosed to Fiel is not documented in the available records.

In the wreck of Fiel's aircraft, the inspectors found a list of radio code-words for the 7th, 8th and 9th Staffeln, as well as the Gruppen Stab, Bodenstelle, Geschwader and the Geschwader Bodenstelle.

Fiel also possessed a combat report dated 27 September 1940. This stated that at 1400 hours at 20,000 feet, five ME109's fought ten British fighters. No German aircraft were lost, but two RAF fighters were claimed, because they, 'Went into an uncontrolled spin.' German combat claim records have a claim by Fiel's colleague, Feldwebel Xaver Ray of 8/JG53, for two Hurricanes at 1400 hours at 20,000 feet over London that day. However, analysis of RAF casualty records, finds no corresponding Hurricane or Spitfire losses for this report.

Fiel may have said very little of military value to his interrogator, but his personal effects, the letter, combat report and his aircraft, told AI1(k) everything they needed to know. The unit was also identified as having bomb release equipment fitted to their aircraft and Walther Fiel's bravado was probably very ill-conceived.

AI1(k) continued to examine and analyse intelligence from prisoners, documents and aircraft obtained over the previous months. This would often entail comparing aircraft that were known to have originated from the same Staffel or Geschwader.

Intelligence log No. 679, dated 2 October 1940, is one such report and examines three Heinkel III crews from KG55 who were shot down on 26 September 1940.

It was established by comparing the accounts of prisoners, that aircraft had been drawn from across the Geschwader for a raid on the Aero Engine works of the Bristol Aeroplane Company on 26 September 1940. The First Gruppe had taken off from Dreux, the Second from Chartres and the Third from Villacoublay near Paris. The three Gruppen had formed up over the English Channel off Cherbourg, comprising of three Gruppen 'vic' formations known as Ketten Kolonne. The central Gruppen formation being slightly ahead of those to the left and right.

Their escort comprised of Messerschmitt 110 fighters who kept formation by weaving about four to five hundred yards from the bomber formation.

The massed formation headed for Poole in Dorset and then on towards their target. Various maps were found in the wrecked aircraft, confirming the target and their flight plans. The bomb load was probably six or seven 250 kg bombs, deduced from the loads of three of the aircraft shot down.

One unidentified prisoner told his interrogators that another Gruppe were to make a diversionary attack with a strong fighter escort, but this was a feint attack, three quarters of an hour before the main assault. The hope was to draw off British fighters, thereby allowing the three Gruppen a clear path to the factory which was the main target.

A number of prisoners claimed the timing and organisation worked perfectly and everything went according to plan. Geschwader operations of this kind were difficult if the weather was inappropriate, as good visibility was required for the formation and accurate bombing.

A comparison of the KG55 prisoners, found that although not identical, their experiences were broadly similar. They appeared to have made about forty war flights in the French campaign and another nine against Britain. They had nearly all taken part in an attack on Portsmouth in early September 1940, when aircraft G1+AA was lost. This machine had contained the Geschwader Kommodore, Oberst Stoeckl, who was killed. Many of those interrogated had operated against the port of Liverpool, stating that they had attacked from the east. (Author's note: this was interesting as many raiders came across Wales and the Irish Sea in 1940/41.)

Lists of war flights were also recovered from one airman's personal diary, which provided a list of operations and detailing the anti-aircraft fire and fighter attacks they encountered.

In one aircraft wreck, a certificate, similar to those found in possession of Messerschmitt 109 pilots was recovered. This stated that B-Ammunition (Explosive) in belts was only to be used on aircraft targets. Troop concentrations and 'living targets' were not to be targeted with this ammunition. The certificate was dated 1/4/1940.

The continued careful examination and analysis of information and material recovered by Air Intelligence was continually providing updated information. This in turn, was used to brief RAF and military partners, as well as providing a starting point for future prisoner interrogations. Even when a pilot or crew were deceased, a wreck, a body and any papers etc. could provide a wealth of intelligence.

Intelligence log No. 683/40, detailed the loss of Messerschmitt 110 (L1+XB) of 13/LG1, which crashed at Halisham in Sussex, on 27 September and was totally destroyed. The crew of Feldwebel Adolf Bruns and Gefreiter Franz Grobl were both killed.

A number of documents, including two operational orders which should not have been taken on the flight, were found in what remained of the aircraft and these provided a great deal of intelligence for AI1(k).

The first operational order dated 25/9/40, stated that at fifty minutes before zero hour, a preliminary attack was to be made by II/LG1 (JU88's) escorted by three Geschwader of fighters. The main attack at zero hour, was to be composed of KG3 (Dornier 17's) with another three Geschwader of fighters.

The ME110's of ZG76 and the ME109's of JG52, were to meet twenty-five minutes before zero hour over Cap Gris Nez at 18,000 feet. They would then make a freelance patrol over Biggin Hill and the Thames Estuary, being ready to cover KG3 as they returned home. The actual target of the bombers mission was not stated in the operational order and there were a number of raids that day.

The second operational order was not dated and did not specify a bomber formation, but it gave a rendezvous for Stab V(z)/LG1, II/ZG76 and one Rotte of III/ZG76. The formation was to climb to 18,000 feet over Cap Gris Nez and patrol for forty minutes, at a point forty-five minutes from their base. The main formation would then meet at twenty minutes before zero hour over Cap Gris Nez and head towards Biggin Hill.

The order of flight for the formation was given as:

Formation *Schwarme* astern:

- JG51 to act as close escort.
- 2 Jagdgeschwader to act as secondary escort.
- 2 Jagdgeschwader freelance fighter action.
- 1 Jagdgeschwader to arrive independently at the objective at zero hour.
- The rendezvous for the whole operation to be at zero hour at Biggin Hill.
- The objective was to be left ten minutes after zero hour, with all aircraft directly supporting the bomber formation.

AI1(k) noted that from their own record of losses, they could not identify the date this operation took place, although on 27 September 1940, several of the units mentioned were known to have taken part in a similar operation.

Information such as these briefing reports was vital for AI1(k) and the wider Air Intelligence community in understanding Luftwaffe tactics etc.

Another airman who passed through and was of interest to Trent Park was Unteroffizier Karl Michael Vogel of 6/JG53. He was shot down on 30 September, landing in the sea off Beachy Head with minor wounds. His preliminary interrogation report was dated 2 October.

Although only twenty years of age, he had two years military service. The preliminary interrogation report, once again signed off by Guy Jepson, noted that his morale was good. Although his aircraft was lost to the sea, AI1(k) still obtained his identity disc number, his Feldpost number and his grey Ausweis which was issued at Merseberg two to three months previously.

Vogel was clearly another very talkative prisoner and explained that he had taken off from Boulogne to escort about forty bombers to London. He became involved in a dogfight over Tunbridge Wells, but had to break away and head for the coast as his engine started to falter. However, he maintained like many others before him, that he had not been hit by a British fighter. It seems many Luftwaffe fighter pilots could not bring themselves to accept they had been hit by an enemy pilot.

As he approached the coastline at Beachy Head, Vogel claimed his faltering ME109 was attacked by a single Spitfire which shot him down into the Channel. He managed to get out and after swimming around for some time, a Royal Navy destroyer picked him up and took him to Portsmouth.

As well as having documents, an identity disc and Feldpost numbers which connected him to 6/JG53, Vogel asked his interrogator about a number of pilots the Geschwader had recently lost. One such man was Hauptmann Makulan and AI1(k) knew from a previous prisoner that this man was missing and known to belong to II/JG53. Because of this, the interrogation log (No. 684/1940) noted that Makulan's loss could now be taken as reasonably established.

In addition to Luftwaffe losses, Vogel was also keen to add that he had been told, the Academy of Arts in Berlin had been destroyed in a recent RAF bombing raid.

The morale of many pilots and airmen remained relatively high and there was a continuing belief that Germany would eventually win. Despite this, many airmen were only too happy to talk about various matters, clearly unaware that any information could be of value to the British. It seems many believed that avoiding questions about their own unit was the correct procedure, but asking about missing colleagues, talking about aircraft, bomb damage at home and even their rations was permissible and could surely be of no use to the British.

Intelligence log No. 686, dated 3 October, was another composite report detailing intelligence gleaned from two Messerschmitt 110's of Grp. 210, shot down on 27 September over south-west England.

While the crew of one aircraft (S9+DH) had been killed, the other from S9+DK, although badly wounded, were very talkative and their comments formed the basis of the report.

Feldwebel Fritz Ebner was injured and his wireless-operator Gefreiter Werner Zwick serious wounded. The report does not state which man talked and gave the most information, but they allowed AI1(k) to form a sound understanding of their unit's hierarchy and its senior officers. The prisoners identified the commanders of the 1st, 2nd and 3rd Staffeln by name and rank. Their unit had suffered the loss of a number of top commanders and were on their third Gruppe-Kommandeur in less than three weeks. Despite these losses, their morale did not seem to have suffered according to the report.

The report covered maps, aerial photos and aircraft of the unit, but the most interesting fact was that the wireless operator (Gefreiter Werner Zwick) had previously served with 4/Stuka 77; his identity disc number being linked to that unit. Further interrogation of this man revealed that until fairly recently, he had in fact been a pilot in the 2nd Staffel of that Stuka unit. A man of some experience, having joined the Army in 1933, he transferred to the Luftwaffe in 1935 and after training joined the Immelmann Geschwader – at that time a fighter unit.

After twelve months, the unit's pilots were trained in Stuka tactics and became St/G.77. Zwick was later selected for ME110 bomber pilot training and posted to 2/KGr. 210 in July 1940. Why he was not piloting the aircraft when shot down is unclear, but certainly provided some interesting information for Air Intelligence.

The issue of ME109 'Jabo' fighter-bombers returned on 2 October, when Gefreiter Heinrich Zag of 8/JG52 was shot down and made a forced landing at Twelve Acre Hopyard, Forge Farm near Goudhurst in Kent.

Intelligence report No. 693 on 3 October, noted that Zag was severely wounded after combat with Spitfires and smashed through a number of hop field poles before finally coming to rest. His aircraft was reported to have been fitted with a bomb release mechanism for a 250 kg bomb, but Zag stuck to the account during his preliminary interview, that he was an escort for other 'Jabo' bombers.

Henrich Zag refused to give his unit details, but the aircraft which was mostly intact, his identity disc number and Feldpost number gave this away. Flight Lieutenant Guy Jepson signed off the preliminary interrogation report, noting that Zag, though wounded, had very high morale which was impossible to shake. He was however, noted as, 'Probably unreliable', but why Jepson made this comment is a mystery.

Some 'Jabo' pilots did talk, and according to Preliminary Interrogation log No. 709, Unteroffizier Georg Morschel of LG2 did just that.

Georg Morschel belonged to LG2 and was brought down near Tunbridge Wells on 7 October by British fighters. Hit in the radiator like so many other

Messerschmitt 109's, he made a forced landing as the machine caught fire. The pilot, who was wounded in the crash, managed to crawl out of the aircraft and was quickly captured. The Messerschmitt had been armed with a single 250 kg bomb, but the aircraft never reached its objective in London. Whether this was still attached to the aircraft is unclear, but it was probably ditched before the forced landing.

Morschel was given a preliminary interrogation and admitted being a member of LG2. His aircraft had unusual markings with a black solid equilateral triangle alongside the German cross and a black letter 'F' on the fuselage sides. The nose and fin were painted yellow with a yellow Mickey Mouse emblem. The pilot was very badly shaken according to the report and gave details of his Gruppen-Kommandeur, Major Weiss and his Staffel Kapitan who was named as Oberleutnant Vogeler. (Major Otto Weiss was indeed the Gruppen-Kommandeur of II/LG2.) Morschel's identity disc number was quickly identified as being one previously encountered with a member of the 4th Staffel of the Geschwader (4/LG2 and II/LG2).

The unit LG2 was something of an oddity for RAF Intelligence. Early in the Battle of Britain a JU88 belonging to 1/LG2 was brought down and then a whole series of ME109's belonging to various Staffeln of LG2. Then an ME110 from 7(F)/LG2 was brought down. AI1(k) would eventually identify that Lehrgeschwader 2 (LG 2) or Demonstration Wing 2 was a mixed Geschwader operating three fighter, night fighter, reconnaissance and ground support Gruppen. In many respects they were originally intended as a form of operational evaluation unit, but over time, they were committed more and more to the front line.

On the same day that Georg Morschel arrived in Kent, another interesting pilot was captured, but AI1(k) and the authorities did not realise who he was for some time (see log No. 712/1940).

At 1100 hours a Messerschmitt 109E made a forced landing at Dole Ham Farm, Guestling in East Sussex. The pilot, who was not wounded, had been on a freelance patrol when he tangled with Spitfires at 22,000 feet and was hit in the radiator. As his engine overheated, he made a forced landing and was quickly captured.

The aircraft, which was relatively intact, was marked with a yellow nose and rudder, together with a number '1' on the fuselage. The pilot gave his name as Oberleutnant Viktor Molders and said he had four years military service. He would not disclose his unit, but his identity disc number and his Feldpost number (L35915) were obtained. The identity disc number allowed Air Intelligence to assume that he belonged to 8/JG26, but this would prove to be totally incorrect.

The intelligence report noted that although the unit was assumed from the identity disc number, this was not a confirmed identification, as the Messerschmitt did not display the regular Schlageter 'S' badge under the cockpit or other JG26 markings. In addition, AI1(k) did not recognise his Feldpost number. Because of these factors, the pilot was marked for further interrogation by Denys Felkin's team at Trent Park.

The initial interrogator had managed to obtain some facts from the pilot. He held the Iron Cross First Class and he had fought in the Polish, Norwegian, Danish and Dutch campaigns. He had made about twenty war flights against Britain and his morale was good. In fact, the report noted that he was 'A good type of regular officer.'

Somewhat surprisingly, Air Intelligence staff and the preliminary interrogator had not taken much notice of the pilot's surname, Molders, a name synonymous with one of the Luftwaffe's top air aces in 1940 (Werner Molders Kommandore of JG51). In fact, it took a week before AI1(k) deduced who this pilot was.

A follow-up report (No. 749/1940), signed by Denys Felkin, stated that the unit suggested in the preliminary report was incorrect, owing to an error in the identity disc classification. He then somewhat sarcastically noted, 'As might be expected from the name (Oberleutnant Molders), this man is a brother of the famous Major Molders, Kommodore of JG51 and in fact he belongs to the 2nd Staffel of his brother's Geschwader.' Felkin's comment is filled with irony and sarcasm. Was this an exasperated head of AI1(k) showing his disgust that his team had failed to put the facts together and missed this prized captive?

The short report appears to be one of the most important in the collection when it adds:

> 'This man confirms the details given of his brother's tactics and was very dismayed that so much should be known, and fears for his brother's safety… His brother apparently had a narrow escape a few days previously when his oxygen apparatus became disconnected at high altitude.'

Although we no longer have the follow-up interrogation reports with exact details of that interview, was this a perfect example of the RAF's master interrogator righting his junior interrogators errors and dismantling the young German officer's defences? Did Felkin, use all his skill to gather intelligence and make Molder's younger brother talk?

The report continued, stating that Major Werner Molders was now credited with forty-two victories in the present war, but his brother hung his head in shame when he confessed to having only seven himself.

Viktor Molders was a fine artist and would later draw a series of sketches portraying his capture and arrival at Trent Park on 8 October 1940.

A total of seven Messerschmitt 109's was brought down on 7 October, one of those being piloted by Unteroffizier Paul Lederer of 5/JG27. Unlike the other pilots, Paul Lederer's morale was reportedly not very good.

Lederer had taken-off from Calais to escort the 'Jabos' of LG2. His schwarm was led by the Staffel Kapitan, Oberleutnant Ernst Dullberg, but before they reached their objective, they were attacked by Hurricanes and he was pursued by three of them. Once again, this ME 109 was hit in the radiator and the engine quickly overheated, causing Lederer to make a forced landing in Bedgebury Wood near Cranbrook in Kent.

The 25-year-old pilot was slightly wounded, but managed to extricate himself from the Messerschmitt which did not catch fire.

Lederer was quickly captured and during a preliminary interrogation, he was happy to talk and disclose that this had been his third sortie of the day. The first two had been escort missions which were uneventful, as had previous flights in earlier days.

Air Intelligence were interested to note that Paul Lederer had been a Coastal Unit pilot until March 1940, when he was sent to a fighter pilot school, before joining JG27 on 18 June 1940.

Lederer was keen to discuss tactics and told his interrogator that he now felt it would have been better if he had climbed when attacked, as the ME109 had a superior rate of climb when compared to the Hurricane. He had completed forty-two war flights over England and considered many of the English pilots to seem young and inexperienced, however, there were obviously a lot of older more experienced hands among them he added.

Like many German airmen, he asked about missing friends from his Staffel (5/JG27), some of whom were now either prisoners of war or dead. The report stated that his morale was not very good, but that he was keen on his job as a fighter pilot, but not very hopeful regarding the outcome of the war!

Air Intelligence and more specifically AI1(k), continued to not only gather intelligence, but assess the morale and attitudes of the captured airmen. While there was a wide variety of morale, there were still a few ardent Nazis among the new arrivals and intelligence log No. 724/1940 identifies two such fanatical Nazis.

A Junkers 88 from 2/806 was shot down on 8 October at 1615 hours after apparently attacking the Rootes aircraft factory next to Speke airport, Liverpool. The aircraft had flown across the Channel to Southampton and on to Ellesmere Port, using the thick cloud as cover. Unfortunately, despite the cloud layer, its progress was tracked and a section of Hurricanes were scrambled to intercept the intruder over Merseyside.

The No. 312 (Czech) Squadron Hurricanes had taken off from Speke airport and riddled the Junkers with bullets, hitting the starboard engine and narrowly missing the pilot. The crew managed to ditch two bombs before the pilot made a forced landing at Bromborough Dock near Port Sunlight, on the other side of the River Mersey from Speke airport.

The pilot, Oberleutnant Helmuth Bruckmann, miraculously escaped injury, but his Observer, Leutnant zur see Herbert Schlegel, was killed. The wireless operator, Unteroffizier Helmuth Weth, was slightly wounded and the fourth man, a war correspondent, Sonderfuhrer Horst Lehmann, was wounded.

The preliminary field interrogation report No. 724/1940, noted that both Bruckmann and Weth were fanatical Nazis, but the war correspondent was older and 'Rather more reasonable.'

AI1(k) managed to deduce from a logbook and other captured documents found inside the aircraft, that this machine belonged to 2/806 and this corresponded with the aircrafts code letters (M7+BK) and a badge on its fuselage. The last aircraft bearing the part-code M7+ known by AI1(k) was in 1939, when the unit operated the Dornier 18 flying boat.

Although Air Intelligence had a very complete list of personnel from this Staffel, neither Bruckmann or Weth were known to them. The war correspondent was a photographer and he had a complete log in his possession, detailing all his war flights and others made by other war correspondent photographers.

The AI1(k) report concluded, stating that further interrogation would be carried out, but sadly there are no longer any surviving documents relating to this.

AI1(k) continued to try and identify deceased airman and bodies washed ashore. While their main aim as we have seen, was to obtain intelligence, they would provide a valuable service to the deceased's families via the International Red Cross.

Intelligence log No. 730/1940, dated 9 October 1940, details a number of these men whose bodies had been washed ashore.

On 3 October 1940, a body was washed ashore at Reculver in Kent, it was quite badly decomposed having been in the sea for about three weeks. The body still had its identity disc attached and the Feldpost number was also identified, but the grey Ausweis was no longer legible. Despite this, the airman wearing a Feldwebel's uniform, was identified as Hermann Bohn of 7/KG53.

AI1(k) quickly deduced this individual was part of a 7/KG53 Heinkel III crew, brought down on or about 5 September. On that date, Air Intelligence already knew another aircraft from the same Staffel had been shot down. What had happened to the rest of Bohn's crew was unknown, but the report did speculate that another body found just along the coastline at Herne Bay, may have been a fellow crew member. That body had been washed ashore a few days previously on 29 September. That man was another Feldwebel named Lorenz Keck, with an identity disc number of Bla 71044/17 and he possessed a yellow Ausweis issued at Langendiebach on 7/2/40.

The man's Ausweis was linked to both III/KG76 and III/KG53, while his identity disc was linked to 3/KG76, but had been encountered with several other units over the summer months. AI1(k) therefore surmised that this may have been a Training School or Ergangzung unit disc. In view of these facts, AI1(k) believed both Keck and Bohn had been part of the same crew.

In reality, when Luftwaffe loss records are examined, Feldwebel Hermann Bohn is identified as an observer on a 7/KG53 Heinkel III (A1+GR), shot down on 5 September off Herne Bay. The rest of his crew were never found, but Lorenz Keck was not one of them, so the AI1(k) assumption was incorrect.

Feldwebel Lorenz Keck was in fact, a pilot with 8/KG76 flying a Dornier 17 (F1+BS), which was shot down off Herne Bay on 15 September, so AI1(k) were initially correct in linking the Ausweis to both III/KG76 and III/KG53. However, it was a bit of a leap of faith, to suggest the two bodies were from the same crew. Although some intelligence is based on educated assumptions, it is always better to avoid making assumptions unless they are backed up with concrete evidence.

On 12 October, Leutnant Bernhardt Malischewski of 4/JG54 was shot down and landed East of Small Hythe, three miles south of Tenterden in Kent. Malischewski was something of a conundrum for AI1(k). He was, in the words of the preliminary field interrogation log (No. 741/1940), 'More than usually silent' and would not discuss anything.

Leutnant Malischewski, who was not wounded, was aged twenty-seven, he held the Iron Cross First Class and his morale was deemed to be 'Very high indeed.' What little he did say, included the fact he had been engaged in combat, but had not been shot down. His engine had just given up and he made a forced-landing. This was the same old story... Either these pilots were trying to deceive their interrogators or uncharacteristically, the Daimler-Benz engines on their Messerschmitt 109's were faltering.

The identity of the pilot's unit like so many before him, was identified by AI1(k) from his identity disc and Feldpost numbers, plus a list of wireless code words found in the aircraft. Most previous lists normally covered a single Gruppe and its three Staffeln, plus the Stab flight, but this one included the Geschwader Kommodore, the six Staffeln of the second and third Gruppen (i.e. Staffeln 4 to 9) and each Gruppen-Kommandeur. The list was quickly sent to AI1(e) for use by the Y-Service.

Unfortunately, there is no surviving later interrogation report for Bernhardt Malischewski, but it is possible the preliminary interrogator missed a few pointers...

Although his aircraft was marked with the fuselage markings for the Geschwader Adjutant (< | +) and he had such a long list of radio call signs, there is no mention of his probable position within the Geschwader on the preliminary interrogation report. Images of the aircraft taken at the time, show four victory bars on the rudder, but these were not mentioned in the report. Later reports state that this man was a member of Stab II/JG54 which is corroborated by the above facts.

Some sources claim Malischewski had only three confirmed aerial victories and therefore the victory bars may have referred to the Messerschmitt, rather than an individual pilot. It has also been claimed that he was shot down by the renowned RAF pilot and ace – Flight Lieutenant Robert Stanford-Tuck, despite Malischewski's claims of a faulty engine.

Malischewski's ME109 was quickly camouflaged and later salvaged for evaluation. It went on to tour the country as the star exhibit for the Spitfire fund and war bond collections.

Intelligence log No. 745/1940 detailed the interrogation of Feldwebel Siegfried Voss of 3/JG52, shot down on 12 October at Bradbourne Down, near Ashford in Kent.

As the month of October continued, larger formations of ME109 'Jabo' bombers, supported by larger groups of escorting fighters swarmed across the south-east of England. Voss had been one of the escorting pilots covering the Jabos to RAF Biggin Hill and Central London when he was shot down and had to bail out.

Voss claimed to have been on his third sortie of the day when he was brought down. He said his formation was about sixty strong and they flew over Biggin Hill at an altitude of about 25,000 feet. He told his interrogator some bombs were dropped and he saw hits on the oil tanks at Biggin Hill which caught fire, although from 25,000 feet this must have been hard to see and the claim is questionable. The formation continued on to London, but he said he did not see anything over London.

Once they turned for home, Voss was over Ashford when his unit speeded up, leaving Voss and his Rottenführer behind. They were attacked by two Spitfires and were holding their own, until a third Spitfire intervened and his controls were hit. His ME109 entered an uncontrolled dive and he bailed out at about 1,500 feet.

During his preliminary interrogation, his morale was noted as good and he was very talkative. The reporting officer noted that Voss apparently tried to be truthful, but was liable to get carried away and start romancing…

Voss said he did not take part in the Polish campaign, but had fought throughout the French campaign. He claimed to have made about sixty war flights over England and had once run out of fuel and ditched in the Channel just off Boulogne. He said he had also escorted bombers to raids on the airfields at Detling, Manston, Kenley and others.

Voss believed the RAF only had three hundred Spitfires remaining and that British pilots were not very enthusiastic. This was because on one occasion, he was with two Staffeln over Ashford when fifteen Spitfires were sighted. He claimed the German listening services heard an order from British fighter controllers ordering the Spitfires to attack the 109's, but they did not do so. The listening service claimed the British said they could not see the ME109's.

The German pilot was scornful of the armour plating in Spitfires. He told his interrogator that his Staffel had recovered a piece of armour from a Spitfire and fired one of their own bullets through it.

In addition, Voss claimed the German radio codes were used for varying lengths of time before being changed and his own code had been in use for the past two weeks.

Siegfried Voss was certainly very talkative and clearly something of a storyteller. The reported attack on the oil tanks at Biggin Hill on 12 October 1940, was certainly overstated. There had been a small raid on the airfield that day, but little damage was reported and no oil tanks were destroyed!

On the same operation as Voss, JG52 lost Oberleutnant Gunter Busgen of the 2nd Staffel (see log No. 747/1940). Busgen's Messerschmitt 109 was hit in the radiator and as the engine overheated, he bailed out at 16,000 feet. As he exited the fighter, he struck the fuselage and fractured an arm.

The preliminary intelligence/interrogation report noted that the pilot, despite his injuries, had tried to mislead in every detail. He was clearly a senior pilot and held the Iron Cross First Class, which he claimed was awarded for having completed more than forty war flights over England.

What was not known at the time, was Busgen was an ace with six victories to his name. His unit was assumed from his identity disc number to be 2/JG52, but in reality, he was from 1/JG52. He was later transferred to the Royal Herbert Military Hospital in Woolwich and was still there in December 1940 (see later chapter on London Cage re his later interrogation).

One of the last Battle of Britain pilots for whom there is a fair amount of information from his interrogations is Feldwebel Horst Hellriegel of 3/JG2. He was shot down on 15 October and subjected to the standard preliminary interrogation (log No. 756) and a longer subsequent report dated 27 October (No. 808/1940).

Horst Hellriegel was the sort of pilot AI1(k) were always keen to interrogate. Hellriegel was twenty-five years old with five years military service, having only joined his Staffel two days before he was shot down on his first war flight. His identity disc number was an old one, indicative that he had more service than most of the other prisoners.

The prisoner quickly admitted to previously being a flying instructor at Berlin and had no Ausweis because he had only just joined JG2. He told his interrogator that his Ausweis would eventually have been signed off by the Gruppen Kommandeur – Hauptmann Helmut Wick.

On his first and final war flight, Hellriegel had been on a freelance patrol at 25,000 feet when his aircraft developed a radiator problem. He descended to about 23,000 feet, when he encountered about twenty Spitfires and was hit in the fuel tank and left wing. A second attack damaged his instruments, so he made a forced landing at Bowcombe Down near Newport on the Isle of Wight and was captured, but unharmed.

His morale was deemed to be not very good and he was very anxious about his family. Once again, a list of call signs was found in the aircraft and he had been unable to destroy this. It was clear this experienced, yet inexperienced war flier was anxious and full of important information. Air Intelligence were keen to interrogate him further.

> The later in-depth interrogation report gave full details of this pilot. He had left school at fourteen, becoming a sailor and a quartermaster. He left and from 1933-1935, worked in his uncle's factory in Hamburg.
>
> In 1935 aged twenty years, Hellriegel joined the Luftwaffe and after obtaining his A2, B1 and B2 flying certificates, he went to Vienna to join I/JG76 and later III/JG54. He was transferred and as a member of I/JG71, flew numerous patrols along the German-French border.

Hellriegel stated that the unit emblem of a cat with an arched back linked to II/JG52, was originally the that of I/JG71. The cat had originally been painted in black, but it was too hard to see and had since become a red cat.

In March 1940, Hellriegel was sent to become an instructor at the Fighter Training School at Werneuchen where he tutored young pilots until his recent move to JG2. He was happy to discuss the training at Werneuchen, stating that each course consisted on average of thirty new pilots. There was one instructor for every nine to ten students and a Chief Instructor. He claimed that on a standard three-month, thirty pupil course five would be found immediately to be unsuitable and discarded. A further five would fail to pass out, while on average, four may be killed while training. This left a total of sixteen pilots who would move on to the Erganzungs unit.

Werneuchen would use a variety of aircraft, including Moranes, Curtiss and Messerschmitt 108's. About fifteen hours would then be put in on Messerschmitt 109's before the course was completed.

The interrogator had told Hellriegel that one prisoner had apparently only 150 hours on all types when he was shot down. Hellriegel was very sceptical of this claim and asked if the man had been an Anwarter (Officer Cadet). He then somewhat brutally claimed there were a number of such pilots and instructors often knew they would never be a good pilot. They therefore pushed these men on to an operational unit to 'make or break' them.

Hellriegel paid tribute to the training of RAF bomber crews, particularly the night bomber navigators. This was noted by AI1(k) as a 'Tacit admission of the effectiveness of our raids, and in any case is sincere praise coming from a trainer from the other side'. Sadly, with hindsight, this was an empty compliment, as we now know RAF night bombing accuracy and navigation was very poor in 1940.

Horst Hellriegel was not the only man from JG2 to provide a good deal of information to AI1(k). A 19-year-old Gefreiter, Alois Pollak of 4/JG2, was shot down in similar circumstances to Hellriegel, but would provide an even greater amount of intelligence. A resident of Bohemia in Czechoslovakia, Pollak joined the Luftwaffe in January 1939 after his home region became part of the German Protectorate in 1938.

After a preliminary interrogation, Pollak was given a more in-depth follow-up interrogation in which he was happy to discuss his military career and postings in great detail.

Pollak recalled joining the Luftwaffe in January 1939 and being sent to Flieger-Ausbildungs-Regiment 63 at Eger, under the command of Oberstleutnant Ritter. At the time, the regiment consisted of one hundred and fifty men, but only five were selected for pilot training. The rest would become ground and technical staff.

Pollak detailed his pilot training, including the number of hours required for various elements and the locations of his training schools. In September 1939 when he first started training, there were no instructors and therefore the students did virtually nothing and enjoyed themselves in a holiday camp atmosphere.

In November 1939, he completed his B1 flying certificate training at Pilsen in Czechoslovakia. There were five flying instructors and twenty to twenty-five student pilots, ten of these had been with Pollak when he did his basic flying training. He completed his B1 certificate with ten hours on the Arado 66 aircraft, this entailed cross-country flights in addition to circuits and landings at the airfield.

In January 1940, Pollak was sent to Starubing for his B2 flying certificate training. This comprised of thirty hours in the W.34 aircraft. AI1(k) noted with interest, that the five instructors moved from level to level with their students, unlike those in the RAF training program.

In June 1940, Pollak was sent to the Fighter School (Jagdfliegerschule) at Herzogenaurach in Bavaria. He was the only student from his previous course selected for fighter pilot training. At Herzogenaurach, there were a total of six instructors, all of whom had combat experience and twenty-three students.

Pollak started his course with about thirty hours on an old Avis aircraft, an old Czech Air Force fighter. He did not like this aircraft, which he claimed was unreliable and he once had to bail out from one. Eventually, he progressed on to Messerschmitt 108's and then the 109 on which he completed ten hours flying. By September 1940, he had a total of one hundred and fifty flying hours and was transferred with two other student pilots to JG2. He added that during his training, there had been no fatalities among the students and this was fortunate and unusual.

Although the information was primarily obtained from interrogation, it was corroborated by a notebook found in Pollak's possession. The notebook gave details of lectures on R/T and various code words and these were similar to intelligence received from other prisoners of war.

Pollak explained that the Avia training aircraft were marked and numbered in a similar manner to that used on Messerschmitt 109's. Messerschmitt 108 and Focke-Wulf 58 aircraft used four-letter registration markings and Pollak had a list of such aircraft and their individual markings in the notebook.

Pollak gave details of basic fighter tactics and lectures on this subject, as well as air combat tactics. ME109 machine guns (in the engine cowling) were set for a convergence of rounds at 400 meters, while the wing guns would converge at 200 meters. If the aircraft was going to be used for ground strafing, both sets of guns were set to converge at 400 meters.

Pollak also gave a detailed explanation of the structure of a Fighter Gruppe, including the various ground staff appointments and even tradesmen. While some of this information was already known to Air Intelligence, other factors were new and other information corroborated earlier intelligence reports.

It was clear that by the end of October 1940, Air Intelligence was receiving some very detailed intelligence which added on a daily basis to their bulging indices and archives at Trent Park. Although naturally some errors were made, in the vast majority of cases, the intelligence was of great value.

Like all good Intelligence units, AI1(k) always strove to gather corroborative information and increase the value of their information. If the assessed validity and provenance of intelligence was high, this allowed for in-depth disseminated reports and further down the proverbial line, much better operational decision making and training. There is no doubt AI1(k) were providing that by the end of the Battle of Britain.

Chapter 22

Oberleutnant Ulrich Steinhilper

One pilot who was shot down and captured at the end of October 1940, was Oberleutnant Ulrich Steinhilper. In many ways he was very different to Franz von Werra – a man he knew personally from military flying school.

Steinhilper was 22-years-old when he was captured at the end of the Battle of Britain. He joined the Luftwaffe in 1936 and after qualifying as a pilot, joined a fighter Geschwader. In September 1939, while the Luftwaffe supported the invasion of Poland, Ulrich Steinhilper and his Gruppe (I/JG52) stayed at home defending the Reich.

During the early summer of 1940, Ulrich Steinhilper's Staffel (3/JG52) supported the invasion of France and then the Battle of Britain.

On 18 August 1940, Steinhilper reportedly destroyed three Spitfires on the ground at RAF Manston. Some records have stated this event took place the following day, but JG52 strafed the airfield on the eighteenth, destroying two and damaging another six Spitfires of No. 266 Squadron as they were being refueled.

The following month, Steinhilper gained his first aerial victories, claiming four Spitfires between18-30 September. These were followed by a Bristol Blenheim off Calais on 4 October, making Steinhilper an ace.

Ulrich Steinhilper continued to fly a variety of fighter sweeps across Kent and Sussex, but on the morning of 27 October 1940, his luck ran out and he was shot down.

Steinhilper had taken off with his wingman, Feldwebel Lothar Schieverhofer and joined up with the rest of the formation before heading across the English Channel to Kent. Over northern Kent, they were attacked by the Spitfires of No. 74 Squadron and Steinhilper was hit in the radiator. Immediately, his engine temperature soared and although he tried to return home, calling on his radio for air-sea rescue services, he eventually had to abandon his Messerschmitt over Chislet near Canterbury. Steinhilper did not know it at the time, but his wingman Lothar Schieverhofer had also been shot down and escaped injury.

In his autobiography, Steinhilper gives an account of how he made a less than standard escape from his doomed ME109. First of all, the emergency release for the canopy failed and he had to open it in the same manner he would on the ground – tilting the entire canopy to one side on its hinges. As the canopy opened, the gush of the slipstream lifted anything that was not secure out into the slipstream.

Releasing his harness, Steinhilper tried to exit the cockpit, only to find his parachute pack was stuck under the non-removable rear section of the cockpit canopy. Buffeted by the howling slipstream, he eventually managed to release himself and somersaulted over the side, just missing the tail as it flashed past him. As he fell, he pulled the ripcord and the parachute streamed out between his legs in a less than exemplary manner. The chute and its rigging lines wrapped themselves around his left leg and as the silk deployed and the lines became taught, a searing pain shot up his leg. With his left leg pulled into an unnatural position above him, Steinhilper was in danger of further injury upon landing. Eventually he managed to free himself and his injured leg hung limply next to the other one.

As Steinhilper considered his injuries and imminent landing, his Messerschmitt 'Yellow 2' dived into the ground a short distance away. He landed in a crumpled heap and started to remove his personal survival equipment which included his dinghy, a flare pistol and sea marker dye.

Suddenly he heard a gunshot and laid himself flat on the damp ground. His tormentor was man in civilian clothes with a rifle. He had an armband with LDV on it – Local Defence Volunteers – the Home Guard. The part-time soldier told his prisoner to get up, but Steinhilper's leg was badly injured and in his best school-boy English, he tried to explain this. Eventually, a crowd of civilians appeared from the nearby village together with two more soldiers.

The LDV man asked for Steinhilper's identity card which he didn't have, neither was he wearing his identity disc. The man and the villagers were soon surprised to find the Nazi airman had his pyjamas on under his flying clothes. The LDV man thought this was quite comical and clearly wanted some sort of a souvenir. To placate him, Steinhilper gave him the only thing he could – a small badge of a wild boar – the insignia of I/JG52. The LDV man quickly put this valuable piece of intelligence, which would have been very useful to AI1(k), into his pocket.

Steinhilper, ably assisted by the two soldiers, was half carried half dragged to a hall in the nearby village of Chislet. He was given a cup of tea by a local nurse and his swollen leg was placed in a bucket of cold water.

About half an hour later, an officer in an RAF uniform arrived. The officer spoke German with a Nuremberg accent and started asking questions about his unit, aircraft etc. Steinhilper quickly told him, that apart from his name, rank and home address, he would say nothing else. The preliminary intelligence officer carried on asking questions and this irritated the German pilot who started to become restless.

In his book, *Ten minutes to Buffalo,* Steinhilper recalls telling the officer that he would gladly confirm his aircraft had been hit in the radiator, so the British pilot could claim his 'kill', but he would give no other information.

The RAF Intelligence Officer appeared to be concerned that Steinhilper did not possess either an identity card or an identity disc. The pyjamas under his outer clothing also made him curious, but that was nothing compared to a letter the prisoner had in his pocket…

A girlfriend's brother was married to an English girl whose family lived in south-west London. If the German Army had invaded the United Kingdom, Steinhilper intended visiting the family and asked for their address. This was contained in the letter together with some other personal details about a recent family birth.

Steinhilper feared the worst. The officer asked him about the letter and after a brief explanation, the Intelligence Officer surprisingly did not follow-up on his initial question. This is unusual and what records there are in the UK National Archives, sadly cannot explain this issue. On face value, the Intelligence Officer had a German with no identification, wearing pyjamas under his flying kit and possessing the details of what could have been a British collaborating family or a spy in south-west London…

The RAF Officer, according to Steinhilper, produced an identity card for another German airman. The interrogator explained the man had been shot down nearby and badly mutilated. He wanted Steinhilper to possibly identify him and his unit, so the man's family could be informed. Steinhilper could see the man's name and service number on the identity card and immediately suspected a trick, he denied knowing the man and the questioning stopped.

Was this another ruse used by Air Intelligence officers? An examination of known German losses for the ten days prior to Steinhilper being shot down, fails to produce any Luftwaffe airmen killed nearby. When those search parameters are reduced to just ME109 pilots, only two were killed in Kent during that period; and they came down at the opposite end of the county in Sevenoaks and Tunbridge Wells. However, one pilot's body was washed ashore at Littlestone Golf Links, near Folkestone on 24 October. That pilot was Unteroffizier Henrich Arp of 2/JG26, a completely different Geschwader to Steinhilper's.

The preliminary RAF Interrogation Officer's identity is unknown, but it may have been Flying Officer C.M.D. Eales who was based at RAF Biggin Hill for most of the Battle of Britain. (He had dealt with Unteroffizier Leo Zaunbrecher on 12 August in Sussex.) Eventually, the RAF man left Ulrich Steinhilper in the care of the Army and departed.

Steinhilper was moved to Westbere House nearby and stayed there for a few days before being transferred. The house was the home of an Army major and his leg was treated by a local doctor. A pair of crutches were obtained from Ashford hospital by a lieutenant and he was given a good dinner.

Steinhilper did have one poor interaction with a young officer, but in the main, he was well received and very well treated by the soldiers. He stayed two nights in the house and remained on good terms with the soldiers.

The AI1(k) initial report signed by Felkin and dated 29 October 1940, indicates that Steinhilper had been detained and given an initial interrogation. Although signed by Felkin, this appears to have been the initial Interrogating Officer's report, but there was no mention of the compromising letter, the lack of an identity card, his pyjamas etc.

It appears Steinhilper may have given away more information than he recalled in his autobiography… the report states that although he did not have his Ausweis with him, he stated it was grey in colour and issued at Zerbat. In addition, it appears he may have stated that his mission started at 0900 hours from the Calais area and he was escorting Messerschmitt 109 bombers to London. He was at 26,000 feet when attacked and his radiator damaged. The report added that the pilot refused all information about his unit, but the Ausweis and the Feldpost number, which was on the parachute pack certificate, indicates this was I/JG52. Two other aircraft from that Gruppe were also brought down in the same action (one of which was clearly his wingman).

Although Steinhilper says he did not give anything away, the report concludes that he enquired after three other prisoners of war from I/JG52. Two were from the 2nd Staffel and one the Staffel Kapitan shot down on 12 October (Oberleutnant Karl Sauer). As a result of these comments, the Ausweis and the parachute pack's Feldpost number, Air Intelligence believed they had positively identified Steinhilper's unit. His morale was noted as being extremely high. The report did not mention knowing he was a five-victory ace.

On 30 October, Steinhilper was transferred to what he called an interrogation camp. After a three-hour drive, during which it started to rain heavily, Steinhilper arrived at what he thought was a chicken farm with a barbed wire fence. He had his crutches taken from him and he had to hop in the rain to his new accommodation, a long dark barn.

A non-commissioned officer with a 'stick' shouted endless orders and abuse at the injured pilot, as he hopped up the staircase of the barn and into what he described as a hayloft with plasterboard partitioned areas. Each area had a cement floor with an iron bed, a straw-filled palliasse and a rough blanket. This was his new lodgings, guarded by a soldier in his fifties together with a rifle and fixed bayonet. Unlike Trent Park and the London Cage, which had lockable rooms, the accommodation in this camp was not secure and there was no door to each area. Instead, the soldier with a rifle and fixed bayonet stood guard.

While those held at Trent Park were held in solitary confinement with no one to talk to, Steinhilper claimed to have chatted happily with his guard who was an older soldier. However, whenever his guard changed, some would remain silent, while others seemed only too happy to engage in conversation. This regime appears to have been much laxer than that which von Werra and others experienced at Trent Park.

From the description, the camp appears to have been Lingfield race course in East Sussex, which had been requisitioned in 1939 and Steinhilper's lodgings appear to have been the old stable block. Initially, in the spring of 1940, Lingfield race course held civilian internees, before they were sent to other camps and the Isle of Man.

On 15 of October 2014, Freddy Godshaw told the BBC Peoples War of his internment and arrival at Lingfield in the spring of 1940, the description sounds similar to Steinhilper's:

'Next morning a convoy of army lorries took us to Lingfield, which had been hurriedly converted into an Internment Camp. We were given paliasses, mattresses stuffed with straw, to sleep on. Some put down their mattresses on the grandstands, while we were taken to the stables, which had been cleaned out.'

In June 1940, after the internees had been moved on, Lingfield Park and a number of other race courses became Prisoner of War 'Cages'. They were adapted from June 1940 for MI19's Prisoner of War Interrogation Section (Home) – otherwise known as PWIS(H) – which was part of the Combined Services Detailed Interrogation Centres (CSDIC) and therefore, part of the larger overall unit, which included AI1(k) and Air Intelligence at Trent Park.

Ulrich Steinhilper saw several other injured Luftwaffe men in the adjoining guarded areas with fresh blood-stained bandages. He had a feeling of foreboding and even thought he could be killed – this was not the sort of prison camp he expected.

After a night's sleep, the next morning Steinhilper was made to hop on one leg to another building near the main gate. He was confronted by more British officers and armed soldiers, before being stripped naked and having his personal effects, including his wrist watch removed. Steinhilper was questioned about his physical exercise and he thought this was just a medical examination.

Steinhilper was allowed to dress before being questioned by what he called a friendly looking man, who spoke fluent German, in front of a number of officers and armed guards. Unfortunately, Steinhilper does not say whether this interrogator was a military man or a civilian.

The friendly man offered him a cigarette and asked some personal questions. Steinhilper gave his personal details and home address before stating he had been awarded the Iron Cross First and Second Class. This was a mistake. He had not been wearing any decorations when shot down and it is likely the interrogator would not have known about these awards, if he had not offered the information himself. Immediately, the interrogator latched onto this comment and speculated about how many aerial victories his prisoner had achieved. Steinhilper repeatedly refused to give any further information until the interrogator stated:

'Well, we know that you belonged to a fighter unit and we know just about everything about all the German fighter units… look (pointing to a pile of papers on the desk)… there is a whole pile of information we have gathered here.'

Steinhilper apparently continued to refuse to give any further information and was soon sent hopping back to his austere stable lodgings under armed guard.

This interrogation, the lodgings and the guards all appear to have been very different to those at Trent Park. This was almost certainly a Prisoner of War Interrogation Section (Home) – otherwise known as a PWIS(H) site. It was more of an Army Intelligence site than the RAF wing at Trent Park, where the system appears to have been very different.

En route back to his cell Steinhilper was surprised to find his wingman, Feldwebel Lothar Schieverhofer. He was sat in an outside toilet block with the door wide open and closely guarded. Despite the guard, the two pilots managed a few words and Steinhilper discovered his wingman was shot down just before he had been brought down. Eventually, the guards stopped the chattering Germans and he was moved on, back to his cell, happy to know his young wingman was alive.

Lothar Schieverhofer's AI1(k) preliminary interrogation report, was dated 27 October and he appears to have given details of his own demise at the hands of Spitfires (No. 74 Squadron). He did not give the RAF field interrogator details of his unit, but this was assumed from his Feldpost number and from the names of two other prisoners of war he stated were friends. In addition, having belly-landed his Messerschmitt, the aircrafts full markings were noted and greatly assisted in the identification of the 3rd Staffel of JG52.

In his autobiography, Ulrich Steinhilper states that later he met up with his wingman who told him that the RAF knew everything about their unit and their Staffel commanders…

On 31 October, Ulrich Steinhilper states Oberleutnant Hermann Reifferscheidt of 1/JG2 arrived at their interrogation centre, although AI1(k) records state he was shot down on 1 November and their report is dated 2 November, so this may be an error. Like Steinhilper's wingman, Hermann Reifferscheidt had made a successful belly-landing and given the RAF another present of a virtually intact Messerschmitt 109E, together with his radio codes.

On 1 November, Steinhilper was asked further questions by another officer, allegedly working on behalf of the Red Cross. He asked him about his interests and hobbies, as well as his education and family background, but nothing according to Steinhilper of a military value. It is likely the interrogator was testing him and assessing his political beliefs, but Steinhilper chose to avoid mentioning this delicate subject. The interrogating officer then mentioned the fact Steinhilper's sister could not get silk stockings and asked if he had sent her any from France. How the interrogator could know this is unclear from Steinhilper's book, is it possible he had been placed in an M-Room and this was overheard by a *listener*? Steinhilper says this made him aware the interrogation was aimed at military information and he asked for the session to be terminated.

Back in his cell, Ulrich Steinhilper says he spent some time listening to an NCO pilot being interrogated in the room below him. The interrogator shouted at him in German and eventually the prisoner told them everything he knew. Even after he had divulged all his information, the interrogator continued to shout abuse and the man was left crying and pleading for him to stop. Steinhilper saw the guards return the man to his own area and in his own words, the man 'Looked a broken fearful wretch.'

There is no reason to doubt this account, but this does not sound like the interrogation regime of Denys Felkin and AI1(k) at Trent Park, this appears more likely to be the tactics used by Colonel Scotland's team in the 'Cages.'

After three days interrogation, Steinhilper had a final interview with an officer he believed was the camp commandant. The officer told Steinhilper he had been a POW during the First World War, before adding that as unpleasant as it might have been, if it had been up to him, it would have been much worse. Who this man was is unclear, but he may well have suffered as a prisoner in the first war. At the conclusion of this meeting, Steinhilper was told he was moving on to a Prisoner of War camp.

It is clear Trent Park was very busy during the summer and autumn of 1940. As the number of Luftwaffe prisoners increased, the Prisoner of War Interrogation Section (Home) of CSDIC used its new Cages at former race courses such as Lingfield, Kempton Park and Newmarket to supplement AI1(k). They assisted by making a further assessment of a prisoner after the initial RAF Intelligence officer's interrogation, or even an initial assessment of a prisoner, if there had been too many arrivals for the Field Officers to interview.

An assessment of AI1(k) intelligence reports, finds the numbers of Luftwaffe prisoners of war passing through the hands of Air Intelligence from aircraft either brought down over the UK mainland or just off-shore (Other Luftwaffe prisoners had arrived from the Continent having been captured during the Blitzkrieg assault, but these ceased after withdrawal from Dunkirk in June 1940):

May 1940:	7 POWs
June 1940:	21 POWs
July 1940:	89 POWs
August 1940:	371 POWs
September 1940:	351 POWs
October 1940:	132 POWs

It appears that after preliminary assessment, a prisoner would either be sent on to Denys Felkin's team at Trent Park for more detailed interrogation or sent directly to a POW camp if they were deemed to be of no interest. However, due to the number of prisoners and the opening of the London Cage at Kensington Palace Gardens, some prisoners were sent to the London Cage and others to Trent Park from late October 1940 onwards. Which prisoners were sent to Trent Park and who went to Kensington Palace Gardens is unclear, but on 2 November, Ulrich Steinhilper claims he was taken with Oberleutnant Hermann Reifferscheidt to the London Cage in Kensington Palace Gardens. Although there are some surviving interrogation files for the London Cage, Steinhilper's name does not feature in any of them, so we cannot confirm where he went and it might have been Trent Park.

Upon arrival in London, both men were placed in a sparse room together and left alone. The two men chatted in what they thought was privacy, but it was almost certainly an M-Room and Reifferscheidt suspected there were hidden microphones. Steinhilper believed his suspicions were correct, for as soon as they stopped chatting, the guards arrived and they were each placed in a sparsely furnished room on his own.

After a period of solitary reflection, another officer joined Steinhilper. This man claimed to be a Lieutenant Rossi, a submariner of the Italian Navy, captured in the Atlantic. After introductions, the two men spoke to one another in broken English, as neither spoke the other's main language. Rossi soon speculated that they had been brought together as there would be hidden microphones and so they spoke in whispers. A short time later, they agreed to speak loudly about hidden microphones and sure enough, they were quickly separated again.

Lieutenant Rossi is an interesting character and was almost certainly a stool-pigeon. The Italian Navy did send submarines to France in 1940 and they did operate in the Atlantic, but when Rossi spoke to Steinhilper, not one vessel had been lost and no prisoners taken. It therefore would appear Rossi, who Steinhilper did say looked too old to be a submariner (in his forties and bald), was a stool pigeon.

The fact Rossi entered and immediately speculated about hidden microphones, making Steinhilper speak in whispers, was an excellent tactic. It immediately disarmed the suspicions of the genuine prisoner who would continue talking in whispers and giving information. When the stool pigeon believed he has obtained all he could from the prisoner, they agree to 'flush' out the hidden microphone tactic by speaking loudly about the devices and hey-presto! the guards safely remove the stool pigeon with his information. The only problem is no third party can hear and record that information, but against a pilot who is refusing everything, it's a last resort tactic. However, the RCA microphones were so sensitive, maybe they could hear a whispered conversation.

The next day (3 November 1940), Steinhilper and Reifferscheidt were placed in another room with two officers, one of whom was Leutnant Ernst Busch and an old fishing boat captain.

Leutnant Ernst Busch was another Messerschmitt 109E pilot of Stab I/JG3. Like Ulrich Steinhilper, he had been shot down on 27 October and was slightly wounded. His aircraft was wrecked, but the less than talkative pilot had his unit assumed from his identity disc and Feldpost numbers, just like Steinhilper.

One by one the men were taken out and interrogated separately over a period of time by five different British officers. What Ulrich Steinhilper imparted to these officers was not disclosed in his book, but he claimed to have told them he would tell them nothing. Unfortunately, there are no other records available at the UK National Archives of his repeated interrogations. It is quite possible he did not say too much, as he was soon on the move again.

On 4 November, Steinhilper was moved by road to Swanwick prisoner of war camp in the Midlands. There he soon met up with an old associate – Franz von Werra. He also met Hauptmann Walter Kienzle (Stab/JG26), who knew Steinhilper of old and had been Adolph Galland's wingman when he was shot down on 30 September over Surrey. He lost a leg and would be later repatriated to Germany by the International Red Cross. Other officers included the ardent Nazi, Leutnant Walter Manhart of 6/ZG26, the man who left his inscription on the wall in von Werra's first room; Major Heinz Cramer (Stab II/LG1) and Major Willibald Fanelsa (Stab III/KG1) who had been von Werra's first commandant at Grizedale Hall prison camp in Cumbria.

Franz Von Werra continued to make escape attempts, as did Walter Manhart, Major Heinz Cramer, Leutnant (Dr.) Ernst Wagner (Stab I/JG3) a pre-war lawyer and Hannes Wilhelm. They tunneled out of the camp, but were all recaptured and together with Steinhilper, were transported to camps in Canada, where their escape attempts would continue. Ulrich Steinhilper would make numerous attempts to escape, but only Franz von Werra made the ultimate *home-run* to the Fatherland.

The two separate accounts from Steinhilper and von Werra give a good impression of what CSDIC, AI1(k) and PWIS(H) were doing in 1940 and the different manner in which the prisoners of war were treated.

The exact number of prisoners passing through the Cages and ultimately the London Cage is unknown, many documents have either been destroyed or are not available for public consumption. What is clear, is that quite a number passed through the Cages and the different interrogation techniques.

In the next chapter, we shall examine some of the German airmen who passed through Lieutenant Colonel Scotland's London Cage, their details being recorded and preserved at the UK National Archives.

Chapter 23

The London Cage Interrogations

We have already noted that by late 1940, a number of Luftwaffe airmen were being sent to the London Cage in Kensington Palace Gardens for interrogation. It is also clear that other so-called Cages were being utilised around the country. This raises two questions: Why were these particular men selected and how were they interrogated, compared to those under the management of Denys Felkin's staff at Trent Park?

In the UK National Archives, there is a file (reference WO/208/5163) detailing some of those detained at the London Cage and a brief summary of the intelligence gleaned from them. We know of a number of Luftwaffe airmen captured during the Battle of Britain and interrogated at Kensington Palace Gardens from November 1940 to February 1941 and it is these nineteen men we shall concentrate on in this chapter.

Like the AI1(k) intelligence files, it is clear the London Cage file contains only interrogation summaries and all other detailed material, including transcripts and information about each prisoner, is either no longer available or possibly still withheld from public view.

In a bid to understand why these prisoners went to the London Cage, rather than to Trent Park, we shall examine the available AI1(k) records, the Cage interrogation summary and any other facts concerning these airmen.

While the assistance of the London Cage may have been appreciated at the peak of the Battle of Britain in August and September 1940, it did not start operating until the last week of October 1940 – basically the end of the battle. It is therefore unclear why these particular men went to the London Cage in the winter months of 1940-1941.

The number of new Luftwaffe prisoner arrivals peaked in August and September, but there was a reduction in October, November and December. The period January to mid-April 1941, saw just 154 new arrivals for AI1(k) to interrogate, so when this figure is compared to the number of arrivals during the summer and autumn of 1940, these were very low figures.

If the earlier Battle of Britain prisoners had been injured and hospitalised, surely upon release in the autumn and winter of 1940–41, they could have been interrogated at Trent Park, which must have had greater capacity due to falling prisoner numbers? It is because of the falling new prisoner numbers, that I suggest prisoner numbers is not the reason for sending these men to the London Cage for interrogation. Many of these men were still hospitalised in December 1940 and upon release went to the London Cage. They could have been handled by Trent Park, so we must therefore examine each prisoner more carefully.

In the next chapter, we shall consider the use of the Royal Herbert Hospital in Woolwich, south-east London to guard and treat Luftwaffe prisoners of war; but at this point we just need to recognise that in 1940, two wards were used for Luftwaffe prisoners. One was on an upper level for officers and a lower level for non-commissioned officers.

Feldwebel Willi Hohenstadter was interrogated at the London Cage on 29 November 1940. Report Ref. No. MI9(a)/IS/137 only records him being a wireless operator on a Dornier 17 (U5+LR) belonging to 7/KG2 and brought down on his first war flight at Highman's Farm Thaxted, Essex on 26 August. It therefore appears the interrogators considered him a *small fish* with little in the way of intelligence and sent him off to a prisoner of war camp. Hohenstadter and the flight mechanic, although wounded from enemy fire, managed to bail out successfully, but their pilot and observer were killed when the Dornier exploded upon crashing. Which hospital Hohenstadter attended is unclear, but as a Feldwebel (Sergeant) it is likely to have been the Royal Herbert Hospital's lower ward.

Unteroffizier Erwin Kramer was interrogated at the London Cage on 29 November 1940. He was the wounded wireless operator from a Heinkel III (V4+KL) of 3/KG1, shot down by Spitfires at Hildenborough, Kent on 11 September. It appears from the records that Kramer and some of the crew had previously been shot down over France, just prior to the French armistice and captured. They were eventually released and the crew had either been on leave or in hospital before returning to their unit in France. Again, it is possible as a non-commissioned officer, Kramer was held at the Royal Herbert Hospital's lower ward, but this cannot be confirmed.

When he was interrogated at the London Cage, Kramer was identified as being a wireless operator on his first flight over England. He provided little of intelligence value and was quickly sent on his way to a POW camp.

Leutnant zur See Karl-Heinz Kemper was interrogated at the London Cage on 12 December 1940. Kemper was the wireless operator on a Heinkel 115 (S4+AH) which was attacked off the coast of Norfolk by a Hampden bomber on 26 October 1940. The British aircraft damaged the Heinkel's engines, causing the crew to abandon the aircraft on the water. Unlike many of the prisoners known to have been interrogated at the London Cage, Kemper was uninjured and had been previously shot down by a Blenheim while a crew member of a Heinkel 59 deployed on air-sea rescue work in the Channel. He had been rescued by an E-boat.

Karl-Heinz Kemper was a better source of information for the London Cage interrogators. He informed them that he had been seconded from the Navy to the Luftwaffe since May 1940 and that was why he still wore his naval uniform. He had not yet ordered a Luftwaffe uniform, but was expected to serve with them for four years, eventually returning to the Kriegsmarine for promotion.

Kemper told the interrogators he had seen bomb damage to civilian property in Bremen in September 1940, but he was told that most RAF bombs had failed to detonate. He had seen similar damage in Dusseldorf and heard that some military targets had been hit in the city.

Kemper had been stationed at Nordeney, which had seldom been bombed and never effectively. Losses in his Staffel were about ten per cent.

Kemper told his interrogators he could not understand why the invasion of England had not taken place, and he did not believe excessive German losses were the reason for this. He had high morale and expected an invading army to free him in three to six months' time.

The prisoner was happy to discuss the German rescue buoys anchored in the sea, stating that he believed these were operated under the auspices of the Red Cross. He added that the British black-out was good, better than that in France and that he often used civilian radio broadcasting for radio direction finding purposes, but his apparatus was not up to date.

Feldwebel Georg Engel was interrogated at the London Cage on 29 December 1940, (reference MI9(a)/IS/MISC/97), but it appears he may have been interrogated on a previous date at Kensington Palace Gardens, as the document mentions another previous reference MI9(a)/IS/MISC/78.

Engel was the radio operator on a Heinkel III (G1+DN) of 5/KG55, shot down by anti-aircraft fire over Somerset on 25 September. Unlike Hohenstadter and Kramer, Engel was not injured. While the first two could have been in hospital recovering before transfer to the London Cage, why Engel was held for three months prior to his attendance at the London Cage is unknown.

When he was interrogated (ref. MI9(a)/IS/MISC/97), Engel told his interviewers he was of the opinion Germany would lose the war. He added that he thought there is a good deal of opposition to the war in Munich, Augsburg, Donauworth and Regensburg, having heard people discussing it there in July. However, people could not say this in Berlin or Cologne for fear of reprisals. Despite these comments, he told the interrogators that he did not think there was sufficient material for a revolution in Germany.

Engel was asked what he knew about *Gas Brillen*. He explained that these were the pieces of glass fitted to a gas mask. They could be taken out and replaced. He said, there were four different types of glass for different gases and two could be used simultaneously for use against two gas types. Despite these comments, the interrogation reports author noted that Engel's statements on this matter had been inconsistent and seemed a little far-fetched!

Feldwebel Georg Engel was an experienced wireless operator who possessed an Iron Cross First Class. He appears to have been interrogated again on 28 February 1941 (reference MI9(a)/IS/MISC/135) which would appear to indicate he was at the London Cage for over two months. If correct, he must have been providing some very useful information as this extended period appears to reflect the time Gerd Kahle spent at Trent Park providing intelligence to AI1(k).

Engel said he did not carry his gas respirator in his aircraft. He did not believe British radio broadcasts and gave as an example the Daimler works in Stuttgart, saying that contrary to British claims, they had not been hit in July 1940.

According to the intelligence summary, Engel was also keen to state that the Poles had slaughtered their German prisoners of war in 1939.

It would appear from these first prisoners, the London Cage was concentrating on wireless operators, but they soon moved on to other crewmen…

Unteroffizier Ludwig von Lorentz was interrogated in London on 29 and 31 December 1940. He was the pilot of a Junkers 88 (4D+KL) of 3/KG30, shot down at Barnstown near Bridlington, Yorkshire, on 15 August.

When interrogated (ref. MI9(a)/IS/155), von Lorentz, who had been injured, was keen to show his gratitude to his interrogators for his kind treatment in hospital. He was an Austrian and said his opinion was that if Germany was to win the war, they must do so soon.

Von Lorentz had served in the Polish campaign, telling his interrogators that he had not seen much bomb damage in Poland and they had only attacked military targets.

While on leave in Konigsberg in July, he had the same rations as civilians with plenty of everything except coffee. There was however, less meat than before the war. Von Lorentz concluded his initial interview by stating that he did not like the war and was prepared to think for himself. He did not approve of everything Hitler did.

Oberfeldwebel Erich Slotosch was interrogated at the London Cage on 2 January 1941, having been brought down almost six months before on 11 July 1940. He was pilot of a Heinkel III (G1+LK) belonging to 2/KG55 when they made a forced landing on the beach at Selsey in Sussex. Slotosch suffered serious wounds and was hospitalised, possibly at the Royal Herbert Hospital in Woolwich.

When he was interrogated, (ref. MI9(a)/IS/MISC/98), Slotosch told the interviewer that he did not think gas would be used as a weapon and the English were unnecessarily frightened of it. He was asked what he knew about *Gas Brillen,* but said he had never heard of it.

Unteroffizier Edo Flick visited the London Cage on 27 January 1941. He was the wireless operator of a Heinkel III (1G+OT) of 9/KG27, shot down on 14 August 1940.

The aircraft was attacked by Spitfires and the crew successfully abandoned the Heinkel, but Flick was wounded and needed hospital treatment at an unknown hospital (again possibly the Royal Herbert) until December 1940.

It would appear he was sent to the London Cage upon his release from the hospital. His London Cage record states he had been a Signal Instructor near Cologne before joining his present unit at Rennes in July 1940. He was shot down on his second war flight over England and no other detail of intelligence value was provided by Flick.

Leutnant Heinz Schnabel, a contemporary of Franz von Werra was shot down on 5 September and interrogated in London on 29 and 31 January 1941. He was flying a Messerschmitt 109E of 1/JG3 when attacked by British fighters and wounded. He made a forced landing at Banks Farm, Aldington, East Kent and was taken to the Royal Herbert Hospital in Woolwich. As we have already seen, he would later make an audacious escape with fellow Royal Herbert Hospital patient Harry Wappler in late 1941, before being recaptured in East Anglia.

Schnabel, like von Werra, refused to discuss any of his military operations and activities. Like Franz von Werra his political comments were eye-opening for his interrogators. He told them that Germany was fighting for her existence and if she lost, the Treaty of Versailles would be nothing compared to a new defeat. He added that he had been taught that Britain had made a prime blunder in not attacking Germany as a preventative measure in 1933. He had been taught that France was stronger than she proved to be, and the entry of Italy into the war was a bad mistake, as he felt sure Germany had overestimated Italy's military effectiveness and strength.

In a strange display of changing attitudes, Schnabel added that he never expected England to enter the war and there was a certain amount of profiteering in Germany. The German government were minimising this, but he quickly added that profiteering is far more rampant in England.

Despite generally regurgitating propaganda, he told his interrogators Nazi leaders were making fortunes, but this was nothing compared to the wealth of the Reich and the same thing was going on in Britain and other countries too.

Interestingly, Schnabel believed the pact between Germany and Russia was a political necessity to keep the Soviets out of the clutches of England. The French were far less hostile than he had expected and he believed they would make first class collaborators. In many ways his comments were similar to those of his Geschwader colleague Franz von Werra.

The interrogators, like those at Trent Park, were clearly obsessed with the risk of a gas attack and asked Schnabel about this. He told them he had never received any gas training and did not know of its military use. He also did not expect Hitler to use gas as a first use weapon.

Schnabel expected Germany to invade Britain and he had no doubts over a Germany victory. The report ended by stating that full copies of these extracts had been sent to AI1(k).

Leutnant Franz Schad was interrogated at the London Cage on 11 February 1941 (ref. Nos. MI9(a)/IS/MISC/122 & MI9(a)/IS/178). He was shot down by Hurricanes and anti-aircraft fire on 12 August 1940, while the observer in a Heinkel III (9K+AA) of Stab/KG51. The pilot (Oberst Johann Fisser the Geschwader Kommodore) was killed, but Franz Schad and the other crew members were wounded and taken to hospital. Schad was treated in the officers' ward at the Royal Herbert Hospital in Woolwich.

Franz Schad, like Schnabel, gave the London Cage interrogators quite a bit to think about. In many ways, he was the complete opposite to Schnabel.

Schad told his interrogators that he had been in hospital for the past six months since being shot down. He had been a member of the Centre Party in Germany before 1933 and knew Heinrich Bruining the party leader personally, but he joined the Nazi Party in 1933. He blamed the Centre Party for the war, as it had not secured a customs treaty with Austria. The union between Germany and Austria was not possible through arbitration, and therein lay Hitler's apology for the Anschluss.

Schad stated that in Wuerttemberg, not many men were reserved at the start of the war, but after the Polish campaign, many men were returned to civilian life and others were called-up to replace them.

The London Cage interrogators noted that Schad possessed all the usual specious arguments, but after they had established that he despised the Italians and resented religious persecutions, he finally admitted Britain only had peaceful intentions. After discussing the international outlook as he saw it, Schad gave the impression that he was, at heart, desperately afraid of the outcome of the war despite his politics.

The prisoner had been a council lawyer in Stuttgart before the war and was a Roman Catholic. As a student of international law, Schad said his activities had been viewed with a certain amount of suspicion by the Nazi Party, even though he was a member. He never made any secret of his religion, but this did sometimes cause difficulties and business was sometimes delayed.

Schad admitted to reading the London *Times* newspaper with interest and admiration. He was a great believer in the British as a people and had a friend who was a former English lecturer at Tubingen University named Barnes.

Hauptmann Joachim Roth was interrogated at the London Cage on 15-16 February 1941, (references MI9(a)/IS/MISC/123 & 129), six months after he was shot down on 18 August 1940. Roth was the commanding officer and lead observer on one of the 9/KG76 Dornier 17's (F1+DT) which made an audacious low-level raid on RAF Kenley. Roth's Dornier was hit by anti-aircraft fire and struggled away from Kenley, before being attacked by Hurricanes of No. 111 Squadron. Three of the crew bailed out at low-level, surviving with injuries commensurate with their low altitude exit.

Roth and his pilot, Oberleutnant Rudolf Lamberty, remained inside the aircraft as it slid to a halt and caught fire at Leaves Green next to RAF Biggin Hill. The wrecked Dornier with its British Army guard, would become one of the most iconic photographic images of the Battle of Britain. Roth and his pilot suffered serious burns as they managed to scramble out of the wrecked Dornier before fire consumed the cockpit area. Roth said that after their escape, they both stood and watched as Heinkel's bombed the adjacent airfield.

As commanding officer and lead navigator of such an audacious low-level raid and elite Staffel, there is no surprise Roth ended up at the London Cage. However, he spent a number of months in the officers' ward of the Royal Herbert Hospital in Woolwich before he visited London.

Roth told his interrogators that his father owned a 400 hectares farm. They received as much petrol as necessary for farming, but only enough for business use of their car. The Nazi authorities inspected their fruit and vegetables every month to ensure quality was maintained. In addition, before the war, there was an annual animal census. They made butter and could keep as much of their product as they liked.

After the war in France concluded, French farm produce was imported to Germany, but Germany had plenty before this.

Roth said he had convinced a French farmer with whom he was billeted, of the justice of the German cause and that they had everything to gain by co-operating with the Germans. Despite being billeted with a French farmer, Roth added that German soldiers were discouraged from mixing with the French population. He believed the ultimate aim was to make the French partners if not friends of the Reich.

Roth believed that if an invasion of Britain failed, the war would last for many years, but conversely, Britain could never succeed in invading Germany. He was convinced Germany would invade, but did not have high hopes for its success. He stressed the possibility of landings by airborne troops and had seen with his own eyes, what he called amphibious tanks. Like previous prisoners, he was asked about the use of gas, and he said he was surprised neither side had used it, but he thought the fear of reprisals may deter the German command from doing so.

Although, like most airmen, Roth stayed clear of military operational matters, he did remark on the comparative lack of German air raids by day. He attributed this to the necessity to rest the aircrews and the poor condition of the French aerodromes.

Roth said he believed Germany had derived little assistance from a Fifth Column in their invasion of Holland, in fact the Germans were hated by the Dutch. He thought Germany had anticipated a British move and that was why the Wehrmacht invaded the neutral countries, while Denmark had to be invaded as an approach to invade Norway.

Roth admired the British and would expect any act of heroism from them, however, the Italians who have a good army and air force were fooled. After the Jews, the Germans hate the Poles, but the destruction of Warsaw was necessary to bring an end to that campaign.

Feldwebel Rudolf Poh a member of 7/KG76 was shot down in his Dornier 17 on 6 October 1940. He was interrogated at the London Cage over 16-17 February 1941 (ref. MI9(a)/IS/182).

Rudolf Poh was the aircrafts flight mechanic when they were attacked by fighters near Wadhurst in East Sussex. Badly damaged they made a forced landing but hit a tree, the observer being killed and the pilot and wireless operator being injured. Poh sustained serious injuries and ended up in an unknown hospital, possibly the Royal Herbert.

Poh told his interrogators that anti-aircraft fire did not worry him, although it was severe over London. He did not carry his gas mask in the aircraft and civilians in Germany did not carry them either. He said he felt Germany would not use gas unless the British did so first.

Poh had flown daylight and night-time operations. He said the two methods of spotting British night-fighters were to see them in the searchlight beams or by looking for 'watch light' signals from the fighters to the ground defences and vice-versa.

Oberleutnant Gerard Goetz (sometimes spelt Gotz) was a pilot and Staffel Kapitan of a Messerschmitt 110 of 1/ZG2 (3M+AH), shot down by Spitfires on 25 August 1940, near Wareham in Dorset. He was badly wounded and ended up in hospital before he also attended the London Cage on 16/17 February 1941 (ref. MI9(a)/IS/183). Like Hauptmann Roth, he was a Staffel commander and clearly was a target for detailed interrogation.

Goetz was full of Nazi bravado when interrogated and was keen to tell the British that Germany had so many soldiers, they did not need to use 'old men' such as his 37-year-old brother. He did not consider the educational standards of the Luftwaffe to be any higher than the German Army. He believed the German-Soviet pact had caused amazement in Germany, but it was purely a political union. Goetz also refused to believe the Germans were treating the Poles badly.

Goetz told the interrogators that politics could not be conducted with truth and honour and therefore, Hitler could not be blamed for the Czechoslovakian invasion. The losses by Italy were also, in his eyes, no doubt foreseen and part of the overall German plan!

Once again, the interrogators appear to have been fixated with the possible use of poison gas and Goetz thought the weapon would be of more benefit to a defending force than an attacker.

His views on a possible invasion of Britain were deemed to be uncertain. On the one hand he thought it would be tried on a large scale and was inevitable, but on the other hand, he was sure the German General Staff would not try anything crazy.

Goetz was asked about the reduced number of air attacks on Britain, but he told his interviewers this was caused by nothing more than weather issues.

Leutnant Karl-Ernst Wilke was interrogated at the London Cage on 22 February 1941, (reference MI9(a)/IS/187), having been shot down by Spitfires on 15 September 1940.

The observer on a Dornier 17 of 3/KG76 tasked with bombing an airfield in North London, Wilke was seriously wounded when the aircraft came down at Sturry in Kent. Three of his crew were killed and the final member wounded. Wilke was taken to the Royal Herbet Hospital in Woolwich and was still there in December before finally attending the London Cage.

Wilke stated that in 1936 he had friends in the Göring Parachute Regiment based at Renigendorf, Berlin. The unit used to guard the home of Hermann Göring.

Wilke said he took no special action in avoiding anti-aircraft fire other than changing altitude or direction. He did however, think British anti-aircraft fire was of a good standard.

In peacetime his gas mask was checked every six months, but he had not changed his mask since the start of the war. Wilke said he had not received any special training regarding the use of gas.

Karl-Ernst Wilke said he would have been interested in listening to BBC radio broadcasts, but he could not receive them in mid-France. However, he thought little of British propaganda and though it was misdirected.

As we have seen, Oberleutnant Harry Wappler would be one half of a famous escape attempt with Leutnant Schnabel in 1941. Wappler was the pilot of a Heinkel III of 8/KG27 (1G+DS), which bombed a target in Ellesmere Port in the early hours of 13 September 1940. They had bombed their target and were en route to their base via South Wales, when they struck at least two barrage balloon cables which caused the aircraft to become uncontrollable. Wappler managed to gain some control but the aircraft was doomed and he ordered the crew of four to bail out. Unfortunately, they did not hear Wappler who was the only man to exit the bomber as it fell from the sky, landing on a newsagents and house in Stow Park Avenue, Newport killing two children.

Wappler received injuries and was sent to the Royal Herbert Hospital in Woolwich. He was eventually interrogated at the London Cage on 22 February 1941 (ref. MI9(a)/IS/189).

Harry Wappler gave very little information to his interrogators. His father had an engineering business and he had been employed there before he joined the Luftwaffe. He was convinced Hitler had improved Germany's position, but he admitted the unemployment issue had only been solved by rearmament and an enlarged military. Wappler told his interrogators that he was very surprised England had survived past the autumn (of 1940), but he bore no hatred of the British.

Unteroffizier Frederich Dilthey was serving as a pilot with 4/JG2, when he was caught by Spitfires on 23 September 1940 and shot down off Folkestone. His Messerschmitt 109 provided the local cameras with some excellent images of the aircraft, one of its main under-carriage legs hanging down as it was ditched just off Folkestone Pier. Dilthey was wounded in the crash and had to be rescued by soldiers who dived into the English Channel to extricate him from the sinking fighter. He was transferred to an unknown hospital, possibly the non-commissioned officers ward at the Royal Herbert, before he too visited the London Cage on 28 February 1941.

Dilthey was an engineer in the family business pre-war, the company were wool manufacturers based in Rheydt near the Dutch border. The business employed 1,600 people before the war and now they used a lot more artificial materials instead of wool. There had been daily air raids in Rheydt and he said there had been a good deal of bomb damage.

Gefreiter Alfred Hoffmann was a flight mechanic on a Dornier 17 of 9/KG2 (U5+FT). He was shot down on 15 September off Herne Bay, Kent and had to be rescued by the Royal Navy along with two of his colleagues – the fourth crew member was killed. Hoffmann was injured and treated in an unknown hospital, possibly the Royal Herbert in Woolwich, before he visited the London Cage on 28 February 1941.

Hoffmann appears to have given away little information, but did state that he did not carry his gas mask, which had been tested, on the aircraft.

Oberleutnant Gunter Busgen (sometimes spelt Buesgen) was the Staffel Kapitan of 1/JG52, when he was shot down at Dean Hill, Harrietsham, Kent on 12 October 1940. Busgen the holder of the Iron Cross First Class, was attacked by a fighter and he had to bail out at an altitude of 16,000 feet. Busgen struck the tail of his Messerschmitt 109 and fractured his arm as he bailed out, being taken to the Royal Herbert Hospital in Woolwich.

In his preliminary RAF Field Officer interrogation, as we have seen earlier in this book, he appeared to deliberately mislead his interviewing officer who also appeared to miss the fact he was a six-victory ace. Whether he ever attended Trent Park is unknown, but it appears he went straight from the Royal Herbert Hospital to the London Cage on 28 February 1941, for further interrogation – possibly because of his attempts to mislead the interrogators and or the fact they eventually discovered his status as a top pilot.

His interrogation appears to have obtained little intelligence. He was noted as thinking the Germans would win the war by a combination of air power and submarine warfare. Invasion was still just possible he claimed.

Feldwebel Gunter Kramer was a Messerschmitt 109 pilot with 1/JG77 when he was shot down by a Hurricane on 31 August 1940. His 109 started to burn and he came down, making a forced landing at Shornemead Fort near Gravesend. He was badly burned and taken to an unidentified hospital, very likely the Royal Herbert in nearby Woolwich. He was interrogated at the London Cage on 28 February 1941, almost five months after his arrival in captivity.

Gunter Kramer gave little information to his interrogators, but he was happy to announce he earned RM260 per month as a Feldwebel. He also explained that a Reserve Offizieranwärter was an ROA – someone identified with officer potential and had done particularly well.

It appears upon examination of the London Cage documents, that the most likely reason these eighteen Luftwaffe men were sent to the London Cage for interrogation is:

1. Half of the total were wireless operators and observers, men who were of interest because of intelligence on radio beacons, *X-Gerät* etc.
2. Most, sixteen out of the eighteen, had been badly injured/wounded/burned and hospitalised, in most cases at the Royal Herbert Hospital in Woolwich.
3. Three of the eighteen were Staffel Kapitan, one of whom commanded a specialist low-level raid.
4. A number of the men gave clear Nazi and political comments – especially Schnabel.

Many other experienced and high-ranking men passed through AI1(k) at Trent Park at this time, so the issue of them being injured and hospitalised in most of these cases, appears to take on an added relevance.

The question is this, considering the reputation of the London Cage later in the war, were these men subject to any mistreatment or threats? It would appear that many were not and giving little intelligence they were quickly sent on to a POW camp.

In the next chapter we shall examine whether there were any breaches of the Geneva Convention at AI1(k) and the London Cage…

Chapter 24

Was there a breach of the Geneva Convention?

In the last chapter, we examined the interrogation of Luftwaffe airmen at Lieutenant Colonel Alexander Scotland's London Cage. We have already identified that while there were a great number of Luftwaffe prisoners arriving in the latter stages of the Battle of Britain, those numbers were decreasing when the first prisoners were sent to the London Cage in the autumn and winter of 1940–41.

In later years, the London Cage would earn itself a reputation for mistreatment of the prisoners held there, while avoiding any oversight from the International Committee of the Red Cross – otherwise known as the Protecting Powers.

The reasons why certain Luftwaffe prisoners of war were interrogated at the London Cage are as we have seen complicated, especially when one tries to identify why certain men were sent there and not just to Trent Park and Denys Felkin's team of experienced interrogators. As we have already noted, we know of at least eighteen (sixteen of whom had been injured) Battle of Britain Luftwaffe POWs who were sent to the London Cage; but from other records held in The National Archives, there were at least another sixty who attended between the end of the battle and May 1941. In each case, the prisoners were given a preliminary interrogation and a report submitted to AI1(k). This was signed off in most cases by Denys Felkin or Guy Jepson at Trent Park.

What the criteria and communication system was for transfer to the London Cage is unclear. As we have seen in a previous chapter, nearly all eighteen Battle of Britain prisoners were injured. Some had high-level connections in Germany or belonged to a specialist unit. The sixty-plus men identified as having been transferred to the London Cage from November 1940 to May 1941 covered a wide variety of units and aircraft, their ranks ranging from a lowly Gefreiter to a Hauptmann and Staffel Kapitan.

In the last chapter, we examined the number of Luftwaffe prisoners sent to the London Cage for interrogation between December 1940 to February 1941, a number having been treated at the Royal Herbert Hospital in Woolwich for many weeks or even several months. A few others appear to have possibly been sent to the London Cage after treatment at regional hospitals. The medical care given to the injured Luftwaffe men at the Royal Herbert and other hospitals, appears to have been the best available in 1940.

In 1990, *After the Battle* magazine *(No. 70)* published an account about the Royal Herbert Hospitals Luftwaffe prisoners. It included a sketch plan of the officers' ward giving the names of thirty-two Luftwaffe prisoners and the date they were captured. The date of the sketch was not given, but it appears to be post 11 December 1940, when the last of the named men was captured. Sadly, there was no similar list of non-commissioned patients in the adjacent ward and we can only assume who was held there at that time.

Hospitalised prisoners were guarded by soldiers with fixed bayonets from the nearby Royal Artillery Barracks at Woolwich. Security was very strict and although the medical staff were not part of the intelligence system, they were very well briefed to keep a look-out for anything suspicious.

The nursing staff and the doctors were first rate and one, Sister Sheila McDermott, later recalled her work during the Battle of Britain. She remembered most of the German airmen being polite and grateful for their care, however, some could be unpleasant, but they were the exception.

Sheila McDermott recalled treating Leutnant Adam Nothelfer who had apparently competed at the 1936 Berlin Olympics. He had badly burned legs, but with care, he was soon walking again. Further enquiries have found Nothelfer to be an interesting character, he was a Sonderführer, equivalent in rank to a Leutnant, but in a specialist role. What his role on board his aircraft was is unknown, but he was on board as the air mechanic and may have been a specialist engineer.

In addition, his aircraft, a Heinkel III of Stab/KG51, was piloted by the Geschwader Kommodore, Oberst Johann Fisser, who was killed. His observer was Leutnant Franz Schad who was injured and treated alongside him at the Royal Herbert Hospital. Schad was later interrogated at the London Cage, but it appears Nothelfer did not attend Kensington Palace Gardens. This appears odd considering his apparent unspecified specialist role on the aircraft.

Some have claimed that Adam Nothelfer took part in the 1936 Berlin Olympic Games despite having Jewish ancestry. This, it has been claimed, was a propaganda ploy by the Nazis, however, I have been unable to confirm this or his Jewish ancestry. There is no mention in the AI1(k) intelligence log (Ref: No. 247/1940) of a specialist role for Adam Nothelfer – surely, they would have investigated this further and possibly missed some vital intelligence?

After the war, Thames Television introduced a former patient and prisoner – Leutnant Heinz Mollenbrok to Shiela McDermott. He brought her dedication to nursing the Luftwaffe men to the German public's attention, and the German Ambassador to Britain presented her with a valuable book, in appreciation of her work and care. Mollenbrok was repatriated via the Red Cross in 1943 because of the severity of his injuries.

As we have seen, some Luftwaffe prisoners were not very happy with their care. One such man was Oberleutnant Joachim Schlichting of Stab III/JG27, the son-in-law of Luftwaffe General Erhard Milch. He was treated by Sheila and her colleagues in the Royal Herbert Hospital after he was shot down and his legs were badly burned, in early September 1940.

It is unclear whether he was sent to the London Cage, as no documents are available to the public stating that he went to Kensington Palace Gardens, but if he was, it could have been because of his family links and his rank. What is clear, is that in 1980, having served as an Oberst in the post-war Luftwaffe, Joachim Schlichting was still very unhappy with his treatment in England. When contacted by the *After the Battle* magazine, he said he did not wish to discuss his wartime experiences, and furthermore, 'His treatment throughout was beneath human dignity and contravened the Geneva Convention.' Exactly what treatment and where he received it, he would not discuss, but it appears unlikely to have been at the Royal Herbert hospital in 1940 and he was possibly referring to his interrogation.

Another patient at the Royal Herbert Hospital with high-ranking family links was Major Johann Hackbarth, a Junkers 88 pilot and Gruppen-Kommandeur with Stab III/KG30, shot down on 9 September 1940. He was the son-in-law of Luftwaffe General Albert Kesselring. Whether he was sent to the London Cage is unknown, as like Schlichting, no publicly available files exist regarding his interrogation, other than the basic preliminary interrogation report.

We have seen how Denys Felkin's team interrogated airmen at Trent Park and in a moment, we shall look at the alleged interrogation techniques at the London Cage, but before we do that, we shall consider whether the treatment by Air Intelligence and the London Cage, breached the Geneva Convention on the handling of prisoners of war during the Second World War.

There have been a number of Conventions convened in Geneva, dealing with the conduct or handling and interrogating of prisoners of war. In 1940, the most recent was the second convention, dating from 1929. That Convention is a very convoluted document with nearly 100 articles, so I shall not examine every one, as that would be too laborious and it would detract from the point of this book. Instead, I shall describe the articles which apply to the interrogation and treatment of prisoners of war.

Article 2

POW are in the power of the hostile Government, but not of the individuals or formation which captured them. They shall at all times be humanely treated and protected, particularly against acts of violence, from insults and public curiosity. Reprisals against them are forbidden.

Article 3

POW are entitled to respect. Women shall be treated with all consideration due to their sex.

Article 4

The detaining Power is required to provide for the maintenance of a POW in its charge.

Differences of treatment between prisoners are permissible, only if such differences are based on the military rank, the state of physical or mental health, the professional abilities, or their sex.

Article 5

Every POW is required to declare, if he is interrogated on the subject, his true name and rank, or his regimental number. If he infringes this rule, he exposes himself to a restriction of the privileges accorded to prisoners of his category.

No pressure shall be exercised on prisoners to obtain information regarding the situation in their armed forces or their country. Prisoners who refuse to reply may not be threatened, insulted, or exposed to unpleasantness or disadvantages of any kind whatsoever.

If, by reason of his physical or mental condition, a prisoner is incapable of stating his identity, he shall be handed over to the Medical Service.

Article 6

All personal effects and articles in personal use, except arms, horses, military equipment and military papers shall remain in the possession of a POW, as well as their metal helmets and gasmasks. Their identity tokens, badges of rank, decorations and articles of value may not be taken from prisoners.

Also:

The questioning of prisoners of war shall be carried out in a language which they understand.

Article 5 is the vital part of the 1929 Convention for us. It clearly states that a POW is required to give his true name and rank, or his regimental number. If he infringes this rule, he exposes himself to a restriction of the privileges accorded to prisoners of his category.

No pressure should be used against a prisoner in order to obtain information about their unit, their armed forces or their country. Prisoners who refuse to reply may not be threatened, insulted or exposed to any unpleasantness or disadvantages of any kind whatsoever.

If, by reason of his physical or mental condition, a prisoner is incapable of stating his true identity, he shall be handed over to the Medical Services.

In 2025, these articles seem at best a little 'wooly', especially around the issue of interrogating an injured prisoner of war, as there is no specific statement that interrogating injured prisoners is contrary to Article 5 or any other part of the 1929 Convention. An injured POW could be interrogated as long as they were capable of giving their identity.

In addition, Article 13 of the Convention states that POWs shall at all times, be treated humanely and protected against acts of violence, intimidation and insults. It is against these rules that we must consider the interrogation of the Luftwaffe prisoners of war in 1939 and 1940.

The AI1(k) preliminary intelligence reports give details of numerous wounded prisoners who were interrogated upon capture. Many reports clearly state that men were very badly injured or burned, and two men even died soon after their preliminary questioning in 1940:

> Log 259: On 14 August, Unteroffizier Gerhart Kemen of 1/JG26 was shot down and **badly wounded**. Despite the log stating, 'The pilot is badly

wounded and is not expected to recover,' he was still interrogated and supplied some information.

Log 264: On 13 August, Unteroffizier Wilhelm Hohenseldt of 5/JG53 was captured and **badly wounded**. The pilot could not give much information, but said the bombers had dropped their bombs when he was attacked.

Log 292: On 24 August, Unteroffizier Wilhelm Kaiser of 2/JG26 was captured with **badly burned face and hands**. He refused to give any information and was noted as having an obstinate and aggressive personality.

Log 332: On 28 August, Leutnant Hans Herbert Landry of Stab I/JG3 was **badly wounded**. His report notes that he was extremely aggressive and stubborn and would give no information. **He died in hospital on 23 September 1940**.

Log 373: On 31 August, Feldwebel Gunther Kramer of 1/JG77 was **badly burned** when he came down near Gravesend. The pilot gave no information when questioned.

Log 387: On the same day another pilot from the same unit, Leutnant Jura Petrenko, received a **head injury** when shot down. He was also noted as being very uncommunicative and his head injury did not help matters.

Log 544: On 15 September, a Messerschmitt 110 of 14/LG1 crashed at Hothfield near Ashford, Kent. The pilot was killed, but the **seriously injured** wireless operator, Feldwebel Andreas Hoffmann, was captured. The preliminary intelligence report notes that Hoffmann **was 'Dying/ Dead' and died shortly after being interrogated**.

These logs, as well as the comments by Oberleutnant Joachim Schlichting, who was badly burned and mentioned earlier in this chapter, tend to indicate that injured and severely wounded airmen were being interrogated – perhaps while in need of urgent medical treatment and pain relief, but this technically, was not a breach of the Convention if they could give their name and rank.

Although the 1929 Convention does not specifically rule out interrogation of injured or wounded prisoners of war, one has to wonder whether medical agreement was obtained in these cases. The Convention does state that no physical or mental torture, nor any form of coercion, may be inflicted upon prisoners of war to secure from them information of any kind what so ever.

It could be argued that once a prisoner gave their name and rank, they could be interrogated, even if they needed medical attention. However, it can also be argued, that allowing a prisoner to remain in pain and in urgent need of medical treatment, was a form of physical or mental torture, and withholding that treatment until they gave information was coercive. In 2025, such treatment is naturally frowned upon.

It is clear that after the war, the interrogation methods used were considered unfair and a clear breach of the spirit of the 1929 Convention. Treatment at locations like Trent Park, the London Cage, as well as those in Germany and Japan, were considered to be illegal.

In 1949 a new updated Convention stated that during the Second World War, certain categories of prisoners (e.g. airmen and submariners) considered as having important valuable intelligence were placed in special interrogation camps, before being sent to a POW camp. In these camps, 'Great hardship was inflicted upon them.' These practices the 1949 Convention ruled were, therefore a breach of Article 5 of the 1929 Convention.

The 1949 Convention added that interrogation camps were outside the control of the so-called Protecting Powers and the delegates of the International Committee of the Red Cross. In most cases the Red Cross had no knowledge of their existence. As we shall see in a moment, this clearly included the London Cage and its linked establishments, but did that include AI1(k) at Trent Park?

The 1949 Geneva Convention stated that the holding of prisoners 'incommunicado' at an interrogation camp away from other prisoners of war was forbidden, although to this day, this tactic still continues across conflict zones.

Although this book is primarily concerned with the interrogation of Luftwaffe airmen, we have already seen that some of them were sent to the London Cage for examination. This location would become infamous for its alleged mistreatment of prisoners later in the war, but other prisoners in RAF custody would be sent there in 1945…

At the end of the war, the Royal Air Force was desperate to bring to justice those responsible for the murder of fifty British, Commonwealth and Allied prisoners of war who escaped from Stalag Luft III at Sagan in 1944. The team responsible for bringing these criminals to justice belonged to the RAF Provost (Police) services. They were a different breed from AI1(k) being police rather than intelligence officers.

The investigation team was led by Wing Commander Wilfred Bowes. He was commissioned directly to the rank of Flying Officer on 16 May 1940 and by the 1 September 1941, he was appointed Deputy Assistant Provost Marshal.

Flight Lieutenant Francis Peter McKenna came from a family of police officers and he joined the Blackpool Police before the war, reaching the rank of Detective Sergeant. In a reserved occupation, McKenna could not join the RAF, but he was later admitted and became a Sergeant Flight Engineer with Bomber Command. He was later commissioned and at the end of 1944, having operational experience himself over Germany, he joined the RAF Provost (Police) Special Investigation Branch (SIB) at Princes Gate Court in London.

In the summer of 1944, Flight Lieutenant Wilfred Bowes took command of the RAF Special Investigation Branch at Princes Gate Court and was joined by the newly promoted Squadron Leader McKenna.

The *Great Escape* had taken place on the night of 24-25 March 1944, when seventy-six men tunnelled out of Stalag Luft III at Sagan. The vast majority were recaptured and the German High Command ordered the execution of fifty of the recaptured officers. SS-Gruppen-Fuhrer Arthur Nebe selected the fifty men who were shot by the Gestapo and efforts were made to hide evidence of the murders.

The British government and the RAF heard of the war crime in May 1944 and this news was re-enforced when Group Captain Herbert Massey was repatriated to the UK because of ill-health. As a former POW at Sagan he gave full details when he was debriefed by Air Intelligence.

A full-scale investigation was initiated with Bowes (now a Squadron Leader) in command and McKenna as his deputy. Also part of their team was Squadron Leader William Thomas and Flight Lieutenant S.H. Courtney. Thomas was a very experienced SIB officer who had been officer in charge of a number of investigations relating to RAF POWs who allegedly collaborated with the Nazis. Courtney was a pre-war solicitor. As a collective group, they were an experienced team of investigators and legal minds.

In July 1945, with the war in Europe over, Bowes and his team moved to Rinteln in Germany to conduct their investigation into the atrocity. The investigators travelled across Germany and Soviet occupied Poland and Czechoslovakia, attempting to gather evidence and arrest the murderers. Eventually, they tracked down and detained a number of those deemed to be responsible over the next two years.

In February 1946, Lieutenant Colonel Scotland, the head of the London Cage POW interrogation centre, recommended Flight Lieutenant A.R. Lyon to the RAF investigation team. He was a former Metropolitan Police Inspector and spoke fluent German. He had previously worked with the RAF Directorate of Intelligence and was therefore also known to Denys Felkin and his team.

Although most of the interrogations took place at Minden in Germany, some of the suspects were flown back to the London Cage in Kensington Palace Gardens – just a short walk from the RAF SIB offices in Princes Gate. The London Cage had been engaged since 1944, interrogating suspects relating initially to what we would now call weapons of mass destruction and war crimes, so it is possible they were deemed to be experts in dealing with such prisoners.

One of the suspects detained in relation to the Stalag Luft III murders was Enrich Zacharias. After the RAF team detained his Gestapo driver Frederich Kiowsky, who broke under interrogation in Germany, they located Zacharias who had shot one of the handcuffed RAF officers in cold blood. He soon admitted to McKenna that he had shot Squadron Leader Kidder on the orders of the local Gestapo head Hans Ziegler, but being detained in an American zone, the allies surprisingly would not release him into British custody and Zacharias promptly escaped.

Three weeks later, Zacharias was rearrested and taken to Minden where he retracted his initial confession. He was therefore taken to the London Cage where he was interrogated by Flight Lieutenant A.R. Lyon. Under examination and confronted by the driver Frederich Kiowsky's statement, he again admitted the murder of Squadron Leader Kidder.

Another man sent to the London Cage was Kripo Chief Josef Gmeiner. He initially stated he was on sick leave at the time of the murders, but later assisted with disposal of the remains in cremation urns.

Johann Schenider was also detained as being involved in the murders. He told the RAF SIB interrogators, that the prisoners had been arrested for burglary of air raid shelters and looting. They were told that if the prisoners attempted to escape, they were to be shot. The interrogators thought he was being evasive and misleading, so he too was sent to the London Cage.

Walter Herberg, another Gestapo man, was detained and gave misleading accounts of his actions and involvement. He too was sent to the London Cage.

The London Cage held a number of other war crimes suspects, and one Dr Hans Merton told Flight Lieutenant Lyon that he had been a Kripo officer in Berlin working with Gruppen-Fuhrer Nebe, who selected the fifty officers to be shot. He was not indicted for being part of the Stalag Luft III murders.

Emil Schulz was detained and interrogated at Minden by the RAF SIB, but started giving conflicting accounts and he was quickly dispatched to the London Cage. Later, a number of other prisoners who had even made confessions in Germany, were sent back to London for 'further interrogation.'

Gestapo chief Hans Ziegler was sent to London and interrogated, but on 23 February 1948, he committed suicide by cutting his own throat. In his book *London Cage,* Alexander Scotland claimed the prisoner had obtained a razor blade and cut his own jugular vein. What caused him to do this is debatable, could it have been the interrogations? How could an alleged war criminal have accessed a razor in such a high security establishment?

Ziegler's death certificate from the Kensington Registry Office, signed by the Registrar C.H. Stark and dated 25 February 1948, states that he died on 23 February 1948 at 7, Kensington Palace Gardens. His occupation was given as 'Police Office (German) Prisoner of war.' A Coroner's Inquest and a post mortem had been held within two days of his death and a death certificate issued by the Coroner, H.M. Stafford. The cause of death was given as:

> 'Haemorrhage from wound of the neck (self-inflicted). Did kill himself while the balance of his mind was disturbed.' PM.

The letter PM almost certainly referred to a post mortem, but the whole process seems to have been expedited.

In June 1947, eighteen suspects were flown back to Germany being indicted with the murders. In total twenty-one Gestapo officers were accused and thirteen would hang.

When Erich Zacharias stood trial, the only evidence against him was his confession which, MI5 noted in its assessment of Scotland's later memoir in the 1950's, had been signed only because 'being a prisoner in their hands, he had been worked upon psychologically.' Zacharias insisted that he had been beaten, but he was convicted and hanged at Hamburg on 27 February 1948. Johann Schneider, Josef Gmeiner, Walter Herberg and Emil Schulz were also found guilty and went to the gallows in Hamburg on the same day as Zacharias.

A number of the Great Escape defendants who were interrogated at the London Cage, claimed to have been sprayed repeatedly with ice-cold water, abused, beaten and threatened with electric shock treatments. They were constantly woken, not allowed to sleep and starved of food.

While the Stalag Luft III suspects were being held at the London Cage, the International Committee of the Red Cross tried to gain access to the interrogation centre. Lieutenant Colonel Scotland refused them access, as he did not believe it fell within their jurisdiction and these were civilians or military criminals, not prisoners of war. (During the war years the Red Cross did not even know of the London Cage and only became aware of its existence after an officer accidently added it to a list of POW camps.) Scotland told the War Office that if the Red Cross were permitted access, he would send the RAF SIB prisoners back to Germany and stop any further transfers back to the London Cage.

It is hard to have sympathy for hard core Nazis and Gestapo murderers and they are not central to the subject of this book. However, if the RAF SIB were utilising the London Cage post-war, sending back evasive and contradictory prisoners for further interrogation, could the Luftwaffe airmen interrogated there in 1940–41 have been sent there for similar reasons?

This appears to be a subject many people chose to ignore in the hope it will go away with time. There is no doubt Denys Felkin and his team carried out some sterling work at Trent Park, but did they know anything about the Luftwaffe POWs transferred to the London Cage in 1940–41, the reasons for their attendance and their treatment there?

At the end of the day, Trent Park, CSDIC and the various Prisoner of War Cages all came under one central command. Denys Felkin and his team had shown great skill in extracting intelligence from German airmen, so why would he allow someone to be extracted from his sphere of influence and taken to Kensington Palace Gardens? Especially when there appeared to be room at Trent Park for their interrogation. That is one question we may never know the answer to.

Chapter 25

JG3 – Arrogant Nazis or educated gentlemen?

Throughout the course of this book, it appears a number of pilots were what many people would call arrogant. Whether it was Franz von Werra or Heinz Schnabel, it appears members of JG3 displayed a particular attitude and arrogance, but is that a fair description? In this chapter, we shall take a closer look at the captured pilots of JG3 and AI1(k)'s perception of that Geschwader.

On 29 September 1940, AI1(k) completed an intelligence summary for this particular Geschwader (reference No. 651/1940).

The report opened by stating that AI1(k) first identified JG3 on 24 August 1940. Since that time, further losses over Britain had enabled the intelligence team to build a picture of the Geschwader and its main personalities. At the time of the report, Air Intelligence had identified a number of losses and this included many that were previously unknown, with the pilot's names being mentioned during interrogations with other JG3 prisoners.

The Kommodore of JG3 was known to be Major von Lutzow, son of Admiral A.D. Lutzow who gave weekly radio talks about the maritime situation. Major Lutzow was apparently not popular and was even accused by some pilots of 'pot-hunting', meaning he liked to collect aerial victories. The term 'pot-hunting' referring to the engraved silver goblets, some First World War German pilots collected for each victory they achieved. (Author: Whether this was a fair accusation is debatable.)

The Gruppen-Kommandeure on 14 October 1940 were as follows:

I/JG3 .... Hauptmann Keller,
II/JG3 ... Hauptmann von Selle and
III/JG3 ... Hauptmann Koenitz.

The AI1(k) report deemed the pilots from this unit to be:

> 'So far of an extremely good type, including a Staffel Kapitan of 3/JG3 who held a doctors degree, an international hockey player who had played in England on numerous occasions and a Professor of Military History, who regarded the present war as quite ridiculous.'

The Staffel Kapitan of 3/JG3 was Helmut Rau and the professor was Oberleutnant Hasso von Wedel of Stab/ JG3. Von Wedel was discussed earlier in this book, but the 1940 intelligence report repeated many of those details in its summary. The international hockey player was Feldwebel August-Wilhelm Muller of 4/JG3.

The report continued and it is no surprise it mentions Franz von Werra, although not by name:

> 'A further interesting character in JG3 is the Oberleutnant who shortly before he was taken prisoner, gave a talk on the German radio describing an entirely fictious exploit over England, during which he shot up a number of our fighters as they came in to land. He has strenuously denied this broadcast, even when confronted with a text of his speech, but confirmation was obtained from the Oberleutnant, who was very shocked to hear that the story was untrue.'

It is clear this man was discussed with other prisoners from JG3, ten of whom had been captured between 18 August and 5 September when Franz von Werra arrived. The report continued:

> 'This Oberleutnant has a reputation for tall stories and is regarded by his fellow officers as a hell of a fellow and keeps a lion-cub.'

The intelligence report signed off by Flight Lieutenant Guy Jepson, noted that the morale of JG3 had up to that date been very high, although the pilots have a healthy respect for the RAF fighters. This the author assumed was because they had very few losses during the French campaign compared to this one, with 'About a third of the entire Geschwader wiped out against this country in a month.'

It was clear AI1(k) had a degree of respect for the Jagdgeschwader 3, but believed there were a few personalities amongst its ranks such as Franz von Werra.

Oberleutnant Helmut Teidmann, Staffel Kapitan of 2/JG3 was the first pilot to arrive on 18 August 1940, he was not wounded and it appears gave little information to his interrogators.

Leutnant Franz Achleitner of 9/JG3 was 22-years-old, when he was shot down into the Thames Estuary on 24 August. He claimed to have shot down a Spitfire and damaged a third before he was himself brought down. It is possible this is correct, but the opponents were likely to have been the Hurricanes of 32 and 151 Squadrons who lost a number of aircraft at the time and location of this combat.

Achleitner said he had shot down his first success on 10 July 1940 when he destroyed a Bristol Blenheim, the crew were buried at Abbeville. He held the Iron Cross First Class. Although not a known 'ace', checks of losses indicate that his comments, particularly in regard to the Spitfires were somewhat inflated.

Unteroffizier Wilhelm Kaiser of 9/JG3 was also brought down in the same dogfight as Achleitner, but he force-landed his Messerschmitt at Camber in Sussex. He refused to give any information and said his identity disc was a pre-war version. He also told the preliminary interrogator that this had been his first war flight and he had been attacked by Spitfires which attacked from out of the sun. He had a badly burned face and hands and was noted as having an obstinate and aggressive personality – which is hardly surprising if he was in pain.

Leutnant Hans Herbert Landry of Stab I/JG3 was attacked by a Spitfire and crashed to earth at Whitfield near Dover on 28 August. He was seriously wounded in the attack and bailed out when his ME109 caught fire. After landing by parachute his captors gave immediate first aid and he was taken to hospital with life threatening injuries. The preliminary interrogation report, completed two days after his capture, noted him as being extremely aggressive and stubborn. He would give absolutely no information to his interrogator, but he held the Iron Cross Second Class.

This man must have been in great pain and died in hospital on 23 September 1940 – so it is hardly surprising he did not want to be interrogated, gave nothing away and was aggressive and stubborn.

Feldwebel B. Lamskemper of 2/JG3 was attacked by Spitfires and brought down on 29 August near the Pevensey RDF base in Sussex. Very little recorded information can be found in relation to this prisoner and his interrogation.

Oberleutnant Helmut Rau Staffel Kapitan of 3/JG3, made a forced landing on Shoeburyness beach in Essex, after combat with British fighters on 31 August. When attacked he tried to climb, but saw his wingman shot down. He then broke the golden rule of not following an aircraft down and attempted to watch the fate of his colleague, when a Spitfire hit him and he had to force land. He was not wounded and asked about his colleague giving his name – Johann Loidolt. Rau's aircraft was noted as having three victory bars on its fin.

Oberleutnant Johann Loidolt of 3/JG3 was the wingman of Rau when he was shot down and slightly wounded, his ME109 crashing to earth at Chadwell Heath, Essex.

Loidolt was admitted to hospital and after two days given a preliminary interrogation. He refused to give any information, but it was noted Rau had already given this pilot's details when interrogated. Loidolt refused to give his unit, but a certain 'amount of bluff and a memory loss story' by the interrogator was eventually successful in gathering some intelligence.

Leutnant Karl Westerhoff aged 24-years-old of 6/JG3 was also brought down on the 31 August, one of five losses for JG3 that day. Westerhoff was attacked by British fighters and made a forced landing at Lydd army ranges, Dungeness in Kent. He received very slight wounds and exited his aircraft, before setting it alight.

Upon interrogation, Westerhoff gave his Geschwader as JG3, but he would not give his Staffel or Gruppe number. Like other pilots he claimed to have shot a Spitfire down before he was shot down. (This may have been the Spitfire of No. 72 Squadron's Flight Lieutenant Smith. He bailed out over Dungeness at the same time Westerhoff came down.) Karl Westerhoff then made the claim he was hit by another Messerschmitt 109 and a Spitfire. He admitted to having three years Luftwaffe service, with another year in the infantry, he had served in the Polish and French campaigns and held the Iron Cross Second Class.

Karl Westerhoff would later feature in the story of Franz von Werra at Trent Park, allegedly being placed in an M-Room together.

Leutnant Heinz Schnabel aged 24-years-old of 1/JG3, was another man who knew Franz von Werra and as we have seen, would make a name for himself as another escape artist. Schnabel was shot down and slightly wounded on 5 September, making a forced landing at Handen near Aldington, Kent.

His aircraft had two victory bars on the tail, but Schnabel said these belonged to a previous pilot. He did admit to being a pre-war civil flying instructor and was called-up at the start of the war. He had been wounded at Lille during the French campaign and would need further treatment for this and the injuries he sustained in his forced landing.

Heinz Schnabel claimed to have been with JG3 since July, been awarded the Iron Cross Second Class and to have taken part in raids to Portland, Eastchurch and even Manchester. The last raid clearly being far beyond the range of the ME109, must have made interrogators wonder whether he was being truthful.

Oberleutnant Franz von Werra of Stab II/JG3 was, as we have already seen, a bombastic, arrogant man with Nazi affiliations. He continually refused to give any military information and would become the notorious escaper.

Unteroffizier Heinz Grabow of 3/JG3 was also shot down on 5 September, coming to earth with a forced landing at Wichling in Kent. He was badly wounded and taken to hospital, although he did manage to state that he was new to the Geschwader, having previously acted as escort pilot to Red Cross aircraft.

Feldwebel August-Wilhelm Muller of 4/JG3 was a pre-war international hockey player. He was brought down on 9 September. Initially he gave his unit as Stab II/JG3 and he may have been trying to hide his actual unit. He had fought in France and been injured, making twenty-two flights against England in addition to those over France. Muller claimed to have been in combat but not hit. However, his engine began to fail and he headed home. It eventually failed completely and he came down in the English Channel off Newhaven. He was picked up by boat and brought ashore to captivity.

Unteroffizier M. Massmann of 7/JG3 was also brought down on 9 September, he claimed to have been a pre-war reservist and fought in the French campaign.

Oberleutnant Hass von Wedel aged 47-years-old of Stab/JG3 has been discussed in detail elsewhere in this book. In summary, the First World War veteran and professor, was sent to gain experience of tactics when he was hit by a Hurricane on 15 September. He was a man who greatly impressed the interrogators.

Oberfeldwebel Franz Hessel of 1/JG3 was shot down on 15 September near Tenterden in Kent. He was very seriously wounded and as such little information was gleaned at the time.

Oberleutnant Helmut Reumschessel Staffel Kapitan of 2/JG3 was the third Geschwader pilot captured on 15 September. Hit in the radiator like so many other Messerschmitt 109 pilots, he bailed out near Pluckley in Kent. To Air Intelligence, he was another man with an impeccable background, his father having been an officer who was killed in Russia in 1915.

Unteroffizier Karl Ebling of 7/JG3 was shot down over Deal on 23 September. He bailed out before swimming to shore where he was captured. Unusually, this pilot gave his Staffel number, but not the Geschwader details. Unfortunately for him, the AI1(k) records system soon identified it as JG3 from his identity disc and Feldpost numbers.

He appears to have been quite a communicative prisoner, giving details of when he gained his flying licence and his recent postings. He also gave details of a number of other airmen posted to various Staffeln of JG3.

Feldwebel Fritz von Herwarth-Bitteffeld of 1/JG3 was hit in the fuel tank and his Messerschmitt burst into flames over Bethersden, Kent on 5 October 1940. The pilot was wounded and badly burned as he bailed out into captivity. He was taken to hospital refusing to give any information to his interrogator. His identity disc and Feldpost numbers allowed AI1(k) to identify his unit from their database.

Oberleutnant Werner Voigt Staffel Kapitan of 4/JG3, was shot down on 8 October and he force landed in the sea just off Folkestone before wading ashore. A number of photographs were taken of the pilot having a cigarette and smiling with his captors. In reality, the preliminary interrogation report states that he refused to say a word to them, but AI1(k) believed he belonged to the 5th Staffel of JG3, his identity disc number being aligned to that unit. Whether he eventually talked is unknown, as any later interrogation reports have long since disappeared.

Gefreiter Hurbert Rungen aged 22-years-old of 7/JG3 was shot down when his radiator was hit by a Spitfire on 13 October and he force landed at Hastingleigh, Kent. The young NCO appears, from his preliminary intelligence report, to have been very helpful and AI1(k) were given quite a bit of information, which resulted in a two-page report rather than the standard single page report.

Rungen told them all about his last sortie and that there had been 50-60 fighters including the entire Third Gruppe of JG3, involved in escorting bombers to East London.

A pre-war civilian pilot, he had been called up and served a year in the Luftwaffe when he was captured. He had a notebook with full details of his operational flying with JG3, since the first flight on 18 September. The notebook was very detailed and for each mission, it gave the date, his aircraft number, flying times (duration) and the duty he performed such as bomber escort.

The wireless call signs for his Geschwader, Third Gruppe Stab and the 7th, 8th and 9th Staffeln were found in his aircraft with a title stating 'From 9/19 to 16/10/40'. The prisoner was questioned about this and stated that the period during which such codes were valid varied. Sometimes they could change that day, but could also last for up to two weeks.

Another piece of paper found in the aircraft gave code names for English and French towns and cities. Both lists were quickly disseminated to AI1(e) and were undoubtedly used by the Y-Service listening in on Luftwaffe transmissions.

Although Hubert Rungen had clearly been very helpful to Air Intelligence, it appears the interrogators may have thought he was too helpful and bordering on the unpatriotic – even for a German. The preliminary report signed off by Flight Lieutenant Guy Jepson stated:

> 'Morale average. Rather a poor type.'

Oberfeldwebel Willi Bauer of 8/JG3 was the next prisoner from the Geschwader, arriving on 15 October. It seems that although he would not give his unit and AI1(k) had to incorrectly deduce it as being 7/JG3, he did give them some details.

Bauer claimed to have undertaken forty war flights, nearly half of them over London. He had apparently made three victory claims over Belgium, France and England. He had however, been shot down, bailing out into the English Channel before being rescued by the ever-efficient Seenotdienst air-sea rescue service in August. His morale was deemed to be average.

Leutnant Ernst Busch of Stab I/JG3 was shot down by British fighters and wounded at New Addington, Surrey on 27 October. He managed to bail out despite being wounded and was taken to hospital for treatment. AI1(k) appear to have received little other information about him and his Staffel and Geschwader were deduced from his identity disc and Feldpost numbers. As we have seen, Busch, according to Ulrich Steinhilper, was interrogated with him at the London Cage in Kensington Palace Gardens and apparently gave little intelligence to his interrogators.

Oberleutnant Egon Troha the Staffel Kapitan of 8/JG3, was shot down on a freelance patrol over Kent on 29 October. Hit in the radiator 'by a Spitfire' (it was always a Spitfire!), he made a forced landing at Shepherdswell in rural Kent and was quickly detained.

Egon Troha's Messerschmitt 109 had six victory bars painted on the rudder and he held the Iron Cross Second Class. AI1(k) probably assumed he was an ace.

During interrogation, he gave his unit details and this was confirmed by comparing his Feldpost number against the Trent Park database, but there was some confusion when his identity disc number related to Stab III/JG3.

Eventually Troha admitted his unit details and that he was actually an Austrian, who had served with that nation's air force before the Anschluss when he transferred to the Luftwaffe.

Unteroffizier Fahrian of 6/JG3 was shot down and received a head injury over Meopham, south of Gravesend, Kent on 30 October. He bailed out and was taken to hospital. It appears very little was established in interrogation, possibly because of his head wound.

Gefreiter Eugen Schuller of 6/JG3 had only joined his unit six weeks before he was shot down on his very first war flight. His morale was deemed to be not very good and he told the interrogator that he thought the war was all nonsense. He could see no hope of the war ending unless England sued for peace.

Schuller had been flying the last aircraft of a Schwarm in line astern when he was hit, claiming his engine had not been pulling very well. He made a forced landing in a hop field and was captured.

The tail of his Messerschmitt displayed ten victory bars. Schuller said this was not his own aircraft and being a newcomer, he had been permitted to use this old aircraft which had belonged to the previous Kommodore of JG3, an Oberst, who had been shot down into the Thames Estuary four weeks previously. AI1(k) was quick to identify that this did not correspond with their own database of information, which gave Major Lutzow as the commander and he had only just been promoted from Hauptmann. Air Intelligence did speculate that, like Hasso von Wedel, there may have been another unidentified Oberst attached to JG3 and he had used this aircraft.

These were the pilots of JG3 captured during the Battle of Britain. It is clear some were arrogant, Nazi supporting and mischievous, but others were gentlemen, former sports stars, professors, doctors and educated men. Many were content to talk, but almost all of them refused to give military secrets and information to their interrogators.

It is hardly surprising there was such a varying degree of personalities in the Geschwader. In many ways they reflected those in the Royal Air Force squadrons in 1940 and society in general. It is therefore unfair to label JG3 with any form of label.

Postscript

As the war moved into 1941 and beyond, AI1(k) was quickly expanded with sub-sections being sent to the Middle East, Malta and further afield. The system developed and expanded by Denys Felkin was very successful, although like all new systems there were some teething problems.

The tactics developed by Felkin and his team, coupled together with the vast database they compiled and the use of M-Rooms and stool pigeons paid dividends. Many prisoners were shocked into giving vital information to Air Intelligence.

For many decades, until the tactics of CSDIC and AI1(k) became public knowledge, very few people knew of the organisation or the work it carried out. Now, well over eighty years after these events, it is easy to claim the London Cage and to some extent AI1(k) may have breached the Geneva Convention; but the fact is, the 1929 version was somewhat poorly worded and allowed the formation of interrogation camps like Trent Park and Dulag Luft in Germany. It did not specifically forbid the interrogation of a wounded airman, but more specifically threats and coercion. The 1929 Convention and specific acts throughout the Second World War, led to a complete rewriting of the Convention in 1947. Whether you choose to critise AI1(k) for its tactics, depends on your opinion of the 1929 Convention and its interpretation. Clearly, there were issues with its wording.

In this book we have looked at the available documentary evidence relating to AI1(k) in 1939-1940. Most of the intelligence reports available were preliminary reports, as well as some composite reports. The M-Rooms SRA transcripts were important and I believe we have managed to identify some of the prisoners involved. In most of these cases, I am satisfied these names are correct, but there is always an element of error, so I would like to add one final time, that the attributed identities should not be accepted as one hundred per cent correct.

Sadly, the main interrogation records are no longer available and there has been some speculation they were destroyed to prevent disclosure etc. The same naturally appears to apply to documents referring to the specific use of stool pigeons and the names of those men.

However, those documents that are available, when coupled with various books and articles, plus the loss and victory records, allows one to create the history contained within this book. Like RAF and allied airmen who went through the Luftwaffe POW regime at Dulag Luft in Oberursel, the system worked and vital intelligence was obtained.

The fact Franz von Werra was so keen to return to Germany and tell of the AI1(k) system developed by Squadron Leader King (Felkin), speaks volumes for the efficiency of the process at Trent Park. It is no wonder the Luftwaffe appeared to copy many of its tactics.

Volumes have been written about CSDIC and their excellent work later in the war with German Generals, the uncovering of the Holocaust and the vengeance weapons under development; but in many respects it was the work of AI1(k) and Denys Felkin's team that laid the ground work for those discoveries.

Appendices

List of Appendices

Appendix I

Luftwaffe Prisoners of War Detained in Britain and Surrounding Waters

September 1939 – October 1940

Date	Location	Aircraft	Unit	Prisoners	Injured
29/9/39	Gt. Fisher Bank, North Sea.	Do. 18 M7+YK	2/KuFIGr506	Lt. W von Reitzenstein Lt. E. Korner Uffz. W. Heckt Uffz. F. Schmalfeldt	N N N N
16/10/39	Off Port Seton, Scotland.	Ju. 88 4D+DH	1/KG30	Oblt. Hans Storp Fw. H. Kohnke Fw. Hans Hielshar	N N N
16/10/39	Off Crail, Fifeshire, Scotland.	Ju. 88 4D+AK	2/KG30	Haupt. H. Pohle	Y
17/10/39	Off Whitby, Yorkshire.	He. 111 F6+PK	Stab I(f)/122	Uffz. E. Lange Uffz. B. Hochstuhl	N Y
17/10/39	Hoy, Orkneys.	Ju. 88 4D+EK	2/KG30	Uffz. F. Ambrosius	Y
17/10/39	Off Hoy, Orkneys.	DO18 8L+DK	2/KuFIGr606	Fw. Grabbett Oblt. S. Salonga Oberfunk. H. Grimm	Y Y N
21/10/39	Off Spurn Head, Yorkshire.	He. 115 S4+GH	1/KuFIGr406	Fw. R. Findeisen Oblt. G. Reymann Uffz. H. Schultze	Y N N
21/10/40	The Wash, Lincolnshire.	He. 115 S4+DH	1/KuFIGr406	Uffz. G. Panke Oblt. A. Peineman Uffz. H. Einbaus	Y Y Y
22/10/39	Off St. Abb's Head, Berwickshire.	He. 111 F6+DH	1(F)/122	Lt. A. Fischer Oblt. G. Awater Uffz. W. Ungar	N N Y
28/10/39	Humbie, Edinburgh.	He. 111 1H+JA	Stab KG26	Uffz. K. Lehmkuhl Lt. R. Neihoff	Y N
13/01/40	Off coast of Fife.	He. 111 F6+LH	1(F)/122	Uffz. Gerd Kahle	N
03/02/40	Off Tynemouth, Northumbria.	He. 111 1H+GK	2/KG26	Oberfw. F. Weimer Fw. F. Schnee Uffz. A. Dietrich	N Y Y

Date	Location	Aircraft	Unit	Prisoners	Injured
03/02/40	Sneaton, Whitby, Yorkshire.	He. 111 1H+FM	4/KG26	Fw. H. Wilms Uffz. Karl Missy	Y Y
09/02/40	North Berwick Law, Scotland.	He. 111 1H+EN	5/KG26	Uffz. H. Meyer Uffz. J. Sangl Obergefr Hegemann	N N N
22/02/40	St. Abb's Head, Berwickshire.	He. 111 T5+OH	Aufklr GrOb. D.L.	Lt. E. Grote Fw. F. Sprigath Uffz. W. Berger Uffz. W. Bachmann	N N N Y
27/02/40	Off St. Abb's Head, Berwickshire.	He. 111 1H+AK	2/KG26	Oblt. Ernst Heinrich Uffz. H. Jonas Fw. Karl Henrici Uffz. Kurt Weinert	N Y N N
07/03/40	North Sea, 64 miles off Aberdeen.	He. 111 T5+AH	1/Aufklr GrOb. D.L.	Fw. E. Breiler	Y
03/04/40	Off Whitby, Yorkshire.	He. 111 1H+AC	Stab II/KG26	Lt. R.G. Behnisch Oberstlt. H. Hefele Lt. Georg Kempe Uffz. A.W. Weber Uffz. Alfred Bachle	N N N N N
08/04/40	Sea off Copinsay Light, Orkney.	He. 111 1H+FM	4/KG26	Uffz. Willi Rolf Oblt. A. Donike Oberfw. H. Koch	N N Y
08/04/40	RAF Wick, Caithness.	He. 111 1H+DP	6/KG26	Lt. K.H. Weigel Oberfw. B. Rehbein	N N
10/04/40	Off Kinnairds Head, Aberdeenshire.	He. 111 1H+M	4/KG26	Oblt. H. Vogel	Y
10/05/40	North Sea.	Do. 17 K6+CH	1/KuFIGr406	Oblt. Hermann Oblt. Wiethoff Fw. Ehrich ? Wollgast	N N N N
11/05/40	North Sea, off the Wash.	Ju. 88 F6+-M	4(F)/122	Uffz. R. Krulich Lt. F. Meyer Uffz. W. Hobel	Y N Y
12/06/40	Sea, north-east of Margate, Kent.	He. 111 4T+BH	Wettererkun. Staffel 51	Oblt. G. Nissen Oberfw. H. Peckhaus	Y Y
19/06/40	Springfield Road, Chelmsford, Essex.	He. 111 5J+GA	Stab/KG4	Lt. Erich Simon	Y

Date	Location	Aircraft	Unit	Prisoners	Injured
19/06/40	Cley next the sea, Norfolk.	He. 111 5J+DM	Stab II / KG4	Oblt. U. Jordan Maj. D. Von Massenbach Oberfw. M. Leimer Uffz. K. Allenberger	N N N Y
19/06/40	Six Mile Bottom, Cambridgeshire.	He. 111 5J+AM	4/KG4	Fw. Wilhelm Maier Oblt. J. von Arnim Fw. K. Hauck	N N Y
19/06/40	Off Margate, Kent.	He. 111 5J+KP	6/KG4	Lt. H. J. Bachaus Uffz. T. Kuhn Uffz. F. Boeck	N N N
26/06/40	Firth of Forth, Scotland.	He. 111 1H+BL	3/KG26	Haupt. H. Schmilden	Y
26/06/40	Off Turnhouse, Lothian	He. 111 1H+GL	3/KG26	Uffz. H. Wilm Gefr. L. Riede Flgr. J. Schwehr	N Y N
27/06/40	North Sea, off Middlesbrough	He. 111 5J+EK	2/KG4	Fw. S. Gessert Uffz. K-H. Beck Uffz. W. Dieter Gefr. H. Filihowski	N N N N
01/07/40	North Sea off Middlesbrough.	He. 59 D-ASAM	Seenotflug Kdo.3	Uffz. E. Ielsen Lt. H-J. Fehske Ogfr. E. Phillipp Uffz. Stuckmann	N N N Y
01/07/40	Off Whitby, Yorkshire.	He. 115 M2+CL	3/106	Oberfw. R. Worms Lt. G. Schroeder Uffz. S. Soest	N N N
02/07/40	North Sea off Hull.	He. 111 5J+EL	3/KG4	Oberfw. H. Raisbach Oblt. F.W. Kock Fw. A. Weber Oberfw. R. Ernst	N N Y Y
03/07/40	Off Dyce, Aberdeen.	Ju. 88 4D+IS	8/KG30	Uffz. R. Heringlehner	N
03/07/40	Paddock Wood, Kent.	Do. 17 3Z+GS	8/KG77	Uffz. R. Brandes Oblt. H-G. Gallion	Y Y
04/07/40	Gillingham, Dorset.	He. 111 B3+DM	4/KG54	Uffz. H. Karwelat	Y
05/07/40	Channel off Folkestone.	He. 111 V4+GS	8/KG1	Oberfw. H. Frischmuth Uffz. G. Wagner	Y Y
08/07/40	Elham, Kent.	Me. 109 White 4+	4/JG51	Lt. Johann Boehm	N
08/07/40	Hornsea, Catfoss, Yorkshire.	Ju. 88 5J+AT	9/KG4	Uffz. Georg Abel Uffz. A. Kuhnapfel Uffz. H. Oechler	Y Y Y

Date	Location	Aircraft	Unit	Prisoners	Injured
08/07/40	Buckland Farm, Sandwich.	Me.109 ?	3/LG2	Lt. Albert Striberny	N
09/07/40	Goodwin Sands, off Deal.	He. 59 D-ASUO	Seenotflug Kdo.1	Uffz. H. Bartmann Uffz. W. Anders Uffz. E. Schiele Fw. G. Maywald	N N N Y
10/07/40	Bouy, Kent.	Do. 17 U5+FL	3/KG2	Haupt. W. Krieger Oberfw. W. Thalman	N N
10/07/40	Channel - East of Folkestone Gate Light.	Me. 110 3U+GS	8/ZG26	Oberfw. W. Meyer	Y
11/07/40	East Beach, Selsey, Sussex.	He. 111 G1+LK	2/KG55	Oberfw. E. Slotosch Oblt. S. Schweinhagen Fw. H. Steiner	Y Y Y
11/07/40	Grange Heath, Lulworth, Dorset.	Me. 110 2N+EP	9/ZG76	Oblt. G. Kadow Gefr. Helmut Scholz	Y Y
11/07/40	Sea off breakwater, Portland, Dorset.	Me. 110 M8+-T	9/ZG76	Lt. Joachim Schroeder	N
12/07/40	Sea off Shipwash Light, Orfordness, Suffolk.	He. 111 A1+-S	8/KG53	Fw. P. Baumeister	Y
12/07/40	Sea off Aldeburgh, Suffolk.	He. 111 A1+ES	8/KG53	Fw. Hans Boete Fw. K. Hartmann	N Y
12/07/40	Hipley, Southampton.	He. 111 G1+FA	Stab/KG55	Fw. J. Mohn Fw. H. Kalina Oberfw. F. Knecht Oberfw. P. Muller	N Y Y Y
13/07/40	Off Chesil Beach, Dorset.	Do. 17 4U+DK	2(F)/123	Oblt. Max Graf Kesselstadt	Y
15/07/40	Off Peterhead, Scotland.	He. 111 1H+EK	2/KG26	Oblt. O. Hollmann Uffz. Walz Ogefr. Probst Ogefr. Trefzger	N N N Y
16/07/40	Off Fraserburgh, Scotland.	He. 111 1H+KT	9/KG26	Oblt. G. Lorenz Uffz. H. Beer	N Y
16/07/40	Off St Catherine's Point, Isle of Wight.	Ju. 88 B3+GP	6/KG54	Fw. R. Fortmann Gefr. H. Augustin	Y N
19/07/40	North Sea off Sunderland.	Fw. 200 F8+EH	1/KG40	Fw. H. Kulken Fw. Karl Nicolai	N N

Date	Location	Aircraft	Unit	Prisoners	Injured
20/07/40	St. Osyth, Clacton, Essex.	Ju. 88 F6+BM	4(F)/122	Uffz. T. Hermsen Oberfw. H-B. Prolss Obergefr. W. Plock Flgr. R. von Hasse	N N N Y
21/07/40	Goodwood Home Farm, Chichester, Sussex.	Me. 110 5F+CM	4(F)/14	Oblt. F-K. Runde Fw. W. Baden	N N
21/07/40	Nutford Farm, Blandford, Dorset.	D0. 17 5F+OM	4(F)/14	Fw. F. Bohnen Oblt. G. Thiel Uffz. A. Werner	Y Y Y
21/07/40	Channel off Selsey, Sussex.	Do. 17 7A+DM	4(F)/121	Lt. Gert Bormann	Y
24/07/40	North Down, Margate, Kent.	ME109 <I+1	Stab III/JG26	Lt. Werner Bartels	Y
24/07/40	Martinhoe Common, Lynton, Devon/	Ju. 88 L1+DL	3/LG1	Haupt. D. von Malpitz Fw. P. Weilmaier Fw. G. Pliefke	N Y N
24/07/40	Sea off Belfast, Northern Ireland	Fw. 200 F8+BH	1/KG40	Haupt. V. Zenker Gefr. L. Hohmann Uffz. H. Hocker	N N N
25/07/40	Pentland Firth, Scotland.	He. 111 T5+AL	Wetterkung. Staffel I	Gehr. E. Franken	N
25/07/40	Elvington Court, Deal, Kent.	Me. 109 6+~	8/JG52	Uffz. Max Reiss	N
25/07/40	Oakridge Lynch, Stroud.	Ju. 88 9K+GN	5/KG51	Uffz. F. Dorner Uffz. W. Hugelschafer Gefr. G. Treue	Y N N
26/07/40	Smeatharpe, Honiton, Devon.	He. 111 5J+AH	1/KG4	Uffz. Georg Strickstock	Y
27/07/40	East Woodhay, Newbury, Berks.	He. 111 G1+CS	8/KG55	Fw. T. Metzner Fw. J. Markl Uffz. K. Bocker Gefr. H. Morgenthal Gefr. E. Ostheimer	N N N N N
28/07/40	Sidley, Bexhill, Sussex.	Ju. 88 9K+HL	3/KG51	Oberfw. J. Bier Lt. W. Ruckdeschel Uffz. H. Ohls Uffz. M. Multhammer	N N N N
30/07/40	Off Happisburgh, Norfolk.	Ju. 88 F6+BK	2(F)/122	Uffz. G. Lehm Lt. H. Rabbow Uffz. J. Kehres Gefr. R. Reimer	Y N N Y

Date	Location	Aircraft	Unit	Prisoners	Injured
08/08/40	Sea off Isle of Wight.	Ju. 87 S1+-B	Stab I/StG3	Oblt. Martin Muller	N
08/08/40	Sea off Portsmouth.	Ju. 87 S2+-C	Stab II/StG77	Haupt. W. Plewig	Y
08/08/40	St Lawrence near Ventnor, Isle of Wight.	Ju. 87 S2+LM	4/StG77	Uffz. Fritz Pittroff	N
09/08/40	Sea off Whitburn near Sunderland.	He. 111 1H+ER	7/KG26	Uffz. O. Denner Fw. W. Haertel Uffz. F. Feinekat Uffz. G. Karkos	N N Y Y
11/08/40	Newton Moor, Whitby, Yorkshire.	Ju. 88 7A+KH	1(F)/121	Fw. O. Hofft Oblt. Hans Marzuch Fw. K-H. Hacker	N N N
11/08/40	Sea off Portland, Dorset.	Ju. 88 B3+-L	3/KG54	Gefr. F. Kleindl	N
11/08/40	Blacknor Fort, Portland, Dorset.	Ju. 88 B3+DC	Stab II/KG54	Oblt. K. Wette Oberfw. K. Meier Gefr. W. Gehre Flgr. G. Kagenbauer	Y N N N
11/08/40	Sea off West Bay, Portland.	Ju. 88 B3+CC	Stab II/KG54	Uffz. Herbert Klatte	Y
12/08/40	Off Folkestone Pier, Kent.	Me. 109 +>	2/JG26	Lt. Hans Werner Regenauer	N
12/08/40	St. Mary's Farm, Selmeston, Lewes.	Me. 109 Red 14+	2/JG52	Uffz. L. Zaunbrecher	Y
12/08/40	Hengrove, Margate, Kent.	Me. 109 <-+	III/JG54	Oblt. Albrecht Dress	Y
12/08/40	Sturminster, Wimbourne, Dorset.	He. 111 1G+AC	Stab II/KG27	Oberfw. H. Frey Maj. H-J Brehmer Maj. F-K Schlichting (2nd observer) Oberfw. G. Lohneng Oberfw. W. Bendrich	N Y N N Y
12/08/40	Godshill Park, Isle of Wight.	Ju. 88 9K+AA	Stab KG51	Lt. F. Schad Oblt. W. Luderitz Sonderf. A. Nothelfer	Y Y Y
12/08/40	Godstone, Gosport, Hampshire.	Ju. 88 9K+CL	3/KG51	Uffz. K. Zimmermann Obergefr. Fahrenhain Obergefr. Hansmann	Y Y N
12/08/40	Westbourne near Thorney Island, Sussex.	Ju. 88 9K+EL	3/KG51	Gefr. G. Fleischmann	Y

Date	Location	Aircraft	Unit	Prisoners	Injured
12/08/40	Sea off Portsmouth Docks.	Ju. 88 9K+FS	8/KG51	Oblt. E. Wildermuth Oblt. O. Stark Uffz. H. Droese	N N N
13/08/40	Denton, Elham, Kent.	Me. 109 ?	5/JG26	Uffz. H. Wemhoner	Y
13/08/40	Salts Farm, Shoreham, Sussex.	Me. 109 <+	Stab I/JG2	Oblt. Paul Temme	N
13/08/40	Sea off Poole Harbour, Dorset.	Me. 109 10+	5/JG53	Uffz. W. Hohenseldt	Y
13/08/40	Barham, Kent.	Do. 17 U5+KA	Stab KG2	Oblt. H. Schlegel Oblt. G. Oszwald Obergefr. G. Babbe Obergefr. E. Holz	N Y Y Y
13/08/40	Stodmarsh, near Canterbury, Kent.	Do. 17 U5+ER	7/KG2	Uffz. G. Vogel Uffz. H. Arndt Uffz. W. Mehringer Gefr. H. Bahr	N Y N N
13/08/40	Mudflats, Seasalter, Kent.	Do. 17 U5+DS	8/KG2	Fw. Rudolf Hansten	Y
13/08/40	Phillis Wood, Treyford, Sussex.	Ju. 88 B3+DB	Stab I/KG54	Uffz. F. Rossler Obergefr. K. Brieger Uffz. K. Seitz	N N N
13/08/40	Swanbourne Lake, Arundel, Sussex.	Ju. 88 B3+-C	Stab II/KG54	Oblt. H. Rosse Uffz. H. Scholz	N N
13/08/40	Tangmere, Sussex.	Ju. 88 ?	6/KG54	Gefr. G. Niessl (baled-out but a/c got home)	N
13/08/40	Sea off Weymouth, Dorset.	Me. 110 L1+-X	13(Z)/LG1	Fw. Hans Datz	Y
13/08/40	Swalland Farm, Kimmeridge, Dorset.	Me. 110 L1+FL	15(Z)/LG1	Uffz. K. Schumichen Obergefr. Giglhuber	N N
13/08/40	Sea off Lulworth, Dorset.	Ju. 87 T6+-N	5/StG2	Fw. H. Schulz	Y
13/08/40	North Baddesley, Hampshire.	Me. 110 3M+LH	1/ZG2	Lt. W. Munschmeyer	Y
14/08/40	Balcombe, Sussex.	He. 111 6N+-K	2/KG100	Uffz. F. Dorner (A/c caught fire and he baled out, but a/c returned home)	N
14/08/40	RAF Manston, Kent.	Me. 110 S9+MK	2/Erpo. Gr210	Gefr. E. Schank	Y

Date	Location	Aircraft	Unit	Prisoners	Injured
14/08/40	Coldred, Dover, Kent.	ME109 <+8	1/JG26	Uffz. G. Kemen	Y
14/08/40	Sea off Charmouth, Dorset.	He. 111 IG+CS	8/KG27	Fw. O. Dubral Fw. W. Gietz	N N
14/08/40	Border House Farm, Chester.	He. 111 1G+FS	8/KG27	Oblt. A. Wiesemann Fw. H. Rodder Uffz. H. Kochy Uffz. W. Schaum Uffz. G. Ullmann	N Y N N Y
14/08/40	Charterhouse near Cheddar, Somerset.	He. 111 1G+NT	9/KG27	Lt. E. Ohlenschlager Uffz. K. Sulzbach Uffz. A. Blumenthal Fw. J. Nikolaus Gefr. K. Kupsch	N N N N N
14/08/40	Puriton, Somerset.	He. 111 1G+OT	9/KG27	Lt. O. Uhlane Obergefr. Ramstetter Uffz. Edo Flick Uffz. J. Kremm Gefr. G. Rother	N N Y N N
14/08/40	Turf Hill, N. Charford, Hampshire.	Ju. 88 L2+-H	1/LG2	Gefr. E. Sauer	N
14/08/40	Dean Hill, East Dean, Hampshire.	He. 111 G1+AA	Stab KG55	Fw. H. Grimmstein Fw. J. Thiel	N Y
15/08/40	School Farm, Hooe, Sussex.	Me. 110 S9+CB	Stab Erpo. Gr.210	Lt. K-H. Koch Uffz. R. Kahl	N Y
15/08/40	Redhill airfield, Sussex.	Me. 110 S9+BB	Stab Erpo. Gr.210	Uffz. Johann Werner	N
15/08/40	Ightham, Kent.	Me. 110 S9+K	Stab Erpo. Gr.210	Lt. H. Ortner	N
15/08/40	Hawkhurst, Kent	Me. 110 S9+CK	Stab Erpo. Gr.210	Oblt. A. Habisch Uffz. E. Efner	N Y
15/08/40	Lightlands Farm, Frant, Sussex	Me. 109 Yellow 3+	3/Erpo. Gr.210	Lt. Horst Marx	N
15/08/40	The Jumps, West Tisted, Hampshire.	Ju. 88 L1+SC	Stab II/LG1	Oblt. S. de Boutmard Oberfw. H. Grund Fw. Willi Luder Uffz. K. Weigang	N N N N
15/08/40	Greatham Farm, Earnley, Sussex.	Ju. 88 L1+FM	4/LG1	Uffz. F. Dieter Uffz. O. Rezeppa Gefr. W. Hohbom	N N N
15/08/40	Priors Leaze, Woodmancote, Sussex.	Ju. 88 L1+SM	4/LG1	Oberfw. W. Richter Fw. H. Dittmann	Y Y

Date	Location	Aircraft	Unit	Prisoners	Injured
15/08/40	Hazeley Down, Twyford, Hampshire.	Ju. 88 L1+BM	4/LG1	Uffz. H. Buckhardt Uffz. E. Kusche Uffz. R. Muller Uffz. E. Poggensee	N N N N
15/08/40	Off Margate, Kent.	Me. 109 2+	5/JG51	Fw. O. Steigenberger	N
15/08/40	Off Reculver, Kent.	Do. 17 5K+LP	6/KG3	Obergefr. W. Duda	N
15/08/40	Off Deal, Kent.	Do. 17 5K+-P	6/KG3	Lt. H-E. Walter Fw. F Schauer Uffz. E. Kirchubel Uffz. A. Pieronczyk	N N N N
15/08/40	Cresswell Bay, Northumbria.	He. 111 1H+MH	1/KG26	Uffz. W. Zimmermann Oblt. R. Roch Gefr. E. Kulick Gefr. A. Machalett Flgr. E. Heinrichsen	N N N N N
15/08/40	North Sea off Middlesbrough.	He. 111 1H+FS	8/KG26	Fw. F. Baldauf Lt. A. Renner Obergefr. W Rossiger Gefr. W. Lorenz Uffz. C. Schumann	N N N N N
15/08/40	Hamilton Hill Farm, Bridlington, Yorkshire.	Ju. 88 4D+KL	3/KG30	Uffz. L. von Lorentz Uffz. H. Kenski Obergefr. H Prumann Gefr. Johann Gobel	N N N N
15/08/40	Bridlington Reservoir, Yorkshire.	Ju. 88 4D+DR	7/KG30	Oblt. W. Bachmann Uffz. W. Evers Flgr. R. Walther	N N N
15/08/40	Panmure Estate, Angus.	He. 115 S4+BH	1/KuFIGr506	Lt. Hand E. Tonne	Y
15/08/40	South of Folkestone Gate Lightship, Kent.	Ju. 87 L1+-U	10 St/LG1	Haupt. Munchenhagen	Y
15/08/40	North Sea off Newcastle.	Me. 110 M8+EK	2/ZG76	Fw. Klaus Ladwein	N
15/08/40	North Ashley Down, Isle of Wight.	Me. 110 M8+BP	6/ZG76	Uffz. M. Guschewski	Y
15/08/40	Weymouth Bay, Dorset.	Me. 110 2N+BC	Stab III/ZG76	Uffz. Herbert Templin	N
16/08/40	Turzes Farm, Etchingham, Sussex.	Me.109 ?	4/JG2	Oblt. W. Mockel	N

Date	Location	Aircraft	Unit	Prisoners	Injured
16/08/40	Hacklinge, Kent.	Me. 109 6+	4/JG51	Uffz. Ernst Buder	N
16/08/40	Farmland, Godshill, Isle of Wight.	Me. 109 2+	2/JG53	Fw. C. Hansen	N
16/08/40	Summerfield, Staple, Kent.	Do. 17 U5+LL	3/KG3	Lt. H-G. Mollenbrok Uffz. P. Hess	Y Y
16/08/40	Annington's Farm, Bramber, Sussex.	He. 111 G1+HP	6/KG55	Oblt. W. Wieland Fw. Hans Langstrof Uffz. W. Appell	N N N
16/08/40	High Salvington, Worthing, Sussex.	He. 111 G1+FR	7/KG55	Lt. R. Theobald Uffz. R. Hornbostel Gefr. H. Glaser	N N Y
16/08/40	Church Norton Junction, Selsey, Sussex.	Ju. 87 T6+HL	3/StG2	Uffz. Ernst Konig Uffz. Josef Scmid	Y Y
16/08/40	Sea off Selsey Bill, Sussex.	Ju. 87 T6+-L	3/StG2	Uffz. P. Bohn Obergefr. J. Bader	N N
16/08/40	Poole Harbour, Dorset.	Ju. 87 T6+-R	7/StG2	Fw. G. Grafenhain	Y
16/08/40	East Dean, Sussex.	Me. 110 2N+CC	Stab II/ZG1	Lt. R. Marchfelder Obergefr. H. Jentsch	N N
16/08/40	Lee Farm, Rackham, Sussex.	Me. 110 2N+AP	9/ZG76	Oblt. U. Schlaffer Obergefr. F. Obser	N N
18/08/40	Tapnall Farm, Freshwater, Isle of Wight.	Me.109 ?	6/JG2	Oblt. Moller-Freidrich	Y
18/08/40	Abbey Field, Leeds near Maidstone, Kent.	Me.109 13+	2/JG3	Oblt. H. Tiedmann	N
18/08/40	Elmstead Court, Barham, Canterbury, Kent.	Me.109 ?	7/JG26	Oblt. Walter Blume	Y
18/08/40	Channel off Sandown, Isle of Wight.	Me.109 6+	1/JG27	Lt. G. Mitsdorfer	N
18/08/40	Shanklin Down, Isle of Wight.	Me.109 6+-	6/JG27	Oblt. J. Neumann	N
18/08/40	Derring Farm, Lydd, Kent.	Me. 110 U8+BB	Stab I/ZG26	Oblt. Rudiger Proske Uffz. Hans Mobius	N Y
18/08/40	Leysdown, Isle of Sheppey, Kent.	Me. 110 3U+AM	4/ZG26	Uffz. Thodor Rutters	N

Date	Location	Aircraft	Unit	Prisoners	Injured
18/08/40	Off the North Foreland, Kent.	Me. 110 3U+CM	4/ZG26	Fw. F. Gierga	N
18/08/40	Channel off Folkestone, Kent.	Me. 110 3U+?P	6/ZG26	Fw. Herbert Strang	N
18/08/40	Blackmanstone, Newchurch, Kent.	Me. 110 3U+EP	6/ZG26	Lt. H-J. Kastner Uffz. W. Kaffenberger	N N
18/08/40	Snargate, Dymchurch, Kent.	He. 111 V4+GK	2/KG1	Lt. R. Ahrens Oberfw. Katzmarski Uffz. G. Schneider Flgr. K. Natzke	N N N N
18/08/40	Channel off Ramsgate, Kent.	He. 111 A1+FR	7/KG53	Oblt. F Zipse Uffz. W. Grasser Gefr. W. Reinhardt Gefr. G. Worch Gefr. H. Mailander	N N N N N
18/08/40	Small Gains Farm, Foulness.	He. 111 A1+FS	8/KG53	Lt. Walter Weber Fw. H. Feick Uffz. K. Hilgert Gefr. K. Erfurt	N N N N
18/08/40	Mill Lane, Hurst Green, Surrey.	Do. 17 F1+IH	1/KG76	Fw. J. Beck Oberfw. Lautersack	Y Y
18/08/40	Church Farm, Aylesford, Kent.	Do. 17 F1+GP	6/KG76	Lt. Buchmeier Fw. O. Watermann Uffz. H. Loffler	N N N
18/08/40	Leaves Green, Biggin Hill, Kent.	Do. 17 F1+DT	9/KG76	Oblt. R. Lamberty Haupt. Joachim Roth Haupt. Gustav Peters Oberfw. V. Geier Fw. Hugo Eberhardt	Y Y Y Y Y
18/08/40	Spring Gardens, Cutmill, West Ashling, Sussex.	Ju. 87 S2+?K	2/StG77	Lt. Hans Sinn	N
18/08/40	Bosham, Chichester, Sussex.	Ju. 87 S2+?K	2/StG77	Oblt. J. Wilhelm Uffz. A. Worner	N N
18/08/40	Off Selsey Bill, Sussex.	Ju. 87 S2+?L	3/StG77	Oberfw. G. Riegler Gefr. Oskar Langwost	Y Y
18/08/40	Ham Manor Golf Course, Angmering, Sussex.	Ju. 87 S2+JN	5/StG77	Oberfw. Kurt Schweinhardt	Y
20/08/40	Chapel Farm, Leysdown, Isle of Sheppey, Kent.	Do. 17 5K+FT	9/KG3	Fw. K. Boke Fw. K. Brehmer Gefr. R. Heinrich	Y N Y

Date	Location	Aircraft	Unit	Prisoners	Injured
20/08/40	Patrington, Hull, Yorkshire.	Ju. 88 4D+IS	8/KG30	Uffz. F-G. Wolff Fw. Hugo Keller	N N
21/08/40	Conifer Hill House, Harleston, Suffolk.	Do. 17 U5+FK	2/KG2	Lt. K. Rasche Uffz. H. Hermen Uffz. G-D. Wulf	Y Y Y
21/08/40	Gippeswyke Park, Ipswich, Suffolk.	Do. 17 U5+CS	8/KG2	Lt. K. Kzienzyk Uffz. H. Behnke Gefr. J. Sollfrank Flgr. H. Sterz	Y N N Y
21/08/40	Bilsby, Alford, Lincolnshire.	Do. 17 5K+AP	6/KG3	Oblt. H. Schwartz Oblt. U. Matschoss	N N
21/08/40	Bilsby, Alford, Lincolnshire.	Do. 17 5K+BP	6/KG3	Uffz. F. Paterrok Uffz. G. Pollmann Gefr. H. Langer Gefr. K Ludwig	N N N N
21/08/40	North Sea off Berwick.	Ju. 88 4D+LT	9/KG30	Obergefr. K. Tutschek Fw. P. Porrmann	N N
21/08/40	Marsch Farm, Warnley, Sussex.	Ju. 88 B3+BM	4/KG54	Oberfw. H. Apollony Haupt. L. Maiwald Uffz. K. Meithner Uffz. Helmut Hempel	N N N N
22/08/40	Beaford, Torrington, Devon.	Ju. 88 7A+AL	3(F)/121	Oblt. Baudler Lt. R. Pfundtner Flgr. A. Leber	Y Y Y
23/08/40	Spring Wood, Wickenhambrook, Suffolk.	Do. 17 U5+EA	Stab KG2	Oberfw. G. Wagner Oblt. H. Hellingers Fw. A. Dietl Uffz. P. Seidel	N N N N
24/08/40	Sea off Herne Bay, Kent.	Me. 109 8+I	9/JG3	Lt. Franz Achleitner	N
24/08/40	Broomhill Farm, Camber, East Sussex.	Me. 109 12+I	9/JG3	Uffz Wilhelm Kaiser	Y
24/08/40	East Langdon, Dover, Kent.	Me. 109 10+	6/JG51	Oberfw. Fritz Boeck	N
24/08/40	Minster Road, Westgate, Kent.	Me. 109 9+	1/JG52	Fw. H. Bischoff	N
24/08/40	North Ockendon, Romford, Essex.	He. 111 A1+KT	9/KG53	Fw. A. Fraas Lt. W. Lutticken Uffz. O. Lackner Uffz. H. Hermans Uffz. K. Platzer	N N N Y Y

Date	Location	Aircraft	Unit	Prisoners	Injured
24/08/40	Abberton Reservoir, Colchester, Essex.	He. 111 A1+-T	9/KG53	Uffz. G. Schaffner	N
24/08/40	Langford, Essex.	He. 111 A1+BT	9/KG53	Gefr. Hans Zaunigk	Y
24/08/40	Samuel's Corner, Gt. Wakering, Essex.	He. 111 A1+LT	9/KG53	Oblt. G. Winter Fw. A. Engelhardt Uffz. H. Schmidt Uffz. O. Wieck Gefr. W. Maurer	N N Y N Y
24/08/40	Sea off Brightlingsea, Essex.	He. 111 A1+DT	9/KG53	Haupt. H. Lonicer Uffz. E. Pegatzki	Y Y
24/08/40	Canewdon RDF Station, Essex.	Me. 109 ?	2/LG2	Uffz. A. Buschmeyer	N
25/08/40	Tatton House Farm, Buckland Vipers, Dorset.	Me. 109 White 15+	1/JG53	Gefr. Josef Broker	Y
25/08/40	Creech Barrow, nr. Wareham, Dorset.	Me. 110 3M+AH	1/ZG2	Oblt. Gerhardt Gotz Uffz. Kurt Haupt	Y Y
25/08/40	Priory Farm, East Holme, Dorset.	Me. 110 3M+KH	1/ZG2	Uffz. S. Becker Obergefr. W. Wopzel	N Y
25/08/40	English Channel off Hastings, Sussex.	He. 111 G1+CT	9/KG55	Uffz. A. Schmaderer	Y
26/08/40	Blendworth, Horndean, Hampshire.	Me. 109 ?	2/JG2	Oblt. H-T. Grisebain	N
26/08/40	Acol, Isle of Thanet, Kent.	Me. 109 1+I	2/JG52	Obergefr. W. Malecki	N
26/08/40	Sandwich Golf Course, Kent.	Me. 109 2+	2/JG52	Fw. Alfons Bacher	N
26/08/40	Sea off Copt Point, Folkestone, Kent	Me. 109 ?	3/JG52	Fw. Adolf Zieger	Y
26/08/40	Rochford airfield, Essex.	Do. 17 U5+LK	2/KG2	Haupt. H. Fosse Obergefr. J. Roeder Uffz. E. Schmidt Uffz. T. Lunghard	Y Y Y Y
26/08/40	Eastchurch, Kent.	Do. 17 U5+GK	2/KG2	Uffz. A. Schmolzer Uffz. Helmut Buhr Maj. M. Gutzmann	N N N

Date	Location	Aircraft	Unit	Prisoners	Injured
26/08/40	Higham's Farm, Thaxted, Essex.	Do. 17 U5+LR	7/KG2	Fw. W. Hohenstadter Uffz. R. Gussmann	Y Y
26/08/40	Cole End, Safron Wadlen, Essex.	Do. 17 U5+TR	7/KG2	Lt. P. Krieger Uffz. K. Winter Gefr. G. Schneider Uffz. S. Illing	Y N N Y
26/08/40	Whepstead, Bury St Edmunds, Suffolk.	Do. 17 U5+??	7/KG2	Uffz. F. Knorky Uffz. W. Simon Gefr L. Schadt	Y Y N
26/08/40	Foulness Point, Isle of Thanet, Kent.	Do. 17 5K+ER	7/KG3	Uffz. R. Haupt Obergefr. K. Ramm	Y Y
26/08/40	Goodwin Sands, Kent.	Do. 17 5K+AR	7/KG3	Uffz. R. Ritzel Fw. W. Essmert Uffz. H. Reinhardt	N Y N
26/08/40	Wick, Littlehampton, Sussex	He. 111 G1+BB	Stab I/KG55	Oblt. I. Krenn Uffz. H. Morrack Uffz. Hans Degen Uffz. W. Schneiders Fw. A. Schreek	N N Y Y Y
26/08/40	Sea off East Wittering, Sussex.	He. 111 G1+DM	4/KG55	Lt. A. Metzger	Y
26/08/40	Westbrook Farm, Cowplain, Hampshire.	He. 111 G1+GM	4/KG55	Lt. Klaus Walter Uffz. O. Schufft Uffz. F. Marmer Flgr. J. Wimmer	N Y Y Y
27/08/40	Hurdwick Farm, Tavistock, Devon.	Do. 17 5D+JL	2(F)/31	Lt. W. Haffan Fw. G. Klauschenke Gefr. J. Schlesjel	N N N
27/08/40	Manor Avenue, Caterham, Surrey.	He. 111 V4+CD	Stab III/KG1	Maj. W. Fanesla Oberfw. Braunsberger Oberfw. A. Vetter Fw. F. Meyer Gefr. G. Zimpel	N N N N N
28/08/40	Church Farm, Church Whitfield, Dover, Kent.	Me. 109 ?	Stab I/JG3	Lt. Hans H. Landry	Y died 23/9/40
28/08/40	Chartham Downs, nr. Canterbury, Kent.	Me. 109 ?	Stab JG26	Oblt. Georg Beyer	Y
28/08/40	Race Hill, Lewes, Sussex.	Gotha Go. 145	5/JG27	Uffz. L. Buckle	N
28/08/40	South Barham Farm, Denton, Kent.	Me. 109 ?	Stab JG51	Oblt. E. Kircheis	Y

Date	Location	Aircraft	Unit	Prisoners	Injured
28/08/40	Poulton Farm, South Alkham, Kent.	Me. 109 14+	7/JG51	Oberfw. Artur Dau	N
28/08/40	Colt's Hill Farm, Capek, Kent.	Me. 109 4+	1/JG54	Fw. Otto Schottle	N
28/08/40	English Channel off Foreness, Isle of Thanet, Kent	Do. 17 5K+LP	6/KG3	Lt. P. Krug Gefr. A. Burhardt Gefr. W. Gailer Flgr. A. Bruchmann	Y Y Y Y
29/08/40	Pevensey RDF station, Sussex.	Me. 109 8+	2/JG3	Oberfw. B. Lamskemper	N
29/08/40	Hale near Fordingbridge, Hampshire.	He. 111 1G+EL	3/KG27	Uffz. J. Schlosser Oblt. H. Hunerbein Uffz. D. Siebers Obergefr. P. Walpert	Y N Y Y
30/08/40	Westcourt Farm, Faversham, Kent.	Me. 109 12+	3/JG27	Fw. E. Arnold	N
30/08/40	Park House, Westwell, Ashford, Kent.	Me. 109 6+	3/JG27	Oblt. E. Axthelm	N
30/08/40	Laymans Farm, Oxted, Surrey.	Me. 109 White 5+	Stab II/JG54	Lt. R. Ziegler	N
30/08/40	Fickleshole Farm, Chelsham, Surrey.	Me. 109 6+	4/JG54	Oblt. Hans Rath	N
30/08/40	Swires Farm, Newdigate, Surrey.	He. 111 V4+BV	5/KG1	Oblt. P. Frohlisch Haupt. R. Bass	N Y
30/08/40	Blackboys, Uckfield, Sussex.	He. 111 V4+DV	6/KG1	Oberfw. K. Riemann Fw. R. Keter Uffz. W. Stein	Y Y N
30/08/40	Lower Beeding, Sussex.	He. 111 V4+GV	5/KG1	Gefr. H. Struger Gefr. W. Hofer Obergefr. Walter Monninghoff	Y N Y
30/08/40	Haxted, Lingfield, Surrey.	He. 111 V4+MV	5/KG1	Fw. H. Schnabel Gefr. H. Groth Uffz. E. Paeslack Uffz. E. Stark	N N Y N
30/08/40	Channel off Folkestone, Kent.	He. 111 V4+HV	5/KG1	Uffz. Emil Burger Gefr. H. Hildebrandt Gefr. W. Feierbend Gefr. H. Roggermann Gefr. W. Klappholz	N N Y N Y

Date	Location	Aircraft	Unit	Prisoners	Injured
30/08/40	Lifstan Way, Southend, Essex.	He. 111 A1+JL	3/KG53	Uffz. H. Gall Lt. W. Rosler	N N
30/08/40	Colne Engaine, Halstead, Essex.	He. 111 A1+BN	5/KG53	Fw. F. Steinberg Fw. A. Hummel Fw. A. Fellner Uffz. T. Hugelschutz	Y Y Y N
30/08/40	Goodmans Farm, Manston, Kent.	He. 111 A1+JP	6/KG53	Gefr. A. Klapp Fw. K. Stockl Gefr. F. Gluck	Y N Y
30/08/40	Hunsdon Rectory, Herts	He. 111 A1+CR	7/KG53	Lt. E. Fischbach Fw. W. Kusserow Fw. G. Distler	N Y Y
30/08/40	Thames Estuary off Isle of Sheppey, Kent.	He. 111 A1+GP	6/KG53	Uffz. G. Rascher Uffz. W. Roempert Uffz. H. Wagner Uffz. A. Schall Uffz. G. Keuerleben	N N N N N
30/08/40	Mill Hill Harm, Rettenden, Essex.	Me. 110 3U+KP	5/ZG26	Uffz. R. Franke Uffz. W. Hubner	N N
30/08/40	Barley Beans Farm, Kimpton, Hertfordshire.	Me. 110 M8+MM	4/ZG76	Uffz. H. Nordmeier	Y
31/08/40	Whalebone Lane, Chadwell Heath, Essex.	Me. 109 ?	3/JG3	Oblt. J. Loidolt	Y
31/08/40	Shoeburyness, Essex.	Me. 109 4+	3/JG3	Oblt. Helmut Rau	N
31/08/40	Lydd ranges, Kent.	Me. 109 ?	6/JG3	Lt. K. Westerhoff	Y
31/08/40	Knatts Valley, West Kingsdown, Kent.	Me. 109 ?	7/JG26	Uffz. Horst Liebeck	Y
31/08/40	Mill House Farm, Allington, Kent.	Me. 109 ?	7/JG26	Uffz. Martin Klar	Y
31/08/40	Jubilee Hall Farm, Ullacombe, Kent.	Me. 109 10+I	9/JG26	Lt. W. Fronhofer	N
31/08/40	Wagstaff Farm, High Halden, Tenterden, Kent.	Me. 109 13+I	1/JG77	Oblt. H-J. Ehrig	N
31/08/40	Jenkins Farm, Stapleford Abbots, Essex.	Me. 109 4+	1/JG77	Lt. J.B. Petrenko	Y

Date	Location	Aircraft	Unit	Prisoners	Injured
31/08/40	Boxley, Maidstone, Kent.	Me. 109 8+	1/JG77	Uffz. X. Keck	Y
31/08/40	Shornemead Fort near Gravesend, Kent.	ME109 5+	1/JG77	Fw. G. Kramer	Y
31/08/40	Elham Park Wood, Elham, Kent	Me. 109 ?	2/JG77	Oblt. E. Priebe	Y
31/08/40	Stanstead, Wrotham Hill, Kent.	Me. 110 S9+GK	2/Erpo. Gr.210	Uffz. E. Glaeske	N
31/08/40	Sea off Colne Point, East Mersea, Essex.	Me. 110 3U+HS	8/ZG26	Lt. E. von Bergen Uffz. Hans Becker	N N
31/08/40	Sandwich Golf Course, Kent.	Do. 17 5K+LM	4/KG3	Oberfw. W. Lange Uffz. F. Krostopotsch Fw. H. Berndt Fw. Hans Wunsch	Y Y Y Y
31/08/40	Burnham on Crouch, Essex.	Do. 17 5K+KM	4/KG3	Oberfw. A. Bulach Oblt. H. Gahrtz Gefr. E. Neumann	Y Y Y
31/08/40	Goodwin Sands, Deal, Kent.	Do. 17 5K+GN	5/KG3	Uffz. H. Blasche Fw. E. Gudat Uffz. W. Sonntag	N Y Y
31/08/40	Newchurch, Dungeness, Kent.	Do. 17 F1+BK	2/KG76	Lt. J. Kleppmeier Fw. H. Pfaehler Uffz. A. Bloss Oberfw. H. Lang	N Y Y Y
31/08/40	English Channel off Isle of Thanet, Kent.	Me. 110 L1+BK	14(Z)/LG1	Lt. K-J. Eichhorn	N
31/08/40	English Channel off Kent.	Me. 110 L1+AK	14(Z)/LG1	Fw. Gottlob Fritz Obergefr. K. Dopfer	N N
31/08/40	Chathill Park Farm, Crowhurst, Surrey.	Me. 109 ?	3/LG2	Oblt. H. von Perthes	Y died 14/9
01/09/40	Iden, near Rye, Sussex.	Me. 109 11+I	7/JG26	Lt. J. Burschgens	Y
01/09/40	Winchelsea Bridge, Rye, Sussex.	Me. 109 10+I	7/JG53	Lt. H. Strasser	N
01/09/40	Ruckinge, Bonnington, Ashford, Kent.	Me. 109 14+	5/JG54	Oblt. A. Stangl	N

Date	Location	Aircraft	Unit	Prisoners	Injured
01/09/40	Tarts Field, Lydd, Kent.	Do. 17 F1+AT	9/KG76	Uffz. M. Maasen Oberfw. W. Illg Fw. H. Wohner	Y N Y
01/09/40	Tarpot Farm, Bilsington, Ham Street, Kent.	Me. 110 L1+OH	13(Z)/LG1	Oberfw. R. Kobert Fw. W. Meining	N N
02/09/40	Coles Hill, Little Chart, Kent.	Me. 109 ?	4/JG2	Uffz. Anton Glomb	Y
02/09/40	Near Lympne Castle near Hythe, Kent.	Me. 109 12+ -	4/JG2	Uffz. E. von Stein	Y
02/09/40	Abbey Farm, Leeds Castle, Kent.	Me. 109 ?	1/JG51	Lt. Helmut Thoerl	Y
02/09/40	Hoath, Westbere, Canterbury, Kent.	Me. 109 12+	1/JG52	Fw. H. Verlings	N
02/09/40	Ranges, West of Hythe, Kent.	Me. 109 14+	1/JG53	Uffz. Werner Karl	Y
02/09/40	Bridge Farm, Bilsington, Kent.	Me. 109 ?	3/JG53	Oblt. H. Riegel	N
02/09/40	Finns Farm, Kingsnorth, Ashford, Kent.	Me. 109 2+	8/JG54	Uffz. Heinrich Elbers	Y
02/09/40	St. Radigund's Abbey, West Hougham, Kent.	Me. 110 3M+HK	2/ZG2	Lt. G. Schipper Gefr. T. Schockenhoff	N N
02/09/40	White Horse Wood, Birling, Maidstone, Kent.	Me. 110 U8+DK	2/ZG26	Uffz. H. Stuwe	Y
02/09/40	Thames Estuary off Kent.	Me. 110 3U+GN	5/ZG26	Oberfw. K. Rochel Uffz. W. Schoffler	N N
02/09/40	Rochford airfield, Essex.	Do. 17 5K+BT	9/KG3	Oblt. U. Rohr Fw. O. Sprink Uffz. K. Seidel	Y Y Y
03/09/40	Langenhoe, Essex.	Do. 17 U5+AN	5/KG2	Fw. Martin Kriegl	N
03/09/40	Woodham Ferrers, Essex.	Me. 110 3M+CB	Stab I/ZG2	Oblt. R. Messner Obergefr. A. Santoni	N N
03/09/40	Sea off Herne Bay, Kent.	Me. 110 3M+BK	2/ZG2	Oblt. S. Gottschalt Uffz. M. Hoffmann	Y N
03/09/40	Rye Hill, Thornwood, Harlow, Essex.	Me. 110 3M+HL	2/ZG2	Oblt. K. Muller	N

Date	Location	Aircraft	Unit	Prisoners	Injured
03/09/40	Pudsey Hall Farm, Canewdon, Essex.	Me. 110 3M+EL	3/ZG2	Oberfw. G. Winkler Gefr. O. Weiler	Y N
03/09/40	Road south of Maldon, Essex.	Me. 110 3U+EP	6/ZG26	Lt. W. Manhart Uffz. W. Drews	N Y
03/09/40	North Shoebury House, near Southend, Essex.	Me. 110 3U+KR	7/ZG26	Fw. Hans Grau	Y
04/09/40	Long Reach, West Horsley, Surrey.	Me. 110 L1+BK	14(Z)/LG1	Uffz. J. Jackel	Y
04/09/40	Mill Hill, Shoreham by Sea, Sussex.	Me. 110 3M+AA	Stab/ZG2	Oblt. W. Schafer Uffz. H. Bendjus	N Y
04/09/40	Little Butts Farm, Cousley Wood, Wadhurst, Sussex.	Me. 110 M8+AC	Stab II/ZG76	Oblt. H. Wieber Uffz. M. Michael	N Y
04/09/40	English Channel off Pevensey, Sussex.	Me. 110 M8+IM	5/ZG76	Oblt. E. von Schotheim. Uffz. G. Hommel	N Y
04/09/40	Honeysuckle Lane, High Salvington, Sussex.	Me. 110 2N+BM	Stab III/ZG76	Oblt. W. Schiller Fw. H. Winkler	N Y
04/09/40	Strivens Farm, Steyning, Sussex.	Me. 110 2N+HM	7/ZG76	Uffz. W. Schultis Uffz. R. Bileck	N Y
04/09/40	Patching, Angmering, Sussex.	Me. 110 2N+CN	8/ZG76	Lt. Hans Munich Uffz. Adolf Kaser	N N
05/09/40	Banks Farm, Aldington, Kent.	Me. 109 6+	1/JG3	Lt. Heinz Schnabel	Y
05/09/40	Winchet Hill, Marden, Kent.	Me. 109 <+-	Stab I/JG3	Oblt. Franz von Werra	N
05/09/40	Wichling, Kent	Me. 109 7+	3/JG3	Uffz. H. Grabow	Y
05/09/40	Monkton Farm, Manston, Kent.	ME109 <I-+-	Stab/ JG53	Haupt. Wilhelm Meyerweisflog	N
05/09/40	English Channel off Hastings, Sussex.	Me. 109 ?	9/JG53	Fw. A. Ochsenkuhn	N
05/09/40	Hardy Street, Maidstone, Kent.	Me. 109 +6	1/JG54	Uffz. Fritz Hotzelmann	N
05/09/40	Sea off Dover, Kent.	Me. 110 3U+-C	II/ZG26	Oblt. Friedrich Viertel	Y

Date	Location	Aircraft	Unit	Prisoners	Injured
05/09/40	Rendlesham, Suffolk.	He. 111 V4+AB	Stab 1/KG1	Oblt. H-D. Biebrach	N
05/09/40	Thames Estuary off Sheerness, Kent.	He. 111 A1+CR	7/KG53	Fw. A. Maier Uffz. H. Lenger	N Y
06/09/40	Plumtree Farm Headcorn, Kent.	Me. 109 <+	Stab / JG2	Lt. M. Himmelbeber	Y
06/09/40	Bleakwood, Walderslade, Chatham, Kent.	Me. 109 2+~	8/JG2	Oblt. Karl Heinz Metz	N
06/09/40	Hothfield, Kent.	Me. 109 1+I	7/JG27	Lt. Hans Markwart Christinnecke	Y
06/09/40	Sea off Sheerness, Kent.	Me. 109 11+	3/JG27	Oblt. W. Schuller	Y
06/09/40	Bank Farm, Tudeley, Tonbridge, Kent.	Me. 109 6+-	5/JG27	Fw. Erich Braun	Y
06/09/40	Thames Estuary off Shoeburyness range, Essex.	Me. 109 ?	Stab III/JG27	Haupt. Joachim H. Schlichting	Y
06/09/40	Blean, Canterbury, Kent.	Me. 109 8+	7/JG27	Uffz. E. Nittmann	N
06/09/40	Stone Street, Sevenoaks, Kent.	Me. 109 ?	3/JG53	Oblt. H. Waller	N
06/09/40	Vincent's Farm, Manston, Kent.	Me. 109 5+I	7/JG53	Uffz. H-G. Schulte	N
06/09/40	Cannons Hill Golf Course, Coulsdon, Surrey.	Me. 110 U8+CL	3/ZG26	Uffz. E. Neuss	Y
06/09/40	Foyle Farm, Crowhurst, East Sussex.	Me. 110 S9+BH	1/Erpo. Gr. 210	Gefr. Edmund Ernst	N
06/09/40	North Sea off Harwich.	He. 111 A1+AB	Stab I/KG53	Oberfw. M. Winter Oblt. A. Weber Fw. F. Kempgens	N N N
06/09/40	Tanyards Farm, Tonbridge, Kent.	Ju. 88 F1+HP	6/KG76	Lt. J. Kernbach Oberfw. Schumacher Gefr. R. Riedl Uffz. H. Agel	N N N N
06/09/40	Thames Estuary off Sheerness, Kent.	Me. 109 O+	4/LG2	Lt. H. Gultgen	N

Date	Location	Aircraft	Unit	Prisoners	Injured
06/09/40	RAF Hawkinge, Kent.	Me. 109 +C	6/LG2	Fw. W. Gottschalk	Y
07/09/40	Mallwyd, Machynlleth, Wales.	Ju. 88 4U+BL	3(F)/123	Lt. E. Bohle Oblt. Hans Kauter Uffz. G. Leisler Fw. W. Kobald	Y Y Y Y
07/09/40	St. Radigund's Abbey, West Hoogham, Kent.	Me. 109 8+	1/JG2	Oblt. Adolf Gotz	N
07/09/40	English Channel off Folkestone, Kent.	Me. 109 6+-	5/JG2	Uffz. W. Melchert	N
07/09/40	Sheerlands Farm, Pluckley, Kent.	Me. 109 12+-	4/JG26	Lt. Hans Krug	N
07/09/40	English Channel between Dover and Folkestone.	Me. 109 +-	6/JG26	Uffz. Ernst Braun	N
07/09/40	Rainham Road, Hornchurch, Essex.	Me. 109 ?	1/JG27	Lt. G. Genske	N
07/09/40	Oad Street, Sittingbourne, Kent.	Me. 109 9+	3/JG51	Gefr. H. Werner	Y
07/09/40	Bethersden, Kent.	Me. 109 7+	3/JG51	Uffz. H. zur Lage	N
07/09/40	Little Clacton, Essex.	Me. 109 11+I	9/JG51	Uffz. Kurt Koch	N
07/09/40	Rolvenden, Tenterden, Kent.	Me. 109 11+	1/JG77	Oberfw. G. Goltzsche	N
07/09/40	Laindon Common, Essex.	Me. 110 3M+BB	Stab I/ZG2	Oblt. G. Granz Fw. W. Schutel	N N
07/09/40	Hoath, Herne Bay, Kent.	Me. 110 3M+LM	3/ZG2	Obergefr. R. Dahmke	N
07/09/40	Bullers Farm, Little Burstead, Essex.	Me. 110 A2+JH	4/ZG2	Lt. Karl Stix	Y
07/09/40	English Channel off Birchington, Kent.	Me. 110 A2+ML	6/ZG2	Oblt. W. Brede	N
07/09/40	Thames Estuary off Isle of Grain, Kent.	He. 111 5J+JP	6/KG4	Uffz. R. Klein Gefr. H. Beckmann	N N

Date	Location	Aircraft	Unit	Prisoners	Injured
07/09/40	Old Marsh, Isle of Grain, Kent.	He. 111 A1+DN	5/KG53	Oberfw. A. Pitzka Oblt. H. Brauer Gefr. E. Urich Uffz. F. Bergmann	N N Y Y
07/09/40	Sundridge, Sevenoaks, Kent.	Do. 17 F1+BA	Stab / KG76	Fw. Erich Rosche	Y
07/09/40	Wickhambreaux, near Canterbury, Kent.	Me. 109 11+	1/LG2	Uffz. W. Gotting	N
08/09/40	Farningham Road Station near Dartford, Kent.	Do. 17 U5+FN	5/KG2	Oberfw. M. Strobel	Y
08/09/40	As above.	Do. 17 U5+BN	5/KG2	Oblt. J. Schneider Uffz. J. Schumacher Obergefr. Hoffmann Flgr. W. Kohl	Y Y Y Y
09/09/40	English Channel, off Newhaven, Sussex.	Me. 109 ?	4/JG3	Fw. A-W. Muller	N
09/09/40	Rosemary Farm, Flimwell, Sussex.	Me. 109 6+I	7/JG3	Uffz. M. Massmann	N
09/09/40	Mayfield, East Sussex.	Me. 109 <+	Stab I/JG27	Oblt. Gunter Bode	N
09/09/40	Charity Farm, Cootham, Sussex.	Me. 109 13+-	5/JG27	Oblt. Erwin Daig	N
09/09/40	Mounts Farm. Benenden, Kent.	ME109 7+-	6/JG27	Uffz. G. Rauwolf	N
09/09/40	Near Old Jail Inn, Jail Lane, Biggin Hill, Kent.	Me. 109 5+	1/JG53	Fw. H. Honisch	Y
09/09/40	English Channel, off Newhaven, Sussex.	Me. 110 2N+EP	9/ZG76	Fw. Hermann Koops	N
09/09/40	Sundridge near Sevenoaks, Kent.	He. 111 V4+BL	3/KG1	Oblt. E. Kiunka Uffz. A. Stumbaum Uffz. E. Marks Oberfw. A. Heidrich Gefr. H. Reinecke	N N Y N Y
09/09/40	Newells Farm, Nuthurst, Sussex.	Ju. 88 4D+AA	Stab/ KG30	Oblt. Rold Heim Uffz. Josef Beck Fw. A Fuhs Uffz. W. Baustian	N N N N

Date	Location	Aircraft	Unit	Prisoners	Injured
09/09/40	Court House Farm, Barcombe, Sussex.	Ju. 88 4D+KK	Stab I/KG30	Lt. H-G. Gollnisch Uffz. W. Rolf Uffz. W. Hamerla	N N N
09/09/40	Pagham Harbour, Sussex	Ju. 88 4D+AD	Stab III/KG30	Maj. J. Hackbarth Oberfw. H. Manger	Y Y
09/09/40	Chawton, Alton, Hampshire.	He. 111 A1+ZD	Stab III/KG53	Fw. O. Broderix Oblt. K. Meineke	Y Y
10/09/40	West Hoathly, West Sussex.	Do. 17 F1+ET	9/KG76	Uffz. E. Nurenburg Gefr. A. Greza	Y N
11/09/40	Broomhill Farm, Camber, Sussex.	He. 111 V4+FA	Stab/KG1	Fw. J. Sommer Lt. O. Behn Uffz. P. Moeck Uffz. G. Arndt Gefr. M. Mannich	N N Y Y Y
11/09/40	Stocks Green, Hildenborough, Kent.	He. 111 V4+KL	3/KG1	Uffz. H. Steinecke Uffz. W. Hirsch Uffz. E. Krammer Gefr. W. Pfeiffer Gefr. H. Pumpel	N N Y Y Y
11/09/40	Broomhill Farm, Camber, Sussex	He. 111 V4+RW	6/KG1	Uffz. B. Hanzen Uffz. K. Markert Uffz. H. Wildenhopf Uffz. J. Krall Gefr. G. Wilhelm	N N Y N N
11/09/40	Between Mayfield and Crowborough, Sussex.	He. 111 1H+KH	1/KG26	Fw. W. Jabusch Lt. H. Zimmermann Fw. G. Schilling Oberfw. W. Hasebrink	Y N N N
11/09/40	Burmarsh, Kent.	He. 111 1H+CB	Stab I/KG26	Fw. H. Freidrich Fw. H. George Uffz. K. Hoffmann Uffz. A. Breyer Uffz. H. Stirniman	N Y N N N
11/09/40	Staplecross, Sussex.	He. 111 1H+AH	1/KG26	Fw. E. Buttner Haupt. W. Kunstler Gefr. E. Schmidt	N N N
11/09/40	New Barn Farm, Dormansland, Surrey.	He. 111 1H+ML	3/KG26	Oblt. W. Abendhausen Uffz. H. Hauswald	N Y
11/09/40	English Channel off Hastings, Sussex.	He. 111 1H+IN	5/KG26	Oblt. G-O. Bertram Gefr. G. Schroter Gefr. R. Entrich	N N N

Date	Location	Aircraft	Unit	Prisoners	Injured
11/09/40	Cobham Farm, Lenham, Kent.	Me. 110 U8+HL	2/ZG26	Fw. H. Brinkmann Uffz. E. Gruschow	N N
13/09/40	Stow Park Avenue, Newport, South Wales.	He. 111 1G+DS	8/KG27	Oblt. Harry Wappler	Y
14/09/40	Boxley, Detling, Kent.	Me. 109 4+	1/JG77	Fw. H. Ettler	Y
14/09/40	Newman's End, Sheering, Essex.	He. 111 5J+BL	3/KG4	Oblt. Hermann Kell Fw. Walter Hobe	N N
14/09/40	New Street Farm, Great Chart, Kent.	Me. 109 +1	6/LG2	Uffz. V. Blazejewski	N
15/09/40	Hans Farm, Ruckinge, Kent.	Me. 109 -+-	Stab JG3	Oblt. H. von Wedel	N
15/09/40	St Michael's near Tenterden, Kent.	Me. 109 ?	1/JG3	Oberfw. F. Hessel	Y
15/09/40	Thorn Farm, Pluckley, Kent	Me. 109 ?	2/JG3	Oblt. Helmut Reumschussel	N
15/09/40	Isfield, near Uckfield, Sussex.	Me. 109 5+	2/JG27	Uffz. A. Walburger	N
15/09/40	St Margarets at Cliffe, near Dover, Kent.	Me. 109 ?	7/JG51	Lt. Kurt Bildau	N
15/09/40	Biddenden Green, Kent.	Me. 109 <I+	Stab I/JG52	Lt. Hans Bertel	N
15/09/40	Adisham Court, Bekesbourne, Kent.	Me. 109 <<+	1/JG53	Fw. H. Tschoppe	Y
15/09/40	Grand Redoubt, Dymchurch, Kent.	Me. 109 2+	3/JG53	Uffz. K-H. Feldmann	N
15/09/40	Westfield, near Hastings, Sussex.	Do. 17 U5+CN	5/KG2	Oblt. Ulrich Latz Fw. Kurt Hasse Uffz. Franz Reinisch	Y Y N
15/09/40	City Way, Chatham, Kent.	Do. 17 U5+PS	8/KG2	Uffz. J. Stampfer Oblt. W. Kittmann Uffz. P. Langer Flgr. W. Kohler	N N N N
15/09/40	Kilndown, Goudhurst, Kent.	Do. 17 U5+ET	9/KG2	Uffz. Jaakob Sehrt	Y
15/09/40	Thames Estuary off Herne Bay, Kent.	Do. 17 U5+FT	9/KG2	Gefr. Josef Zierer Gefr. A. Hoffmann	Y Y

Date	Location	Aircraft	Unit	Prisoners	Injured
15/09/40	Gladstone Road, Laindon Hills, Essex.	Do. 17 5K+DM	4/KG3	Uffz. Gerhard Friebe	N
15/09/40	Perry Street, Barnhurst Golf Course, Bexley, Kent.	Do. 17 5K+JM	4/KG3	Lt. H. Michaelis Flgr. H. Bormann	Y Y
15/09/40	Allhallows, Isle of Grain, Kent.	Do. 17 5K+CM	4/KG3	Fw. M. von Gortz Uffz. G. Wien Gefr. E. Schild Gefr. H. Weymar	Y Y N Y
15/09/40	Thames Estuary.	Do. 17 5K+DN	5/KG3	Fw. Kurt Falke	N
15/09/40	Skinners Farm, Beltring, Kent.	Do. 17 5K+JN	5/KG3	Ober Fw. H. Howind Ober Fw. Zimmermann Ober Fw. H. Hobel	N N N
15/09/40	Asplins Farm, Foulness, Essex.	He. 111 1H+IH	1/KG26	Lt. H. Straubel Fw. H. Schwarz Fw. W. Marnbach Fw. K. Potenberg Gefr. E. Domes	N N Y Y Y
15/09/40	Woolwich Arsenal, Kent.	He. 111 A1+DA	Stab/KG53	Fw. Michael Cionber	Y
15/09/40	Botany Farm, Orsett, Essex.	He. 111 A1+EL	3/KG53	Lt. H. Boeckh Uffz. A. Gerding Obergefr. Kurzawski Uffz. K. Altmann	Y N Y Y
15/09/40	Bourne Farm, Sandhurst Cross, Kent.	He. 111 A1+GL	3/KG53	Oblt. G. Buchler Gefr. H. Stamminger Gefr. H. Richter	N Y Y
15/09/40	Payne Land Farm, Frittenden, Kent.	He. 111 A1+GM	Stab II/KG53	Maj. Max Gruber Oberfw. G. Schmidt Fw. M. Nagl Uffz. E. Schilling	N N N Y
15/09/40	RAF West Malling airfield, Kent.	He. 111 A1+AN	5/KG53	Fw. K. Behrendt Fw. R. Lichtenhagen Uffz. O. Zilling	N Y Y
15/09/40	Trafford Farm, Benenden, Kent.	He. 111 A1+LN	5/KG53	Lt. H. Bahmsch Uffz. S. Bauer Uffz. E. Buttler	N N Y
15/09/40	Victoria Station, London.	Do. 17 F1+FH	1/KG76	Obergefr. Armbruster Uffz. Hammermeister	N Y
15/09/40	Alcroft Farm, Sturry, Kent.	Do. 17 F1+FL	3/KG76	Oblt. K-E. Wilke Uffz. H. Zrenner	Y Y

Date	Location	Aircraft	Unit	Prisoners	Injured
15/09/40	Lullingstone Castle Farm, near Eynsford, Kent.	Do. 17 F1+FS	8/KG76	Fw. Rolf Heitsch Fw. Hans Pfeiffer Fw. Martin Sauter	N Y Y
15/09/40	Underriver, Sevenoaks, Kent.	Do. 17 F1+DT	9/KG76	Fw. W. Raab Oberfw. H. Steit Fw. W. Seuffert	N Y Y
15/09/40	Ripper's Cross, Hothfield, Kent.	Me. 110 L1+IH	12(z)/LG1	Fw. A. Hoffman	Y died after Interrog.
15/09/40	Hartlip Church, near Sittingbourne, Kent.	Me. 109 ?	1/LG2	Uffz. H. Streibring	N
15/09/40	Shell Ness, Isle of Sheppey, Kent.	Me. 109 -+2	3/LG2	Uffz. August Klick	N
16/09/40	North Sea off Eyemouth, Northumbria.	He. 115 S4+CL	3/KuFIGr506	Oblt. C. Lucas Haupt. E-W. Bergemann Fw. E. Kalinowski Haupt. H. Kripendorf	N N N N
16/09/40	New Aberdour, near Frazerburgh, Scotland.	He. 115 8L+GH	1/KuFIGr906	Haupt. H. Kothe Lt. H-O. Aldus Uffz. H. Meissner	N Y N
16/09/40	Withybrook, near Coventry.	Ju. 88 B3+HH	1/KG54	Fw. K. Perlberg Fw. H. Baur	Y Y
17/09/40	Ladywell Barn, Warminster, Wiltshire.	Ju. 88 L1+XC	Stab II/LG1	Maj. Heinz Cramer Oberfw. P. Stutzel Fw. Fritz Schultz	N Y Y
17/09/40	Broomhill Farm, Camber, Sussex.	Me. 109 2+I	7/JG26	Uffz. Karl-Heinz Bock	N
18/09/40	Royal St. George's Golf Course, Sandwich, Kent.	Me. 109 1+	9/JG27	Gefr. W. Glockner	Y
18/09/40	Harringe Farm, Sellinge, Kent.	Me. 109 7+	9/JG27	Uffz. E. Schutz (shot att. to escape scene)	Y died 26/9
18/09/40	Guilton Ash, Sandwich, Kent.	Me. 109 10+-	4/JG53	Lt. E. Bodendiek	Y
18/09/40	Collier Street, Yalding, Maidstone, Kent.	Do. 215 G2+KH	4/Auf. Grp. Ob.d.L	Lt. Hans Poser Uffz. A. Wiesen Uffz. A. Linsner	N Y N
18/09/40	Eastry Mill, near Sandwich, Kent.	Ju. 88 3Z+ED	Stab III/KG77	Fw. F. Himsel Uffz. F. Probst	N N
18/09/40	Thames Estuary off Southend on Sea, Essex.	Ju. 88 3Z+AS	8/KG77	Uffz. P. Weidmuller	Y

Date	Location	Aircraft	Unit	Prisoners	Injured
18/09/40	Thames Estuary off Sheerness, Kent.	Ju. 88 3Z+HS	8/KG77	Fw. Walter Haret	Y
18/09/40	Thames Estuary off Sheerness, Kent.	Ju. 88 3Z+FS	8/KG77	Fw. Hans Stier Obergefr. P. Baumann	Y Y
18/09/40	Cooling Court, Cooling, Kent.	Ju. 88 3Z+DT	9/KG77	Uffz. K. Burkant Uffz. H. Glaeseker	N N
18/09/40	Bowers Gifford Marshes, Essex.	Ju. 88 3Z+FT	9/KG77	Fw. Otto Graf	Y
19/09/40	RAF Oakington, Cambridgeshire.	Ju. 88 7A+FM	4(F)/121	Uffz. H-J. Scheket Lt. Helmut Knab Uffz. Josef Thoring Obergefr. E. Bresch	N N N N
19/09/40	Spellbrook, Bishops Stortford, Hertfordshore.	He. 111 G1+GL	3/KG55	Uffz. Walter Gerss	Y
19/09/40	Culford School, Bury St. Edmunds, Suffolk.	Ju. 88 3Z+GH	1/KG77	Uffz. Ernst Etzold	Y
20/09/40	Richmond Avenue, Merton, Surrey.	Ju. 88 B3+HM	4/KG54	Fw. W. Schlake	Y
21/09/40	Trawsfynydd, North Wales.	Do. 215 VB+KK	2(F)/121	Fw. Kurt Jensen Lt. Rolf Book Fw. Hans Kuhl	Y Y Y
21/09/40	Mulberry Farm, Old Fishbourne, Bosham.	Ju. 88 L1+AL	3/LG1	Oblt. K. Sodemann Uffz. O. Bergstrasser Fw. W. Lorenz Gefr. E, Bosert	Y N N N
22/09/40	English Channel off Newhaven, Sussex.	Ju. 88 7A+AM	4(F)/121	Lt. H. Bottscher Fw. T. Vater Uffz. W. Muller Uff. Peter Rabe	Y Y Y N
23/09/40	English Channel off Folkestone harbour wall, Kent.	Me. 109 2+-	4/JG2	Uffz. Frederich Dilthey	Y
23/09/40	English Channel off Deal, Kent.	Me. 109 3+I	7/JG3	Uffz. Karl Elbing	N
23/09/40	Grain Fort, Isle of Grain, Kent.	Me. 109 4+I	8/JG26	Uffz. Arnold Kupper	Y

Date	Location	Aircraft	Unit	Prisoners	Injured
23/09/40	Biddenden, Kent.	Me. 109 9+I	8/JG26	Fw. Gerhard Grzymalla	N
24/09/40	West End, Chobham, Surrey.	He. 111 1H+GP	6/KG26	Uffz. K. Niemeyer Gefr. H. Leipnitz Gefr. S. Weinlick Gefr. W. Jenreck	N N N N
25/09/40	Ballard Down, Swanage, Dorset.	He. 111 G1+BH	1/KG55	Fw. F. Jurgens Haupt. K. Kothke Gefr. R. Weisbach Flgr. Otto Muller	Y N N N
25/09/40	Racecourse Farm, Portbury, Somerset.	He. 111 G1+DN	5/KG55	Oblt. G. Weigel Oberfw. A. Narres Fw. G. Engel Uffz. K. Gerdsmeier Gefr. K. Greib	N N N N N
25/09/40	Church Farm, Wolverton, Somerset.	He. 111 G1+EP	6/KG55	Haupt. Helmuth Brandt	Y
25/09/40	Westminster Road, Branksome Park, Dorset.	He. 111 G1+LR	7/KG55	Gefr. Kurt Schraps	N
25/09/40	Well Bottom, Boyton, Somerset.	Me. 110 3U+GS	8/ZG26	Fw. W. Scherer	Y
26/09/40	Bleak Down Hill, Isle of Wight.	Me. 110 U8+HH	1/ZG26	Fw. H. Rohde Fw. E. Feder	Y N
27/09/40	Sea off Porlock Bat, Somerset.	Ju. 88 4U+RL	3(F)/123	Fw. H. Ackenhausen Oblt. W. Rude Oberfw. E. Riehle	N N N
27/09/40	Preston Hill, Iwerne Minster, Dorset.	Me. 110 S9+DK	2/Erpo Gr. 210	Fw. Fritz Ebner Gefr. Werner Zwick	Y Y
27/09/40	Lower Mays Farm, Selmeston, Sussex.	Me. 109 11+-	7/JG27	Gefr. Hans-Dieter John	N
27/09/40	Broad Street, Hollingbourne, Kent.	Me. 109 8+-	Stab II/JG52	Oblt. C. Treiber	Y
27/09/40	Petham near Canterbury, Kent.	Me. 109 4+-	4/JG52	Lt. Heinz Geist	Y
27/09/40	St. Nicholas at Wade, Kent.	Me. 109 5+-	4/JG52	Fw. F. Bogasch	N
27/09/40	Northbourne Park, Sandwich, Kent.	Me. 109 12+-	4/JG52	Gefr. Ernst Bosch	Y

Date	Location	Aircraft	Unit	Prisoners	Injured
27/09/40	Brick House Farm, High Halden, Kent.	Me. 109 3+-	5/JG52	Fw. H. Hoffmann	Y
27/09/40	Seamans Home, Cudham, Kent.	Ju. 88 3Z+DH	1/KG77	Oberfw. H. Muller Uffz. Kollmansberger Oberfw. R. Muller	N Y Y
27/09/40	Folly Farm, South Holmwood, Surrey.	Ju. 88 3Z+HK	2/KG77	Uffz. R. Schumann Uffz. H-J. Tenholt Uffz. A. Ackermann	N N Y
27/09/40	English Channel off Lydd, Kent.	Ju. 88 3Z+IK	2/KG77	Uffz. G. Schmidt Uffz. H. Sergocki	N N
27/09/40	Lodge Farm, East Grinstead, Sussex.	Ju. 88 3Z+BL	3/KG77	Fw. A. Brautigam	Y
27/09/40	Graveney Marshes, near Faversham, Kent.	Ju. 88 3Z+EL	3/KG77	Uffz. F. Ruhlandt Uffz. G. Richter Uffz. E. Richter Gefr. F.J. Reiner	Y N Y Y
27/09/40	Honninton Park, Brenchley, Kent.	Ju. 88 3Z+CL	3/KG77	Uffz. R. Ludwig	Y
27/09/40	Vexour Farm, Penshurst, Kent.	Ju. 88 3Z+DC	Stab II/KG77	Fw. A. Zeller Uffz. E. Brodbeck	Y Y
27/09/40	English Channel off Hastings, Sussex.	Ju. 88 3Z+DN	5/KG77	Gefr. J. Freichtmaier	Y
27/09/40	Chiddingstone, Kent.	Ju. 88 3Z+DP	6/KG77	Fw. H. Zindsmeister	Y
27/09/40	Stickets Manor, Ozted, Surrey.	Me. 110 L1+LL	15(Z)/LG1	Oblt. O. Weckeiser Gefr. H. Bruggow	N Y
27/09/40	Horam Manor Farm, Horam, Sussex.	Me. 110 L1+GL	15(Z)/LG1	Uffz. Hans Bechthold	N
27/09/40	Haydon Farm near Radstock, Somerset.	Me. 110 U8+GL	3/ZG26	Lt. Joachim Koepsell	N
27/09/40	Kimmeridge, Wareham, Dorset.	Me. 110 3U+DS	8/ZG26	Uffz. F. Schupp Gefr. K. Nechwatal	Y Y
27/09/40	Does Ash Farm, Piddletrenthide, Dorset.	Me. 110 3U+FT	9/ZG26	Gefr. G. Jackstadt	Y
27/09/40	English Channel off Hastings, Sussex.	Me. 110 M8+X?	Stab II/ZG76	Oblt. W. von Eichborn	Y

Date	Location	Aircraft	Unit	Prisoners	Injured
28/09/40	English Channel off Beachy Head, Sussex.	Ju. 88 5J+GS	8/KG4	Gefr. F. Marchardt	N
30/09/40	Hides Farm, North Chapel, Surrey.	Me. 109 ?	Stab/JG26	Haupt. Walter Kienzle	Y
30/09/40	East Dean, Eastbourne, Sussex.	Me. 109 4+-	4/JG26	Uffz. Horst Perez	Y
30/09/40	Pelsham House, Peasmarsh, Sussex.	Me. 109 -+7	4/JG27	Uffz. R. Hammer	Y
30/09/40	Grayswood, Haslemere, Surrey.	Me. 109 3+-	6/JG27	Lt. Herbert Schmidt	Y
30/09/40	Queen Anne's Gate, Windsor Great Park	Me. 109 9+	7/JG27	Oblt. Karl Fischer	N
30/09/40	Channel off Newhaven, Sussex.	Me. 109	Stab I/JG52	Lt. Kurt Kirchner	Y
30/09/40	Clayton Farm, Peasmarsh, Sussex	Me. 109 14+-	3/JG52	Uffz. Kurt Wolff	Y
30/09/40	Near RAF Detling, Maidstone, Kent.	Me. 109 2+-	4/JG52	Gefr. E. Mummert	N
30/09/40	Kingswood Church, Dorking, Surrey.	Me. 109 ?	6/JG52	Gefr. G. Strasser	Y
30/09/40	Langney, Eastbourne, Sussex.	Me. 109 13+-	3/JG53	Fw. Walter Scholz	N
30/09/40	English Channel off Beachy Head, Sussex.	Me. 109 3+-	6/JG53	Uffz. Karl Michael Vogel	Y
30/09/40	Strood, Rochester, Kent.	Me. 109 12+I	7/JG53	Uffz. E. Poschemrieder	Y
30/09/40	Rock House Banks, Normans Bay, Pevensey.	Me. 109 4+	7/JG54	Uffz. F. Marcks	N
30/09/40	Gatwick race course, Sussex.	Ju. 88 3Z+DK	2/KG77	Oblt. F. Oeser Gefr. R. Hulsmann Fw. G. Goerke	Y Y Y

Date	Location	Aircraft	Unit	Prisoners	Injured
01/10/40	Shadoxhurst, near Ashford, Kent.	Me. 109 9+	1/JG51	Uffz. E. Gerneth	N
02/10/40	North Sea off Kinnaird Head, Fraserburgh.	HE115 S4+AH	1/506	Uffz. R. Schwedtke Oblt. G. Lenz Obergefr. H. Neuborg	N N Y
02/10/40	Twelve Acre Hop Yard, Goudhurst, Kent.	Me. 109 3+I	8/JG53	Gefr. Heinrich Zag	Y
02/10/40	Addlested Farm, East Peckham, Kent.	Me. 109 7+I	8/JG53	Oblt. Walter Fiel	N
02/10/40	Rookery Farm, Cretingham, Suffolk.	Ju. 88 U5+FA	Stab/KG2	Oblt. Hans Langer Oblt. Erich Eitze Uffz. Robert Seidel Uffz. H. Bellmann	N N N N
02/10/40	West Marsh Point, Brightlingsea, Essex.	Ju. 88 5J+US	8/KG4	Uffz. H. Mairhofer Obergefr. Preugschs Obergefr. Hansheir Obergefr. Scholtz	N N N N
02/10/40	Beach at Chapel St. Leonards, Skegness, Lincolnshire.	He. 111 A1+CH	1/KG53	Oberfw. K. Zinner Oblt. Hans Seigel Fw. W. Zickler Oberfw. V. Weidner Obergefr. A. Kreuzer	N N N N N
03/10/40	Eastend Green Farm, Hartingfordbury, Hertfordshire.	Ju. 88 3Z+BB	Stab I/KG77	Oblt. Fiebig Fw. H. Rethof Oberfw. E. Goebel Uffz. Kurt Seifert	N N N N
04/10/40	Gypsum mine, Mountfield, Battle, Sussex.	He. 111 V4+FW	II/KG1	Gefr. Fritz Zuckrigel	N
05/10/40	Runsell Farm, Bethersden, Kent.	Me. 109 2+	1/JG3	Fw. F. von Herwarth-Bitteffeld	Y
05/10/40	Sheerlands Farm, Pluckley, Kent.	Me. 109 3+	1/JG53	Lt. Alfred Zeis	N
05/10/40	New Bank Farm, Blisington, Kent.	Me. 109 10+	1/JG53	Uffz. Willi Gehsla	Y
05/10/40	Pelsham Farm, Peasmarsh, Sussex.	Me. 109 1^+M	6/LG2	Fw. Erhard Pankratz	Y
06/10/40	Snape Wood, Wadhurst, Sussex.	Do.17 F1+FR	7/KG76	Lt. F. Mohr Uffz. F. Mrossinsky Fw. Rudolph Poh	Y Y Y

Date	Location	Aircraft	Unit	Prisoners	Injured
07/10/40	Thornton Farm, Eastry, Kent.	Me. 109 10+-	5/JG27	Uffz. Paul Lederer	Y
07/10/40	Oak Farm, Headcorn, Kent.	Me. 109 ?	9/JG27	Uffz. Lothar Bartsch	N
07/10/40	Lidham Guest Farm, Guestling, East Sussex.	Me. 109 1+	2/JG51	Oblt. Viktor Molders	N
07/10/40	English Channel off Sandgate, Kent.	Me. 109 12+	2/JG51	Lt. Erich Meyer	N
07/10/40	Up Sydling, Dorchester, Dorset.	Ju. 88 9K+SN	5/KG51	Oblt. Sigurd Hey Lt. Frederich Bein Oberfw. C. Konig Oberfw. Josef Troll	N Y Y Y
07/10/40	English Channel off Greatstone, Kent.	Me. 109 ^+A	4/LG2	Uffz. Heinrich Bley	N
07/10/40	Spa Golf Club, Tunbridge Wells, Kent.	Me. 109 ^+F	4/LG2	Uffz. G. Morschel	Y
07/10/40	English Channel off Ringstead Bay, Dorset.	Me. 110 3U+FM	4/ZG26	Oberfw. E. Gensler Uffz. F. Haefner	N Y
07/10/40	Bowleaze Cove, Weymouth, Dorset.	Me. 110 3U+DD	Stab III/ZG26	Lt. B. Sommer Uffz. P. Prauler	N Y
07/10/40	English Channel off Weymouth, Dorset.	Me. 110 3U+GT	9/ZG26	Oblt. H. Grisslich Uffz. L. Obermeier	N Y
07/10/40	Near Corfe Castle, Dorset.	Me. 110 3U+JT	9/ZG26	Gefr. Berhardt Demming	N
08/10/40	Mudflats, Bromborough, near Liverpool.	Ju. 88 M7+DK	2/806	Oblt. H. Bruckmann Uffz. H. Weth Sonderfuhrer Hans Lehmann	N Y Y
08/10/40	North Sea off Rattray Head, Aberdeenshire.	Do. 17 4N+GK	2(F)/22	Oblt. E. von Eickstedt Haupt. K. Hardt Oberfw. H. Freund	N N N
08/10/40	English Channel near Folkestone, Kent.	Me. 109 ?	4/JG3	Oblt. Werner Voigt	N
08/10/40	Little Grange Farm, Woodham Mortimer.	Me. 109 2+	4/JG52	Fw. Paul Boche	Y

Date	Location	Aircraft	Unit	Prisoners	Injured
08/10/40	Vensons Farm, Eastry, Kent.	Me. 109 10+	1/JG77	Lt. Heinz Escherhaus	N
09/10/40	Lyminge, Kent.	Me. 109 6+	7/JG54	Fw. Fritz Schweser	Y
10/10/40	Horseshoe Corner, Foulness, Essex.	Ju. 88 9K+HS	8/KG51	Uffz. R. Metschllat Fw. Hans Wolff Uffz. A. Schrogl	N N N
11/10/40	Marthalyn, North Wales.	Do. 17 7T+HH	1/606	Fw. Hans Staas	N
11/10/40	Irish Sea off Bardsey Island, North Wales.	Do. 17 7T+EH	1/606	Lt. J. Krause Gefr. H. Sudermann Uffz. H. Arpert	Y N N
12/10/40	Dean Hill, Harrietsham, Kent.	Me. 109 11+	1/JG52	Oblt. Gunter Busgen	Y
12/10/40	Hollingbourne, Kent.	Me. 109 <1+	2/JG52	Oblt. Karl Sauer	Y
12/10/40	Weeke's Lane, West Brabourne, Kent.	Mr. 109 3+	3/JG52	Fw. Siegfried Voss	N
12/10/40	Small Hythe, Kent.	Me. 109 <I+	4/JG54	Lt. B. Malischewski	N
13/10/40	Roberts Dane, Hastingleigh, Kent.	Me. 109 7+I	7/JG3	Gefr. Hubert Rungen	N
15/10/40	Bowcombe Down, Newport, Isle of Wight.	Me. 109 8+	3/JG2	Fw. H. Hellriegel	N
15/10/40	Everton, Lymington, Hampshire.	Me. 109 12+-	4/JG2	Gefr. Alois Pollak	N
15/10/40	Princes Golf Course, Sandwich, Kent.	Me. 109 7+I	8/JG3	Oberfw. Willi Bauer	N
15/10/40	Trimworth Manor, Crundale, Kent.	Me. 109 ?	8/JG27	Oblt. G. Deicke	N
15/10/40	Owl Castle Farm, Cousley Wood, East Sussex.	Me. 109 2+	4/JG51	Uffz. Erich Hohn	N
15/10/40	Little Butts Farm, Wadhurst, Sussex.	?	3/KG2	Gefr. Hans Fellerman	N
16/10/40	Creaseys Farm, Hutton, Essex.	He. 111 1T+BB	2/KGr126	Lt. Kurt Newald Gefr. H-J. Granetz	N N

Date	Location	Aircraft	Unit	Prisoners	Injured
17/10/40	RAF Manston, Kent.	Me. 109 1+	3/JG53	Oblt. Walter Rupp	N
20/10/40	Mereworth Woods, Kent.	Me. 109 4+	5/JG52	Fw. Ludwig Bielmaier	N
20/10/40	North Fording House, nr. New Romney, Kent.	Me. 109 6+	9/JG54	Fw. Adolf Iburg	Y
20/10/40	Court Wood, Foxhunt Green, Waldron, Sussex.	Me. 109 11+	3/JG77	Fw. Karl-Heinz Wilhelm	N
20/10/40	Bockingfold Farm, Horsmondon, Kent.	Me. 110 L2+MR	7(F)/LG2	Oblt. Roland Semmerich	N
22/10/40	Ness Point, Shotley, Suffolk.	Do. 17 7T+AH	1/606	Lt. W. Stirnat Lt. H. Wurdemann Uffz. F. Schornich Uffz. R. Kuttner	N N N N
22/10/40	English Channel off Hastings, Sussex.	Me. 109 10+	3/JG51	Kurt Muller	N
25/10/40	North Sea off Yarmouth, Norfolk.	Me. 110 F6+MK	2(F)/122	Lt. Konrad Wacker	N
25/10/40	New Barn Farm, Yalding, Kent.	Me. 109 7+-	8/JG26	Fw. Josef Gartner	Y
25/10/40	Milebush, Marden, Kent.	Me. 109 <-+-	Stab/JG51	Haupt. Hans Asmus	Y
25/10/40	Lidham Hill Farm, Guestling, East Sussex.	Me. 109 <+	7/JG51	Fw. W. Koslowski	Y
25/10/40	Stonewall Farm, Hunton, Kent.	Me. 109 4+-	7/JG51	Fw. Leonhard Birg	N
25/10/40	Scotney Farm, Lydd, East Sussex.	Me. 109 7+	5/JG54	Oblt. Joachim Schypek	N
25/10/40	Lydd Ranges, Kent.	Me. 109 2+	5/JG54	Lt. Ernst Wagner	Y
25/10/40	Harvey's Cross Farm, Ilford, East Sussex.	Me. 109 13+	3/JG77	Gefr. Karl Raisinger	N
26/10/40	North Sea off Norfolk coast.	He. 115 S4+AH	1/506	Uffz. G. Grotefendt Lt. K-H. Kemper Obergefr. K. Forster	N N N

Date	Location	Aircraft	Unit	Prisoners	Injured
27/10/40	Wickham Court Farm, New Addington, Surrey.	Me. 109 <-+	Stab I/JG3	Lt. Ernst Busch	Y
27/10/40	Hooks Wood, Lenham, Kent.	Me. 109 10+	8/JG27	Oblt. Anton Pointner	N
27/10/40	East Park House, Newchapel, Surrey.	Me. 109 5+	2/JG52	Gefr. Carl Bott	N
27/10/40	Pemshurst airfield, Kent.	Me. 109 4+	3/JG52	Fw. Lothar Schieverhofer	N
27/10/40	Upstreet, Kent.	Me. 109 2+	3/JG52	Oblt. Ulrich Steinhilper	Y
27/10/40	Lydd Water Tower, Kent.	Me. 109 13+	7/JG54	Uffz. A. Zimmermann	Y
27/10/40	North Sea off Clacton, Essex.	He. 111 V4+HW	1/KG1	Uffz. W. Saumsiegel Uffz. R. Heinhold Gefr. K. Rosenberg Uffz. M. Berens Gefr. R. Hartleib	N N N N N
27/10/40	Duggleby, Malton, Yorkshire.	Ju. 88 5J+ER	7/KG4	Oblt. F-J. Podbielski Uffz. Hans Heier Uffz. Von Kidrowski Uffz. O. Piontek	N N N Y died 15/11
28/10/40	London Road, Leybourne, Kent.	Me. 109 2+ -	5/JG27	Uffz. A. Gonschorek	Y
28/10/40	North Common, Chailey Sussex.	Me. 109 3+ -	4/JG53	Fw. Alfred Berg	N
28/10/40	Boughton Malherbe, Kent.	Do. 17 5K+CH	1/KG3	Fw. K. Vosshagen	Y
29/10/40	Sheerlands Farm, Pluckley, Kent.	Me. 109 6+	3/Erpo. Gr.210	Oblt. Otto Hintze	Y
29/10/40	Wootton Crossroads, Shepherdswell, Kent.	Me. 109 5+I	9/JG3	Oblt. E. Troha	N
29/10/40	Tillingham, Essex.	Me. 109 1+I	8/JG26	Fw. Konrad Jackel	N
29/10/40	Gate Inn, West Elham, Kent.	Me. 109 13+	3/JG51	Fw. K. Bubenhofer	N

Date	Location	Aircraft	Unit	Prisoners	Injured
29/10/40	Parkstone Quay, Essex.	He. 111 A1+LT	9/KG53	Oberfw. K. Penzel Uffz. F. Sigger Uffz. J. Klitscher Oberfw. H. Metzer Uffz. H. Ludicke	N Y Y Y Y
29/10/40	Langenhoe, Essex.	Me. 109 ^+N	4/LG2	Oberfw. Harmeling	Y
30/10/40	Meopham, Kent.	Me. 109 9+ -	6/JG3	Uffz. A. Fahrian	Y
30/10/40	East Fairleigh, Kent.	Me. 109 1+-	6/JG3	Gefr. Eugen Schuller	Y
30/10/40	Priggs Yard, Ely, Cambridgeshire.	Ju. 88 L1+GS	8/LG1	Uffz. Willi Arnt Uffz. A. Brommer Obergefr. P. Fliger Gefr. W. Kellner	N N Y N
31/10/40 or 01/11/40	Mapson's farm near Chichester.	Me. 109 6+	1/JG2	Oblt. Hermann Reifferscheidt	N

Appendix II

Messerschmitt Me 109E Markings as noted by Air Intelligence

June – October 1940

Note: From AI1(k) records, it does not cover every operating unit and this is not an exhaustive list of markings for the Me 109 Geschwader at that time. Markings also changed over that period.

Unit	Markings
Stab I/JG2	Badge: Richthofen Geschwader with a Gothic 'R' in red on white shield.
1/JG2	Badge: Red 'Bonzo' character with white tongue & feet badge, yellow rudder & spinner.
3/JG2	Badge: Richthofen Geschwader with a Gothic 'R' in red on white shield. Engine cowling & rudder painted orange-yellow colour, Mickey Mouse in shorts wearing boxing gloves badge below cockpit.
4/JG2	Badge: Richthofen Geschwader with a Gothic capital 'R' in red on white shield outlined in red.
8/JG2	White engine cowling with red band around spinner.
Stab /JG3	Yellow nose, rudder and fin with white ring on spinner.
Stab I/JG3	Yellow nose and rudders in late October 1940.
Stab II/JG3	White wing tips & rudder, black & white quartered spinner. An eight segmented alternating black and white shield under the cockpit windscreen which was outlined in red.
1/JG3	White rudder and wing tips, white worm/snake with a red tongue outlined in black. Later in period changed to yellow nose and engine cowling.
2/JG3	White rudder and wing tips, later in period changed to yellow nose and engine cowling.
3/JG3	Yellow snake with red tongue on engine cowling, yellow tipped spinner with green and white sections.
6/JG3	Nose rudder and fin painted yellow in late October, unit crest of eight segmented alternating black & white shield under cockpit windscreen which was outlined in red.
7/JG3	Nose, cowling and rudder painted yellow, spinner and propellor blades green.
8/JG3	Nose and rudder painted orange with red spinner.

Unit	Markings
Stab I/JG26	Badge: Schlageter Geschwader badge of Gothic black letter 'S' on white shield by cockpit. Yellow cowling.
1/JG26	Badge: Schlageter Geschwader badge of Gothic black letter 'S' on white shield by cockpit.
2/JG26	Badge: Schlageter Geschwader badge of Gothic black letter 'S' on white shield by cockpit.
3/JG26	Badge: Schlageter Geschwader badge of Gothic black letter 'S' on white shield by cockpit.
4/JG26	Badge: Schlageter Geschwader badge of Gothic black letter 'S' on white shield by cockpit. Tigers head badge below cockpit. Yellow nose, cowling & rudder, later changing to white spinner, cowling and rudder yellow.
5/JG26	Yellow cowling and rudder in late October 1940.
6/JG26	Brown ID numbers, yellow spinner and cowling with Goat badge on fuselage below cockpit. Schlageter Geschwader badge of Gothic black letter 'S' on white shield by cockpit still seen in late October.
7/JG26	Badge: Schlageter Geschwader badge of Gothic black letter 'S' on white shield by cockpit. Later seen with a heart on cowling. White wing tips and rudder, changed to yellow nose in mid-September 1940.
8/JG26	Yellow nose and fin in late October 1940. Black Hellhound badge on fuselage below cockpit. Also seen a badge of an old man with walking stick above head, known as 'Adamson'.
9/JG26	Badge: Schlageter Geschwader badge of Gothic black letter 'S' on white shield by cockpit. Also seen with black Hellhound under cockpit.
Stab I/JG27	Geschwader badge of a lioness & native face superimposed on black map of Africa on the nose. Yellow nose and rudder.
Stab III/JG27	Badge of black cross with brown edging & three aircraft in brown along horizontal bar of cross.
2/JG27	Black ID numbers outlined in red, yellow cowling with red & white spinner.
4/JG27	Geschwader badge of a Lioness & native face superimposed on black map of Africa on nose. Yellow nose, rudder and fin, green & white spinner, Badge of black bear rampant on red shield with red castle above it.
5/JG27	Yellow cowling & rudder, red stripe on tail, 2nd Gruppe shield with a bear on it (Oct 1940).
6/JG27	2nd Gruppe badge of a red crown above black rampant bear on engine cowling. Yellow cowling.
7/JG27	Badge of Red cross on black background with a gold aircraft, Cowling painted white with aircraft ID number in white on grey rectangle on cowling.
9/JG27	Yellow rudder & nose, ID number on cowling, three concentric yellow rings on spinner.
1/JG51	Yellow nose & rudder, shield featuring a Mountain Goat (Gems Bok).
2/JG51	Yellow cowling.

Unit	Markings
3/JG51	ID numbers in Brown, shield featuring a Mountain Goat; yellow nose late October.
4/JG51	Badge on rear fuselage featuring a black Raven wearing spectacles with an umbrella under its wing on some with the words: 'Gott strafe England.' Yellow rudder.
6/JG51	Badge on rear fuselage featuring a black Raven wearing spectacles with an umbrella under its wing.
7/JG51	Part yellow cowling, Latter third of rudder painted yellow, green & white spinner with a red tip.
8/JG51	Cowling and rudder painted yellow. Spinner has red band around it.
9/JG51	Yellow cowling, rudder and wing tips.
Stab II/JG52	Yellow cowling and rudder.
Stab II/JG52	Yellow nose and tail late October 1940.
1/JG52	Wing tips and rudder painted white, badge of a white shield with a black bear on it. In late October 1940 white replaced by yellow.
2/JG52	Geschwader badge featuring a red devil with a bow and arrow in white circle on cowling. In late October 1940, a different badge of a wild boar on cowling.
3/JG52	Yellow cowling.
4/JG52	Yellow cowling and nose. Badge of a red cat with an arched back in a white circle.
5/JG52	Geschwader badge featuring a red devil with a bow and arrow.
6/JG52	Yellow cowling and spinner, large blue eagle head and one extended wing on cowling. In late October red extended to rudder.
8/JG52	Identification number outlined in white edging.
Stab / JG53	White rudder & wing tips, half red half white spinner with red band around cowling.
1/JG53	In late October 1940, yellow nose and rudder with a red band around fuselage. Dark green spinner.
3/JG53	Yellow nose & rudder in early Sept 1940, changing to Orangey-yellow nose and fin with a green spinner tip in late Sept 1940 with a red band around cowling.
4/JG53	Yellow wasp badge, yellow nose and faint red nose band in October 1940.
7/JG53	White wing tips and red spinner, others with white cowling, spinner & rudder, plus a red band around cowling was painted out. In late Sept. 1940 changed to yellow nose and rudder.
8/JG53	Yellow nose, cowling & rudder, red band around cowling and red spinner.
9/JG53	Yellow nose, cowling & rudder.
Stab III / JG54	Badge: Oval black & white crest featuring two ME109 profiles. White spinner.
1/JG54	Black chimney sweep wearing a top hat and carrying a ladder badge. Top of rudder painted white.

Unit	Markings
3/JG54	Yellow nose. White ID markings outlined in black, badge consisting of a red shield with a black cross outlined in white with 3 aircraft on cowling.
4/JG54	Yellow nose and cowling with a green spinner.
5/JG54	Cowling painted yellow. Later in October 1940, upper part of cowling painted yellow, lower half orange, a green spinner with a white flash and a red ring on the tip. Rudder painted yellow.
7/JG54	Cowling & rudder painted yellow; badge of a winged wooden clog outlined in black.
8/JG54	Wing tips and top of rudder painted white, spinner ¾ white ¼ black. Aircraft number under the cockpit. In late September 1940 cowling painted yellow.
9/JG54	Yellow nose with a white spinner. Later Red devil's head on a yellow shield and a crude tigers head below port side of cockpit.
Stab I /JG77	White rudder & wing tips, Red letter R in a shield on fuselage.
1/JG77	Yellow cowling, spinner and wing tips. Later, a 45 degrees red line pointing from the cockpit on the fuselage side.
3/JG77	Yellow rudder and fin, brown aircraft ID number.
8/LG1	Red spinner, crest on port side of red griffin on white background. On starboard side three white swans flying over sea.
Stab I / LG2	Yellow nose and yellow fuselage stripe.
3/LG2	Yellow Mickey Mouse with an umbrella on fuselage, brown ID numbers.
4/LG2	Badge of Mickey Mouse holding a pistol, yellow nose and rudder October 1940.
6/LG2	White rudder & wing tips, blue spinner with white & black stripes. Black triangle on fuselage. Badge of black Puss-in-Boots in a white circle. Later in September 1940, yellow nose & rudder, pale blue & white spinner, with same Puss-in-Boots badge.
1/Erpo. Gr.210	Blue ID letter outlined in white.
2/Erpo. Gr.210	Badge of red map of UK with a superimposed bomb sight over it.

Appendix III

Bomber Kampfgeschwadern Markings noted by Air Intelligence

September 1939 – October 1940

Note: From Air Intelligence records, therefore it does not cover every operating unit and this is not an exhaustive list of markings for the bomber units at that time.

Unit	Markings
II/KG1	Badge: Black owl with yellow eyes on aircraft nose.
3/KG1	White eagle attacking a yellow 'British' lion.
Stab/KG2	Shield bearing a man with a telescope, sitting on a cloud with bomb falling from it, a red wavy line at the top of the shield which was placed under the cockpit. Green spinners.
5/KG2	Wide red band around aircraft nose.
8/KG2	Red spinners.
KG3	Red & white shield, white upper half, red lower half, with a Maltese cross in each section in the opposite colour i.e. red on white, white on red.
1/KG3	Crest: Blue shield with a man with a cockatoo's head carrying a bomb under his arm and an owl sat on his other hand.
4/KG3	White circle with a black jackdaw/bird on a branch. White ring on spinners. In Sept-October 1940: Pink stripes on wing tips and rudder.
9/KG3	Badge: Red heart on white square.
Stab/KG4	Kampf-Geschwader Badge: Red shield under cockpit with letter 'C' inside vertical wavy white shape.
1/KG4	Kampf-Geschwader Badge: Red shield under cockpit with letter 'C' inside vertical wavy white shape.
7/KG4	Badge: Silver bat on a yellow crescent moon, white tips of spinners.
Stab/KG26	Kampf-Geschwader White Shield under cockpit featuring a green sitting lion with gothic words 'Vestigium Leonis' in black.
Stab I/KG26	Port wing tip & rudder white stripes.
1/KG26	Kampf-Geschwader White Shield under cockpit featuring a red sitting lion with gothic words 'Vestigium Leonis' in black.
2/KG26	Yellow spinners, Kampf-Geschwader White Shield under cockpit featuring a red sitting lion with gothic words 'Vestigium Leonis' in black.
3/KG26	Yellow tail, leading edge of tailplane had yellow stripe.

Unit	Markings
4/KG26	Kampf-Geschwader White Shield under cockpit featuring a red sitting lion with gothic words 'Vestigium Leonis' in black.
5/KG26	Kampf-Geschwader White Shield under cockpit featuring a sitting lion with gothic words 'Vestigium Leonis' in red.
6/KG26	Kampf-Geschwader White Shield under cockpit featuring a sitting lion with gothic words 'Vestigium Leonis.'
3/KG27	Large ID letter in yellow on upper side of both wings.
5/KG27	Red spinners.
6/KG30	Kampf Geschwader Red shield with a diving eagle in black on white background.
8/KG30	Kampf Geschwader Red shield with a diving eagle.
3/KG51	Kampf Geschwader badge of a blue shield with white edelweiss with yellow centre under cockpit. Yellow spinners.
5/KG51	Shield featuring a diamond with red & black stripes, plus Kampf Geschwader badge of shield bearing a 'sunflower' with white petals and yellow, on blue background. Also red spinners.
3/KG53	Red & Yellow on spinners, later, aircraft ID letter in yellow on upper wing.
5/KG53	Red spinners, later, three or five vertical pink stripes on rudder.
6/KG53	Yellow spinners.
7/KG53	Shield bearing red 'M' with a bomb through it.
Stab II/KG54	Red band around fuselage of aircraft.
3/KG54	Yellow spinners.
Stab/KG55	Green shield outlined in red bearing red griffon with black wings & yellow claws. Also later described as badge of a red lion carrying a pike on a yellow or gold background. (Kampf Geschwader badge.)
3/KG55	Badge: Yellow shield with red dragon & blue wings. (Kampf Geschwader badge.)
4/KG55	Kampf Geschwader Badge: Gold shield with red & white dragon/griffon with blue wings.
6/KG55	Kampf Geschwader Badge: Red Lion/dragon on shield with yellow spinners.
7/KG55	Kampf Geschwader Griffon on a shield, white spinners.
8/KG55	Kampf Geschwader Yellow shield on rudder bearing three red fishes.
1/KG76	Figures '7+' on upper wing surface.
2/KG76	Badge: Shield of a bomb falling on a British lion, red spinners with red band around fuselage.
6/KG76	Yellow spinners.
7/KG76	Large pink stripe on rudder & top of port wing.
8/KG76	Black shield with red downward falling bomb & three white aircraft across it. Later, red band around fuselage and red spinners, or horizontal pink band around rudders.

Unit	Markings
9/KG76	Yellow spinners and yellow band around fuselage behind wings, later, black tail fins with two pink horizontal stripes on them.
Stab I/KG77	Badge: Grey shield with a Black eagle on yellow outlined in black.
1/KG77	Badge: Black dragon on yellow background, white spinners.
2/KG77	Black eagle with yellow flag and words, red spinners.
3/KG77	Kampf Geschwader Black eagle on yellow banner with words 'Ich wil das si vorvechten.'
8/KG77	Kampf Geschwader Badge: Red & Yellow shield bearing yellow banner with black German eagle on it. Later, broad white lines 54"x18" on wings and red spinners.
9/KG77	One broad white line 54"x18" on wings and red spinners. Later still, various white panels on aircraft.

Appendix IV

Heavy Fighter, Stuka and Miscellaneous Geschwadern Markings noted by Air Intelligence

September 1939 – October 1940

Note: From Air Intelligence records, therefore it does not cover every operating unit and this is not an exhaustive list of markings for all other units at that time.

Unit	Markings
Stab II/LG1	Green spinners.
Stab V/LG1	Green & white spinners.
3/LG1	Badge: Red dragon on white background with yellow claws.
4/LG1	Badge: Shield with a black winged griffon under the cockpit.
8/LG1	Badge: Red griffin on a white shield.
13(Z)/LG1	Badge: Black wolfs head outlined in yellow.
14(Z)/LG1	Badge: Wolfs head, green heart with white edging & Belgian & French flags across it.
15(Z)/LG1	White nose & white spinners.
1/KuFIGr.506	Badge: Blue/grey shield with three black & white sea birds over waves.
3/KuFIGr.506	Badge: Black shield outlined in white with animal skull with horns.
2(F)/121	Red ring around spinners.
3(F)/123	Badge: Eagle by cockpit.
4(F)/123	Badge: white circle with an owl wearing spectacles sat on a pencil with clouds above it.
1/606	White spinner tips.
2/606	Badge: Grey & Black eagle standing on red map of England, attacking it with beak and claws. Cliffs on map in white.
2/806	Badge: German eagle in flight carrying Iron Cross with small swastika.
3/St.G77	Geschwader Badge: Yellow topped shield, lower red part, with German eagle in black, lower black & white iron cross.
4/St.G77	Badge: Red topped shield, lower part yellow and bearing a black cockerel.
5/St.G77	Geschwader Badge: Yellow shield with white rabbit and black cat. Red tipped spinner.

Unit	Markings
Stab/Erpo. Gr.210	Badge: red map of England in yellow circle through gunsight.
2/Erpo.Gr.210	Badge: Shield with red map of British Isles, but Eire in white, viewed through a yellow bomb/gunsight.
Stab/ZG2	Horizontal red lightning flash.
Stab II/ZG2	White 'N' on upper wing.
1/ZG2	Large white ID letter on upper wing.
4/ZG2	Badge: A dragon.
Stab I/ZG26	Badge: Red crocodile, German aircraft chasing a black fish, British aircraft in a circle on nose.
1/ZG26	White nose.
2/ZG26	White nose, white band around fuselage in front of tail, white rings on spinners, small steam engine on nose.
4/ZG26	Badge: White diamond bearing ladybird on nose.
6/ZG26	Badge: White diamond outlined in red, with red diamond at centre on aircraft nose.
8/ZG26	Red spinners, white nose and yellow stripe on rudders.
Stab II/ZG76	Red snake on white fuselage (actually red and white shark's teeth on nose).
Stab III/ZG76	White rings on spinners.
1/ZG76	White tips on spinners.
6/ZG76	Badge: Red and white emblem on nose – no further details known.
8/ZG76	Yellow spinners.
9/ZG76	Badge: Three yellow wasps above clouds. ID Letter on wing in yellow.

Appendix V

SRA Covert Microphone Transcripts, Airmen Identification Codes

Note: The author has cross-checked various records and believes the following AI1 (k) codes refer to these airmen POWs, but he cannot be 100% certain in every case. This list ***should not*** *be accepted as fully confirmed.*

ID. Code	Additional Comment	Believed to be The Following Airman	Captured	Unit
A1	Oberfunk	Hilar Grimm	17/10/1939	2/KuflGr.606
A2	Pilot	Lt. Arndt Fischer	22/10/1939	1/(F)/122
A3	Observer	Oblt. Gustav Awater	22/10/1939	1(F)/122
A4	Gunner	Uffz. Wilhelm Unger	22/10/1939	1(F)/122
A5	Radio Operator	Uffz. Berhard Hochstuhl	17/10/1939	Stab I (F)/122
A6	Radio Operator	Uffz. Walter Heckt	26/09/1939	2/KuFIGr506
A23	Pilot	Lt. Zur see Reitzenstein	26/09/1939	2/KuFIGr506
A24	Radio Operator	Uffz. Fritz Ambrosius	17/10/1939	2/KG30
A25	Pilot	Haupt. Helmut Pohle	16/10/1939	2/KG30
A26	Observer	Lt. Ernst Korner	26/09/1939	2/KG30
A27	Radio Operator	Uffz. Hans Schultze	21/10/1939	1/KuFIGr406
A29	Pilot	Uffz. Gerd Kahle	13/01/1940	1(F)/122
A30	Pilot	Fw. Hermann Wilms	03/02/1940	4/KG26
A32	Observer	Fw. Franz Schnee	07/02/1940	2/KG26
A34	Pilot	Uffz. Helmut Meyer	09/02/1940	5/KG26
A35	Mechanic	Obergefr. Heinz Hegemann	09/02/1940	5/KG26
A36	Pilot	Lt. Erich Grote	22/02/1940	AufKir Gr. Ob.d.L
A37	Observer	Fw. Fritz Sprigath	22/02/1939	AufKir Gr. Ob.d.L
A38	Radio Operator	Uffz. Wilhelm Berger	22/02/1940	AufKir Gr. Ob.d.L
A40/1	Radio Operator	Fw. Kark Henrici	27/02/1940	2/KG26
A44	Observer	Fw. Franz Schnee	03/02/1940	2/KG26
A45	Radio Operator	Uffz. Alfred Detrich	03/02/1940	2/KG26
A46	Pilot	Fw. Ernst Breiler	07/03/1940	1/AufKir Gr. Ob.d.L
A47	Gruppen-Kommandeur	Oberstlt. Hans Hefele	03/04/1940	Stab II/KG26

ID. Code	Additional Comment	Believed to be The Following Airman	Captured	Unit
A48	Pilot	Lt. R.G. Behnisch	03/04/1940	Stab II/KG26
A50	Mechanic	Uffz. Alfred Detrich	03/04/1940	Stab II/KG26
A51	Observer	Lt. Georg Kempe	03/04/1940	Stab II/KG26
A52	Pilot	Lt. K.H. Weigel	08/04/1940	6/KG26
A53	Observer	Ober Fw. Bruno Rehbein	08/04/1940	6/KG26
A55	Pilot	Uffz. Willi Rolf	08/04/1940	4/KG26
A70	Pilot	Oblt. H. Vogel	10/04/1940	4/KG26
A76	Pilot	Oberfw. F. Weimer	03/02/1940	2/KG26
A150	Observer	Oblt. Wilifried Gerling	26/05/1940	5/KG54
A187	Pilot	Lt. Hans Strehl	23/05/1940	1/JG51
A201	Pilot	Oblt. Theodor Beermann	10/05/1940	4/KG30
A258	Pilot	Lt Zur see Gottfried Schroeder	01/07/1940	3/106
A260	Pilot	Either: Oblt. Joachim von Arnim *or* Oblt. Ulrich Jordan	Both captured 19/06/1940	4/KG4 Stab II/KG4
A266	Pilot	Lt. Johann Bohm	08/07/1940	4/JG51
A269	Pilot	Lt. Albert Striberny	08/07/1940	3/LG2
A275	Pilot	Lt. Joachim Schroeder	11/07/1940	9/ZG76
A285	Observer	Obergefr. Walter Plock	20/07/1940	4(F)/122
A289	Radio Operator	Fw. Willi Baden	21/07/1940	4(F)/122
A294	Pilot	Haupt. Dieter von Malpitz	24/07/1940	3/LG1
A296	Pilot	Haupt. Von Zenker	24/07/1940	1/KG40
A299	Pilot	Uffz. Max Reiss	25/07/1940	8/JG52
A302	Observer	Gefr. L. Hohmann	24/07/1940	1/KG40
A303	Radio Operator	Uffz. Heinrich Otto Hocker	24/07/1940	1/KG40
A312	Mechanic	Gefr. H. Morgenthal	29/07/1940	8/KG55
A313	Gunner	Gefr. E. Ostheimer	29/07/1940	8/KG55
A315	Pilot or wireless operator	Either: Uffz. G. Lehm *or* Uffz. Justus Kehres	30/07/1940	2(F)/122
A317	?????	Either: Uffz. Herbert Klatte *or* Uffz. H. Karwelat	11/08/1940 04/07/1940	Stab II/KG54 4/KG54
A331	Observer	Maj. Franz-Karl Schlichtling	12/08/1940	Stab II/KG27
A339	Pilot	Lt. Hans Werner Regenauer	12/08/1940	2/JG26
A345	Observer Staffel Capt.	Oblt. Gerhard Oszwald	13/08/1940	Stab/KG2
A346	Pilot	Oblt. Heinz Schlegel	13/08/1940	Stab/KG2
A349	Pilot	Oblt. Heinz Rosse	13/08/1940	Stab II/KG54

ID. Code	Additional Comment	Believed to be The Following Airman	Captured	Unit
A351	?	Uffz. Friedel Dorner	14/12/1940	2/KG100
A354	Mechanic	Uffz. Josef Kremm	14/08/1940	9/KG27
A376	Pilot	Obergefr. Franz Obser	16/08/1940	9/ZG76
A383	Pilot	Haupt. H. Loncier	24/08/1940	9/KG53
	Mechanic	Gefr. G. Fleischmann	12/08/1940	3/KG51
A427	Pilot	Lt. Johann Kernbach	06/09/1940	6/KG76
A433	Pilot Staffel Kapitän	Oblt. Helmut Rau	31/08/1940	3/JG3
A436	Pilot	Oblt. F. Zipse	18/08/1940	7/KG53
A445	Pilot	Lt. Karl Stix	07/09/1940	4/ZG2
A469	Radio Operator	Fw. Willi Schutel	07/09/1940	Stab I/ZG2
A473	Pilot	Uffz. K. Koch	07/09/1940	9/JG51
A483	Pilot	Oberfw. G. Goltzsche	07/09/1940	1/JG77
A488	Pilot	Fw. Hermann Koops	09/09/1940	9/ZG76
A493	Pilot	Fw. August-Wilhelm Muller	09/09/1940	4/JG3
A504	Gruppen-Kommandeur	Maj. M. Gruber	15/09/1940	Stab II/KG53
A509	Pilot	Lt. Kurt Bildau	15/09/1940	7/JG51
A519	Pilot	Lt. Karl Westerhoff	31/08/1940	6/JG3
A520	Pilot	Oblt. K. Fischer	30/09/1940	7/JG27
A593	Pilot	Oblt. K. Sauer	12/10/1940	2/JG52
A594	Leutnant Fighter-Pilot	Lt. B. Malischewski	12/10/1940	4/JG54

The above individual identifications were made by reference to information in the transcripts, dates and other AI1(k) POW records. Although the author believes they are correct, they may not be and the reader should use discretion.

Appendix VI

Selected RAF Intelligence Officers 1939 – 1940

Samuel Denys Felkin

Known as Denys Felkin. Squadron Leader (later Group Captain) born in Edinburgh on 28 August 1894, he died in Mont Cochon, Jersey in January 1973 aged 78. Felkin was OC of Trent Park, Cockfosters, managing the RAF element of the interrogation centre where he was the Chief Interrogation officer. He later received the OBE and an MBE. He joined the Artists' Rifles regiment and then the RNAS in 1915 and qualified as a pilot at Eastbourne in July 1915. He later served as a Field Intelligence Officer in Paris, Berlin and Vienna. He joined the Assistant Directorate of Intelligence in August 1939 as second in command (behind Pollak). He took command of the unit and oversaw its move and operations at Trent Park.

Squadron Leader Edmund R.H. Pollak

Served in the air force in First World War, he worked as a businessman in Germany in the 1930s before being detained by the Gestapo and his assets frozen. A close pre-war associate of Kendrick, his friend managed to obtain his release and return to the United Kingdom. It is highly likely he was working for British intelligence at the time. He rejoined the RAF and was made CO of the Air Intelligence Section AI1(k) at the Tower of London with Felkin as his deputy. However, within weeks he was replaced by Felkin.

Flight Lieutenant William Allean O'Moore Brayton RAFVR

Was born in St John's Wood in May 1910. He joined the RAF reserve in 1934 moving into the RAFVR. He was commissioned on 17 June 1940 (RAFVR) and joined AI1(k), before moving on to 502 Squadron in 1943 and earning a DFC. He was a member of the Directorate of Intelligence, working under the Assistant Chief of the Air Staff Intelligence.

Flight Lieutenant Guy Brooks Jepson

Stationed at Cockfosters in summer 1940 as Felkin's deputy.

Flying Officer W.O. Brayton

Listed in KV4/302 as being one of the initial Tower of London officers in October 1939 and at Cockfosters in summer 1940.

Flying Officer H.N. Roffey

Listed in KV4/302 as being one of the initial Tower of London officers in October 1939.

Flying Officer H.O. Gregory

Listed in KV4/302 as being one of the initial Tower of London officers in October 1939, and at Cockfosters in summer 1940.

Flying Officer C.H. Smith

Listed in KV4/302 as being one of the initial Tower of London officers in October 1939 and at Cockfosters in summer 1940.

List of AI1(k) Liaison Officers in July 1940

From file KV4/302 in the UK National Archives:

Flight Lieutenant H.L. Benson, RAF Turnhouse.
Flight Lieutenant B,E. Bishop, RAF Wick.
Flight Lieutenant A.K. Boning, RAF Wyton.
Flying Officer M.D.M. Cochrane, RAF Ponteland.
Flying Officer R.M.C. Day, No.61 Group, Belfast.
Flying Officer C.M.D. Eales, RAF Biggin Hill.
Flying Officer H.R. Gray, RAF Dyce.
Flying Officer L.F. Hartje, RAF Thornaby.
Flying Officer L.P. Hodson, RAF Watnall.
Flying Officer J.X. Hunt, RAF Tangmere.
Flying Officer D.S.R. Kent, RAF Abingdon.
Flying Officer E.P. Kohn-Speyer, RAF Pembroke Dock.
Flying Officer W.W. Marks, RAF North Weald.
Flying Officer N.J. Miller, Fighter Command HQ, Stanmore.
Flying Officer A. Moore, RAF Hooton Park.
Flying Officer J.E. Mulholland, RAF Manston.
Flying Officer P. Pralle, RAF Warmwell.
Flight Lieutenant R.L.S. Raffles, RAF Castle Bromwich.
Flying Officer J.R. Robinson, RAF Leconfield.
Flight Lieutenant J.F.A. Segner, RAF Mount Wise.
Flying Officer C.K. Squires, RAF Horsham St. Faith.
Flying Officer P.E.S. Toll, RAF Digby.
Flying Officer R.N. Walford, No. 61 Group Belfast.
Flying Officer J.R. Woods, RAF Filton.

Other Air Intelligence Officers of Note:

Flight Lieutenant Derek Rownsley, RAF Fort Grange, Gosport.

Appendix VII

Luftwaffe Officers Held in Royal Herbert Hospital, Woolwich

Circa mid-December 1940

Rank/Name	Unit	Date Captured	London Cage; Date
Haupt. H. Von Loncier	9/KG53	24/08/1940	No
Oblt. Carl Treiber	Stab II JG27	27/09/1940	No, but badly wounded
Lt. F. Morr (Mohr)	7/KG76	06/10/1940	n/k
Oblt. H-M Christinnecke	7/JG26	06/09/1940	n/k
Oblt. W. Blume	7/JG26	18/08/1940	n/k
Oblt. W. Bartels	Stab III JG26	24/07/1940	No, but badly wounded
Lt. H-G Mollenbrok	3/KG2	16/08/1940	n/k
Oblt. S. Gottschalt	2/ZG2	03/09/1940	n/k, had fractured ankle
Oblt. W. von Eichborn	Stab II ZG76	27/09/1940	n/k, but badly burned
Haupt. R. Bass	5/KG1	30/08/1940	n/k
Oblt. Rolf Heim	Stab KG30	09/09/1940	n/k
Oblt. K-E. Wilke	9/KG76	15/09/1940	Yes, interrogated 22/02/1941
Lt. H. Bottcher	4(F)/121	22/09/1940	n/k
Haupt. G. Peters	9/KG76	18/08/1940	n/k
Oblt. W. Schuller	3/JG27	06/09/1940	n/k
Lt. K. Kzienzyk	8/KG2	21/08/1940	n/k
Oblt. G. Busgen	1/JG52	12/10/1940	Yes, interrogated 28/02/1941
Lt. Max Himmelheber	Stab JG2	06/09/1940	Badly injured
Oblt. H. Wappler	8/KG27	13/09/1940	Yes, interrogated February 1941?
Oblt. Viktor Kraft	Stab II LG2	11/12/1940	n/k
Haupt. J. Roth	9/KG76	18/08/1940	Yes interrogated 15/02/1941
Maj. J. Hackbarth	Stab III KG30	09/09/1940	n/k, badly wounded
Oblt. A. Gotz/Goetz	1/JG2	07/09/1940	n/k
Lt. H. Schnabel	1/JG3	05/09/1940	Yes, interrogated 31/01/1941

Rank/Name	Unit	Date Captured	London Cage; Date
Lt. F. Schad	Stab KG51	12/08/1940	Yes, interrogated 11/02/1941 badly burned
Sonderfur. A. Nothelfer	Stab KG51	12/08/1940	n/k, but badly burned
Haupt. J-H Schlichting	Stab III/JG27	06/09/1940	n/k buy badly burned legs
Lt. H. Michaelis	4/KG3	15/09/1940	n/k
Oblt. Freidrich Oeser	2/KG77	30/09/1940	n/k
Haupt. W. Plewig	Stab II/StG77	08/08/1940	n/k

Appendix VIII

Luftwaffe Fighter Aces Captured During the Battle of Britain

Rank/Name	Unit	Date Shot Down	Number of Victories
Oblt. Paul Temme	Stab I/JG2	13/08/1940	5
Lt. Richard Marchfelder	Stab III/ZG76	16/08/1940	10
Oblt. Helmut Tiedmann	2/JG3	18/08/1940	7
Lt. Walter Blume	7/JG26	18/08/1940	6
Lt. Franz Achleitner	9/JG3	24/08/1940	5
Oberfw. Artur Dau	7/JG51	28/08/1940	7
Oblt. Georg Beyer	7/JG26	28/08/1940	7
Oblt. Rudolf Ziegler	II/JG54	30/08/1940	6
Lt. Josef Burschgens	7/JG26	01/09/1940	10
Oblt. Anton Stangl	5/JG54	01/09/1940	6
Oberfw. Kurt Rochel	II/ZG26	02/09/1940	5
Lt. Walter Manhart	3/ZG26	03/09/1940	13
Lt. Hein Schnabel	1/JG3	05/09/1940	6
Oblt. Franz von Werra	II/JG3	05/09/1940	8-13*
Oblt. Joachim Schlichtling	III/JG27	06/09/1940	8 (5 in Spanish Civil War)
Uffz. Hans-Georg Schulte	7/JG53	06/09/1940	7
Oblt. Hans Krug	4/JG26	07/09/1940	9
Fw. Heinrich Hohnisch	1/JG53	09/09/1940	6
Lt. Hans Berthel	Stab I/JG52	15/09/1940	6
Fw. Gerhardt Grzymalla	8/JG26	23/09/1940	8
Lt. Alfred Zeis	1/JG53	05/10/1940	5
Oblt. Viktor Molders	2/JG51	07/10/1940	9
Lt. Erich Meyer	2/JG51	07/10/1940	6
Lt. Botho Sommer	III/ZG26	07/10/1940	9
Oblt. Gunther Busgen	1/JG52	12/10/1940	6
Fw. Josef Gartner	8/JG26	25/10/1940	6
Oblt. Ulrich Steinhilper	3/JG52	27/10/1940	5

* Franz von Werra's total is subject to question.

Source Material

UK National Archives

KV4/302 Policy & arrangements for interrogation of enemy POWs in British hands.
WO 208/3513 Training of Intelligence Officers in interrogation of POWs.
WO 311/566 Alleged ill-treatment of German POWs at London District Cage 1945-1948.
WO 208/4158 Combined Services detailed interrogation SRX 1-250 (1939-1941).
AIR 40/2336 Radio Countermeasures 1940.
AIR 40/2962 AI 1(k) Reports Nos. 3-200 (1940) info obtained from refugees & POWs.
AIR 40/2963 AI 1(k) Reports Nos. 201-986 (1940) info obtained from refugees & POWs.
AIR 40/2428 Fighter Command Pow Interrogation reports & correspondence.
AIR 40/2429 Interrogation report of Luftwaffe prisoners of war by AI 1(R) & AI (K).
AIR 40/2636 Intelligence from Interrogation – the work of ADI (k) 1939-1945.
AIR 40/3070 CSDIC (UK) reports SRA 1-499 Jan '40 – 11 Sept 40: info from German POWs.
AIR 40/3071 CSDIC (UK) reports SRA 500-899 11 Sept 40 – 12 Nov 40: from German POWs.
AIR 40/2394, Vol. 1, Interrogation of German & Italian POWs (Sept – Dec 1939).
AIR 40/2395, 1-50 Vol. 2, Interrogation of German & Italian POWs.
AIR 40/2396 51-100 Vol 3 Interrogation of German & Italian POWs.
AIR 40/2397 101-200 Vol. 4 Interrogation of German & Italian POWs.
AIR 40/2398 201-300 Vol. 5 Interrogation of German & Italian POWs (1/7/40 – 31/8/40).
AIR 40/2399 301-500 Vol. 6 Interrogation of German & Italian POWs (1/8/40 – 30/9/40).
AIR 40/2400 501-700 Vol. 7 Interrogation of German & Italian POWs (1/9/40 – 31/10/40).

AIR 40/ 2401 701-902 Vol. 8 Interrogation of German & Italian POWs (1/10/40 – 30/11/40).
WO 208/4117 Combined Services Detailed interrogation SRA 1-110 (Nov 1939 – May 1940).
WO 208/4118 Combined Services Detailed interrogation SRA 111-440 (1 June – 31 Aug 1940).
WO 208/4119 Combined Services Detailed interrogation SRA 441-651 (September 1940).
WO 208/4120 Combined Services Detailed interrogation SRA 652-861 (October 1940).
FO 898/320 Reports of interviews with POWs by C H Brooks (1940-1942).
WO/208/5163/89 Interrogation at London Cage of Oblt. Frederich Dilthey JG2.
WO/208/5163/21 Interrogation at London Cage of Ober Feldwebel Erich Slotosch KG55.
WO/208/5163/44 Interrogation at London Cage of Haupt. Joachim Rath KG76.
WO/208/5163/90 Interrogation at London Cage of Gefr/Uffz. Alfred Hoffmann KG2.
WO/208/5163/56 Interrogation at London Cage of Leutnant Heinz Schnabel JG3.
WO/208/5163/42 Interrogation at London Cage of Oblt. Gerhardt Goetz ZG2.
WO/208/5163/67 Interrogation at London Cage of Feldwebel Gunter Kramer JG77.
WO/208/5163/88 Interrogation at London Cage of Oblt. Harry Wappler KG27.
WO/208/5163/41 Interrogation at London Cage of Feldwebel Rudolh Poh KG76.
WO/208/5163/27 Interrogation at London Cage of Uffz. Edo Flick KG27.
WO/208/5163/37 & 43 Interrogation at London Cage of Leutnant Franz Schad KG51.
WO/208/5163/5 Interrogation at London Cage of Uffz Rolf Kahl Erg. 210.
WO/208/5163/66 Interrogation at London Cage of Oblt. Gunter Buesoen / Busgen JG52.
WO/208/5163/65 & 135 Interrogation at London Cage of Feldwebel Georg Engel KG55.
WO/208/5163/8 Interrogation at London Cage of Feldwebel Willi Hohenstadter KG2.
WO/208/5163/65 Interrogation at London Cage of Oblt. Karl-Ernst Wilke KG76.
AIR 40/2169 AI 1 (g) Air Tactics & Technical intelligence May 1940- Sept 1941.
AIR 40/2980 AI 1(g) Aircraft reports 1940-1941.
AIR 40/2265, AIR 40/226-2293 RAF SIB investigation papers in Stalag Luft III murders.
WO 235/424-432 Case Papers for Stalag Luft III trial.
WO 258/105 Sentences from the court.
TS 50/3 Publication of London Cage by Lt. Colonel Alexander Scotland.
WO 208/5381 Draft of Alexander Scotland's book from War Office.
TS 50/3/1 Previously closed extracts from London Cage book.

RAF Air Historical Branch:

Intelligence Narrative 1939-1945 Parts 1-6. *Air Ministry Intelligence in War* by S.D. Felkin.

BBC Peoples War archives:

15 of October 2014, Freddy Godshaw civilian internee.

Other websites:

www.getsurrey.co.uk/news/nostalgia/battle-britain-flypast-memories-guildford-10058681.

Bibliography

After the Battle magazine No. 70, published 1990.
After the Battle magazine No. 106, published in 1999.
The M Room, by Helen Fry, published by Marranos Press 2012.

The Walls have Ears, by Helen Fry, published by Yale University Press in 2020.
The London Cage, by Helen Fry, published by Yale University Press in 2017.
The One That Got Away, by Leasor & Burt, first published 1953.
A Spitfire on my tail, by Ulrich Steinhilper & Peter Osborne, Independent Books 1990.
Ten minutes to Buffalo, by Ulrich Steinhilper & Peter Osborne, Independent Books 1991.
Einer Kam Durch. Fluchtbericht des Fliegerleutnant Franz von Werra. German language text, (translated by author), 1957 & 1963.
Luftwaffe Aces in the Battle of Britain, by Chris Goss, published by Air World/Pen & Sword books 2020.
JG26 War diary Vol. 1, by Donald Caldwell, Grub Street books 1996.
Luftwaffe Crash Archive volumes 1-5, by Nigel Parker, Red Kite.
Battle of Britain: The Hardest Day, by Alfred Price, M & J Books 1979.
Most Secret War, by Dr R.V. Jones, published by Wordsworth Military Library books 1998.
The Battle of Britain - Then & Now, edited by Winston G. Ramsay, published by After the Battle 1985.
The Battle of France – Then and Now, edited by Peter Cornwell, published by After the Battle 2008.
RAF Fighter Command victory claims of WW2 Part One 1939-1940, by John Foreman published by Red Kite 2003.
Luftwaffe over the North, by Bill Norman, published by Pen & Sword books 1993.
Luftwaffe losses over Northumberland & Durham 1939-1945, by Bill Norman, published by Pen & Sword books 2002.
The Bookseller magazine, October 1954.
Yorkshire Post & Leeds Intelligencer, February 1955.

Other books by M.S. Morgan & published by Pen & Sword Books:

The Hurricane pilot who became a Gestapo agent.
Hitler's RAF Collaborators.
The Death of Guy Gibson
The Death of HRH Prince George, Duke of Kent.

Index

NB: Samuel Denys Felkin is not listed within the Index due to the vast amount of times he is mentioned within the book.